The Feeling Brain

The Feeling Brain

The Biology and Psychology of Emotions

Elizabeth Johnston and Leah Olson

W. W. Norton & Company
New York • London

For information about permission to reproduce selections from this book,
write to Permissions, W. W. Norton & Company, Inc.,
500 Fifth Avenue, New York, NY 10110

For information about special discounts for bulk purchases, please contact
W. W. Norton Special Sales at specialsales@wwnorton.com or 800-233-4830

Manufacturing by Edwards Brothers Malloy
Production manager: Christine Critelli

Library of Congress Cataloging-in-Publication Data

Johnston, Elizabeth (Psychologist)
The feeling brain : the biology and psychology of emotions /
Elizabeth Johnston and Leah Olson. — First edition.
      pages cm. — (A Norton professional book)
Includes bibliographical references and index.
ISBN 978-0-393-70665-9 (hardcover)
1. Affective neuroscience. 2. Emotions—Physiological aspects.
3. Emotions. 4. Neuropsychology.
I. Olson, Leah (Biologist) II. Title.
QP401.J64 2015
612.8'233—dc23
                              2014046923

W. W. Norton & Company, Inc.
500 Fifth Avenue, New York, N.Y. 10110
www.wwnorton.com

W. W. Norton & Company Ltd.
Castle House, 75/76 Wells Street, London W1T 3QT

1 2 3 4 5 6 7 8 9 0

For the sources of my greatest feelings: Ron, Ross, Cam, Addie, and the memory of Nanette—ebj

To Dan, whose belief that I could finish this project never faltered. I could never have done this without you—lo

Contents

Acknowledgments

Joint acknowledgments: This book grew out of a course of the same name that we co-taught several times at Sarah Lawrence College, and we are thankful for the support and interest of many members of the Sarah Lawrence community. We especially thank Barbara Kaplan and Pauline Watts, former Deans of the College, and our colleagues in psychology and biology for encouraging and enabling our initial collaboration on the course. Our special thanks also go to the current Dean of the College, Jerrilyn Dodds, whose willingness to allow us to coordinate our sabbatical schedules was invaluable as we began to adapt our course to book form.

We are also grateful to the wonderful Sarah Lawrence students who took our course, whose characteristic engagement and insightful, probing questions and ideas kept us on our toes, and helped shape our thinking about the field. We give particular thanks to the incomparable Gemma de Choisy who provided help early on in the project by researching and coordinating resources as well as her careful critical reading of some of our earliest attempts at writing. In the later stages of the project, Fiona Mahon and Elena Hall did sterling work checking the extensive bibliography.

Thanks to our editor, Deborah Malmud, who saw the potential for a book in our course syllabus and was patient as we realized it.

Elizabeth only: I am grateful for the love, support, and inspiration that my family provided throughout. I thank my husband and dedicated partner in love and work, Ron Cagenello, my sons Ross and Cameron Johnston Cagenello, and my dad Adam Johnston for their understanding of the importance of the book project, and the welcome relief from its demands that spending time with them provided. In addition, my artistic and technologically savvy older son, Ross, cleaned up some of the figures with great attention to detail. Dody and Bruce Cagenello, the best in-laws a person could ask for, provided constant family support. I also feel fortunate to be related to Cindie Cagenello and Guy Ciccarillo, who were staunch supporters of the work throughout, and excellent people to celebrate with. My relatives in Scotland, John Paul Johnston, and Jane, Nick, Arabella, and Louisa Paterson, cheered me on from afar. My mum, Nanette Johnston, passed away before this project began, but I know that she would have been one of its firmest champions.

Many non-family members also kept me going. Mary Porter, Sarah Lawrence litter mate, close colleague, and dear friend, often boosted my spirits when the work was challenging. Ann Johnson, my valued collaborator on a different project, was a good sounding board and source of encouragement. Jill Koleszar and Nicole Murphy, fellow mothers and book-lovers, helped out many times with my sons, and always inquired so gently about the progress of the book. Dr. Suzanne Davino provided sage expert advice and insightful, practical encouragement. Two inter-connected yoga communities, Blackbird and Open Sky Yoga Barn, have been enormously important in maintaining my physical and mental health; special thanks to Bernadette Birney, Laura Young, and Cathy Whelehan.

What Is an Emotion?

Our emotions are often frustrating and elusive. We frequently ask ourselves searching questions about them: Why am I feeling the way I am? What exactly am I feeling? Why are my emotions so unknowable to me? Why do emotions have such power to direct my life? How can I change the way I feel? Over the last two decades a scientific field has emerged that addresses these puzzling questions by exploring the brain mechanisms of emotions. The field of affective neuroscience has its roots in the work of 19th-century pioneers of biology and psychology: Charles Darwin (1809–1882) and William James (1842–1910). In the early to mid 20th century, a basic model of the emotional brain was developed and came to be known as the limbic system, but it was not until the more recent development of neuroimaging technologies that the field really exploded into a major discipline.

After years of neglect by both mainstream biology and psychology, the study of the neuroscience of emotions is now burgeoning. Although many of the specific brain regions and networks involved in the processing of emotions are beginning to be understood, there is still no single answer to the question "What is an emotion?" Most researchers now agree that emotional systems act to provide meaning and value to the information being processed; emotions tell us what we like and don't like, what is good for us and what is bad for us. But there remain a variety of ideas about how the "hot" emotions interact with "cold" cognitive processes to direct behavior. The evolutionarily old system of automatic emotional reactions that meet survival needs is now housed in the same brain as the slower, more deliberative cognitive processes that evolved to provide humans with the ability to reason, to plan, and to think about the future. While some researchers argue that emotions are essential for "rational" decision-making, others see emotional systems as functioning only as a quick and dirty "gut" feeling that can often lead to irrational behavior.

Different researchers focus on different aspects of emotional processing. It can be frustrating to understand current research because of the many different threads being explored. Our objective in this book is to introduce the dominant research on emotions taking place today, and to integrate that work when possible to provide a more complete view of this rapidly developing landscape. Our hope is to transform that initial frustration into recognition of the complex, multilayered, and fascinating nature of emotion through close consideration of the diverse research that now characterizes the field.

Like all good discussion topics, our guiding question "What is an emotion?" generates many more specific subquestions that have been taken up to varying extents by different groups of investigators. Our goal in this chapter is to introduce the questions to which we will return again and again throughout the book.

What is the function of emotions?

Why do we have emotions in the first place? Darwin first insisted that emotions and emotional expressions should be viewed as adaptive behavior shaped over evolutionary time by natural selection, equivalent to any other physical or physiological feature of an organism. Emotions serve a function. But what exactly is their function? How does their function help explain some of the persistent paradoxes about emotions, such as why we are so attuned to the most subtle expressions of emotion in another's face yet struggle to understand our own emotions? To understand emotions, like any other evolved trait, we need to understand their evolutionary function.

How do emotions differ from other mental states?

In trying to define a complex concept like emotion, it makes sense to contrast it with what it is not. In everyday parlance, emotions are often contrasted with reason or logic and characterized as powerful but mysterious "hot" psychological forces often at odds with our "cooler" reason. The reason/emotion dichotomy is long-standing in Western thought, dating back at least to the time of Plato in Ancient Greece. In the Phaedrus dialogue, Plato provides a compelling visual analogy: The human soul is depicted as a charioteer with two horses moving in different directions. The one on the right is fair and good and listens to the reason of the charioteer, whereas the dark horse on the left is unruly and guided by passion. René Descartes (1596–1650) equated mind with thinking in his well-known cogito argument "I think, therefore I am," and is perhaps the most influential advocate of a dualistic view of mind (soul) and body. However, he also equated the *passions*, such as the experiences of feeling fear and anger, with awareness of the movements of bodily spirits, and thus set up an equally influential dualism equating mind with cognition and emotion with the body.

Much of the Eastern philosophy that has been imported into contemporary Western culture through the growth in popularity of yoga and meditation clearly contrasts with Cartesian mind/body or thinking/feeling dualisms. The Sanskrit word *yoga* can be translated as "yoking" or "joining," referring to the union of mind and body. Modern neuroscience explicitly opposes Cartesian mind/body dualism, but the idea that cognition and emotion are separate mental functions often at odds with each other has long persisted. With increased research on emotions, however, it has become increasingly difficult to parse emotion and cognition at the level of either brain or behavior, and the cognition/emotion dichotomy is coming under increased scrutiny. Indeed, many of the most intriguing studies are those showing the integration of emotion and cognition rather than their separation or the dominance of one over the other.

What is the role of the body in emotional experience?

Emotions feel like something. Is it even possible to have an emotion without having a bodily response? If your heart isn't pounding, your hands aren't sweating, and your breathing doesn't become more rapid, can you still feel afraid? What is the relationship between emotions and their accompanying bodily feelings? The prominent early psychologist William James first challenged common assumptions about the relationship between an emotion and its bodily feeling in 1884, arguing against common sense that our heart doesn't pound because we are afraid; rather, we are afraid because our heart is pounding. Although this idea was roundly criticized in the early 20th century, neuroscience has recently returned to this question to more carefully explore the role of the body in emotions.

How are emotions processed in the brain?

Brain researchers long assumed that brain regions that processed emotional behaviors were distinct from those devoted to cognitive functions. Indeed, introductory brain textbooks today localize emotion to a set of structures identified as the limbic system. The limbic system was proposed as a functional concept in the mid 20th century by the influential researcher Paul MacLean, who argued that emotions and emotional brain structures evolved to serve emerging prosocial behaviors, such as care of offspring, in early mammals. Over evolutionary time, these older emotion structures became overlaid by the neocortical structures we commonly associate with higher cognitive functions seen in humans and primates. The limbic system provided a satisfying anatomical correlate for the cognition/emotion dichotomy. However, as we will see, the division of behavior or brain structures into cognitive or emotional becomes less clear-cut as we more closely examine the pervasive interactions between cognition and emotion.

How many emotions are there, and are some more basic than others?

Do all humans experience the same emotions? Emotion researchers have largely assumed the existence of a small set of core emotions, called basic emotions, thought to have evolved as automatic and adaptive responses to broadly shared environmental challenges, such as finding food, securing mates, and escaping predators. These basic emotions are assumed to be both experienced and recognized by all humans, regardless of their cultural differences, and also evident in a similar form in our close animal relatives. Does the brain have a separate system to process each basic emotion? For example, is there a fear system that is distinct from an anger system? How does the concept of basic emotions fit into the more vaguely defined emotional limbic system concept? As researchers attempt to define and identify the brain substrates of specific emotions, the question of what is core, or basic, in an emotional experience has become much more complex.

What role does memory play in the experience of emotion, and vice versa?

We all have a few vivid and detailed memories of the most significant events of our lives. Yet we remember strikingly few of the more mundane events of our past. Highly emotional events seemingly imprint their memory indelibly into our brains; however, at other times, strong emotions seem to impair memory. Victims of gun crimes can often remember very little about their attacker or other features of the environment at the time; instead, the gun dominates their memory, wiping out all other details, a phenomenon known as "weapon focus." Emotions seem to function as a memory filter, selecting, rejecting, and enhancing what will be remembered. Without an accompanying emotion, most of our experiences are not remembered at all. Understanding the relationship between emotion and memory has been essential in understanding how memory itself works, but much is still unknown about the partnership of emotion and memory. When and how does emotion enhance memory? Can strong or aversive emotions actually suppress critical memories? Which brain structures and neurochemicals associated with emotion enhance or impair memory functions? Investigation of the role of emotions in memory is some of the most exciting work being done in memory research today.

How do motivations relate to emotions?

Emotions compel us to act. Indeed the root of the word *e-motion* expresses this core feature of emotions: They *motivate* us to do something. As psychology was splitting off from philosophy as a distinct academic discipline in the late 19th century, the mind was conceived of as a trilogy of cognition, affection, and conation. *Affection* was the term for emotion, and *conation*, a term that is rarely encountered today, refers to striving or motivation. In their recent work on hedonics, or the study of pleasant and unpleasant states of mind, Kent Berridge and his colleagues have revived the trilogy of mind by separating out learning (cognition), feeling (affection), and wanting (conation). The distinction and interrelationships of these three key aspects of mind in contemporary work have been a major insight emerging from emotion research.

Can we control our emotions?

We know that much of the time we can't immediately act on our emotions. No matter how angry we feel, we don't usually end up hitting the person we disagree with. Much of the work of parenting is teaching children how to control their emotions. How are emotions regulated? What are the best ways to control emotions that may not be socially appropriate or even personally acceptable? The study of emotions holds the promise of better strategies to regulate emotions in ways that don't just bottle them up inside. A relatively new field of inquiry, appropriately known as emotion regulation, addresses these questions, and is one of the most active areas of research within affective neuroscience, with great potential for practical application.

How do basic studies of "normal" emotions inform our understanding of emotional disorders?

Most psychiatric disorders include disturbances of the emotions. Depression and anxiety account for much of the burden of psychiatric disorders, and many of us will encounter them at some point in our lives. Yet our understanding of these debilitating afflictions is still rudimentary, and the available treatments are not always effective. A major promise of emotion research is to provide the foundation needed to develop a more coherent model of emotional disorders. What is being learned about the neuroscience of emotions holds out the hope of our developing a more nuanced understanding of these disorders, with the goal of producing improved and more targeted treatments.

An Overview of the Book

Emotion research is already vast, but it is expanding at an astonishing rate. In this book, we have chosen to introduce emotion research by highlighting the work of a few key researchers. Therefore, each chapter will focus on a small number of select individuals whose work has helped shaped emotion research today as they have addressed the question "What is an emotion?" and the subquestions outlined above. We think of this text not as a comprehensive survey, but rather as a tasting menu that introduces the variety of delicacies available in the vibrant and growing field of emotion research.

In Chapter 1, we look first at the work of William James, the great Harvard psychologist of consciousness and pragmatist philosopher who published an article titled "What Is an Emotion?" in the philosophical journal *Mind* in 1884. This article has become a touchstone for the field today. It created controversy when it was published, and the lively debate surrounding it continues to the present day. James addressed many of our subquestions, but the bulk of his attention was devoted to the role of the body in emotional experience. His paper is an argument for the primacy and necessity of bodily symptoms in producing emotional feelings. James's theory was so roundly criticized by the Harvard physiologist Walter Cannon (1871–1945) that his ideas were not seriously considered again until later in the 20th century. Today, however, there is significant work on the role of the body in emotion by a whole field of emotion research characterized as *neo-Jamesian*.

Although much early work on the brain substrates of emotion implicitly viewed emotions as discrete and identifiable states, an influential experiment by Schacter and Singer in the middle of the 20th century refocused the attention of psychologists on the important role of cognition in determining the kind of emotional reaction that would result. The appraisal theory of emotions, which argues that an identifiable emotional state emerges only after a cognitive assessment of the meaning of an emotional stimulus, effectively recast emotion as a kind of cognitive state for much of the last half of the 20th century. The role of cognitive assessments in the development of emotional reactions continues to be debated today.

Chapter 2 centers on early attempts to identify the brain substrates of emotions. The key players here are a Cornell neuroanatomist, James Papez (1883–1958), and the aforementioned physician and neuroscientist Paul MacLean (1913–2007), who worked at Yale and the National Institutes of Mental Health. Together with a seminal medial temporal lobe lesion experiment reported by Heinrich Klüver and Paul Bucy in 1939, the work of Papez and MacLean resulted in the idea of an emotional brain composed of a set of interconnected structures in the core of the brain, which MacLean named the limbic system. Although the concept of a monolithic limbic system that underlies all emotional processing has been strongly criticized by some researchers, MacLean's seminal paper contains many thought-provoking ideas that are worth reexamining.

Chapter 3 explores the concept of universally shared basic emotions, an idea that goes far back in history and was first advanced as a scientific theory by Charles Darwin. The concept of basic emotions has been most strongly championed in contemporary psychology by Paul Ekman, whose work formalized a detailed description of the prototypical emotional facial expression of each basic emotion. We will also look at the work of Jaak Panksepp, who coined the term "affective neuroscience." Using electrical and chemical stimulation of the brain to evoke behavior, Panksepp has developed a neurobiologically based theory of what he describes as the "core" affective systems, such as rage, fear, seeking, and lust, each of which evolved to meet a specific survival need.

Chapter 4 focuses on the work of NYU researcher Joseph LeDoux. LeDoux is widely considered one of the founding fathers of modern brain-based emotion research. Rather than trying to define an entire "emotional" brain, LeDoux carefully traced the processing of a single emotion, fear, through the brain. His work in the rat has shown that an emotional stimulus is processed simultaneously along two parallel pathways. An emotional pathway concerned with immediate safety takes what he calls the low road directly to the amygdala, which acts to coordinate the whole suite of behavioral and bodily responses needed to respond as rapidly as possible. At the same time, a more deliberative high road to the overlying neocortex performs a more careful, but slower, analysis of the stimulus as well as its context. Because the high road also ends up at the amygdala, it can override any mistakes made by the quick but sometimes sloppy low road. Since LeDoux's seminal work on fear conditioning, the amygdala is now more broadly conceived as registering the emotional salience of a stimulus, and has been shown to play a central role in many emotional behaviors in addition to fear. An understanding of the role the amygdala and related structures play in the processing of fear and threat has led to important insight into and potential therapies for the anxiety disorders such as PTSD

Chapter 5 turns to the groundbreaking work of Antonio Damasio and his colleagues, whose research on the role of emotions in higher brain functions such as decision-making based on neurological patients has revived interest in the role of the body in emotions as first postulated by James. These patients, as exemplified by the prototypical patient Damasio refers to as Elliot, share the puzzling convergence of symptoms of an inability to make advantageous decisions in everyday life and work despite possessing intact cognitive functions as measured by a variety of neuropsychological tests, including the IQ test and disrupted emotional processing. Damasio argues that the inability to make appropriate decisions in these patients is due to damage to key structures of an emotional brain system that normally functions to "tag" experiences as good or bad. He calls these tags "somatic markers," which are stored maps of the body systems activated during the initial emotional events. During subsequent similar situations, these somatic markers will be reactivated, providing clues, often experienced as hunches or "gut" feelings, to an appropriate choice in decisions that are otherwise so complex or uncertain that reasoning systems are overwhelmed. Damasio's somatic marker hypothesis has important implications for the cognition/emotion dichotomy discussed above; rather than disrupting reason, he argues, emotions are instead *essential* to sound decision-making.

In Chapter 6, we turn to the connections between motivation and emotion through the study of hedonics, or the pleasurable or unpleasurable features of a stimulus. One definition of emotions is based on the states elicited by rewards and punishments, or by the expectation of reward or punishment. This view of emotions focuses on understanding the "value" of a stimulus: Is it good or bad? Do I want it? Kent Berridge is one of the researchers beginning to develop a neuroscience of hedonics by investigating how a sensory stimulus we like, such as the taste of sugar, becomes "painted" with the "pleasure gloss" that we call *sweet*, imbuing it with the "incentive salience" that draws our attention like a magnet. His work has uncovered two separable brain systems, one for liking and one for wanting, or incentive salience. Although these two systems normally work together—we usually want what we like—they can be dissociated both anatomically and pharmacologically. This work has significant implications for understanding conditions like drug addiction and eating disorders in which wanting and liking become dissociated.

In Chapter 7, we turn to the work of contemporary pain researcher A. D. (Bud) Craig. Craig's work is a fascinating exploration of what the great early physiologist Charles Sherrington (1857–1952) called the "material me"—how the brain representation of the body contributes to the sense of self. Sherrington also introduced the term "interoception" to distinguish sensing of the internal body from sensing the input to the body from the external world, which he called "exteroception." Craig makes a strong argument for the idea that a buried piece of cortex, known as the insula, brings together interoceptive and exteroceptive information in the ultimate body map that is crucial for assessing the emotional significance of a stimulus based on the needs of the body, as well as giving rise to the "feeling" of a self. Craig's work provides theoretical support for therapies for mental distress that concentrate on monitoring and regulating bodily functions, such as controlling breathing and heart rate.

In Chapter 8, we discuss the extensive work on memory and emotion. Emotional events are arousing and trigger the release of stress-related hormones and neurotransmitters such as epinephrine, cortisol and norepinephrine. California-based psychologist James McGaugh and his many collaborators have demonstrated that the emotional enhancement of memory depends on release of norepinephrine in the amygdala, the same brain structure studied by LeDoux in his fear studies, just after a learning experience. Rockefeller neuroscientist Bruce McEwen and his coworkers have shown that chronically high levels of another stress hormone, cortisol, can result in damage to the neighboring hippocampus, shrinking its volume substantially. The interactions between the overactivated amygdala and depleted hippocampus are thought to be responsible for the paradoxical memory symptoms of posttraumatic stress disorder (PTSD), with its intensification of sensory flashbacks and deleterious effects on memory in everyday life. We will also discuss the work of Elizabeth Phelps, an NYU psychologist who is one of a number of contemporary researchers whose work is inspiring the development of promising new therapies for anxiety and PTSD.

In Chapter 9, we address the relationship between emotion and cognition through consideration of how the less specific but more pervasive affects, what we often refer to as moods, influence what and how we think, make judgments and decisions, and form impressions. Norbert Schwartz and Gerald Clore and their many collaborators have pioneered an approach known as feelings-as-information. With clear parallels to Damasio's somatic marker hypothesis, the feelings-as-information theory posits that how we feel—broadly conceived of as positive or negative, good or bad—provides a crucial assessment about the value of a situation that is needed during "cognitive" processes such as judgment and decisions. Schwartz and Clore's work suggests that how we feel also alters *how* we think, or our "cognitive style." Negative affective states such as sadness and fear have been associated with focused, narrow processing of local features, whereas positive emotions like happiness have been aligned with a broad, relational style of processing that is more globally focused. Although positive affect is most often aligned with global processing and negative affect with a local focus, recent work also points to the context-dependent and situated nature of affect–cognition interactions.

Chapter 10 continues our investigation of how the emotional stimulus or affective state alters information processing in the brain, beginning with the earliest levels of perception and attention and moving on to their role in choices or decisions. Emotional stimuli grab attention by lowering the perceptual threshold and increasing the ability to make fine discriminations. During an emotional event, seeing and hearing literally improve. We also explore the vibrant field of neuroeconomics, which is beginning to develop a neural basis of decision-making. Human decisions often violate basic assumptions about the "rational actor" that inform classical economic models. As shown by Amos Tversky and Daniel Kahneman in behavioral experiments, we are less likely to choose an option presented in terms of loss than an identical one presented as a gain. Thus, our decisions often appear irrational. The phenomenon of loss aversion, and individual differences in susceptibility to it, can now be attributed to the differential responsivity of the amygdala to losses as opposed to gains.

Chapter 11 concerns emotion regulation. One of the really exciting, and even unexpected, consequences emerging from a neuroscience of emotion is new insight into emotion regulation. James Gross, Kevin Ochsner, Matthew Lieberman, and many others have begun to outline the many ways that emotional behavior can be regulated. Their experimental work has started to show how language, meditation, and other strategies can be learned and used to modify emotional behavior beyond simply ignoring or suppressing urgent emotional states. The neural basis of explicit strategies such as reappraisal or reframing of emotional situations has been shown to involve the same control mechanisms involved in other forms of self-regulation. New work is also beginning to uncover the neural mechanisms of implicit emotion regulation processes and the relationship between explicit and implicit forms of modifying emotional experience. The clinical application of basic neuroscience is being effectively realized in investigations of these forms of emotion regulation.

In the concluding chapter, we return to our guiding question "What is an emotion?" and the further questions that it generates in light of the body of work that we have introduced in the heart of the book. We hope that our tour of a few historical sites and the many contemporary affective neuroscience laboratories will do the work of transforming mystery and frustration into more complex and biologically grounded understandings of our feeling brains.

The Feeling Brain

The Early Work on Defining Emotion

From William James to Appraisal Theory

The late 19th-century period when William James was writing has been termed the "Golden Age" of emotions (Gendron & Barrett, 2009). James was part of the first wave of scientific work on emotion initiated by Charles Darwin's 1872 publication *The Expression of the Emotions in Man and Animals*. Darwin's work, together with the publication of James's seminal 1884 essay "What Is an Emotion?," can be seen as the beginning of the scientific study of emotions. Although not as widely known outside psychology and philosophy as his famous novelist brother, Henry James, William James was a key figure in the early days of American psychology. His founding text *The Principles of Psychology*, published in 1890, laid the groundwork for the field. In this influential text, James wrote about many facets of mental life, including habit, perception, attention, memory, will, consciousness of self, and, of course, emotions. James's trademark became his use of a rich and descriptive analysis of subjective experience to supplement his extensive scientific and philosophical knowledge. His unique insights have inspired generations of psychologists, who continue to look to him, as many biologists look to Darwin, as having been able to capture the essence of most core principles in his field.

James's choice to attend to emotion can be understood in part from his own struggles with his emotions. Both James and his father suffered from severe anxiety attacks in their early adulthood (Fancher, 1996; Richardson, 2006). James was also afflicted with persistent depression and a variety of bodily ailments often thought to have a strong psychosomatic component.

As we will see, James used an introspective analysis of his experiences with these mental disorders and the role of the body in illness to inform his model of emotions.

Working barely 30 years after the publication of Darwin's *Origin of Species*, James, like many scientists of his time, was deeply influenced by Darwin's theory of natural selection. In his often overlooked, but increasingly influential, text *The Expression of the Emotions in Man and Animals*, Darwin explored the evolutionary origins of bodily expressions of emotions such as joy, anger, fear, disgust, shame, and surprise in a wide variety of animals, including humans. He argued that the marked similarities of emotional expressions across species, such as the baring of teeth in anger or aggression seen in humans and dogs, and even the hissing of geese when threatened, are evidence of their evolution from common ancestors. Emotions and their physical expressions, just as much as physiology and structure, are the products of natural selection. By focusing on the shared evolutionary functions of emotions and emotional behavior, Darwin's work opened the door to the use of animal models in emotion research.

James's theory of emotions was therefore strongly centered on evolutionary theory. He began "What Is an Emotion?" by chastising his fellow physiologists and neurologists for excluding from their scientific investigations what he called the "aesthetic" sphere of the mind, which James elaborated as "its longings, its pleasures and pains, and its feelings" (1884, p. 188). Evolutionary theory argues that all mental experiences emerge from brain processes similar to those of the more objectively definable perceptual and motor processes. In "What Is an Emotion?," therefore, James put forward one of the first brain-based theories of emotions.

In his essay, James, like Darwin, focused on emotional expression, and he was especially interested in the changes occurring *within* the body during emotional expression. Philosophers and scientists had long shared a central assumption about the relationship between emotional experience, or feelings, and emotional expression. It seemed intuitively straightforward: An emotional stimulus provokes an emotional feeling such as fear, and the emotional experience then initiates the bodily changes we commonly associate with emotion. This is how most of us understand the relationship between our feelings and our emotional expressions. We cry because we feel sad, and when we observe someone else crying, we assume that their tears are caused by feelings of sadness.

In "What Is an Emotion?," James turned this everyday and widely accepted notion on its head. To illustrate his counterintuitive model, James recounted his now-famous bear example. Our commonsense view of the order of events is that we see a bear, feel frightened, and then run. James argued instead that we feel afraid of the bear because we tremble; he inserted bodily changes between the eliciting stimulus and the emotion. "My thesis on the contrary is that *the bodily changes follow directly the* PERCEPTION *of the exciting fact, and that our feeling of the same changes as they occur IS the emotion*" (1884, pp. 189–190, capitalization and italics in original). Contrary to our everyday experience, James not only insisted that "we feel sorry because we cry, angry because we strike, afraid because we tremble" (p. 190), but he claimed that without the bodily manifestations, we have no emotion.

James of course recognized that this theory would be met with incredulity, and most of the paper was devoted to developing several lines of evidence to persuade his readers of his case. He first reminded readers that Darwin's work had shown that evolution equips living organisms with built-in responses to the important features of their environment, stating that "every living creature is in fact a sort of lock, whose wards and springs presuppose special forms of key" (James, 1884, p. 191). A "key" here refers to an environmental stimulus, in this case the bear. The sight of a bear opens its specific lock, triggering a built-in adaptive response. The heart begins to pound, breathing becomes rapid, and the senses are enhanced to help the organism quickly and automatically seek out safety. James argued that there is no need to *feel* fear in order to run from the bear; the sight of the bear simply opens the lock, and the bodily response is released. Evolution has prepared organisms to react to such a threat. It is only once we become aware of the bodily responses that have been triggered—our pounding heart and trembling knees—that we actually "feel" the fear. It is this *feeling* that is the emotion. An emotion is thus a sensory experience—the feeling of the bodily changes that have been triggered by an emotional stimulus. James viewed the body as the "sounding-board" of emotions and emphasized the extent, subtlety, and variety of bodily responses involved, including changes in the glands, muscles, heart, entire circulatory system, bladder, bowels, mouth, skin, liver, and breathing. This great variety of bodily response means that "no shade of emotion, however slight, should be without a bodily reverberation as unique, when taken in its totality, as is the mental mood itself" (p. 192).

The next line of evidence that James presented is another thought experiment. He asked his readers to imagine a strong emotion stripped of all bodily manifestations. If we can do so, "we find we have nothing left behind, no 'mind-stuff' out of which the emotion can be constituted, and that a cold and neutral state of intellectual perception is all that remains" (1884, p. 193). For James, such a "purely disembodied human emotion is a nonentity" (p. 194). He recounted a case of a woman who had lost all feelings of pleasure in formerly joyful activities such as eating, listening to music, and the healthy growth of her children. She described her loss of emotions as a loss of physical sensations: "Each of my senses, each part of my proper self, is as if it were separated from me and can no longer afford me any feeling" (p. 200). To James, this woman was an unfortunate illustration of "how much our mental life is knit up with our corporeal frame" (p. 201). The inconceivability of feeling an emotion without experiencing its bodily manifestations is really the cornerstone of James's theory.

James proposed a test of his theory. If, as he claimed, feelings are caused by feedback from the body as it engages in action initiated by an emotional stimulus, then if we voluntarily alter the body we should be able to alter our feelings. We see proof of this in our everyday experience. James argued that "whistling to keep up courage is no mere figure of speech. On the other hand, sit all day in a moping posture, sigh, and reply to everything in a dismal voice, and your melancholy lingers" (1884, p. 198). He also made use of his own experience with anxiety, a disorder he characterized as the "most distressing of all maladies" (p. 199). James posited that the overwhelming dread provoked during an anxiety attack can be overcome through gaining control of the bodily symptoms. As proof, James gave the example of a friend who told him that the feeling of dread dissipated as soon as he could control his breathing and slow his racing heart. This may seem too simple a solution to all human emotional woes, and it should be noted that James never revealed whether he was able to control his own anxiety using this strategy. However, he was convinced that application of this basic principle would have significant consequences. He urged his reader to consider the profound implications:

> There is no more valuable precept in moral education than this, as all who have experience know: if we wish to conquer undesirable emotional tendencies in ourselves, we must assiduously, and in the first instance cold-bloodedly, go through the outward motions of those contrary dispositions we prefer to cultivate. (p. 198)

Work on the role of the body in emotions has recently become an intensely active area of emotion research and, as James so long ago proposed, is having a direct impact on emotion regulation in clinical practice. In a 2007 review paper, contemporary researcher Paula Niedenthal described work that confirms James's injunction to put on a happy face. For example, in one study, participants forced to smile by holding a pencil between their teeth rated cartoons as funnier than the people who were unable to smile because they were told to hold the pencil between their lips without touching it with their teeth. This simple physical manipulation of bodily expression was enough to alter the emotional experience, as James had asserted.

James's Emotional Brain

Our emphasis in this book is on the brain substrates of emotions, and it might be easy to dismiss James's introspectively based theory as having primarily historical interest. In fact, James was well informed about the physiology of his time, having begun his academic life as a lecturer in anatomy and physiology at Harvard, where he had previously obtained a degree in medicine. Although James was understandably limited by the embryonic state of neurology at that time, he was able to offer some speculation about how the brain processes emotion.

James's hypothesis was simple and sparse; no special emotional structures were necessary. Because an emotion was simply a sensory experience—the sensing of the body—James proposed that the processing of emotions should require nothing beyond already identified sensory cortex: "The emotional brain-processes not only resemble the ordinary sensorial brain processes, but in truth *are* nothing but such processes variously combined" (p. 188). This simple brain theory was later seriously challenged by Walter Cannon (1871–1945), a Harvard physiologist who had studied with William James as an undergraduate.

James-Lange versus Cannon-Bard

James's evidence for the primacy and necessity of bodily manifestations in emotion was introspective and conceptual; he reflected on his own experience of emotion and asked his readers to do the same. A year after James published "What Is an Emotion?," a Danish physiologist, Carl Lange (1834–1900), published a paper proposing a similar theory but with more emphasis on identifying the bodily manifestations of some of the "standard" emotions: sorrow, joy, fright, and anger-rage (Lange, 1885/1912). Although for Lange the important bodily correlates of emotions were exclusively cardiovascular changes instead of the broader visceral and somatic changes proposed by James, the two theories became grouped together as the James-Lange theory. In spite of its lack of experimental support, the James-Lange theory quickly became the dominant theory of emotions until the publication of an exhaustive critique by Walter Cannon in 1927.

Cannon became famous for his work on the concept of homeostasis—the tendency of the body to maintain optimal internal conditions in the face of widely fluctuating external conditions (see the section on homeostasis in Box 1.1 for more on this important concept). He also conducted pioneering work on the autonomic nervous system, the part of the peripheral nervous system that regulates the homeostatic functions of the body, and coined the well-known phrase "fight or flight" to describe the effects of activating the sympathetic arm of the autonomic system (see Box 1.1 for more information about divisions of the nervous system).

Through his work on the regulation of homeostasis by the autonomic nervous system, Cannon had become very knowledgeable about the bodily changes in different emotional states. In fact, one of his major works is titled *Bodily Changes in Pain, Hunger, Fear and Rage* (1915). He had the experimental tools to test James's theory, and his 1927 paper, *The James-Lange Theory of Emotions: A Critical Examination and an Alternative Theory*, sounded the death knell for the James-Lange theory, and with it interest in the role of the body in emotions. This remained true until the recent emergence of a new neuroscience of emotion and the development of much more sensitive measures of both the brain and the body. The James-Lange theory, in modified form, is again generating intense interest.

Cannon's first evidence against the James-Lange peripheral theory of emotion came from experiments directly testing the sufficiency and necessity of bodily changes in emotional expression. Sir Charles Sherrington (1857–1952), an eminent British physiologist and Nobel Prize winner, had already demonstrated that cutting the vagus nerve, the major parasympathetic nerve carrying sensory information from the viscera (see Box 1.1), significantly disrupts the input of visceral information from the body but does not interfere with the ability to express appropriate emotions. Referring to one such vagotomized dog, he reported, "Her anger, her joy, her disgust and when provocation arose, her fear, remained as evident as ever" (quoted in Cannon, 1927, p.108). Likewise, Cannon was able to demonstrate a similar result in sympathetically isolated cats. Emotional expression in cats and dogs did not seem to require intact connections between the visceral system and the central nervous system.

This evidence seemed damning enough on its own, but Cannon furthered his argument by asserting that the autonomic nervous system both is too slow and lacks the specificity to differentiate among different emotions. Cannon claimed that *any* stimulus that provokes arousal of the sympathetic nervous system leads to similar or even identical visceral changes. In fact, similar autonomic activation occurs not only for the negative emotions of fear and rage, but also for positive emotions such as joy. Responses not primarily emotional in character, such as fever and exposure to cold, also lead to similar visceral changes. On the basis of these results, Cannon concluded that it was more appropriate to view the sympathetic nervous system as a unit, which he dubbed the fight-or-flight response (see Box 1.1 for more detail). The fight-or-flight system thus mediates arousal; it simply does not have the requisite specificity to allow emotions to be differentiated.

Cannon also argued against James's idea that emotions result from the sensing of bodily information by claiming that the viscera are "extraordinarily undemonstrative," pointing out that we remain blissfully "unaware of the contractions and relaxations of the stomach and intestines during digestion . . . , of the squeezing motions of the spleen, of the processes of the liver" (1927, p. 111). If we are mostly unaware of visceral activity, how can it inform our subtle and nuanced feelings?

In his final argument, Cannon addressed the idea that altering feedback from the body would alter emotions. He pointed to work by Maranon, one of the first researchers to inject subjects with the adrenal hormone adrenaline and record their emotional responses. Adrenaline is normally released into the blood by sympathetic activation, and it quickly activates the full range of bodily changes observed during intense emotions. Nonetheless, Maranon's subjects almost never reported having specific emotions. Although they did report feeling "keyed up," their subjective experiences had an unreal quality; they seemed to feel "as if" they were afraid, sad, or happy. To Maranon, their reported experiences "were without true feeling" (quoted in Cannon, 1927, p. 113). The only exception to this conclusion occurred when his participants were "primed" by inducing an emotional state before the injection, for example, by talking to them about a sick child or dead parents. In those cases, the emotions provoked by those thoughts and memories sometimes became more intense after an adrenaline injection.

Cannon, working together with his former student Philip Bard (1898–1977), who was becoming a well-known physiologist at Johns Hopkins, then proposed an alternative brain model of emotions. The Cannon-Bard theory, as it is now known, not only attacked the role of bodily feedback in the experience of emotion proposed in the James-Lange model, but it also challenged the proposal that emotional information was processed in the sensory and motor cortices of the brain. Instead, Cannon and Bard identified a subcortical location for emotion: the diencephalon, composed of the thalamus and the hypothalamus (see Box 1.1 for details about the divisions of the central nervous system). The proposed role of the diencephalon in emotion was based on studies that Cannon initially conducted with Britton in 1925 on decorticate animals—cats whose cortices had been surgically removed. Once the decorticate cats recovered from their operation, they readily displayed intense fury, disproving the idea that the cortex is necessary for emotional expression. Cannon and Britton termed this behavior "sham rage" because it could be provoked by innocuous stimuli that would not normally evoke a strong emotional response, such as touching the tail. However, lesions below the level of the thalamus prevented expression of rage (Bard, 1928), pointing to the critical role of the diencephalon in generating emotional behavior. Cannon also pointed to the emotional displays seen when humans are in the early stages of ether anesthesia or suffering from acute alcoholism. The disruption of cortical activity in these states seemed to confirm the importance of subcortical rather than cortical structures in the generation of emotional expression.

Cannon and Bard proposed that an emotional stimulus first travels to the thalamus. The thalamus activates the adjacent hypothalamus, which then organizes the full range of necessary bodily responses through regulation of autonomic, endocrine, and motor centers. Simultaneously, however, the thalamus relays this information upward to the cortex. It is via this thalamocortical projection that the stimulus acquires an emotional meaning. In the words of Cannon, "the thalamic disturbances contribute glow and color to otherwise simply cognitive states" (1927, p. 121). The cortex is thus required for emotional awareness. In the Cannon-Bard model, emotional feeling and emotional behavior are simultaneously activated through different routes.

The evidence of sham rage in decorticate animals also suggested to Cannon and Bard that the thalamus and hypothalamus are ready to discharge upon stimulation with any appropriate stimulus. Since cats with an intact cortex do not show such easily provoked anger, the cortex must act to inhibit or modify this impulsive subcortical activity. Cannon thus proposed that projections from the cortex back to the diencephalon carry the higher-level cognitive information acquired from experience and learning that could be used to tame the trigger-happy emotional subcortical structures.

The Cannon-Bard theory thus provides a mechanism by which emotions can color experience as well as a way for nonemotional information acquired by learning and experience to have a significant impact on our emotions and behavior. Cannon felt his model was superior to James's because he could offer experimental support for it. He also criticized the James-Lange model for focusing only on the sensory, or "felt," side of emotions. Emotions are more than just feelings—they also impel action. The Cannon-Bard proposal that the thalamus and hypothalamus, when unimpeded by the cortex, generate emotional behavior automatically and impulsively, helps us to understand the common "sense of being seized, possessed, or being controlled by an outside force and made to act without weighing of the consequences" (Cannon, 1927, p. 124).

Cannon's emphasis on subcortical processing of emotion expression was immediately influential, and has remained so in contemporary work, although the thalamus itself is no longer highlighted as a key region in modern models. Subcortical structures, which are older evolutionarily and widely shared among animals, reflexively mediate the basic adaptive behaviors that emotions seem designed to elicit. The more recently evolved cortical regions, which are most highly developed in humans, are implicated in cognitive processes and reason.

The Cannon-Bard critique with its seemingly irrefutable experimental evidence was devastating for the James-Lange theory. However, it's worth noting that James based his thinking on the assumption that bodily manifestations are more far-reaching than Cannon assumed and include somatic as well as autonomic changes. Today, with more technically sensitive instruments able to measure more aspects of autonomic activity, more support for James's position is emerging (B. H. Friedman, 2010). While it may not be true, as suggested by James, that bodily changes are so many and varied that it is conceivable that every shade of emotion has a unique bodily reverberation, even in Cannon's time there was evidence that the sympathetic nervous system did not always act as an all-or-none unit. For example, the flushed face of anger can be easily differentiated from the pallor of fear. Clearly, sympathetic activation of the cardiovascular system associated with fear and anger results in very different patterns of blood flow.

Although James and Cannon hinted at the role of higher-level factors in processing emotional experiences, such as being afraid of an imagined bear, it was not until much later that the field of emotion research concerned itself more centrally with cognition. The development of models that focused on how emotional stimuli are assessed by individuals—how they are appraised—led to a refocusing of attention on cognitive aspects of emotion.

Thinking about the Bear

A recent experience I (EBJ) had illustrates the need for further thinking about the potential role of higher cognitive processes in initiating as well as modifying emotional behavior.

At the entrance to a large forest where I was about to walk my dog, I met another dog walker who warned me that his dog had been spooked by something in the woods. Although he himself had not seen anything, he felt sure his dog had detected a bear. In fact, bear sightings had been reported in the area recently, and dogs can clearly smell and hear things quite undetectable by humans. In spite of his warning, I decided to go into the woods, although I would avoid the trail he had taken.

Nonetheless, the mental image of a bear that his words had evoked created a powerful fear response in me. As a way to keep my anxiety from escalating, I thought about how well this experience illustrated the purpose of fear. My senses were heightened: Every little sound seemed amplified and crystal clear. I suddenly had a kind of visual super-sense with an expanded field of view and uncommon clarity. I even seemed to hear the blood pumping through my body, preparing me for the flight part of Cannon's sympathetic response (I had no intention of engaging in the fight part). My perceptions of the sensory world were profoundly altered by my emotional state.

These sensory and bodily changes were not initiated by a stimulus in the external world; they were generated by thoughts and memories, illustrating the vital role of language and thoughts in provoking an emotional response. Another intriguing aspect of this experience was how I used cognitive activity to manage my anxiety about the prospect of meeting a bear. Thinking about this book transformed my fear into other emotions, such as interest in the experience, a sense of achievement in coping with the anxiety, and even the experience of love and caring as I thought about the welfare of my dog and other family members who often walked in the woods with me. However, although neither my dog nor I detected a bear or anything threatening, I have been reluctant to go back to those woods that I used to love walking in.

Appraisal Models of Emotion

The examples of emotions used by James focused primarily on those prompted by intense stimuli, such as predators, that appear to activate built-in locks—innate emotion pathways. Yet many emotions are not triggered by these kinds of powerful stimuli. Cannon and Bard, on the other hand, seem to have simply ignored the question of how different emotional stimuli are able to activate different emotional response programs in the thalamus. They seemed content with having successfully dismantled the Jamesian idea that bodily feedback can be used to identify different emotions. But if the body doesn't carry the information about the nature of the specific emotion, where does that information come from?

This crucial issue of emotion identification was not addressed by the field of emotion research until the so-called "cognitive revolution" of the mid 20th century revived interest in cognitive factors. The cognitive turn in emotion research was initiated by the theoretical work of Magda Arnold (1903–2002), who proposed that a process she termed "appraisal" is the essential first step in emotion processing. In the appraisal model, a cognitive process, the identification of the stimulus and its meaning, is the first step in emotion processing and is what permits activation of a specific emotional program. In the appraisal model, I see the bear in the woods and appraise it as dangerous; it is my appraisal of the bear as a threat that provokes my emotion of fear and my decision to run to safety. If the bear were behind the bars at the zoo, I would likely appraise it differently. Although appraisals can be conscious and deliberate, some appraisal processes can be implicit and automatic.

Schachter and Singer's Experimental Demonstration of Appraisal

Social psychologists Stanley Schachter and Jerome Singer published a compelling and influential study of the role of appraisal in emotion identification in 1962. Noting that the many attempts to identify physiological differences in different emotions had either failed or were at best inconclusive, they devised an experiment to test whether, in addition to arousal, a cognitive assessment of the specific context in which arousal occurs—an appraisal—is needed to actually identify the emotion. Because this study has been so influential, we will take time to explain it in some detail.

Like Maranon, Schachter and Singer induced sympathetic arousal in their subjects with adrenaline injections. In their experiment, however, the subjects were unaware of the true nature of the test or of the injection; they believed that they had been recruited for a test of the effect of vitamin injections on visual processing. Three groups of participants were injected with adrenaline, but each group was given different information about the expected side effects of the supposed vitamin injection. One group was given accurate information about the effects of adrenaline, a second group of subjects was misled about its effects, and a third group was given no information. A control group of subjects received a saline injection.

After the injection, while the participants were supposedly waiting for the drug to take effect prior to the visual study, a confederate of the experimenters, a stooge, entered the waiting room posing as another study volunteer. The stooge then began a scripted emotional performance, acting in either a "euphoric" or an "angry" manner. Participants' reactions to the stooge's behaviors were scored by an observer behind a one-way mirror who was blind to the study conditions. The participants were also asked to rate their own levels of anger and happiness after their time with the stooge. Schachter and Singer predicted that those who had received the adrenaline injections but had been given an adequate understanding of their arousal would be unaffected by the behavior of the stooge. On the other hand, without this information, the misinformed and uninformed groups would use the stooge's behavior as a way to understand and explain the arousal caused by the injection. If their study partner was angry, they would be more likely to interpret their arousal as due to anger, whereas passing the waiting time with a euphoric study partner would make them more likely to judge themselves as happy.

Schachter and Singer did indeed find that the behavior of misinformed or uninformed participants was judged as more similar to that of the stooge than to that of the informed participants. The self-rating measures for the euphoria condition also supported Schachter and Singer's hypothesis.[1] The control group results were more puzzling, however; rather than showing no effect, the control group mirrored the stooge's behavior more than those in the informed group, but not as strongly as those in the uninformed or misinformed groups. Perhaps they were experiencing some naturally induced arousal as a result of waiting to take an experimental test and misinterpreted it as induced by anger or happiness depending on the stooge's behavior?

Although the results of their experiment were more complex than expected, Schachter and Singer used their findings as support for a two-factor theory of emotion. First, the two-factor theory posits that bodily arousal is necessary for emotion, as proposed by James, but also that, consistent with the Cannon-Bard model, arousal alone is too unspecific to identify the kind of emotional state. The second factor in Schachter and Singer's theory provides the information needed to identify the nature of the arousal: a cognitive assessment.

Importantly, the second factor in Schachter and Singer's experiments involved the reactions of other people. The emotions experienced by study participants were substantially affected by the social context—what those around them were expressing. The same experimental situation was appraised differently depending upon the emotion expressed by their companion, the stooge. The social sharing of emotions has become an important theme in contemporary research. Current social psychologists, such as John Bargh and his colleagues at Yale University, have described the chameleon effect: People tend to unconsciously mimic the body postures and facial expressions of other people they are interacting with, and this increases their emotional connection (Chartrand & Bargh, 1999). The participants in Schachter and Singer's study experienced a kind of emotional contagion that was perhaps induced by the bodily based chameleon effect, an explanation that would have pleased William James.

Schachter and Singer's experiment was clever and appealing, and the concept of emotions as composed of two separable components, the bodily

---

1. The self-rating measures for anger did not follow the predictions, but this could be explained by the fact that the participants were reluctant to report their irritation to the experimenter because he was also their psychology professor.

response and the cognitive appraisal, was compelling. Yet in many ways the experiment seemed artificial. In the experimental setting, an injection of adrenaline may produce an artificially undifferentiated autonomic arousal that prompts a search for an explanation of this seemingly inappropriate response, but this may not happen in a more natural setting.

However, another compelling experiment that avoided the artificiality inherent in adrenaline injections added support for the two-factor theory. In this study, Donald Dutton and Arthur Aron (1974) asked male student participants to cross either a bridge that was very stable or a bridge that was suspended across a deep canyon and thus appeared precarious. At the other end of the bridge, participants were met by a female student who asked them to participate in her psychology survey. Once the survey was completed, the men were given the number of the interviewer in case they had further questions or wanted further information about the interview. The participants' degree of sexual interest in the interviewer was measured by whether they subsequently chose to call her as well as by their response to imagery questions on the survey. Crossing the precarious bridge resulted in higher sexual interest scores than crossing a stable bridge. The authors proposed that arousal generated by crossing the nerve-racking bridge would be misinterpreted as sexual interest in the attractive interviewer. The tendency of arousal to be assigned to whatever is present has been shown to occur with emotions themselves (see chapter 9), which appraisal theorist Gerald Clore refers to as the promiscuity of emotion (Clore & Huntsinger, 2007).

The experiments of Schachter & Singer and Dutton & Aron draw our attention to the fact that more than the eliciting stimulus must be considered in attempting to explain the rich phenomenon of an emotional experience. The social context and our cognitive appraisals of it must be taken into account.

Thus, the cognitive revolution in psychology brought cognition into the study of emotion. Unfortunately, as we will see, the cognitive study of emotion soon quickly left behind any role for the "felt" component of emotion that seemed so critical to James. Instead of an emphasis on the heat of emotional passions came a focus on the cold logic of emotions. It was not until the close of the 20th century that researchers began to turn back to James's insight that without the feelings of the body "we have nothing left behind, no 'mind-stuff' out of which the emotions can be constituted, and a cold and neutral state of intellectual perception is all that remains" (1884, p. 193). This neo-Jamesian research, which we will review extensively in chapters 5 and 7, has identified new brain regions in which the representation of the body is central for the processing of emotions. Before we move on to the recent work on the role of the body in emotions, we need to step back in time again to follow the story of the developing understanding of the brain areas and networks involved in emotional processing.

Differentiation of the Emotional Networks of the Brain

James's simple theory of the feeling brain was that no special structures were required to explain the processing of emotions. In his view, there was no exclusive brain-seat for emotion; instead, feelings were generated as a result of brain processing of body states by the same sensory and motor centers that had already been identified for other cognitive and volitional processes. Cannon and Bard's theory was the first real theory of an emotional brain that defined specific sites: The brain center involved in emotions was the subcortical diencephalon, particularly the thalamus. For Cannon and Bard, the thalamus was responsible for giving emotional tone or coloring to sensations and actions, providing a kind of emotional gloss on experience. Their model was also the first to differentiate between the roles of the cortex and subcortical structures. In their model, the more recently evolved cortex was the site of higher cognitive functions, and it could inhibit and regulate the impulsive thalamus. Subcortical structures were in charge of basic homeostatic functions as well as the automatic and reflexlike emotions. However, Cannon and Bard's brain theory also lacked specificity in terms of the brain regions and pathways involved.

The Cannon-Bard theory was influential during the 1920s and 1930s, having successfully turned the tide against the James-Lange emphasis on the body, but with time it too began to lose its prominence in the field. This was not due to disagreements with the basic tenets of the theory; rather, more detailed neuroanatomical knowledge superseded Cannon's thalamic account and Bard's later emphasis on the hypothalamus. The basic insights of their model—the vital role of subcortical structures in emotion and the need for cortical inhibition of the rapid subcortical pathways—remained, but were incorporated into more complex and detailed anatomical theories put forward in the late 1930s, 1940s, and 1950s. The story of those neuroanatomical developments is the subject of our next chapter.

Box 1.1: Divisions of the Nervous System

The sprawling nervous system has typically been divided into structurally distinct subcomponents. The first major division distinguishes between the **central nervous system** (**CNS**), composed of the brain and spinal cord, those parts of the nervous system protected by the hard, bony coverings of the skull and vertebrae; and the **peripheral nervous system** (**PNS)**, which includes everything outside the CNS. The PNS includes the sensory and motor nerves carrying information to or from the CNS, as well as scattered **ganglia**,[2] or collections of neurons, located throughout the body.

The PNS

The PNS contains further subdivisions we refer to throughout the book. The first is between the **somatic** and **autonomic** divisions of the PNS. The somatic division is concerned with the interaction of the body with the external environment, and includes the motor nerves that activate skeletal muscles as well as sensory nerves from the major sense organs, such as the eyes, ears, and skin. The autonomic division senses and regulates the internal environment. It innervates the smooth muscles of the viscera, and cardiac muscle, rather than skeletal muscles, and in turn receives sensory information from the viscera. The autonomic system is thus often referred to as the **visceral system**, the term employed by William James, as the term "autonomic nervous system" was not coined until 1898.

Sensory information coming from the outside world and carried by somatic nerves is often designated as **exteroceptive**, while information about the internal environment carried by autonomic nerves is called **interoceptive**. The autonomic division, as its name implies, acts autonomously. We are not usually consciously aware of visceral sensations, and unless we are highly trained meditators or have received biofeedback training, it is difficult for us to consciously regulate our heart rate or blood pressure.

Finally, the autonomic nervous system is further subdivided into the **sympathetic** and the **parasympathetic** branches. Both divisions innervate the entire viscera, but they have opposing actions on their targets: One system activates, the other inhibits. The sympathetic division, dubbed the **fight-or-flight**

---

2. Collections of neurons are typically referred to as **ganglia** when they are located outside the CNS and **nuclei** when they occur inside the CNS. A major exception to this rule is the large *basal ganglia* of the forebrain.

response by Walter Cannon, prepares the body for action by increasing heart and breathing rates and releasing stored glucose into the blood to provide the energy needed by muscles for flight or fight. The parasympathetic system is concerned with "**rest and relaxation**," restoring and replenishing the body once sympathetic activation is turned off.

Once the need for fight or flight is over, sympathetic activity declines and the parasympathetic nervous system, concerned with rest and relaxation, becomes active, slowing down the heart and decreasing breathing rate. It works to replenish the energy used in sympathetic activation by promoting digestion, which was turned off when sympathetic activity selectively directed energy to skeletal muscles. Almost all the parasympathetic innervations of the body are carried by the **vagus nerve**, which contains both sensory and motor nerve fibers. Thus, it is relatively easy to disrupt parasympathetic function in the body by simply cutting the vagus nerve (vagotomy).

The sympathetic nervous system uses the neurotransmitter **norepinephrine (NE)** at its targets throughout the body, and in addition stimulates the release of its close cousin, the hormone **adrenaline**, or **epinephrine**, from the adrenal medulla, a modified sympathetic ganglion. Norepinephrine and adrenaline have very similar actions on their targets. Thus, an injection of adrenaline, which is commonly used to restart the heart during a heart attack or to counter the effects of an allergic reaction, has been used experimentally to mimic the flight-or-fight response. The parasympathetic system instead uses the neurotransmitter **acetylcholine (ACh)** at its targets.

The Brain

Based on early developmental divisions, the brain is divided into the **forebrain**, **midbrain**, and **hindbrain** (see Figure 1.1).

The major adult structures of the hindbrain include the **medulla** and **pons**, which mediate many basic homeostatic functions, and the **cerebellum**, or little brain, which sits just below the **cerebrum**, or cerebral hemispheres—the big brain. The cerebellum receives input from the organs of balance in the inner ear as well as proprioceptive input from our joints and muscles. Damage to the cerebellum disrupts balance as well as the smooth performance of movements.

The midbrain remains a rather simple structure in the adult, but in addition to important sensory and motor structures, it contains **nuclei**, or groups of neurons, which are the primary source of the brain's **dopamine**. Dopamine is implicated in reward, motivation, attention, and willed movement, and disorders

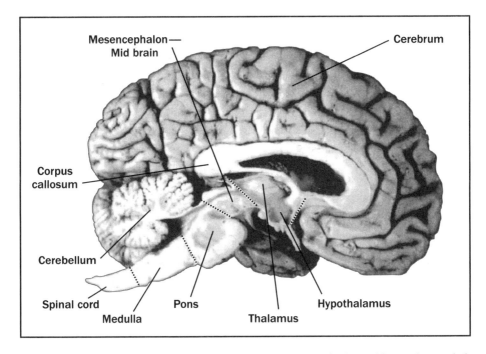

Figure 1.1 Mid-sagittal section of the human brain, showing forebrain (the cerebrum, thalamus, hypothalamus, and corpus callosum) midbrain (mesencephalon), and hindbrain (pons, cerebellum, and medulla) structures.

Source: Adaptation of work, copyright © John A. Beal, PhD, Department of Cellular Biology & Anatomy, Louisiana State University Health Sciences Center, Shreveport, November 30, 2005, CC-BY-2.5, (license: http://creativecommons.org/licenses/by/2.5/legalcode).

of dopamine function are associated with Parkinson's disease, schizophrenia, addiction, and attention disorders.

The forebrain grows dramatically during development, and makes up the major bulk of the adult brain. It is further divided into the **telencephalon** and the **diencephalon**.

The **diencephalon** includes two major structures, the **thalamus** and the **hypothalamus** (see Figure 1.1), as well as the **pineal gland** (epithalamus), which secretes the hormone melatonin. The thalamus is composed of numerous separate nuclei that have a variety of functions. One major function of the thalamus is as a relay station for sensory information en route to primary cortical areas (except for the olfactory system). Other nuclei are important in regulating states of consciousness like sleep and waking, as well as in regulating the level of arousal in the brain as a whole. Permanent coma can result from extensive damage to the thalamus.

As its name specifies, the **hypothalamus** lies directly below the thalamus, at the base of the brain. Like the thalamus, it is composed of many nuclei with diverse functions, but can be most generally described as mediating homeostasis (see below). The hypothalamus is often said to be the master endocrine gland, as it directly regulates the release of hormones from the pituitary gland, to which it is connected, as well as other endocrine glands. Other nuclei within the hypothalamus regulate autonomic activity and basic behaviors critical to survival, such as feeding, drinking, and sexual behavior.

The telencephalon refers to the **cerebrum**, or the two **cerebral hemispheres**, as well as the group of nuclei or ganglia in the center of the brain, the **basal ganglia**.

The basal ganglia are large structures buried in the center of the telencephalon and are most broadly designated as motor structures important for the selection and initiation of willed movements. Parkinson's disease and Huntington's Chorea are both diseases of the basal ganglia that present with major movement disorders. The basal ganglia comprise three main structures, the **caudate**, the **putamen** (together, the caudate and the putamen are referred to as the **striatum**), and the **globus pallidus**. The ventral portions of the striatum and globus pallidus are often referred to as separate structures: The **ventral striatum**, also referred to as the **nucleus accumbens**, and the **ventral pallidum** are considered important components of the **reward system**, which we discuss in chapter 6. The basal ganglia are major targets of the dopamine nuclei in the midbrain; dopamine projections to the striatum are disrupted in Parkinson's disease, thus upsetting the production of willed movement, while dopamine projections to the ventral striatum define the primary reward pathway.

The cerebral hemispheres are covered by the **surface cortex**, or bark, of the cerebrum—the outer layers of **gray matter**, which is nervous tissue composed primarily of cell bodies. The cortex comprises six distinct layers and is referred to as **neocortex**, which is commonly divided into four lobes (see Figure 1.2): **frontal** at the front above the eyes, **temporal** on the lower sides above the temples, **parietal** (the name is derived from the overlying bone and means "wall") on the upper sides, and **occipital** (visual) at the rear. A fifth lobe of the cortex, the **limbic lobe**, is buried underneath the neocortex, and is identified with emotional behavior.

To maximize surface area, the cortex is massively folded, giving it the wrinkled appearance of a walnut. The hills of the folds are referred to as **gyri** and the valleys are termed **sulci** (singular: sulcus). Two major sulci divide the lobes of the

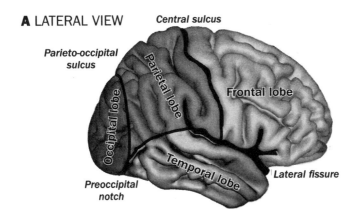

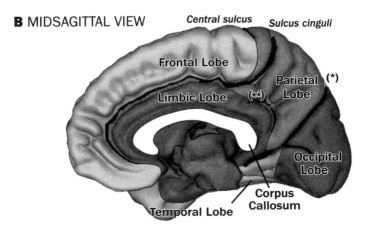

Figure 1.2 The lobes of the human brain. A. In the lateral view the conventional four lobes—frontal, parietal, temporal, and occipital—can be readily seen. The central sulcus divides the frontal from the parietal lobe, and the lateral or Sylvian fissure divides the temporal from the frontal and parietal lobes. The division of the occipital lobe from the parietal and temporal lobes is based on the location of the preoccipital notch and the parieto-occipital sulcus. B. In the mid-sagittal view another lobe of the brain identified by Broca can be seen: the limbic lobe. The cingulate gyrus is the area of the limbic lobe that lies above the corpus callosum and the parahippocampal gyrus is the lower area of the limbic lobe.

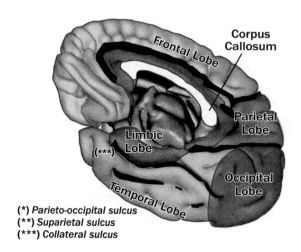

(*) *Parieto-occipital sulcus*
(**) *Suparietal sulcus*
(***) *Collateral sulcus*

Figure 1.2 **The lobes of the human brain.** (continued)

brain. The **central sulcus** divides the frontal from the parietal lobe, and the **Sylvian sulcus** (also known as the Sylvian fissure or the **lateral sulcus** or fissure) divides the temporal from the frontal and parietal lobes. Below the cortex are vast tracts of **white matter**, the myelinated axons that connect the cortex to many other parts of the brain and spinal cord. One broad band of white matter, the **corpus callosum** (see Figure 1.1), forms the bridge that connects homologous regions of the two cerebral cortices. The corpus callosum is sometimes severed to restrict the spread of seizure activity in intractable epilepsy, creating the "split-brain" condition that led to the discovery that the two hemispheres are specialized for different kind of processing functions.

Forming the buried medial surface of each hemisphere is a large band of cortex referred to as the limbic lobe by 19th-century neurologist Paul Broca, who described it as the rim, or hem, of the cortex. The part of this medial cortex just above the corpus callosum is called the **cingulate gyrus**. As it bends around the posterior edge of corpus callosum and returns anteriorly just below the lateral ventricle, it becomes the **parahippocampal gyrus**; slightly medial to the parahippocampal gyrus, and so not visible in Figure 1.2, is the adjacent **hippocampus**. The term *limbic* was subsequently used by Paul MacLean, who included a number of subcortical structures together with the limbic lobe to form the **limbic system**, which composed the structures of the emotional brain.

Structures found below the neocortex are often referred to by the general term **subcortical.** These include buried telencephalic structures such as the hippocampus, the amygdala and basal ganglia, and the diencephalon, but the term is often taken to include structures in the brain stem as well.

Homeostasis

French physiologist Claude Bernard (1813–1878) first focused on the *milieu intérieur*—the environment within—noting that the internal environment is maintained at a constant level in spite of large fluctuations in the external environment. In the 1920s, English physiologist Walter Cannon introduced the term **homeostasis** (from the Greek words *homeo*, meaning same or similar, and *stasis*, meaning standing still or stability) to refer to the processes by which the internal environment is maintained at an optimal state (Cannon, 1929). Homeostasis is regulated by the hypothalamus through its control of the autonomic nervous system and the endocrine system. Importantly, homeostasis is also maintained behaviorally; when we get too hot or cold, the appropriate autonomic responses to shiver or sweat will be activated, but we can also add or remove clothing, or move to a more appropriate environment. Thus, in addition to regulating the internal environment, some hypothalamic nuclei motivate behaviors needed to ensure survival and reproduction, such as feeding and drinking, sexual behavior, sleep, and aggression.

2

The Limbic System Version
of the Emotional Brain

The success of Cannon and Bard in overturning James's notion that emotional processing did not require any "special centers" in the brain spurred further efforts to identify the brain substrates of emotion. Their evidence that emotional behavior could persist in decorticate animals brought attention to the older, buried structures below the cortex. Although work by Bard identified the base of the diencephalon, particularly the hypothalamus, as the neural center controlling emotional *expression*, Cannon and Bard also argued that emotional *awareness* required the neocortex. Their model, however, made no attempt to address the mechanism or pathways by which cortical processes, such as thoughts and memories, could activate emotional expression in the hypothalamus. The first comprehensive brain theory of emotion addressing these unanswered questions was put forth by Cornell anatomist James Papez (1883–1959) in 1937. Making use of the growing knowledge of how different brain structures are interconnected, Papez proposed an entire network or circuit for emotion (Papez, 1937), a circuit that would integrate emotional experience and emotional expression as well as allow feelings and thinking to interact by linking the cortex to the hypothalamus.

Papez was able to identify many structures and pathways that today are known to participate in emotional processes, and his work inspired an even more detailed theory of the emotional brain by Paul MacLean (1913–2007) (see Lambert, 2003). MacLean modified and elaborated Papez's circuit into a set of interconnected cortical and subcortical structures he referred to collectively as the limbic system. Although recent emotion science informed by more sophisticated anatomical knowledge has begun to undermine the notion of a single system that mediates all emotions, a topic we take up in more detail at the end of this chapter, the term *limbic system* today remains practically synonymous with the emotional brain in both the popular and the academic press. Indeed, most contemporary neuroscience textbooks continue to refer to the emotional brain as the limbic system. In this chapter we set up the context for contemporary brain theories of emotion by looking more closely at the founding work of Papez and MacLean.

Papez's Emotional Circuit

James Papez was a medically trained neuroanatomist working in the 1930s and 1940s. Contemporary New York University emotion researcher Joseph LeDoux relates the rumor that Papez put together his seminal paper *A Proposed Mechanism of Emotion* in just a few days to demonstrate to an American donor who had lavishly funded a British group's research on the emotional brain that Americans also had something to say about the neuroanatomy of emotion (LeDoux, 1996, p. 85). At the heart of Papez's theory is an anatomical circuit that links the part of the brain which regulates emotion expression, the hypothalamus, with the neocortical areas that carry out the detailed analysis of sensory stimuli needed to subserve higher cognitive functions, including thinking, memory, and, at least in humans, consciousness awareness.

The Papez Circuit

Papez began his paper by noting that in light of Cannon and Bard's recent work identifying the hypothalamus as the neural center regulating emotional expression, an understanding of how the hypothalamus is connected to other brain structures, particularly the cortex, would be key to answering what he considered to be the two core unsolved questions about emotional processing: First, how do the everyday sensory events that are processed in well-known sensory cortical pathways acquire emotional coloring? And, second, how do our thoughts and memories, such as simply remembering meeting up with an old flame who once broke our heart, cause our heart to begin pounding, our palms to sweat, and our breathing to become rapid?

Differentiating Medial Cortex from Lateral Cortex

Thinking about the problem of how hypothalamic and cortical structures are linked to integrate emotions and higher cortical processes, Papez turned to work being done by evolutionary neuroanatomist C. Judson Herrick (1868–1960). Herrick's work had pointed to the presence of two anatomically distinct cortical circuits. One circuit connected sensory information from the eyes, ears, and skin to the lateral wall of the developing cortex through connections in the dorsal thalamus. In the adult, this lateral wall made up the entire surface of the cerebral hemispheres, or what we commonly refer to as cortex. A different region of developing cortex, the medial cortical wall, participated in a circuit with the hypothalamus. This cortex gave rise to buried, and presumably evolutionarily older, cortical structures such as the cingulate gyrus, lying just above the corpus callosum, as well as structures in the medial temporal lobe, such as the parahippocampus and the adjacent hippocampus (see Figure 2.1).

LeDoux uses the example of a hot dog bun to help us visualize the difference between medial and lateral cortex. The lateral cortex is akin to the brown outer surface of the bun, while the buried medial cortex is like the invisible white part of the roll. This distinction between the deeper medial cortex as being concerned with emotion and the overlying lateral areas that expanded dramatically in higher primates as being involved in cognitive processing continues to have currency in contemporary neuroscience.

The Stream of Feeling and Stream of Thinking

As he began his paper, Papez noted,

> The histories of the two walls of the hemispheres owe their disparity and distinctive structure to two totally different kind of integration—the hippocampus and the cingular cortex participating in hypothalamic activities and the lateral cortex in the general sensory activities. (1937, p. 726)

For Papez, the presence of a hypothalamic connection to the cortex suggested a way to assemble the pieces of the emotion puzzle. Extending Cannon's recent work placing the thalamus at the crossroads between sensory information activating higher cortical regions and that activating the body, Papez also proposed that the two streams of sensory information leaving the thalamus were each associated with their own distinct cortical circuit.

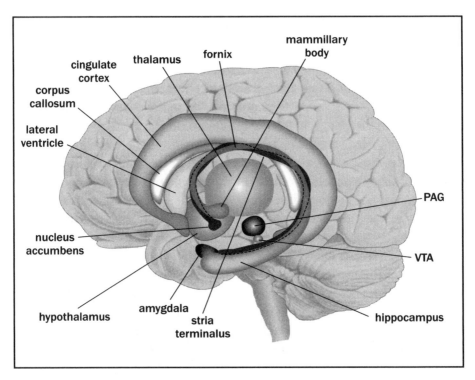

Figure 2.1 A schematic brain, highlighting the structures identified by Papez in his 1937 emotional circuit: the cingulate, the mammillary bodies of the hypothalamus, the hippocampus, and the anterior thalamic nuclei, as well as other important emotion-related structures.

Source: Adapted from a drawing by Daniel Greenberg.

As in the Cannon-Bard model, the dorsal thalamus served the well-known thalamic function of a sensory relay, directing sensory input to its appropriate cortical target to ultimately give rise to conscious cognitive perceptions and memories. Papez labeled this pathway the "stream of thinking."

However, making use of emerging knowledge of detailed brain connections, Papez was able to identify a second thalamic pathway arising from a previously unrecognized and older part of the thalamus, the diffuse ventral thalamus, which projected to a specific nucleus of the hypothalamus, the mammillary body. Papez's identification of the mammillary body as the hypothalamic target of the ventral stream of sensory input was another key piece of the puzzle, as information leaving the mammillary body also gives rise to two projections. One pathway projects deeper into the hypothalamus to activate emotional expression, as proposed by Cannon and Bard. The other pathway, however, was a pathway unknown to Cannon and Bard and carries information upward, passing through yet another thalamic relay, the anterior thalamus, on its way to its medial cortical target, the buried cingulate gyrus. It was here in this buried older cortex, Papez proposed, that sensory stimuli acquire emotional coloring. This pathway from the mammillary bodies to the cingulate gyrus was the first part of Papez's "stream of feeling."

Papez likens the role of the cingulate cortex in the processing of emotional stimuli to that of the occipital cortex as the primary receiving area for visual information: The cingulate serves as the primary cortical receiving area for emotional stimuli. From the cingulate, emotional information then radiates to all parts of the lateral cortex. In Papez's words, this "radiation of the emotive process from the gyrus cinguli to other regions in the cerebral cortex [adds] emotional coloring to psychic processes occurring elsewhere" (1937, p. 728).

In Papez's theory, it is the cingulate that confers meaning and value to all sensory events, including those processed by the stream of thought. As he described it, the cingulate is "the seat of dynamic vigilance by which environmental experiences are endowed with an emotional consciousness" (Papez, 1937, p. 737). Papez found support for the key role of the cingulate in emotional consciousness in neurologists' reports that cingulate damage in their patients resulted in loss of spontaneous emotional expression, thought, and activity and a marked reduction in conscious processes, resulting in a stuporous or even comatose state.

Integrating the Stream of Thinking with the Stream of Feeling

Figure 2.2 depicts a basic circuit diagram of the key structures in Papez's circuit. The Papez circuit also provides a pathway by which thoughts and feelings in higher centers can enter the stream of feeling to activate the hypothalamus via a top-down pathway through the cingulate to the other key structure in the Papez circuit, the hippocampus.

The hippocampus is where Papez envisioned that emotional information about thoughts and memories is elaborated. At the time Papez was writing, the function of the hippocampus was unclear. Earlier anatomists (see below) had suggested that medial cortical structures, including the hippocampus, had an olfactory function, and they were thus collectively named the "rhinencephalon," or smell brain (see Figure 2.1 for the location of the hippo-

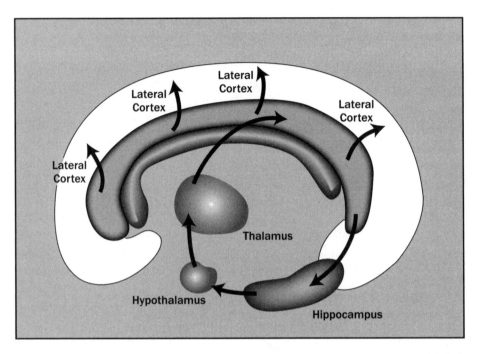

Figure 2.2 Cartoon brain diagram with the four key structures in Papez's circuit labeled: the cingulate cortex, the hippocampus, the anterior thalamus, and the hypothalamus. Arrows indicate the fanning out of signals from the cingulate to the lateral cortex.

Source: Adapted from a drawing by Daniel Greenberg.

campus). Papez explicitly challenged this notion. He noted that little real evidence had accrued to support an olfactory function for these structures; for example, lesions here did not result in olfactory deficits. Furthermore, dolphins and humans rely very minimally on olfactory senses,[1] yet have well-developed hippocampi. Instead, he pointed to work showing that "various parts of the cortex may incite hippocampal activity" (Papez, 1937, p. 732), including input from the cingulate gyrus. Furthermore, the association of the disease of rabies with the hippocampus, whose symptoms include intense emotional outbursts, strongly suggested to Papez that it played a key role in emotional behavior. Finally, the hippocampus is directly connected to the mammillary bodies of the hypothalamus through the fornix, completing the pathway by which thoughts and memories could activate the

---

1. Humans' lack of use of smell information has been seriously questioned by Shephard (2004), who emphasizes its important function in the human sense of flavor.

body. Thus, the enigmatic hippocampus came to serve a central function in Papez's stream of feeling.

The Papez Circuit Today

Many of the structures and almost all of the connections proposed by Papez as key players in his emotional brain network continue to be the focus of intensive study in affective neuroscience. His identification of the cingulate as primary emotional cortex was clearly prescient. As we will see in upcoming chapters, the role of the cingulate (particularly its anterior sections) in emotional processing is under intense current investigation. The list of functions currently linked to the cingulate, which is now parceled into numerous subregions that differ both functionally and in connections, include the valuation of stimuli, motivation, pain, willed behavior, and conflict resolution (Shackman et al., 2011; Torta & Cauda, 2011). As one group of authors recently noted, the "(anterior) cingulate lies in a unique position in the brain, with connections to both the 'emotional' limbic system and the 'cognitive' prefrontal cortex" (Stevens, Hurley, & Taber, 2011, p. 121). As such, another author comments, "it is hard to think of a common cognitive or affective experimental protocol that has not in fact been found to elicit activity in this region" (Egner, 2011, p. 1219). Indeed, some researchers continue to view the cingulate as an important substrate of conscious experience (Dalgleish, 2004).

In contrast, the central role in emotions that Papez allocated to the hippocampus in his circuit is less consistent with contemporary views. Studies that appeared in the 1950s shifted consensus about the function of the hippocampus away from emotion to emphasize its important role in the consolidation of long-term memories (see Box 2.1). A neighboring region directly in front of the hippocampus, the amygdala, has instead become a major focus in emotion science. The connections between the amygdala and hippocampus turn out to be vital for the emotional enhancement of memory, a story that we will explore in depth in chapter 8.

Papez concludes his article with a vital question: "Is emotion a magic product, or is it a physiologic process which depends on an anatomic mechanism?" (Papez, 1937, p. 743). In Papez's view, the function of emotions is to assign meaning to stimuli and prepare the organism to react to those important stimuli. By providing a circuit that links the hypothalamus with the cortex, Papez suggested a mechanism for the integration of emotional and cognitive functions. His early paper did much to dispel magical thinking about the emotional brain by putting forward an inspired and specific model of the emotional brain.

MacLean's Visceral Brain: The Limbic System

Twelve years after the publication of Papez's seminal paper, physician and neuroscientist Paul MacLean (1913–2007) took up the challenge of replacing magic with anatomy and formulated what is probably the most enduring and prevalent model of the emotional brain. Kelly Lambert (2003) has recently provided a brief but cogent biography of MacLean's work and ideas. MacLean's background and route to his work on emotion and the brain were quite different from Papez's anatomical one. After medical training at Yale and work as an army psychiatrist in New Zealand during World War II, MacLean opened a private practice in general medicine in Washington State. He soon became frustrated with this work because he felt that most of the physical symptoms his patients described were actually psychological in nature, and he found himself at a loss about how to treat them. To gain some scientific understanding of the role of emotions on physical processes, he looked to the published literature on brain physiology, immersing himself in the writings of Dr. Stanley Cobb, a neurologist at Massachusetts General Hospital in Boston who was also deeply interested in Freudian psychiatry. MacLean contacted Cobb to further his understanding of this complex material, and this correspondence led to the offer of a research fellowship position. So, MacLean moved his young family across the country to pursue this opportunity (Lambert, 2003).

During his internship, MacLean worked with patients suffering from psychomotor epilepsy, a condition he later described as "one of those cruel experiments of nature" (Holden, 1979, p. 1067). After noting the intense emotional experiences reported by some of his patients who had sustained temporal lobe damage, particularly in the area around the hippocampal formation, MacLean again turned to the scientific literature, and hit upon Papez's 1937 paper. Acting on Cobb's suggestion that he visit Papez, MacLean spent three intense days at Cornell with Papez in the spring of 1948. On the basis of her personal communication with MacLean, Kelly Lambert describes this encounter between these two giants of emotional brain anatomy as "a life-changing experience for MacLean as he was in awe of the neuroanatomical skill of Papez" (2003, p. 344). In her interview with Mac-

Lean 55 years after this formative experience, he described Papez as "*saint-like* and one of the most gifted neuroanatomists of the last century" (2003, p. 344).

In light of Papez's anatomical speculations, MacLean combined his earlier clinical experiences with psychosomatic diseases with his observation that epileptic seizures affecting medial temporal lobe structures gave rise to emotional experiences. It was widely assumed that diseases such as asthma and hypertension were psychosomatic in nature; that is, they emerged due to the disruption of autonomic functions, such as those regulating blood pressure and breathing, caused by emotional distress. However, until his discovery of Papez's paper, MacLean knew of no mechanism by which emotional experiences could act on the hypothalamus to disrupt autonomic function.

The next January, MacLean presented to a staff meeting of the Psychiatric Service of Massachusetts General Hospital his paper connecting Papez's theory of emotional circuitry with the autonomic disruption seen in psychosomatic diseases. This paper became MacLean's first publication on what he would later call the limbic system, although he had not yet coined that term. The paper was instead titled *Psychosomatic Disease and the "Visceral Brain": Recent Developments Bearing on the Papez Theory of Emotion.* In this paper, he described Papez's speculations on an emotional circuit in detail, which he described as a "tour de force" (MacLean, 1949, p. 339). He then related Papez's circuit to his observations that the emotional states provoked by seizures in these structures are often accompanied by a variety of visceral events, including chewing, gastric distress, and even a sense of hunger or urination and bowel movements. He also reviewed work done since the publication of Papez's paper that added support to these ideas. Brain stimulation near the mammillary body had been shown to produce a rise in blood pressure, as did stimulation of parts of the hippocampal gyrus and the cingulate gyrus. Together, both theoretical and clinical work were beginning to suggest specific mechanisms by which emotional disturbances could promote hypertension. The cingulate gyrus was also emerging as an important autonomic center, with powerful effects on respiration as well as blood pressure, and thus relevant to asthma as well hypertension. In addition to demonstrating that many of the structures in the Papez circuit were involved in autonomic regulation, MacLean pointed to work suggesting that other structures, including the amygdala, the orbitofrontal cortex (OFC), and possibly the insula, were also involved in visceral functions (see Figures 2.1, 6.1, and 7.1 for the locations of these regions); later, these structures were added to his emotional brain. As we will see in later chapters, each of these three subsequently introduced structures—the amygdala, OFC, and insula—now figure prominently in accounts of brain processing of emotions, and their respective roles are the focus of much current work.

Klüver-Bucy Syndrome

MacLean also connected the Papez circuit to the findings of another paper, appearing in the same year as Papez's paper, by University of Chicago scientists Heinrich Klüver (1897–1979) and Paul Bucy (1904–1992). It reported the results of medial temporal lobe lesions, and the eponymous Klüver-Bucy syndrome now refers to the constellation of symptoms that result from lesions to medial temporal lobe structures. Klüver had initiated these lesion studies in an attempt to localize the effects of mescaline on monkey oral behavior (Nahm & Pribram, 1998). However, after observing the radical effects of this surgery, which he described as the "most striking behavior changes ever produced by a brain operation" (as cited in Nahm & Pribram, 1998, p. 10), he quickly changed the focus of his research to the study of the temporal lobe. After the surgery, the vicious, intractably aggressive animal known as Aurora, who had been given to Bucy because of his known monkey-handling skills, appeared completely tamed. She exhibited a suite of behaviors later shown to be characteristic of medial temporal lobe lesions and now described as the Klüver-Bucy syndrome. In addition to having a total lack of fear or aggression, animals with these lesions are described as displaying "psychic blindness," or the inability to identify objects by sight, in spite of having intact visual function. They also exhibit "oral tendencies," examining all objects by mouth, including such inappropriate objects as feces and nails. In addition, they show a range of abnormal sexual behaviors and will attempt to copulate with inappropriate partners, including other species. Klüver and Bucy concluded that damage to the cortical and subcortical structures of the temporal lobe had "disrupted the processes by which the meaning of a sensory precept is appreciated" (Nahm & Pribram, 1998, p. 11). For MacLean, Klüver and Bucy's observations were further confirmation of the function of Papez's circuit in emotion: Medial temporal lobe structures were vital for assessing the psychological value of stimuli.

The Visceral Brain

Like Papez, MacLean questioned the primary role of medial cortical structures in olfaction, so he purposefully avoided using the term "rhinencephalon" to refer to his emotional brain. Instead, he chose the term "visceral brain" to draw attention to the visceral function common to these structures. His visceral brain included the members of the Papez circuit as well as the amygdala and regions of the medial prefrontal cortex that had been shown to have autonomic effects. He contrasted his visceral brain, which provided the link between emotions and the body, with the neocortex, the part of the brain that "holds sway over the body musculature and subserves the functions of the intellect" (MacLean, 1949, p. 344).

For MacLean, the visceral brain regulated the body and mediated basic survival behaviors involved in acquiring food, reproduction, and defense. As such, he proposed that these structures evolved early in the evolution of mammals. Furthermore, this "older" brain functioned instinctively and could regulate behaviors and bodily responses independently of the neocortex. The neocortex enabled the inhibition of overt bodily, or somatic, expression of emotional turmoil in order to conform to social standards, and MacLean speculated that in psychosomatic patients, the visceral brain escaped this inhibition. This chronically active "primitive" brain is what gave rise to the visceral dysfunctions related to peptic ulcers, colitis, hypertension, and asthma.

From the Visceral Brain to the Limbic System

In a paper published three years after his paper on the visceral brain, MacLean changed the name of his system to the one that would become synonymous with the emotional brain: the limbic system. In choosing the name "limbic," MacLean was explicitly reaching back to the work of the early French neuroanatomist Paul Broca, who described *le grande lobe limbique* in 1878 (Finger, 1994). Broca selected the Latin word *limbus*, meaning a circular edge or border, to refer to the ring of medial cortex composed of the cingulate gyrus above and around the corpus callosum and the parahippocampal gyrus curving around below the lateral ventricle (see Figure 1.2 for the location of the limbic lobe). Guided by the suggestion of an earlier anatomist as well as his own observations that the size of the limbic lobe seemed to vary by species depending on the degree to which they depended on smell, Broca assigned to the limbic lobe an olfactory function, and thus these structures became known as the "rhinencephalon," or nose brain. These limbic structures were present in all mammals, so must have evolved early in mammalian evolution. Broca thus associated these seemingly primitive cortical structures with basic survival functions, which he contrasted with the intellectual function of the neocortex, the cortex which had expanded so dramatically in the evolution of primates. For Broca, the limbic lobe represented the beast or brute within human brains (Finger, 1994). Unfortunately, because of the limited importance of the olfactory sense in humans, these buried limbic lobes soon became "the unwanted child of brain anatomy books and lectures" (Lambert, 2003, p. 344). Broca's work was even overlooked by Papez as he constructed his emotion circuit.

From the Limbic System to the Triune Brain

Although MacLean rejected Broca's assignment of an olfactory function to these structures, the idea of the beast within sparked his imagination. He came to view the human forebrain as composed of three separate brains that had evolved at different times and for different functions in evolutionary history. Drawing on vocabulary from his upbringing as the son of a Presbyterian minister, MacLean named his three-in-one model the "triune brain." The earliest and most ancient brain consisted of brainstem as well as basal ganglia structures at the core of the forebrain. This *reptilian* brain carried out the most basic instincts, such as feeding and reproductive behavior. Primitive animals such as reptiles, fish, and birds possessed only the reptilian brain and so were capable only of inflexible and stereotyped instinctive behaviors. The *paleomammalian* brain was then added to the reptilian brain with the evolution of early mammals and emerging prosocial behaviors necessary to care for young. This is the brain that corresponds to MacLean's limbic system, and it allowed for the simple emotions needed in basic social behaviors. It was only in the higher-order brains of primates that the crowning third *neomammalian* brain was added, and this is what allowed the development of higher intellectual functions, including, in humans, reasoning and language.

MacLean conceived of these three brains as both chemically and structurally separate and proposed that each could operate independently of the others. In MacLean's view, the human brain contained all three brains set up like a series of stackable Russian dolls. He colorfully described the older parts as the two "animals incognito" within modern man (Maclean, 1964, p. 95). In his own words,

> in evolution the brain develops somewhat like a house to which wings and superstructure are added. Man, it appears, has inherited essentially three brains. Frugal Nature in developing her paragon threw nothing away. The oldest of his brains is basically reptilian; the second has been inherited from lower mammals; and the third and newest brain is a late mammalian development which reaches a pinnacle in man and gives him his unique power of symbolic language. (1964, pp. 95–96)

MacLean felt strongly that the "animals within" had not been given enough attention in human brain science or psychiatry, and that to understand human psychiatric disorders, including psychosomatic disorders, more attention must be given to these brains.

The triune brain concept has been viewed as a flawed scientific theory since its inception. MacLean's conception that evolution works by adding on completely new units, like extensions to a house, is wrongheaded; animals are not like designed manmade structures. Although new brain structures have evolved over evolutionary time, these newer structures must be built on and integrated with older parts of the brain. Moreover, older brain structures can also evolve as needed. Indeed, beginning in the 1970s, neuroanatomists have shown that creatures designated as possessing only the reptilian brain, such as birds or fish, do in fact have neocortex. Thus, MacLean's claim that the neocortex evolved much later than the reptilian brain does not stand up to further scrutiny.

In spite of the failure of MacLean's triune brain theory, his concept of the limbic system as making up the emotional brain garnered considerable attention, as we discussed earlier. Only recently has this aspect of MacLean's work also come under attack. Joseph LeDoux (1996), whose work we discuss in detail in chapter 4, is one of the scientists who has argued most forcefully against the usefulness of the limbic system concept.

LeDoux's Critique of the Limbic Emotional Brain

LeDoux baldly states that the limbic system theory is wrong as an explanation of the emotional brain. Why is he so vehement about this issue? One part of his argument points to the confusion that has developed among anatomists about which brain structures should be considered members of the limbic system. Although the solution to the brain's emotional processing system seemed to be well in hand in the 1950s, the functional criteria MacLean used to define the limbic system—that is, those brain structures which can directly activate visceral function—collapsed. Structures with direct connections to the hypothalamus, an anatomical criterion proposed in an attempt to provide more coherence to MacLean's functional definition, lost ground as a defining feature of limbic structures when it was discovered that the hypothalamus is more widely connected to many other brain areas, including the neocortex, than once thought. Further, the discovery of a cognitive role for the hippocampus, a central structure for both Papez and MacLean, muddies the important emotional/cognitive distinction at the base of their theories.

Although the lack of defining anatomical or functional criteria to determine limbic system membership is a sound reason to reconsider the coherence of the limbic system concept, LeDoux's main argument is a conceptual one. MacLean's limbic system implies that a single brain system processes all emotions. However, distinct emotions have evolved to serve quite different purposes. For LeDoux, lumping together all emotions to be processed by a single brain system goes against the evidence of their distinct evolutionary functions. Aggression, as an adaptation against danger, requires very different brain processing than does the equally important function of caring for and nurturing offspring. LeDoux argues that different brain systems evolved to serve different emotional functions, and that the wide acceptance of the limbic system as defining the whole emotional brain has prevented a more nuanced and detailed search for specific emotional brain processes. As we will discuss in chapter 4, LeDoux began his search for emotional brain systems from a radically different starting point than either Papez or MacLean. Instead of trying to identify an emotional brain, LeDoux instead focused on how one particular emotion—fear—is processed by the brain. This groundbreaking work has led to the identification of the amygdala as a major fear-processing structure as well as a central player in more general emotional processes.

The Importance of the Nonverbal in Emotion

Although LeDoux is critical of the theoretical approach of MacLean and Papez, he acknowledges that some of the structures identified by their work do play key functions in emotional processing. He also comments on the irony that, in spite of the long acceptance of the limbic system concept, a key goal of MacLean's, which was to identify the brain regions involved in integrating information from the internal and external environments, has often been neglected. As we will see in later chapters, it is precisely those structures that integrate signals from the body with those of the outside world that are seen today as the critical structures of emotional processes.

LeDoux also admires MacLean's clear separation of the visceral nonverbal responses of emotion from higher-order linguistic processing, stating, "I am very fond of his idea that the emotional brain and the 'word brain' might be operating in parallel but using different codes and thus are not necessarily able to communicate with each other" (1996, p. 99). In his characteristically speculative style of thinking, MacLean drew out the clinical implications of the division of nonverbal bodily emotions from verbal processing.

The clear nonverbal/verbal separation allowed MacLean to address one of the key confusions that frequently arise when we try to define emotion: It is very difficult to articulate what an emotion is because there is something indescribable about feeling. He attributed this to the animalistic and illiterate nature of the visceral brain. Further, he drew out the implications of this observation for treatment of emotional disorders. In MacLean's view, the creation of a safe, supportive relationship that calms the visceral brain is paramount initially in any kind of psychotherapy. MacLean's ideas accord well with the emphasis on developing an empathic therapeutic relationship that originated with clinical theorist and researcher Carl Rogers (1902–1987) and is prevalent in contemporary approaches to therapy. MacLean's speculations about brain processes linking emotion with physical symptoms in some ways pointed ahead to the contemporary clinical use of mindfulness and other meditation practices that emphasize calming the bodily responses activated by stress and anxiety (Arias, Steinberg, Banga, & Trestman, 2006; Baer, 2003; Hayes, Follette, & Linehan, 2004; Salmon et al, 2004).

The Power of an Evolutionary Perspective

Like many contemporary emotion researchers, LeDoux applauds MacLean's insistence that it is essential to view the emotional brain from an evolutionary perspective. MacLean had a long career at the National Institutes of Health, where he maintained his early focus on researching the brain processes of emotion in an evolutionary context. He increasingly came to emphasize the vital importance of caretaking and social connection in the evolution of the brain. He repeatedly drew attention to a triad of social behaviors that differentiate early mammals from reptiles: Mammal mothers nursing their young, the distress calls of young mammals separated from their mothers, and the rough-and-tumble play behavior that mammals engage in (e.g., MacLean, 1984). Pointing to the presumed absence of cingulate cortex in the reptilian brain, MacLean linked the emergence of social caretaking and playful interaction with the evolution of the thalamocingulate part of his limbic system. MacLean's focus on the importance of social interactions in driving brain development was a precursor to the recently emerging and thriving field of social neuroscience. In the next chapter we will take up modern investigations of the evolution and expression of emotions that expand, refine, and sometimes overturn the early ideas of James, Cannon, Papez, and MacLean.

Box 2.1: Limbic System Structures

Mammillary bodies: The paired mammillary bodies protrude as little bumps at the posterior edge of the hypothalamus (see Box 1.1). In the Papez circuit, they receive sensory input from the ventral thalamus, then project to the anterior thalamus on their way to the cingulate gyrus.

Anterior thalamic nuclei: The anterior nuclei receive input from the mammillary bodies via the mammillothalamic tract and project in turn to the cingulate gyrus. The anterior nuclei are thought to be important in the alertness function of the thalamus.

Hippocampus: The hippocampus is a paired buried structure of the medial temporal lobe. Its name comes from the Latin term for seahorse, which it resembles in shape. Although it was originally considered a part of the olfactory system, its chief function is now known to be the consolidation of short-term memories into long-term memories. Its role in memory first came to light when the hippocampus and surrounding structures were surgically removed from the brain of a patient known in the research literature as H. M., as a treatment for his otherwise intractable epilepsy; H. M. subsequently lost the ability to form any new declarative memories. His case is discussed in more depth in chapter 8.

Fornix: The fornix is a band of axons connecting the neurons in the hippocampus with those of the mammillary bodies of the hypothalamus.

Cingulate gyrus: The cingulate gyrus is the part of the limbic lobe that sits directly above and around the edges of the corpus callosum, the large fiber tract connecting the hemispheres (see Box 1.1 and Figure 1.2). The anterior cingulate gyrus, or ACC, is the part of the cingulate gyrus most commonly implicated in emotional functions. It is intimately connected to many frontal lobe functions and is sometimes considered to be part of the frontal lobe.

Parahippocampal gyrus: Limbic cortex becomes the parahippocampal gyrus as it continues around and below the corpus callosum and lateral ventricle. Just medial to the parahippocampal gyrus sits the hippocampus. The parahippocampal gyrus was at one time referred to as the hippocampal gyrus, leading to considerable confusion, as it is a separate structure from what is now referred to as the hippocampus . Information from the cingulate gyrus flows through a part of the parahippocampal gyrus called the entorhinal cortex on its way to the hippocampus itself.

These buried medial cortical regions originated early in the evolution of mammals and were long considered "primitive" in structure as well as function compared to the neocortex. The hippocampus, for example, consists of only three cellular layers, in contrast to the six layers characteristic of neocortex. Today, however, most anatomists argue that the cingulate gyrus is in fact neocortex, and it is known to be involved in many higher cognitive functions, including detection of conflict, as well as in the processing of emotional value.

3

The Functions of Emotions

Basic Emotional Systems

One of us (EBJ) was a longtime cat owner who recently acquired a dog in response to years of pleas from her sons. I was quickly struck by the vast difference between the two creatures in terms of emotional communications. Our cat, Canoe (who has since passed away), was sweet yet aloof and difficult to read emotionally. She avoided eye contact at all costs. In complete contrast, our dog, Bella, was bursting with emotions from the moment my family met her as an eager almost-two-year-old. Her whole body, not just her tail, wags in delight when she greets us. When the doorbell rings, her fur stands up in an impressive Mohawk-like ridge along the length of her back, and she barks resoundingly until she recognizes the person at the door. When we're in the kitchen, she looks up at us longingly, carefully checking our facial expressions, especially if we're anywhere near where the food and treats are kept. If there is any upset in the house, such as crying or shouting, she goes to the distressed people and stands or sits quietly beside them, watching their faces closely and comforting them with her presence. The extent to which dogs can read the emotional expressions of humans—from both their faces and their voices—is remarkable.

Darwin's Comparative Investigation of Emotional Expression

Contemplation of the shared forms of emotional expression in animals and people makes us think about the evolutionary function of emotions. Charles Darwin initiated the study of the functions of emotions in a comparative framework with his 1872 book *The Expression of the Emotions in Man and*

Animals. In this later contribution to his evolutionary theory, he opened up the scientific investigation of emotions through close analysis of their outward expressions. With his unparalleled skill for detailed observation, he documented similarities in the expression of emotions such as joy, rage, grief, and shame in diverse species. A devoted dog owner himself, Darwin allotted several pages to the description of the range and functions of dogs' emotional expressions, and provided several illustrations of dogs displaying different types of emotional behavior—from humble and affectionate to hostile and aggressive. Darwin understood these outward manifestations of emotion as expressions of different states of mind in animals. For example, he unabashedly attributed the emotion of love to dogs:

> Dogs, when feeling affectionate, like rubbing against their masters and being rubbed or patted by them, for from the nursing of their puppies, contact with a beloved object has become firmly associated in their minds with the emotion of love. (1872, p. 120)

In the theory of natural selection, Darwin argued that the features of an organism were adaptations that had evolved over time to increase survival. In one well known example, he showed how the different shapes of finches' beaks in different parts of the Galapagos Islands were adapted to the different kinds of foods available: The cactus finches' elongated beaks were useful for extracting food from cactus plants, whereas the ground finches' short, stout beaks were better suited to obtaining food from the ground (Cromie, 2006). In *The Expression of Emotions in Man and Animals* Darwin argued that emotional expressions were also the product of natural selection. His argument that emotions had evolved to serve an evolutionary function was a profound conceptual shift away from the long-standing view of emotions as disruptive to rational behavior. Although some of his analyses of how specific emotional expressions first evolved are only partially supported today, he importantly proposed that over time many expressions came to serve a different function from the one they originally evolved for—they came to serve as a communicative signal. For example, because the origins of many bodily expressions take place in preparation for a specific action, these expressions also convey something about animals' inner states, and thus their intentions, to any observers. Over time, some of these intention expressions become exaggerated to better serve the sender. For example, think of a cat being threatened by a dog and preparing to defend itself in

Figure 3.1 Figure 15 from Darwin's *The Expression of the Emotions in Man and Animals*
Source: Reproduced with permission from John van Wyhe ed. 2002—The Complete Work of Charles Darwin Online (http://darwin-online.org.uk).

response. The bodily expressions of that preparation for defense—the arched back, hair standing on end, and a snarling mouth— all make the cat appear larger and more imposing, as illustrated in Darwin's Figure 15, reproduced here as Figure 3.1. Many a hissing "Halloween cat" has frightened off an approaching dog, even when the bigger dog clearly has had the physical advantage. Emotional expressions, in their ability to communicate intentions, enable a form of mind reading in those observing the behavior. The advantages of such an expressive system for survival are obvious. To expand on Darwin's example, the cat wards off the potential threat from the predatory dog without engaging in the energy-consuming and life-threatening behavior of fighting. The reading of others' intentions from their facial and bodily expressions is a key component of successful social interactions. This form of mind reading from the body is a vital aspect of the study of theory of mind in developmental psychology, and difficulties in smoothly achieving it are thought to contribute to the social challenges of autism (Frith, 2003).

Providing a quick signal indicating whether other animals or situations should be avoided or approached is one basic function of many of the emotions that Darwin discussed. Darwin's illustrations of animal emotional expressions show dogs, cats, and even a swan in postures that either ward off or invite approach; they are either threatening or welcoming. Modern writers who view emotions in an evolutionary context express their function succinctly as "the activity of survival circuits related to reward and punishment" (Nettle & Bateson, 2012, p. R712). Communication of the potentially rewarding or punishing consequences of interaction with another animal is a chief function of emotional expressions.

What Is Fundamental about Emotions? How Should We Categorize Them?

Darwin's text set up the scientific study of emotions in an expansive manner. A quick perusal of the emotional terms used in his chapter headings gives a good sense of the broad scope of his work: suffering, anxiety, grief, dejection, despair, joy, high spirits, love, tender feelings, devotion, reflection, meditation, ill temper, sulkiness, determination, hatred, anger, disdain, contempt, disgust, guilt, pride, helplessness, patience, affirmation, negation, surprise, astonishment, fear, horror, self-attention, shame, shyness, and modesty (Darwin, 1872, pp. iii–iv). As Darwin's list indicates, there are a multitude of terms for emotional expressions. What is fundamental or core in these many emotional descriptors that makes them all examples of one overarching category? Also, can they be organized into coherent subcategories? In the wake of Darwin's pioneering comparative studies, many different emotion researchers struggled to find ways to identify and categorize emotions. Their solutions can be grouped into two distinct approaches that developed independently and still constitute the two dominant perspectives in the field. One approach—the *dimensional view*—grew out of an analysis of the underlying semantic structure of the terms that placed all human emotions on a few continuous dimensions, such as the level of arousal evoked. Each emotion word can be uniquely located by its position on two or three dimensions, thus simultaneously simplifying and interrelating the diversity of emotional terms. Note that this language-based classification system really only applies to human emotions. The other approach—the *basic emotions view*—worked to identify a subset of fundamental emotions that were widely shared among species and cultures. The point of departure for the basic emotions approach was to identify specific behavioral expressions, particularly facial ones that were commonly expressed and could be reliably recognized regardless of cultural background; this approach clearly grew out of Darwin's close analysis of emotional expression.

Dimensional Views

The first arrangement of human emotional terms on continuous dimensions was put forward by the person credited with opening the first experimental psychology laboratory: Wilhelm Wundt (1832–1920). A contemporary of William James, Wundt employed the method of introspection—analysis of his own mental experience and that of other trained self-observers—as the basis of his fundamental idea that all feelings could be described by their position on three distinct dimensions: agreeableness–disagreeableness, strain–relaxation, and excitement–calm (G. A. Miller, 1991). A more explicitly linguistic approach was adopted by Charles Osgood (1916–1991), a mid-20th-century psychologist who used semantic comparisons and factor analysis to come up with his three dimensions of evaluation, potency, and activity (Osgood, 1952). Contemporary dimensional theorists tend to stress only two of these dimensions: arousal and valence, or the positivity or negativity of the emotion. For example, Peter Lang, Margaret Bradley, and their colleagues at the University of Florida, Gainesville, generated a standardized set of emotional images by asking a large number of people to rate the arousal and valence of images.[1] The image set they produced—the International Affective Picture Set (IAPS)—is one of the most widely used stimulus sets in contemporary emotion research, and its popularity as a research tool ensures that arousal and valence are commonly investigated aspects of emotional stimuli (Lang, Bradley, & Cuthbert, 2008).

The arousal dimension has a clear psychophysiological foundation: In response to an emotional stimulus, autonomic nervous system (ANS) changes in physiological variables like blood flow, muscle tension, breathing, and heart rate take place as the sympathetic arm of the ANS prepares the body to take action—the "fight or flight" that Cannon memorably described (see Box 1.1 for more details). Arousal in and of itself, however, is not enough to determine what course of action should be taken in response to the emotional stimulus: Sympathetic activation can be triggered by a variety of sources, such as being physically threatened by an animal (e.g.,

---

1. They also measured a third dimension—dominance—but it is less frequently drawn upon in experimental studies and rarely discussed in research papers.

James's bear) or the exhilaration of a roller-coaster ride, and some way to evaluate their impact is needed. A second dimension is needed to more fully characterize the emotion. The valence dimension of the emotion—how positive or negative the feeling is—is a crucial aspect of the motivating power of emotions. The *value* assigned to different stimuli determines the fundamental choice of whether the situation should be approached or avoided.

Dimensional theorists, such as James Russell, a researcher at Boston College, also describe the valence dimension as "core affect," which is "the neurophysiological state consciously accessible as simply feeling good or bad, energized or enervated" (Russell, 2012, p. 3). Russell and another influential contemporary emotions researcher, Lisa Feldman Barrett, now at Northeastern University, have developed and refined a version of the dimensional approach that proposes how core affect interacts with other factors in the psychological construction of emotions (Barrett, 2006; Barrett & Russell, 1999). In the process of developing their constructionist model, they have been openly critical of some of the assumptions made by the other major camp of emotion theorists—those espousing a basic emotions approach (Barrett, 2007; Russell, 1994). We now turn to that other vital thread in the quest to describe and classify emotions.

Basic Emotions

The basic emotions approach is built on the idea that emotions are discrete states, such as fear or anger or happiness. Each of the basic emotions is thought to have evolved as a specific adaptive response to an environmentally salient stimulus. For example, fear is the response to a threat. Such responses are highly conserved across species and broadly similar across human cultures, thus they are often described as "universal." Because they are conceived of as discrete categories, they were also thought to have unique physiological profiles, and even distinct neural profiles. The starting point for the basic emotions approach was fine-grained analysis of the facial expression of emotion. The goal of this work was to identify a core set of emotions with characteristic expressions widely recognized across cultures. As is the case for many of the basic questions about emotions, Darwin made the initial contribution to this literature. To test his idea that emotional expressions are universal and thus innate, he composed a questionnaire about human expressions with detailed questions about facial configuration. For example, here is his query about the expression of sadness:

> When in low spirits, are the corners of the mouth depressed, and the inner corner of the eyebrows raised by that muscle which the French call the "Grief muscle"? The eyebrow in this state becomes slightly oblique, with a little swelling at the inner end; and the forehead is transversely wrinkled in the middle part, but not across the whole breadth, as when the eyebrows are raised in surprise. (1872, p. 16)

Darwin sent his questionnaire out to missionaries and "protectors of the aborigines" around the globe and asked them how well these descriptions of expressions applied to the different groups of people they had encountered. On the basis of 36 responses from observers of diverse societies, Darwin concluded that "the same state of mind is expressed throughout the world with remarkable uniformity" (1872, p. 17).

In addition to his cross-cultural questionnaire, Darwin conducted informal experimental work on the identification of facial expression using his own family and friends as participants. He was fascinated by the photographs of French neurologist Guillaume Duchenne (1806–1875), who had generated facial expressions by applying electric current to activate specific facial muscles. In 1826, visitors to Darwin's country home were presented with several of Duchenne's images and asked to describe the emotion expressed in their own words (Snyder, Kaufman, Harrison, & Maruff, 2010). With Duchenne's permission, Darwin included the images that many of his visitors labeled similarly as illustrations in *The Expression of the Emotions in Man and Animals*. Darwin's experimental approach to the categorization of facial expressions later proved highly productive for the scientific study of emotion, yet it was neglected for many years. This neglect was in large part due to an emphasis on the cultural relativity and social construction of knowledge in 20th-century anthropological and psychological study of emotions. Social constructionism was the dominant approach in the field when the influential and prolific emotions researcher Paul Ekman entered it in the 1960s.

Ekman's Analysis of Human Facial Expressions

Ekman, now retired from his long-term post as professor of psychology at the University of California, San Francisco, revived interest in Darwin's work on human emotional expressions when he started studying them experimentally in the 1960s with his collaborators Wallace Friesen and Richard Sorenson. Inspired by a combination of Darwin's cross-cultural questionnaires and Silvan Tomkins's[2] photographic studies of facial expressions, Ekman and colleagues designed a more controlled experimental study (Ekman, Sorenson, & Friesen, 1969). They presented pictures of the faces of actors posing emotional expressions and asked their participants to match the images to one of six labels: "anger," "happiness," "fear," "surprise," "disgust," or "sadness." Their American subjects were able to do this task with high levels of accuracy, reaching as much as 97% agreement for happiness. Recognition of happiness and anger was also high when they conducted these studies in New Guinea, Borneo, Brazil, and Japan, but consistency was lower for disgust, fear, surprise, and sadness in the New Guinea and Borneo samples. However, participants from all cultures performed at levels significantly above chance for all emotions. Ekman and colleagues concluded from these findings that these six "basic" emotional expressions are panculturally recognized, and this study is widely cited in the literature as proving the universality of basic emotions[3].

Ekman and Friesen collaborated on the study of facial expression of emotions for many years and developed an exhaustive coding system, the Facial Action Coding System (FACS), that is now used for training people who need to become expert at reading intent from expressions, such as security personnel and law enforcement officers (Ekman & Friesen, 1976). FACS catalogs expressions precisely in terms of facial musculature; for example, happiness is expressed by moving muscles 6 (orbicularis oculi—cheek raiser) plus 12 (zygomaticus major—lip corner puller).

The identification of basic emotions has generated much controversy over the years (see, e.g., Barrett, 2007; Ekman, 1992; Izard, 2007, 2009; Ortony & Turner, 1990; Panksepp, 2007; Tracy & Randles, 2011). Different basic emotions theorists have produced somewhat different lists of names

---

2. Silvan Tompkins (1911–1991) was a personality theorist who developed a well-known affect theory that heavily influenced Ekman in the early stages of his career. Tomkins identified six basic affects using two-word descriptors where the first term is the milder form and the second is the more intense form of the emotion: interest-excitement, enjoyment-joy, surprise-startle, distress-anguish, anger-rage, and fear-terror. He also described shame-humiliation as a later development, and included disgust and "dissmell" (his own coinage) as two descriptors without distinct words for variations in intensity (Kelly, 2009).

3. Some later research findings have not supported Ekman and colleagues' universality argument, including recent cross-cultural work by Barrett and colleagues.

Table 3.1
Basic Emotion Lists

Tomkins	Early Ekman	Plutchik	Izard	Panksepp
fear-terror	fear	fear	fear	FEAR
anger-rage	anger	anger	anger	RAGE
distress-anguish	sadness	sadness	sadness	PANIC/GRIEF
enjoyment-joy	happiness	joy	joy	PLAY
surprise-startle	surprise	surprise		
disgust	disgust	disgust	disgust	
interest-excitement		anticipation	interest	SEEKING
shame-humiliation			shame	
dissmell				
		trust	love and attachment	CARE
			contempt	
				LUST

for the basic or primary emotions, and have also varied somewhat in the conditions they emphasize for inclusion and categorization. In later papers, Ekman himself shifted from labeling only six basic emotions to describing all emotions as basic (e.g., Ekman, 1994). Table 3.1 shows the lists prepared by important theorists at various times. Although there are some outliers (e.g., Izard's contempt) and some that are less generally agreed upon (e.g., surprise), four of the basic emotions appear on everyone's list: fear, anger, sadness, and happiness. These four core emotions became the focus in studies of the physiological basis of emotions.

Physiological Signatures of Basic Emotions

Ekman and his collaborators believed that the basic emotions that are universally distinguished by their distinct facial expressions are biologically based. To confirm that hypothesis, they wanted to show that each emotion has a unique physiological signature. Thus, they collected psychophysiological measurements to investigate their correlation with specific facial expressions. Ekman, Levenson, and Friesen (1983) correlated the instructed posing of basic emotions with measures of heart rate and skin conductance

(SCR).[4] In combination, the two psychophysiological measures allowed them to distinguish three groups of emotion from one another: (a) fear and sadness, which generated high heart rates combined with low SCRs, (b) anger, which was high on both measures, and (c) happiness, disgust, and surprise, which were all correlated with low heart rate. This finding of some specificity in the bodily correlates of basic emotional states was one of the first pieces of evidence that threw doubt on Cannon's critique of James's embodied theory; the physiological responses were not as undifferentiated as Cannon had claimed.

In a more recent study, a group of researchers at the University of Iowa (Rainville, Bechara, Naqvi, & Damasio, 2006) extended Ekman et al.'s approach using sophisticated multivariate statistical analysis in combination with more detailed measures of cardiovascular and respiratory responses. Participants were asked to recall vivid autobiographical memories that evoked strong and readily identifiable emotions as their cardiovascular and respiratory activity were monitored. Instead of only considering the overall value of single measures like heart rate and skin temperature, as in the Ekman et al. (1983) study, Rainville et al. analyzed many properties of heart rate and its variability, as well as many aspects of respiration, such as changes in the respiratory period and the interval between respiration waves. Principal components analysis, a statistical means of detecting patterns in multivariate data sets, enabled the researchers to reliably differentiate the physiological signatures of the four basic emotions that appear on most theorists' lists: anger, happiness, sadness, and fear (see Figure 3.2 for a flowchart illustration).

Anger could be distinguished physiologically from the three other emotions because the variability of the participants' heart rates did not decrease when they recalled an event that enraged them, whereas it did for the other three emotions. Fear could be differentiated from happiness and sadness because there were significant changes in respiration—the rapid breathing that people experience when they feel panicky. Notably, the patterns for happiness and sadness were most physiologically alike, distinguished only by an increase in respiratory variability when participants recalled sad memories. Thus, a single physiological measure of autonomic activation

---

4. The skin conductance response (SCR) is a well-established physiological measurement that forms the basis of lie detector tests. When the sympathetic nervous system is activated, people start to perspire more, which leads to an increase in skin conductance that can be measured with sensors on the skin.

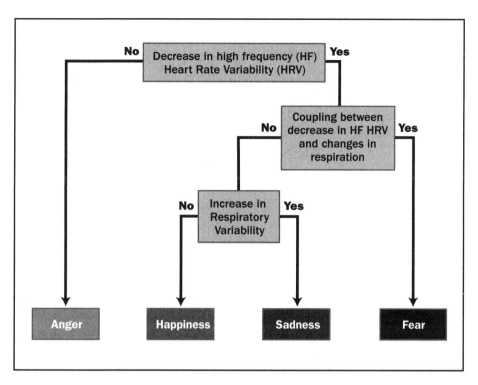

Figure 3.2 A flowchart showing Rainville et al.'s (2006) physiological differentiation of the basic emotions of anger, happiness, sadness, and fear.

Source: Adapted from International Journal of Psychophysiology, Volume 61, Issue 1, Daniel Tranel, Pierre Rainville, Antoine Bechara, Nasir Naqvi, Antonio R. Damasio, "Basic emotions are associated with distinct patterns of cardiorespiratory activity," pages 5–18, copyright © July 2006, with permission from Elsevier.

does not provide enough information to discriminate between emotional feelings; rather, multiple factors have to be considered simultaneously. To return to James's analogy, "not only the heart, but the entire circulatory system, forms a sort of sounding-board, which every change of our consciousness, however slight, may make reverberate" (1884, p. 191).

Are There Unique Neural Signatures for Basic Emotions?

Thus, some evidence has accumulated for unique peripheral psychophysiological signatures of basic emotions, prompting the question of whether the neural responses to the basic emotions can also be differentiated. Ekman and Friesen teamed up with brain researchers from Richard Davidson's group at the University of Wisconsin, Madison, to explore the neural activity associated with people's responses to films designed to induce either happiness or disgust (Davidson, Ekman, Saron, Senulis, & Friesen, 1990). They used Ekman et al.'s (1983) FACS coding system to categorize their participants' facial expressions as they viewed silent film clips of scenes such as puppies playing or leg amputations. Using EEG measures of brain activity, they found that disgust activated the right frontal and anterior temporal regions more than happiness, which produced more activity in the left temporal region. They interpreted their findings in terms of a model of hemispheric asymmetry in responses to positive versus negative emotional stimuli that Davidson had already proposed: more *left* frontal activity associated with positive emotions and more *right* frontal activity associated with negative emotions. This model is also consistent with the dimensional model discussed above, with left frontal activation being associated with approach and right with avoidance.

In this early foray of Ekman and colleagues (1983) into the study of brain activation, two basic emotions could be distinguished by asymmetries in the patterns of frontal and temporal activation, suggesting that there are differences in the neural responses to discrete basic emotions. More comprehensive tests of a larger range of basic emotions and more differentiated localization of the brain areas involved were conducted once functional magnetic resonance imaging (fMRI) became widely used to study emotion. Early meta-analytic reviews that examined the pattern of results across multiple positron emission tomography (PET) and fMRI studies associated discrete basic emotions with specific brain regions. Phan, Wager, Taylor, and Liberzon (2002) linked fear with amygdala activation, and sadness with subcallosal cingulate activity. Murphy, Nimmo-Smith, and Lawrence (2003) linked fear with the amygdala, disgust with the insula and globus pallidus, and anger with the orbito-frontal cortex.[5] In a more recent article, Lisa Barrett and her colleagues reported on a meta-analysis of many neuroimaging studies that showed clearly that there is not a simple one-to-one equation of specific brain areas with different basic emotions that have been associated with them (Lindquist, Wager, Kober, Bliss-Moreau, & Barrett, 2012).

5. Interestingly, Murphy et al. (2003) could not differentiate between the neural patterns for happiness and sadness, a finding that accords well with Rainville et al.'s (2006) observation that the peripheral psychophysiological signatures of happiness and sadness were the most alike.

This simple one-basic-emotion-to-one-brain-area mapping is something of a straw man, however, as Stephan Hamann (2012) points out in his equally recent review of the host of neuroimaging studies mapping discrete basic emotions. Both Lindquist et al. and Hamann argue that a simple one-variable mapping is not sufficient to capture the complexity of emotion signatures. One brain region may participate in more than one emotion, and a single emotion may require activation of a network of brain regions. Hamann and Lindquist et al. argue for more complex models involving networks that may show significant overlap between different emotions, as shown in the peripheral psychophysical experiments described above. Currently, the imaging evidence on whether or not there are neural correlates of different emotions is equivocal, with some evidence supporting each model.

The empirical support for Davidson and colleagues' hemispheric asymmetry model for the valence of emotions is also mixed. Meta-analytic reviews that cover a large range of emotions and brain regions do consistently support the linkage of affiliative emotions with left hemisphere activity, but when all negative emotions are considered activation is more often bilateral rather than strongly right lateralized (Duerden, Arsalidou, Lee, & Taylor, 2013; Murphy et al., 2003).

The Evolutionary Value of Emotions

Ekman outlined a number of criteria for defining basic emotions but ultimately emphasized one aspect over others: their adaptive function for important and elementary life tasks. In a review article, he summarized his conception of emotions concisely: "What is unique is that when an emotion occurs we are dealing with current fundamental life tasks in ways that were adaptive in our evolutionary past" (1999, p. 56). Many other emotion researchers share Ekman's fundamental assumption, including Jaak Panksepp, who has developed an alternative taxonomy of basic emotions that overlaps to some extent with Ekman's but also differs substantially. In language that is similar to the quote from Ekman above, Panksepp described basic emotions as "inherited tools for living from our ancestral past" (2005, p. 158). While Panksepp shared Ekman's focus on the adaptive function of basic emotions, he approached their experimental investigation from a quite different perspective, that of mapping their brain substrates in animal models.

Panksepp's Neurally Based Basic Emotional Systems

Panksepp is an Estonian-born American psychologist who was a longtime professor of psychobiology at Bowling Green State University in Ohio and is now at the College of Veterinary Medicine at Washington State University. Panksepp coined the term "affective neuroscience" that is now widely used to refer to research on the brain bases of emotion and wrote a textbook with the same title that was published in 1998. Panksepp has identified seven fundamental affective systems of the brain that provide animals with ancestral tools for living, using electrical stimulation of key neural regions to provoke complex behaviors. He capitalizes the names of these affective systems to emphasize that he is referring to the neural substrates for emotional constructs only, rather than everything that is implied by the common language terms. The first fundamental system—SEEKING—provides motivation to explore the environment in order to search out necessary resources like food, water, and mates. The next system—FEAR—is a basic defensive system that mobilizes the organism to avoid and escape from predators. RAGE functions to protect the animal when competing for basic resources; LUST is an essential tool for procreation that ensures survival of the species; CARE and PANIC/GRIEF systems are basic social bonding systems that are crucial for the nurturance of immature animals and form the basis of separation distress; and the final and most recently delineated system—play—is also a social interaction system that is crucial for learning.

Panksepp distinguishes three levels of emotion: (a) the *primary* instinctual level of basic affects based in subneocortical structures, (b) the *secondary* conditioning and habit learning dependent on the amygdala and basal ganglia, and (c) the *tertiary* cognitive level that requires the neocortex. His major research focus is on what he identifies as the primary or most basic level. Panksepp's basic emotional systems overlap substantially with the basic emotions defined by many other theorists who identify discrete emotions that aid in survival. FEAR, RAGE, PANIC/GRIEF, and CARE and PLAY are clearly related to the fear, anger, sadness, and happiness that are staples of basic emotions taxonomies such as those of Silvan Tomkins, Paul Ekman, Robert Plutchik, and Carroll Izard. However, rather than focusing on emotional expressions, Panksepp's criterion for a basic emotion specifies a core brain system that can activate basic emotional behaviors. He is hoping to identify the basic unconditioned responses animals evolved in response to environmentally important stimuli. For example, the behaviors that he investigates in the FEAR system are the freezing or rapid escape responses that occur automatically when animals encounter threats. A key assumption of his approach is that these innate survival mechanisms are linked to emotional feelings that reflect the affective value of stimuli. His goal is to understand "how the brain generates *affective feelings*—the valenced phenomenal experiences (qualia) that come in desirable (positive) and undesirable (negative) forms and varieties" (Panksepp, 2011, p. 1791).

Measuring Affect

As a young researcher starting out in the 1960s, Panksepp was inspired by two classic behavioral neuroscience studies. The first was performed by Walter Hess (1881–1973), who was awarded the Nobel Prize for his work showing that electrical stimulation of distinct regions of the hypothalamus in cats elicited a wide range of discrete behavioral responses that were basic to survival, such as eating, drinking, and sexual and defensive behaviors. Panksepp was most intrigued by Hess's finding that localized stimulation of the hypothalamus could evoke expressions of anger, an intense emotional behavior. The other now-classic work that intrigued Panksepp at this time was the then-recent discovery of the phenomenon of brain stimulation by James Olds and Peter Milner at McGill University, Montreal, in the 1950s that gave rise to the concept of the reward system of the brain. Olds and Milner accidentally uncovered this phenomenon when they were attempting to record from the reticular activating system, a brain stem area involved in sleep and waking cycles. They mistakenly placed the electrode a little further forward, landing in the septum, and found that the rat would repeatedly press a lever to activate this electrode, turning it on thousands of times in a row, even ignoring basic needs like eating and sleeping in order to engage in brain stimulation (Linden, 2011; Olds, 1958). We will discuss this work further in chapter 6 on hedonics—how the brain processes pleasure and pain.

Panksepp combined the techniques of Hess and Olds and Milner in studies on aggression in rats for his doctoral thesis. He electrically stimulated regions of the hypothalamus that had earlier been shown by John Flynn, a physiological psychologist based at Yale Medical School, to evoke two distinct types of aggressive behavior, described by Flynn as "predatory" and "affective" aggression. Predatory aggression, or "quiet-biting attack," was directed at prey—live or dead mice—but not other rats, whereas affective attack was directed defensively at other rats and live but not dead mice. Panksepp's important finding was that his rats would engage in Olds and Milner–style self-stimulation if the electrical current intensity and duration produced quiet-biting attack, but if the stimulation produced affective attack, they would choose to escape it instead. The two types of aggression had different value to the animals. Panksepp realized that by choosing to continue or discontinue the stimulation, the rat was indicating whether or not its effects were pleasurable.

By combining the techniques of these two groups of researchers, Panksepp was able to operationalize core affect as whether or not an animal chooses to experience the brain stimulation that generates emotional behaviors. Panksepp also used conditioned place preference as another measure of affective experience. In conditioned place preference, whether or not a rat chooses to return to or avoid an area where it has previously received brain stimulation is a measure of whether the stimulation's affective impact was positive or negative.

Determining the affective value of electrical or chemical stimulation that generates basic emotional behaviors became Panksepp's primary methodology for mapping discrete emotional systems of the brain. For Panksepp, then, a basic or core emotional system is one which when stimulated provokes an identifiable behavioral sequence that the animal can indicate it likes or dislikes. Panksepp has identified different types of behavior that serve as indices for his affective systems. For example, exploratory sniffing is one behavior that results from the electrical stimulation of brain areas that form what Panksepp calls the SEEKING system, whereas distress calls are emitted when brain areas that are part of the PANIC/GRIEF system are stimulated. Rats will repeat the stimulation that evokes exploratory sniffing but avoid the stimulation that evokes distress calls. Panksepp's seven core systems are defined by both behaviors and affects; he links behaviors which are provoked by stimulation of specific brain areas to affect.

Subcortical and Brain Stem Primal Emotional Systems

Most of the brain areas involved in Panksepp's seven core systems are subcortical and brain stem structures located deep in the middle of the brain and include the hypothalamus, thalamus, amygdala, and periaqueductal gray (PAG) of the brain stem (see Figure 2.1 for the relative locations of these structures), each of which can participate in more than one affective system.

Single emotional systems are not mapped onto individual brain areas in a one-to-one fashion; rather, overlapping, interdigitated subcortical and brain stem networks subserve the distinguishable but related basic systems. Panksepp argues that the lower subcortical and brain stem regions of the brain are primary in generating emotional feeling. As electrodes are placed lower within the brain, less current is required to evoke the primal affective behaviors that Panksepp studies. For example, when Panksepp is stimulating what he calls the FEAR and RAGE systems, less current is required to evoke displays of fear and anger from the lower brain stem PAG than from the hypothalamus or amygdala (Panksepp, 2011). In contrast, Panksepp and his colleagues have had great difficulty producing emotional displays in their laboratory animals by electrically stimulating their neocortex.

The older subcortical and brain stem systems are more conserved between species than the more recently evolved cortical regions that have diversified and specialized more over the course of evolution. The human prefrontal cortex in particular is disproportionately larger than that of the rats studied by Panksepp. Because the subcortical and brain stem systems that mediate basic survival behaviors are highly conserved, the use of animal models as a means of investigating emotional brain pathways with techniques that are not available for the study of human brains is justified.

The Neurochemistry of Core Emotional Systems

The use of animal models to investigate the core emotional systems opened up the study of the neurochemistry underlying each system Although it is not the only neurotransmitter involved in SEEKING, dopamine is the chief neurotransmitter identified with this basic emotional system. The dopamine system that Panksepp connects to SEEKING is the mesolimbic system, which projects from the ventral tegmental area (VTA) in the midbrain to a variety of limbic structures (see Figure 6.1 for the location of the VTA and dopamine pathways). Dopamine is widely implicated in reward systems, and Panksepp's linkage of dopamine to SEEKING emphasizes its role in both reward and the exploratory behavior motivated by anticipation of finding a reward. We will return to the role of dopamine in later chapters.

Panksepp has also connected the endogenous opiates or endorphins and the hypothalamic neurohormone oxytocin to core emotional systems. The endorphins are involved in endogenous pain relief systems as well as reward states, and had just been discovered in the 1970s when Panksepp and his coworkers decided to explore their effects on a social rather than physical form of pain. They found that they could substantially decrease the yelping distress calls made by socially isolated puppies with injections of opiates. Panksepp reasoned that the social distress system, which he then called PANIC but has now renamed GRIEF, piggybacked on the alarm system for signaling physical pain during the course of evolution. The role of affect in pain and the overlapping neural systems encoding physical and social pain will be taken up in more depth in chapter 7.

Oxytocin is well known as the reproductive hormone that triggers uterine contractions at parturition as well as the milk let-down reflex in response to suckling, but hypothalamic oxytocin also projects throughout the brain and has been implicated in a variety of behaviors, including maternal-offspring and pair bonding. Panksepp links oxytocin with three of his core affective systems: CARE, LUST, and PANIC/GRIEF. Oxytocin has recently been extensively studied, and was first linked with prosocial behaviors in an animal model, where it acts to increase maternal behaviors and decrease separation distress in young animals that are left alone (Young, Lim, Gingrich, & Insel, 2001). In humans, oxytocin also appears to facilitate social interactions, and genetic variation in the oxytocin receptor has been related to variation in levels of empathy, stress reactivity, and psychological resources such as optimism, mastery, and self-esteem that predict physical and psychological health (for recent reviews, see Kumsta, & Heinrichs, 2013 and Meyer-Lindenberg, Donnes, Kirsch, & Heinrichs, 2011). Studies in humans are simplified by the fact that oxytocin crosses the blood-brain barrier when administered via a nasal spray. Neuroeconomics researcher Paul Zak of Claremont Graduate School and his colleagues discovered that spraying oxytocin into the noses of their participants increased their levels of trust and generosity when playing economic games (Kosfeld, Heinrichs, Zak, Fischbacher, & Fehr, 2005; Zak, Stanton, & Ahmadi, 2007).

These positive findings that oxytocin facilitates bonding, trust, and social perceptiveness motivated the labeling of oxytocin as the "love" or "cuddle" hormone, and the development of commercially available sprays, such as Vero Labs' "Liquid Trust" (Azar, 2011). However, some recent work has identified circumstances where increases in oxytocin can result in decreases in levels of trust, throwing doubt on the simple equation of oxytocin with increased closeness to others. In economic games, oxytocin increased people's trust for members of their own team, but they were also more likely to punish members of the other team preemptively, suggesting that bonding within groups or pair-bonds may be strengthened but members of out-groups may be treated more suspiciously. Panksepp's linkage of his basic emotional systems involved in social connection with an easily manipulated neuromodulator is important, but other contemporary researchers advise that any interventions based on this insight for conditions such as social anxiety or autism should proceed with caution. Studies of long-term use in animal models has just begun, but those completed so far have revealed complex and troublingly inconsistent results, raising concerns about the rapid translation of oxytocin therapy to psychiatric disorders, especially in children, before a fuller understanding of its effects, especially long term ones, is reached.

Applications to Psychiatric Disorders

A major goal of explorations of the neurochemistry of affective systems in animal models is the development of new and more targeted drugs for treating psychiatric disorders. Panksepp argues that psychiatric disorders often involve imbalances in the primary affective systems that can over-whelm humans' ability to control and regulate their feelings. He has recently become involved in preclinical animal research on depression, work that has supported the development of new potential antidepressant substances and renewed interest in older uncondoned medications that can be effective with otherwise treatment-resistant depression (Panksepp, 2010b, 2011).

Panksepp and his coworkers' discovery of what they argue is a rat equivalent of human laughter has produced a potential behavioral tool for the assessment of antidepressant medications. In collaboration with colleagues, such as Jeffrey Burgdorf and Joseph Moskal at Northwestern University in Illinois, Panksepp documented that rats emit 50-kHz ultrasonic vocalizations (USVs) in response to pleasurable experiences such as rough-and-tumble play (Burgdorf, Panksepp, & Moskal, 2011; Burgdorf, Wood, Kroes, Moskal, & Panksepp, 2007). Videos of Panksepp causing rats to emit 50-kHz USVs by tickling them on the nape of the neck and belly earned him the moniker "the rat tickler."[6] Electrical currents applied directly to reward-

---

6. Panksepp's rat tickling can be viewed at http://graphics8.nytimes.com/packages/video/science/rat.mov.

related areas of a rat's brain[7] cause the same vocalizations in the absence of tickling. Panksepp and colleagues reasoned that any chemicals that would increase 50-kHz USVs in rats had the potential to reduce depression in humans by increasing their positive feelings. One of the drugs that they found increased 50-kHz USVs in rats—GLYX-13[8]—is now at the stage of phase 2 clinical testing with humans and is a promising future treatment for depression that does not produce troublesome side effects (Burgdorf et al., 2011). If other clinically effective antidepressants can be shown to also increase 50-kHz USVs, then these vocalizations could provide a useful positive counterpart to existent behavioral indices used in animal models of depression that rely on negative measures such as giving up on difficult tasks.

Animal Feelings

Panksepp has developed his version of a basic emotions theory using animal models over the course of a long and productive career. He has published numerous research papers with many students and coworkers and recently came out with an updated and more accessible version of his founding text (Panksepp & Biven, 2012). Yet, despite his seminal role in affective neuroscience and extensive publication record, he feels that his work has been marginalized and ignored (Panksepp, 2010a). One possible reason that he gives for this neglect is the difficulty that many behavioral scientists have with his attribution of emotional feelings to nonhuman animals. Panksepp links the primary unconditioned response systems of the brain with emotional feelings. His work showing that animals will seek out or avoid brain stimulation that evokes primary emotional behaviors convinces him that they are experiencing feelings. The shift in perspective required to attribute subjective emotional experiences to other animals is one that many neuroscientists are reluctant to embrace.

---

7. Specifically, the prefrontal cortex, nucleus accumbens, ventral pallidum, lateral preoptic area, lateral hypothalamus, ventral tegmental area, and raphe (Burgdorf et al., 2007).
8. An allosteric modulator of the NMDA glutamate receptor that binds to the glycine binding site.

A Critique of Panksepp's Approach: Barrett's Questioning of the ESB Evidence

Not all contemporary emotions researchers are as convinced by the electrical stimulation (ESB) data as Panksepp and his coworkers. In a critique of Panksepp's version of a basic emotions theory, Lisa Barrett and her colleagues question his reliance on electrical brain stimulation data. Barrett, Lindquist, et al. (2007) argue that the results of electrical brain stimulation are more variable than Panksepp suggests. Stimulating the same brain area in rats does not inevitably lead to the same characteristic behavior that indexes a preprogrammed basic emotional system. Instead, temperamental and contextual factors influence and modulate the behavior produced. Barrett, Lindquist, et al. (2007) cite Eliot Valenstein's 1973 book *Brain Control*, which reviewed work that predated Panksepp's delineation of his primary affective systems, quoting his statement that "the experimental data clearly indicate that electrodes that seem to be in the same brain locus in different animals often evoke different behavior, and electrodes located at very different brain sites may evoke the same behavior in a given animal" (p. 89). It is surprising that Barrett et al. reach back to a much older source to support their critique of Panksepp's methodology, but perhaps this is due to the fact that not many contemporary emotion researchers use brain stimulation techniques and current replications of Panksepp's experimental work by independent groups are difficult to find.

Another major stumbling block for Barrett and many other researchers is the applicability of Panksepp's animal work to the human experience of emotions. Some of the human brain stimulation work that Panksepp frequently cites in support of his argument comes from a controversial source: the research psychiatrist Robert Heath of Tulane University who worked with psychiatric patients in the 1950s, 1960s, and early 1970s (Heath, 1972). Heath inserted electrodes deep into the brains of patients in an effort to treat a range of psychiatric disorders, and reported that stimulation of deep brain areas resulted in strong emotional feelings. The ethics of Heath's treatment protocols have come under scrutiny (Baumeister, 2000). For example, he "treated" a suicidally depressed and epileptic male patient, B19, for his homosexuality by stimulating the septal area of his brain while he engaged in intercourse with a female prostitute hired to "convert" him. At that time, homosexuality was still listed as a psychiatric disorder in the *Diagnostic and Statistical Manual of Mental Disorders* (DSM) published by the American

Psychiatric Association. Both patients that Heath described at length in his 1972 report suffered from epilepsy and had serious, long-standing psychiatric conditions; there could well have been abnormalities and dysfunctions in their brain structures, connectivity, and neurochemistry. Heath's findings do not provide strong verification of Panksepp's claim.

Beyond Primary Affects

Panksepp's focus has been on what he calls the primary process level of emotion processing: basic survival related affect systems that indicate approach or retreat, pleasure or displeasure. In a triune model reminiscent of MacLean's work which greatly influenced Panksepp's approach, he delineates two further levels of emotional processing: secondary involving unconscious associative learning and memory processes, and tertiary which involves higher-order thinking, language, and metacognition, functions that depend on cortical processing Although he stresses the primary level in his own experimental work, Panksepp recognizes that the secondary and especially tertiary levels are vital for "cognitivized" human emotions. Panksepp characterizes much of the work of other emotion researchers as taking place at what he describes as the secondary and tertiary levels. The role of cortical processing and the interaction and integration of emotions with brain systems related to attention, perception, memory, thinking, planning, and self-control are the focus of much of the research to be discussed in the following chapters (although subcortical structures are also given a lot of attention).

Precisely how the primary affective systems identified by Panksepp interact with higher-level brain processes is a key question. Treating the three levels as separate systems to be investigated independently harkens back to the modular "Russian dolls" idea of a triune brain promoted by MacLean. As we will see, other researchers often approach the study of emotions very differently than Panksepp, and do not share his conviction that his primary level analysis successfully identifies the basic components out of which emotional systems develop, or that his characterization of the core systems will allow a more complicated or complete structure of emotions to emerge. In our discussion of other streams of contemporary work to follow, we will see many examples of researchers who have taken different approaches to investigating how the dynamic and richly interconnected brain processes emotion.

4

The Neural Substrates of Fear and Anxiety

One of us (LO) has a daughter who developed a persistent and disabling fear of fish when she was quite young, in spite of never having had a threatening or alarming encounter with a fish. This fish fear first surfaced when she was five and refused to go on a scenic boat ride during a vacation (and after the tickets had already been purchased). The fear intensified and became more focused on a different outing when a joking stranger warned her that a river we were planning to float down on inner tubes contained piranhas. Trying to convince her that there were no piranhas in the United States or even anywhere else she might be traveling simply did not work. At 18, she learned she would be expected to travel a river in Bolivia as part of a gap semester in South America, and this river really did have piranhas. Although it wasn't easy, she had to confront her fear or choose not to go on this unique adventure she had been planning for almost a year.

How did my daughter come to fear fish? How did her fear response become activated simply by thinking about being in a boat on a body of water which might contain fish? Why was she so unable to use what she had learned about where piranhas live to help her overcome her fear? How do emotional stimuli come to acquire their great power?

Fearful responses to objects and situations in a person's environment can be so overwhelming that they lead to anxiety disorders. Anxiety disorders, which include phobias, panic attacks, posttraumatic stress disorder (PTSD), obsessive-compulsive disorder, and generalized anxiety disorder, are among the most common and debilitating psychiatric disorders. They interfere with day-to-day functioning in the schoolroom, workplace, and social sphere, and bring with them significant negative health outcomes, including increased risk of depression and substance abuse. These disorders, characterized by excessive fear that leads to an often obsessive avoidance of the feared stimuli, are very common, with a lifetime prevalence of almost 30% (Shin & Liberzon, 2010).

How did the young girl described above develop a fear of fish? How do any stimuli come to be perceived as emotionally salient? William James, like Darwin before him, proposed that each species acquires appropriate emotional responses to evolutionarily relevant stimuli, and suggested that such stimuli act as keys to automatically activate a survival response. His argument, as was usual for James, relied on persuasive inferences and colorful examples:

> In advance of all experience of elephants no child can but be frightened if he suddenly finds one trumpeting and charging upon him. No woman can see a handsome little naked baby without delight, no man in the wilderness see a human form in the distance without excitement and curiosity. (1884, p. 191)

Although James was probably right that an emotional *response* such as the fear response can be described as an innate system, research has shown that *learning* is often required to know what to fear or avoid; indeed, very few innate emotional keys have been found in mammals. Our opening anecdote is one example of a learned fear, a type of learning now called emotional learning. Although emotional learning is critical for learning what is safe and what should be feared, it can sometimes lead to seemingly irrational fears of innocuous or neutral stimuli, such as the fish in our story.

In this chapter, we explore the emotional brain using the powerful tools of modern neuroscience to better understand how emotional stimuli are processed as well as to learn about the logic of emotional learning and memory, one of the key functions of the emotional brain. It has been work on learned fear that has begun to reveal most clearly the outlines of the emotional brain, and this work has helped us to develop better treatments for many emotional disorders, such as anxiety, as well as to understand why seemingly irrational fears can emerge and why some fears are so difficult to overcome. We start by describing the seminal experiments that first showed how and where emotional stimuli are processed in the brain.

The contemporary researcher who first explicitly explored this question is Joseph LeDoux, a neuroscientist working at New York University. Beginning in the 1980s, his work on the neural basis of fear conditioning in the rat spurred a whole new approach to the neuroscience of emotions and has begun to establish the outlines of a detailed neural substrate of the emotion of fear and the emotional brain, the foundation that is needed to understand anxiety disorders.

A Fear Module

As LeDoux first began to explore the neuroscience of emotion, he broke with the dominant view of a unitary "emotional brain" established by Papez and MacLean. Why should the many different emotions all depend on a common brain substrate? LeDoux proposed that, instead of there being a monolithic limbic system for emotions, each emotion had evolved its own module, just as each sensory system (e.g., vision, hearing) had done. This proposition simplified LeDoux's approach to the study of emotions. Rather than tackling the amorphous "emotional brain," he set out to uncover the neural processing of the *single* emotional module of fear—the highly conserved basic emotion that has evolved to detect the presence of a threat and to initiate the response needed to survive that threat.

How does one start to construct such a neurally based study of an emotion? LeDoux decided to adopt the same approach as neuroscientists[1] who had painstakingly mapped sensory pathways by following the activation caused by a stimulus through the brain in a stepwise fashion. Because many of the molecular tools needed for such a study cannot be used on human subjects, LeDoux broke with the majority of psychological researchers of human emotion and decided to work with an animal model: the laboratory rat.

Learning to Be Afraid

It's relatively straightforward conceptually, if technically challenging, to trace the brain pathways activated by a sensory event, such as a visual or auditory stimulus. But how can a pathway that is activated *only* when the visual or auditory stimulus is an emotional stimulus be identified? LeDoux

---

1. For example, David Hubel and Torsten Wiesel, who were awarded the Nobel Prize in Physiology or Medicine in 1981 for their pioneering studies of the visual system.

began by teaching rats to fear a neutral tone, using the conditioning technique developed by Pavlov. Instead of pairing the tone (the conditioned stimulus, or CS) with food (the unconditioned stimulus, or US), he paired it with a brief electric shock. Rats quickly learned to fear the tone, which now provoked the characteristic fear behavior. The first response to a fearful stimulus or potential threat is to freeze—the deer-in-the-headlights response. This is suicidal for a deer with a car speeding toward it, but freezing is usually an adaptive behavior. Think of your own response to hearing a sudden noise late at night. Not moving helps avoid detection[2] and provides time to assess the environment more carefully. The stress hormones epinephrine and cortisol are released to prepare the body to respond, increasing heart and respiratory rates, blood pressure, and glucose levels in the blood, all of which helps to bring maximal amounts of oxygen and nutrients to the muscles that will be activated for fight or flight (see Box 1.1). These characteristic behavioral and physiological responses allowed LeDoux to precisely measure the emotional responses in his rats.

Fear conditioning, which turns an initially nonemotional stimulus into a feared stimulus, allowed LeDoux to dissociate the pathway of a particular sensory *stimulus*—the tone—from the pathways activated only when the sound provoked *fear*—the emotion he wanted to study. Not incidentally, the use of fear learning also made his rat studies more relevant to an understanding of human fear pathologies, such as panic, phobias, and PTSD, which are in most cases learned fears. In fact, throughout his years of research on the fear response in rats, LeDoux has been committed to using basic research on rats to find more effective treatments for human psychiatric disorders.[3] As we will see later in the chapter, the hope that research on fear and anxiety in the rat will be translatable to human disorders appears to have been justified.

LeDoux was now ready to begin tracing the conditioned fear pathway. The primary auditory pathways in the brain had already been well described. For example, it was known that auditory information from receptors in the ears first stops at its thalamic relay (see Figure 1.1 for the location of the thalamus) before continuing to its main target, the primary auditory cortex

---

2. The visual system is highly sensitive to movement; when a stimulus is not moving, most predators cannot detect it.

3. LeDoux is founder and director of the Emotional Brain Institute (EBI), which is a collaboration between New York University and the Nathan S. Kline Institute for Psychiatric Research to explore issues related to anxiety disorders, such as vulnerabilities, as well as to develop and test strategies for their treatment and prevention.

(AI) in the lateral temporal lobe (see Box 1.1). AI is the first stage of the complex cortical processing required to fully characterize an auditory stimulus, so that even tones very similar in pitch will be discriminated. Once a sensory stimulus is fully characterized in its sensory-specific cortex, it becomes integrated with other incoming sensory information to assist in planning an appropriate response. Along the way, past memories of the stimulus are accessed, and as new memories of the ongoing events are formed, the stimulus in turn becomes associated with other correlated events. Cortical processing of sensory stimuli also gives rise to perceptual awareness of the stimulus; the cortex is where stimuli become accessible to consciousness, so it is where "hearing" or "seeing" occurs.

Since AI was known to be crucial for characterizing an auditory stimulus, LeDoux's first experiment was to attempt to disrupt the fear learning by lesioning the auditory cortex. This was the easy part of his research strategy; being able to follow the feared tone beyond AI was expected to be challenging. Instead, the result of this very first experiment helped to catapult LeDoux into the neuroscience hall of fame. To his amazement, the tone continued to elicit a fear response, and subsequent experiments even showed that rats can learn to fear the tone without an auditory cortex. It's hard to convey how confounding this first result was. How could rats learn to fear a stimulus they couldn't "hear"? And where could learning occur if the stimulus was not first analyzed in the cortex?

This was the kind of moment scientists spend their lives waiting for; when the obvious answer is wrong, the most basic assumptions about how a system works have to be overthrown. Fear learning had to take place before the tone information arrived at the auditory cortex, but where could this happen if not in the established thalamocortical pathway? Recall that most sensory information stops at a thalamic "relay" station (see Box 1.1) on its way to the cortex. LeDoux's seminal discovery was that more than one auditory pathway leaves the thalamus: In addition to the established route to AI cortex, there are several noncortical pathways, and one of these new noncortical pathways was the conditioned fear pathway that allowed LeDoux to develop a neuroscience of fear and anxiety.

Two Roads to the Amygdala

The auditory pathway that carried information about the fear-conditioned tone projected from the thalamus along a previously unidentified pathway to target a subcortical structure called the amygdala, a collection of forebrain nuclei buried in the medial temporal lobe (see Figure 2.1 for the location of the amygdala). Derived from the Greek word for almond,[4] the amygdala is a complex structure made up of 13 or so separate nuclei engaged in a variety of functions, only some of which participate in fear learning. Although discovered and named early in the 19th century (see LeDoux, 2007), the amygdala had attracted little interest from neuroscientists[5], with the exception of the lesion work implicating the amygdala in Klüver-Bucy syndrome beginning in the 1930s (see chapter 2). In work now spanning many years and numerous labs (see Phelps & LeDoux, 2005), a subset of amygdala nuclei—the basal nucleus, the lateral nucleus, the accessory nucleus (these three are often grouped together as the basolateral complex [BLA]), and the central nucleus—were identified as mediating all aspects of the fear response to stimuli that directly cause physical pain and trauma, such as being shocked, as well as to conditioned fears.[6] Fear both is learned and has its memory stored in the BLA,[7] while the central nucleus coordinates all elements of the fear response. LeDoux's initial discovery, together with prolific research from his as well as that of many other labs on many aspects of fear conditioning since that time, has elevated the once-overlooked amygdala to one of the most intensely studied regions of the brain today. The amygdala, which mediates all aspects of fear learning, truly seems to represent the fear module that LeDoux set out to discover.

The auditory information entering the BLA is quite distinct from that traveling in the cortical pathway; it has not been highly analyzed, suggesting that a careful characterization of the tone is not necessary for fear learning. This makes sense if the amygdala functions as a threat detector. Like the principle behind the frustratingly oversensitive smoke detector, the amygdala has been built to be safe rather than sorry; responding to any tone that is somewhat similar to a learned threat keeps one safe, even if frequent mistakes are made.

---

4. The almond-shaped area actually refers to only a few of the 13 or so nuclei that are now referred to as the amygdala.

5. However, some early work in the mid-20th century did implicate the amygdala in conditioned fear learning; see Orsini and Maren, 2012.

6. Recent work has shown that other innate fears, such as fear of predators or aggression by conspecifics, are mediated by the hypothalamus and not the amygdala.

7. Throughout the chapter we will refer to the amygdala generally, although it is important to remember that there are many other amygdala nuclei whose function in still unknown; it is not even clear that all parts of the amygdala play a role in emotions.

Further work has shown that the BLA receives coarsely processed information from all sensory pathways; visual, somatosensory, olfactory, and taste information as well as auditory information provide the BLA with quick access to a coarse sketch of all sensory information entering the brain. LeDoux refers to the auditory pathway carrying coarsely processed information as the "low road." As we will see, the same tone is simultaneously being processed by the cortical pathway to provide a much more detailed characterization of the same stimulus. LeDoux refers to this complementary, more precise but slower pathway as the "high road," and it also eventually reaches the amygdala, meeting up with the low road in the BLA.

The difference between the indirect cortical high-road pathway to the amygdala and the direct amygdala low-road pathway was first demonstrated by exposing rabbits to *two* different tones of similar pitch (in experiments by Neil Schneidermann, Phil McCabe, and colleagues, described in LeDoux, 1996, pp. 161–162). One tone was consistently paired with the shock, whereas the other was randomly presented and thus did not predict the timing of the shock. After extensive training, the rabbits learned to react with fear only to the paired tone. If the auditory cortex was lesioned, however, both tones evoked a fear response. The high road is thus necessary for discrimination of similar tones.

LeDoux illustrates the difference between the low road and the high road using a Jamesian story: a walk in the woods. Rather than having you picture meeting a bear, LeDoux has you imagine stepping on a small stick, which breaks, producing a sound that could be mistaken for the rattle of a rattlesnake. Before the high road has time to consciously identify the sound, the low road has activated the amygdala and you jump back. Only after your heart rate has doubled and adrenaline has poured through your body to respond to the potential threat does the more precise high road identify the stimulus as an innocent stick and inhibit the fear response. As your stress hormones and heart rate begin to drop, you probably laugh at your silly mistake. Just as rabbits without their auditory cortex can no longer discriminate between different tones, LeDoux's hiker cannot tell the difference between a snake and a stick until the slower high-road analysis arrives. The quick but dirty pathway is prone to mistakes, but can be relied on to keep us safe. However, this better-to-be-safe-than-sorry principle has a significant downside: The vigilance required to be constantly on the alert for potential threats can result in anxiety.

The Fear Response

The BLA projects to the central nucleus, which as the output nucleus of the amygdala is critically connected to the many brain structures (see Box 4.1) that activate the fear response. One output activates behavioral freezing, others simultaneously activate the fight-or-flight and stress responses (see Box 1.1) to prepare the body to respond to the threat, and yet others activate brain arousal systems and selectively bias attentional systems to attend to and preferentially process the salient stimulus (Vuilleumier, 2005; Vuilleumier & Huang, 2009). We explore the mechanisms by which an emotional stimulus captures attention and biases sensory processing in chapter 10, and as we will see in detail in chapter 8, although activation of the amygdala often enhances the learning and memory of emotional events, it may also impair these functions during extreme trauma.

Emotional Learning and Memory

LeDoux's work has shown for the first time that the amygdala is a major brain structure involved in learning and memory. Tone and shock information come together by having inputs to the same BLA neuron. Shock information, but not auditory input, can always activate BLA neurons strongly enough to activate the central nucleus and the fear response. In fear conditioning, the temporal pairing of the tone and the shock selectively strengthens the tone input, so that after conditioning the tone can activate the fear response on its own. Intriguingly, LeDoux's lab has also shown that the BLA neurons engaged in initial fear learning do not store the fear memory. Instead, BLA neurons rapidly reset after fear conditioning, allowing them to participate in new learning, while the learned fear memories are transferred to a separate population of BLA neurons for storage (Phelps & LeDoux, 2005); learning and the memory of what was learned are two distinct processes, an organization we will see repeatedly in learning and memory systems.

The subcortically processed amygdala-based learning is unconscious or *implicit* learning, so it bears little resemblance to the learning of facts and details or being able to recall memories of our past, the kind of learning we usually think about when we think of human learning and memory. Those memories are consciously accessible, or *explicit*; explicit learning and memory is known to be mediated by other medial temporal lobes structures, especially the hippocampus, which is located just posterior to the amygdala (see Figure 2.1). In contrast to implicit amygdala-dependent learning, hippocampal-dependent explicit learning relies on the highly processed sensory information of the cortical high road. Both kinds of learning occur during fear conditioning; while the tone–shock pairing is learned in the amygdala, the hippocampal-dependent learning records the details about when and where fear conditioning occurred. For LeDoux's rats, this contextual learning would include the cage in which the conditioning took place. Clearly, the environment in which a reward or punishment occurs is just as important as the specific reward or punishment. The associations made in context learning are flexible and don't require the rigid temporal association that is required for conditioning.

Remembering where you were when you first learned of the 9/11 attack is another example of contextual explicit memory, also called declarative memory because in humans it can be expressed in language. As we'll see in chapter 8, although emotions generally enhance memory formation, periods of very high stress resulting from traumas such as combat or rape may selectively disrupt hippocampal-dependent explicit memories even while implicit fear conditioning remains easily triggered. The loss of explicit contextual memories normally used to discriminate seemingly similar innocuous from threatening stimuli means that these innocuous events can automatically trigger intense and uncontrollable fear. For example, war veterans exposed to traumatic gunfire can find themselves reacting with intense fear to something as simple as a car backfiring. Further complicating treatment of these disorders, the disruption of explicit learning means it may not be possible to remember the source of some fears.

LeDoux argues that although the hippocampus allows the specific context of an emotional event to be recalled, these memories by themselves are not emotional. The *emotional* aspect of the memory instead requires activity in the amygdala. Further, he argues that the critical association that is learned during fear conditioning is between the tone and the *emotional representation of the shock*, rather than the sensory features of shock. As LeDoux describes it, the amygdala is the crucial site of the *emotional memory* itself.

In humans, the amygdala participates in kinds of fear learning unique to humans (reviewed in Shin & Liberzon, 2010) in addition to basic fear conditioning. For example, simply being told that a blue box predicts getting a shock will cause the amygdala to become activated at the sight of a blue box, as does seeing someone else shocked when a blue box is presented (Olsson, Nearing, & Phelps, 2007). In our opening example, the daughter's fear of fish could have been acquired when listening to a story or watching a cartoon, or even from a casual comment by someone at some point when she was very young. The very basic survival logic of the amygdala helps us understand that her association of fish with fear may not be as irrational as it first appeared.

The Prepared Amygdala

Although research has shown that very few fears are innate, some stimuli come to be feared quickly with little previous experience, so they give the appearance of an innate fear (Seligman, 1971). Researchers Arne Öhman and Susan Mineka (2001) argue that the amygdala evolved to learn to fear those threats that recurred frequently over a species' evolutionary history very quickly.[8] This so-called "prepared" fear learning can explain why human phobias typically develop to a very limited set of stimuli, including snakes, spiders, and heights, which were likely to be some of the major threats faced by our human ancestors. Supporting the idea that some stimuli have special status, Öhman and Mineka (2001) have shown that humans more quickly pick out images of snakes and spiders embedded in a complex visual display than visually comparable stimuli, such as flowers or mushrooms. Furthermore, spider phobics more quickly detect a spider than a snake in complex images, while snake phobics pick out the snake more readily. Fears of something innocuous such as fish can be learned, but usually require more effort and are also more easily unlearned; it is notoriously difficult to unlearn prepared fears. The ability of the daughter with the fear of fish to go on the trip to Bolivia might mean her fear was not a "prepared" fear.

---

8. Although it appears that most fears in mammals are learned, there are a few examples of innate fears; the fear rodents express to the smell of cat urine appears to be innate, for example. The bed nucleus of the stria terminalis (BNST), and not the amygdala, may mediate these unconditioned fear responses. The BNST is considered by some to be part of what is referred to as the "extended" amygdala, extensions of the medial and central nuclei. It has projections that parallel those of the central nucleus, and thus is capable of coordinating a full fear response essentially identical to that of the central nucleus (Rosen, 2004).

Anxiety and the Amygdala

So far we've talked as if fear and anxiety are the same, and this is supported by research that has demonstrated that anxiety is associated with alterations in the fear circuitry described above. For example, anxious individuals not only respond more quickly to threat-related stimuli, but they also respond more slowly to nonthreat, or neutral stimuli. Imaging studies have begun to link such biases to amygdala activity. Subjects with anxiety show enhanced amygdala activity when passively viewing neutral faces, and are more likely to interpret ambiguous or neutral stimuli as negative in comparison to non-anxious participants (Hartley & Phelps, 2012). During fear learning in the lab, subjects with trait anxiety show more amygdala activity and fear behaviors are enhanced.

However, there are also significant differences between fear and anxiety. Fear is a response to a specific stimulus and recedes quickly once the stimulus is no longer present. Anxiety does not require a triggering stimulus; it's the *anticipation* of a threat that is feared, and so anxiety can result in becoming chronically vigilant for potential threats. In the fish anxiety story we opened with, the daughter's anxiety was provoked by the fear that a body of water might contain fish, and it persisted in spite of the knowledge that she would be in a boat well away from any possible fish and that most fish are harmless. Anxiety is thus an ongoing state of vigilance that persists in the absence of any true danger. As we will see later in the chapter, such heightened activity can in part be explained by oversensitivity of the amygdala itself, as described above, and in part by deficient regulation of the amygdala by other brain regions that normally act to modulate its activity (reviewed in Hartley & Phelps, 2012).

The most conclusive evidence for the role of the amygdala in anxiety and fear comes from studies in which the amygdala is either electrically stimulated or lesioned. Recall from chapter 2 that monkeys with medial temporal lobe lesions (the Klüver-Bucy syndrome) lost their fear of evolutionarily relevant stimuli, such as snakes and spiders, as well as their fear of humans. Indeed, monkeys with such lesions often approached dangerous stimuli with a highly uncharacteristic—and unsafe—curiosity, and later studies have been able to show that these changes are specific to amygdala lesions (see Rosen, 2004).

Finally, as we'll discuss in more detail later, an understanding of how the amygdala learns and remembers fear has provided insight into why anxiety disorders are so difficult to treat; unlike (too) much of our school learning, amygdala-based learning appears to be highly resistant to the process of forgetting (although possible recent exceptions to this will be discussed later in chapter 8).

The High Road: Extinction

We've now introduced two ways that the cortical high road modulates the subcortical amygdala: First, a detailed analysis of a stimulus by the cortex can correct any mistakes made by the quick and dirty low road by projections to the amygdala that inhibit the output of the central nucleus; second, information from the high road about the context in which learning occurs can be used to generalize the fear to related stimuli in the learning environment (such as the cage of the shocked rats). A third way that higher brain structures modulate the amygdala occurs when the feared tone is repeatedly presented without the presence of the shock. The rat will gradually learn that it's no longer necessary to fear the tone, a process called extinction. Extinction is the basis of exposure therapy, one of the most widely used treatments for phobias and PTSD today.[9] Unfortunately, exposure therapy often fails over the longer term. The conditioned fear response often reemerges, during periods of stress or if the unconditioned stimulus occurs unexpectedly or, critically, when the stimulus occurs in contexts other than that in which treatment occurred. It can even emerge spontaneously with the passage of time.

Extinction was first described by Pavlov, who noted that the tendency of extinguished fear to reappear meant that extinction could not be explained as forgetting. The frequent reemergence of the fear response after successful extinction is a testimonial to the exceptional persistence of amygdala-based learning. Indeed, LeDoux once made the discouraging observation that emotional fear learning is likely to persist for the lifetime of the organism. Although, as we will describe in more detail in chapter 8, recent laboratory research has successfully "erased" a simple conditioned fear in humans (Schiller et al., 2010), the better-safe-than-sorry principle dictates that most

---

9. While it may seem counterintuitive to treat trauma with exposure to traumatic images, the idea is that by confronting reminders of the trauma in a safe setting, the fear associated with the images will gradually become replaced by feelings of safety and over time suppress the ability of traumatic memories to hold the patient captive through flashbacks or nightmares.

of the time the amygdala keeps a tight grip on its memories; the cost again is a high vulnerability to anxiety.

If amygdala memories last a lifetime, why does the fear response to the tone gradually decline in the extinction paradigm? Extinction turns out to require *new* learning that the tone no longer predicts the shock; instead, the tone now represents a period of safety. The new safety learning actively competes with the old fear learning by inhibiting fear expression from the central nucleus of the amygdala. Nonetheless, the ever-present old fear learning can reappear with any reminder of the initial fear-conditioning situation, or with exposure to a context that hasn't yet been experienced with safety.

Lesion and pharmacological studies have implicated three brain structures in extinction (Hartley & Phelps, 2010; Maren, 2011; Pape & Pare, 2010). The first, of course, is the amygdala, which, in addition to being needed for fear learning, is also required for learning about the new safety cue. The second structure is the hippocampus,[10] which carries information about the context in which safety learning occurred. However, context is used somewhat differently in safety learning than it is in fear learning. In fear learning, context allows fear learning to be *generalized* to any stimulus in the learning environment. In extinction learning, on the other hand, context learning is used to *restrict* extinction to the specific context in which extinction training occurs. Unfortunately, this is why fear learning returns in contexts other than where extinction learning occurred, which of course seriously limits the effectiveness of extinction training to the therapeutic setting.

Why can fear learning be generalized but extinction learning cannot? Generalizing fear learning is clearly the safest strategy; it makes sense to assume that anytime and anywhere the tone occurs, a shock is possible, and that all stimuli in the shocked environment could predict shock. Generalizing safety learning beyond the context in which it is learned, however, is clearly risky. What's safe will always be favored by natural selection.

However, life has to be lived outside the therapeutic environment. New therapies for phobias and PTSD that use virtual reality technology to simulate a variety of contexts are beginning to show some success. Rothbaum and colleagues have devised "Virtual Vietnam" and "Virtual Iraq" programs

---

10. The role of the hippocampus in context-specific recall of extinction has been studied in both rats and humans by cuing extinction learning with changes in background color.

to expand the range of contexts associated with safety for soldiers with PTSD (Cukor, Spitalnick, Difede, Rizzo, & Rothbaum, 2009). Such therapies offer dramatic confirmation that basic animal research can be productively translated to humans.

The third and final brain structure involved in extinction learning is a region of prefrontal cortex on its underside (ventral) near the midline (medial), appropriately named the ventromedial prefrontal cortex (vmPFC) (see Box 4.2). The vmPFC, a new structure in our emotional brain, is one of the major prefrontal structures with direct and bilateral connections with the amygdala as well as other limbic structures. Because of its direct connectivity to emotional structures, its function is often described as modulating or regulating emotional behaviors by updating the value or salience of the stimulus as new information becomes available. This appears to be its role in extinction; the vmPFC updates the value of the tone when it no longer predicts shock. In the next chapter, we will encounter a tragic example of what happens when the ability to flexibly update the emotional value of stimuli is impaired by damage to the vmPFC.

Although the role of the vmPFC in extinction is complex and not yet fully understood, it has been implicated in both extinction learning and in modulating the recall of extinction memories (Maren, 2011). In one study, vmPFC lesions on the day of training did not disrupt the acquisition of extinction, while lesions performed the day after training did, suggesting that, as in fear conditioning, the processes of extinction learning and its memory are mediated by different structures. Although extinction learning occurs in the amygdala and its memory is also stored in the amygdala, its recall involves the vmPFC, (Maren, 2011) which acts to inhibit the fear-conditioned memory in the amygdala.

PTSD and Extinction

An early explanation for the recurring and persistent fear memories that characterize PTSD was that the associations formed with traumatic events when memories were acquired at the time of the trauma were "hyperconditioned." These strong associations were thought to be resistant to extinction (for a brief history of these ideas, see Milad & Quirk, 2012). However, as we learned earlier in the chapter, *all* fear learning can be characterized as exceptionally persistent. Fear memories are not easily forgotten, and instead, their expression must be regulated or inhibited by further learning. Thus,

PTSD and phobic disorders are now commonly seen as extinction disorders. From what we've just learned, the difficulty that PTSD patients have in recognizing when they are safe could be due either to impaired extinction learning, or to impaired retention or recall of the extinction memory. Although deficits in extinction learning have been described, most research has pointed to a problem in the appropriate recall or retrieval of the extinction learning (for recent reviews, see Maren, 2011; Myers & Davis, 2007). As we learned earlier in the chapter, the brain regions involved in extinction learning and retrieval include the amygdala, vmPFC, and the hippocampus. In addition, work on extinction has recently identified another key area, a dorsal region of the anterior cingulate cortex (dACC; see Milad et al., 2009). In the normal population, the level of activity in vmPFC and hippocampus has been positively correlated with the level of extinction recall, while that of dACC is associated with fear expression (Milad et al., 2009). Activity in the vmPFC and hippocampus activates inhibitory circuits in the amygdala to suppress fear expression, while the dACC has been shown to have excitatory connections to the amygdala, and both its activity and thickness have been correlated with level of fear expression in the normal population (Milad et al., 2009). The role of the hippocampus, however, is complex. In the context in which extinction training occurred, it acts together with the vmPFC to extinguish fear expression. Recently, however, activity in a region of the ventral hippocampus has been shown to activate fear expression in the amygdala. It is this pathway that is activated when the feared cue occurs outside the learning environment (Knapska et al., 2012), and which serves to restrict extinction learning to the learning context.

Alterations in the balance of activity of these structures has been seen in functional magnetic resonance imaging (fMRI) studies of PTSD patients compared with trauma-exposed controls who did not go on to develop PTSD (Milad et al., 2009; Hartley, Fischl, & Phelps, 2011). During extinction learning, PTSD patients show higher levels of activity in the amygdala as well as the dACC while during recall, they show reduced activity in the vmPFC and hippocampus. Intriguingly, vmPFC thickness has been positively correlated with how easily extinction was acquired in the healthy population (Milad et al., 2005; Hartley, Fischl, & Phelps, 2011), suggesting that vulnerability to PTSD may be due in part to normal variation in the thickness of vmPFC, which determines the strength of extinction recall (for review of this work, see Mahan & Ressler, 2012; Milad et al., 2009; Milad & Quirk, 2012).

Amygdala activity is required for both fear expression as well as extinction learning to inhibit fear expression, so understanding its role in normal fear responses versus anxiety disorders is complex. Recent work in rat models as well as in humans has begun to dissociate regions of the amygdala that mediate opposing effects on fear expression (Kim et al., 2011; Knapska et al., 2012), although the limited resolution of fMRI makes differentiating activity in these subunits difficult in humans. Adding to that complexity, both fear learning and extinction learning require synaptic plasticity dependent on brain-derived neurotropic factor (BDNF), a neurotrophic substance we discuss in more detail below (see Box 4.3 for more information), as well as NMDA glutamate receptors. The difficulty in dissociating these shared, complex effects has been highlighted in recent research by LeDoux and colleagues that has troubling implications (Burghardt, Sigurdsson, Gorman, McEwen, & LeDoux, 2013). Numerous studies have now shown that although antidepressants are a mainstay of pharmacotherapy for treatment of human anxiety disorders, supplementing exposure therapy with some antidepressants actually reduces its success. In their recent paper Burghardt et al. found that two antidepressants, the selective serotonin reuptake inhibitor (SSRI) citalopram as well as an antidepressant with a different mode of action, impaired extinction learning in rats when present chronically by altering the structural organization of NMDA receptors.[11] These NMDA receptors are required for successful extinction; thus, the reduction in NMDA function that is necessary for the therapeutic action of antidepressants disrupts the very receptors that are needed for successful extinction learning.

The role of NMDA receptors in extinction learning has recently led to the discovery by another group of researchers that a small-molecule NMDA receptor modulator, D-cycloserine, appears to facilitate extinction learning as well as to prevent fear renewal after extinction in animal models (reviewed in Maren, 2011). D-cycloserine facilitates NMDA receptor function by binding to a glycine receptor subunit, so is similar to GLYX-13, the potential antidepressant discussed in chapter 3 that increases 50-kHz USVs— 'laughter' vocalization - in Panksepp's group's work with rats. Recent clinical trials have shown that systemic administration of D-cycloserine, an antibiotic that has a long established pharmaceutical history, improved the out-

---

11. Antidepressant therapies appear to downregulate the NR2B NMDA receptor subunit needed for extinction learning.

comes of exposure therapy in social anxiety and fear of heights in humans, although it was not effective in treating spider phobia (Maren, 2011). Why this molecule can both reduce depression as well as facilitate extinction learning, unlike other antidepressants, is still not known. However, as we mentioned above, Knapska et al (2012) have recently discriminated two amygdala circuits in rats, one activated by a vmPFC input that carries extinction memories and the other activated by input from a region in rats that appears to correspond to the dACC in humans that renews fear expression. It is possible that traditional antidepressants such as the SSRIs may affect a broad range of glutamate circuits, whereas the small-molecule modulators such as D-cycloserine and GLYX-13 have a more selective effect on just the vmPFC input.

As more is being learned about the neurochemistry of extinction, a number of promising new pharmacological treatments for PTSD are being explored in both animal and clinical models (Mahan & Ressler, 2012; Maren, 2011). BDNF, one of the few known genetic risk factors for PTSD,[12] mediates the synaptic plasticity that underlies learning, that of fear learning as well as extinction learning. Humans with a genetic variant of BDNF (Val66Met) that has been shown to reduce the amount of BDNF produced and secreted in the vmPFC, show lower vmPFC activity and higher amygdala activity in extinction learning than those with the normal variant (Rosas-Vidal, Do-Monte, Sotres-Bayon, & Quirk, 2014; Soliman et al., 2010). This variant does not alter fear learning, but carriers of this BDNF variant show exaggerated responses to neutral stimuli, suggesting that carriers have difficulty identifying safety, both in knowing when a cue does not predict a threat and knowing when a previous threat-related cue is now safe. Furthermore, carriers of this variant show reduced hippocampal volume (Hajek, Kopecek, & Hoschl, 2011; Londsdorf et al., 2010; Molendijk et al., 2012). Thus, individuals with this genetic variant are not only more vulnerable to developing anxiety disorders, but because they also show extinction deficits, they also may be less likely to benefit from exposure therapy (Felmingham, Dobson-Stone, Schofield, Quirk, & Bryant, 2013). A critical role of BDNF in extinction has been dramatically demonstrated recently by Peters et al. (2010), who showed that BDNF injections into the hippocampus/vmPFC pathway of rats just after fear training increases the amount of

---

12. A variant allele (the s allele) of the serotonin re-uptake transporter gene has also been shown to be a risk factor for anxiety (Kalin, Shelton, Fox, Rogers, Oakes & Davidson, 2008).

BDNF released in the vmPFC, and produces extinction without the need for extinction training. Thus, the deficits seen in carriers of this variant are beginning to be understood.

The central role of BDNF in extinction and PTSD has focused attention on ways to modulate its activity therapeutically (see Andero & Ressler, 2012, for a recent review). A small molecule agonist of the BDNF receptor, TrkB, 7,8-dihydroflavoral (7,8-DHF), which can reach the brain after being administered systemically, has recently been shown to increase extinction learning in mice. This intriguing molecule has also been shown to decrease stress related memory deficits in rodents, as well as the memory deficits in a mouse model of Alzheimer's disease. Additional molecules that regulate BDNF are also being discovered, such as endocannibinoids, and clinical trials of the effectiveness of drugs affecting this system are also underway.

Drug candidates that enhance extinction learning through yet other mechanisms are also being explored. Drugs that stimulate the arousal system (adrenergic agonists), which are well known to facilitate memory consolidation in general (see chapter 8) also enhance extinction learning. Unfortunately, these drugs also increase anxiety, clearly limiting their use as an adjuvant to cognitive behavioral therapy. Intriguingly, however, a mechanism that facilitates extinction consolidation without increasing anxiety has recently emerged (Fanselow, 2013). Activation of brain arousal directly by stimulating the vagus nerve rather than administering adrenergic drugs appears to enhance extinction training without increasing anxiety; it may even decrease ongoing anxiety. As we will see in chapter 8, the bodily arousal activated by stress is normally used as a feedback signal to the brain to enhance learning about that stress. That feedback normally travels via sensory afferents in the vagus nerve, which ultimately acts to release brain norepinephrine (NE) in the amygdala where it enhances consolidation. As vagal stimulation has been used successfully in many other contexts, such as seizure treatment, with few side effects, it may be a very viable adjuvant. Why vagal stimulation of arousal does not increase anxiety is not currently known. Fanselow (2013) also reports that the acetylcholine receptor antagonist scopolamine given during extinction training may prevent the hippocampally mediated restriction of extinction to the training context, and so prevent the fear renewal that often occurs in non-training contexts.

The identification of extinction as a core feature disrupted in anxiety disorders such as PTSD and phobic disorder has led to exciting new understandings of and potential treatments for these common and disabling disorders. The work first begun by LeDoux to trace the brain substrates for the emotion of fear has clearly met his early hope that this work would allow a better understanding of emotional disorders. We explore the relationship between PTSD and extinction memories in more detail in chapter 8, where we turn to an in-depth exploration of the role of emotions in memory.

The Cortical Modulation of Subcortical Emotional Information

So far in our story a cortical structure, the vmPFC, acts to modulate an emotional response by inhibiting a subcortical emotional structure, the amygdala. This seems to support the traditional cognition/emotion dichotomy, with the slower, deliberative cognitive activity acting to override or inhibit automatically activated emotional structures. It is in fact often true that prefrontal cortex activity is negatively correlated with amygdala activity in fMRI studies, as we will see in chapter 11 on emotion regulation (Goldin, McRae, Ramel, & Gross, 2008). Although there are bidirectional projections between the amygdala and prefrontal cortex, projections from the amygdala to the prefrontal cortex are much denser than those from the cortex back to the amygdala. LeDoux suggests that this asymmetry in amygdala–prefrontal connections may account for our vulnerability to anxiety disorders and explain why it is often so difficult to overcome them. It's easier for emotions to invade our thought processes than it is for us to take cognitive control of our emotions because the amygdala is better at driving the prefrontal cortex than vice versa (LeDoux, 1996, see discussion on pp. 264–265).

The idea that a major function of the cortex is to inhibit or suppress inappropriate or unwanted subcortical emotional behavior has a long history. This concept was first proposed explicitly by the influential neurologist John Hughlings Jackson in 1888 (Sotres-Bayon, Cain, & LeDoux, 2006) and is clearly consistent with the experiments by Walter Cannon and Philip Bard that we described in chapter 1. Recall that in their work, removal of the cortex of cats resulted in spontaneous emergence of a behavior they dubbed sham rage. Cannon interpreted these results to mean that the cortex normally acts to inhibit expression of subcortical emotional behaviors.

The research we have reviewed above appears to support that traditional understanding; in all the examples we have presented, the high road has acted to inhibit the low road. However, recent results are beginning to complicate this picture by showing that input from the vmPFC to the amygdala can sometimes enhance, rather than inhibit, the fear response (see Etkin, Egner, & Kalisch, 2011, for a review). Indeed, two subregions of vmPFC with opposite effects on the amygdala have been identified: one inhibits it, while the other excites it (Quirk & Beer, 2006). The region that enhances amygdala activity, called the prelimbic region, has also been implicated in fear learning by observation or instruction rather than by direct experience (Hartley & Phelps, 2010). Recall Elizabeth's fear after she heard about a potential bear in the woods where she walked her dog (see chapter 1). This account was presented to illustrate that there are many roads to amygdala activation and that memory and the cognitive activity it stimulates can also provide potent inputs that can activate subcortical fear structures. Thus, a simple model in which the more recently evolved cortex acts to inhibit the older automatic, impulsive, and instinctive subcortex obviously does not fully capture the complex relationship between cortex and subcortex.

The Human Amygdala

Given the overwhelming evidence that the amygdala plays a key role in the detection of threat and fear learning, and evidence that stimulation of the amygdala in humans evokes the experience of fear, the earliest human imaging studies of amygdala function looked at the response of the amygdala to facial expressions (both monkey and human amygdalae contain neurons that respond selectively to faces). Facial expressions provide potent signals about another's intentions and internal emotional state as well as their reactions to events in the immediate environment; accurately detecting emotional expressions in others is likely to be critical for survival. Not surprisingly, expressions of fear have been shown to consistently activate the human amygdala. Indeed, the correct identification of fear expressions is correlated with the level of amygdala activation (see review by Adolphs, 2008). The early work demonstrating amygdala activation to facial expressions of fear and the amygdala's role in identification of fear expressions was seen as strong support for the concept of the amygdala as a fear module. Over time, however, as usual, the story has become much more complicated.

While it remains true that expressions of fear are very effective at activating the amygdala, it has now been shown that the amygdala is activated by positive as well as negative stimuli, and activity has been shown to pictures, words, and semantic concepts as well as to facial expressions other than fear, such as happiness, sadness, contempt, disgust, and anger (Ousdal et al., 2008). Although most researchers agree that the amygdala is critical for fear learning, the amygdala does not *selectively* respond to threat. One suggestion to explain these diverse findings is that the amygdala is specialized to assess the valence of stimuli—whether good *or* bad—and to mediate the emotional *arousal* needed to respond to either a rewarding or an aversive stimulus (Anders, Eippert, Weiskopf, & Veit, 2008).

So What Does the Amygdala Do?

Challenging the idea that the amygdala responds to only valenced stimuli is the demonstration that neutral faces also activate the amygdala. This calls into question its role in emotion processing at all. An intriguing idea, making use of the finding that neutral faces activate the amygdala, comes from David Sander, who suggests instead that the role of the amygdala is to interpret ambiguity or uncertainty in order to determine stimulus relevance. For Sander and colleagues, "an event is relevant for an organism if it can significantly influence (positively or negatively) the attainment of his or her goals, or the maintenance of his or her own well-being" (Sander, Grafman, & Zalla, 2003, p. 311). They argue that in an environment filled with mostly irrelevant stimuli, assessing relevance is critical for survival. In real life, a face with no clear expression often demands significant processing effort: Is she really mad and trying to hide it? Can I really trust that he means what he is saying? Experimentally, in fact, such neutral, expressionless faces are often perceived as "harsh" or untrustworthy, or are labeled as expressing a negative emotion. Thus, a neutral face may convey important social cues, and ambiguous cues in general tend to capture attention so they can be resolved.

Sander's concept of the amygdala as a relevance detector finally seems to integrate the diverse findings from imaging and lesion studies and has recently been tested using nonemotional stimuli, such as numbers or letters, the behavioral relevance and salience of which can each be manipulated. In this paradigm, purple letters and numbers were presented, and subjects were instructed to press a response button with one hand whenever any letter except *t* appeared on the screen. When a *t* occurred, which was infrequent, they were to respond with the other hand. The *t* was thus given *relevance* because it required suppression of the more common and therefore dominant hand response. Numbers interspersed in the sequence required no button pressing, again requiring inhibition of the dominant response, so numbers also had relevance. *Salience* was manipulated independently from relevance by occasionally presenting a green *r* that stood out from the other purple stimuli. However, it had no relevance because the usual letter response was all that was required. The study was able to dissociate behavioral relevance—a stimulus that had a consequence for the subject because it affected his or her subsequent behavioral decision—from salience, or a stimulus that stood out just because it was novel or different.

The amygdala was activated only by stimuli that had acquired behavioral relevance. Perceptual salience alone, as represented by the novel color associated with *r*, did not elicit amygdala activation. The amygdala seems to become activated only when a stimulus has personal significance that requires action. The idea of the amygdala as a relevance detector assessing the potential value of stimuli seems satisfying. It also better explains the deficits in nonthreat situations that are seen in monkeys with Klüver-Bucy syndrome, whose tendency to put everything in their mouth can be attributed to a failure to detect the behavioral relevance of stimuli.

Emotions and Feelings in the Amygdala

You may have noticed that we have exclusively used the word *emotion* in our review of the work in this chapter; the word *feeling* has not yet been used. What's behind this choice? LeDoux's research has prompted him to draw a crucial distinction between emotions and feelings, words that in the vernacular are often used synonymously. He considers all emotions to be similar to the conditioned fear he has studied in the rat: They are rapid, automatically evoked, and essentially unconscious. As he has put it, "Emotions did not evolve as conscious feeling. They evolved as behavioral and physiological specializations, as bodily responses controlled by the brain that allowed ancestral organisms to survive in hostile environments" (LeDoux, 1996, p. 40). It is only once and if we acquire a conscious awareness of the processes activated by an emotion that we have a feeling. LeDoux thus believes that feeling requires brain systems involved in consciousness and may be something not present in animals other than humans.

The lay public as well as most beginning students of emotion often object when they first hear this definition of emotions. In our everyday language emotions and feeling are used as synonyms for each other. Emotions are *felt;* they are an *experience.* How can you have an emotion without feeling something? However, the distinction between emotions and feelings turned out to be extremely useful in our initial analysis of emotions, and is particularly compelling from an evolutionary perspective; if emotions are adaptive responses to critical environmental challenges, then an emotional reaction is a core behavior of all organisms. *Awareness* of an emotional response is likely to serve a very different evolutionary function. LeDoux does not deny the existence or importance of feelings—the subjective experience of emotions. However, he argues that an exploration of subjective awareness will never provide insight into the core processes of emotion itself; more importantly, in his view, it is simply not helpful in understanding the emotional brain. This conviction that emotions are largely, maybe even exclusively, unconscious processes is now a central thesis of LeDoux's biologically based theory of emotions (see LeDoux, 1996, pp. 32–33).

Much confusion and ambiguity arises from the lack of consistency in the use of these terms, both within the emotion literature and in the vernacular use of these terms. In this book, therefore, we adopt the definitions of emotions and feelings put forward by LeDoux (although we will examine alternative positions on these definitions later in the book). Hence, when we refer to emotions we are referring to the automatic, largely unconscious responses evoked by emotional stimuli. The term feeling is reserved for the conscious awareness of that response. As you become more familiar with this initially counterintuitive distinction, its value will begin to become apparent. It's worth taking a moment to reflect back on our discussion of James's essay *What Is an Emotion* in chapter 1; using these definitions, James was clearly referring to feelings. The stimulus provoked a reaction, and this occurred automatically. Only once the emotion had already occurred did awareness of the emotion become evident as a *feeling*. LeDoux identifies the automatically activated response as the *emotion.*

LeDoux's notions about the unconscious nature of emotions grew out of work begun by researcher Robert Zajonc (1923–2008) in the 1960s. In this groundbreaking work, Zajonc used subliminal stimuli to produce what he called "the mere exposure effect." The mere exposure effect refers to the finding that simply exposing a subject to a novel stimulus results in a preference for that stimulus when it reappears in the context of other new stimuli. This bias for what's familiar had been first demonstrated with consciously detected stimuli, but Zajonc extended this work by showing that this preference occurred for subliminally presented stimuli for which the subject claimed to have no conscious familiarity (for review see Zajonc, 1980).

As work demonstrating that unconscious emotional stimuli can have important yet unacknowledged consequences for decision-making continued to grow, LeDoux's work on the fear system was also showing that an appropriate reaction to a feared stimulus did not require a conscious recognition of the stimulus or a deliberate decision to make a response. LeDoux became persuaded that conscious verbal reports were not only unreliable as data in emotions, they were even likely to generate "red herrings, detours, in the scientific study of emotions" (LeDoux, 2004, p. 48). Perhaps influenced by MacLean's ideas that the emotional brain does not have reliable access to language processes and his own early research on the unconscious emotional reactions seen in the split brain subjects he worked with as a graduate student, LeDoux believes we may never have more than limited conscious awareness of the unconscious emotions that motivate our behavior.

As we will see in later chapters, although other emotion researchers tend to agree with LeDoux's definition of emotions, they have very different concepts about the relation of emotions and feelings, and about where and how feelings arise.

Living without an Amygdala

As we end the chapter, we look at the unusual case of a woman with no amygdala. Historically, case studies involving human amygdala damage have been difficult to interpret because surgery and accidents usually affect more than just the amygdala. This situation changed dramatically with the discovery of a woman known as S. M. who has Urbach-Wiethe disease, an extremely rare disorder that selectively destroys the amygdala over time through accumulation of an aberrant protein. S. M., now in her early fifties, has complete amygdala tissue loss that probably started when she was about 10. She has normal intelligence, leads a relatively normal family life with her three children, and has been a willing participant in neurological experiments for almost 30 years (Adolphs, Baron-Cohen, & Tranel, 2002; Adolphs, Tranel, Damasio, & Damasio, 1994; Tranel, Gullickson, Koch, & Adolphs, 2006).

Early work on S. M. seemed to confirm the selectivity of the amygdala for fear expression. Although she judged fear faces as unpleasant, she did not report any of the arousal normally elicited by a fear expression (Adolphs, Tranel, & Buchanan, 2005). Her recognition of other negative facial expressions such as anger and disgust was intact, as was her ability to recognize positive emotions such as happiness. Intriguingly, S. M. tends to judge unfamiliar faces as more trustworthy and approachable than does a normal neurological comparison group, and her trustworthy judgments even increased for faces the control group rated as suspicious or unpleasant.

When cues other than facial expression were explored, it became clear that S. M. does not have a general deficit in fear detection. She can recognize fear from voice cues and identify fearful body expressions. Eye-tracking studies revealed that S. M.'s difficulty with recognizing fearful facial expressions is due to her lack of attention to the eye region when she looks at faces. In the prototypical fear expression, the eyes are widened, possibly permitting a wider field of vision and maximizing light access (Susskind et al., 2008). A clear border of white surrounding the iris also allows fear to be unambiguously identified. Once S. M. is instructed to direct her gaze at the eye region, she can correctly identify fear expressions, but she seems unable to ascertain the relevance of the eyes for detecting fear unless directed to do so. However, although S. M. can identify fear from facial expressions when she is instructed about how to do so, some recent studies throw doubt on the idea that she actually experiences fear in a normal way.

Feinstein, Adolphs, Damasio, and Tranel (2011) found that S. M. did not experience fear when they took her to a haunted house said to be the most frightening in the world, when they brought her to a pet store specializing in dangerous animals such as spiders and snakes, or when they had her watch frightening films. At the pet store, they even had to restrain her from touching a deadly tarantula. Two clinical psychologists who were unaware of S. M.'s amygdala damage rated her as emotionally healthy and exceptionally resilient because she was able to talk about significant traumas in her life so dispassionately. What they did not realize is that her lack of fear and excessive trust in others prevented a healthy avoidance of potentially dangerous situations. A finding by Kennedy and colleagues that S. M. lacks any measurable peripersonal space—she is comfortable with strangers coming extremely close to her—may help explain her lack of fear and excessive trust of strangers (Kennedy, Gläscher, Tyszka, & Adolphs, 2009). In her personal life, S. M.'s lack of fear has put her in danger repeatedly. For example, once, while taking a walk through a nearby park, she was assaulted by a man who held a knife to her throat. She claimed to react very calmly, was released, and returned to walk in the same park the very next night. S. M.'s childrens confirm that they have never seen her afraid, even though she lives in a neighborhood "replete with crime, drugs and danger" (Feinstein et al., 2011, p. 36) and was almost killed by her former husband. S. M. knows that these types of events cause fear in other people, but what she understands about fear personally seems to come from distant childhood, probably before the disease process began to destroy her amygdala.

Will the study of S. M. help uncover the function of the amygdala? Only time and more ingenious experiments will tell. At the moment of writing, she remains an interesting enigma.

Concluding Comments

LeDoux's conviction that brain sciences could no longer ignore the role of emotions in behavior, and his brilliant research strategy to provide a detailed description of a single emotion pathway, have opened the door to the neural study of emotion in a way that was barely conceivable as late as the 1980s. The amygdala has become the rock star of brain structures.[13] The word *amygdala* has become part of our vernacular vocabulary, and LeDoux's work has uncovered one of the key structures governing our most basic and automatic emotional reactions. The continuing explication of the role of the amygdala in fear conditioning holds great promise for the development of new therapeutic strategies for the treatment of anxiety disorders.

Complicating a simple version of the emotional low road and cognitive high road for fear perception, however, is the finding that the amygdala is one of the most densely interconnected brain structures; it projects to and receives projections from many, even most, other brain structures. As more is learned about the varied and complex interactions between the amygdala and the rest of the brain, the idea that the fear function of the amygdala is encompassed within a larger, more abstract function, such as behavioral relevance, is increasingly compelling. After all, what is more relevant than fear?

---

13. This is meant to be a pun; LeDoux has organized a rock band called the Amygdaloids, which plays locally and at some of his academic talks. The lyrics of his songs are based on his ideas about emotions and the brain. You can look up the Amygdaloids on YouTube!

Box 4.1: The Stress System

As we've seen, the amygdala is one of the major brain systems for detecting highly salient or relevant stimuli such as threats, and through its connections to hypothalamic and brainstem systems regulating the autonomic and endocrine systems it initiates the stress response. The autonomic and endocrine systems make up two legs of the stress response.

The Fight-or-Flight Response

The sympathetic neurons that make up the fight-or-flight response (see Box 1.1) release the neurotransmitter norepinephrine at targets throughout the body, rapidly preparing the body for action. In addition, activation of the sympathetic nervous system stimulates the release of the hormone epinephrine, or adrenaline, from the adrenal medulla. Norepinephrine and epinephrine have very similar actions on the body, and cross-react with their receptors; receptors for norepinephrine and epinephrine are referred to as *adrenergic receptors*.

The HPA Axis

The other leg of the stress response[14] activates the endocrine cascade called the hypothalamic-pituitary-adrenal (HPA) axis. The amygdala stimulates the release of the hypothalamic hormone corticotropin-releasing hormone (CRH), which in turn releases adrenocorticotropic hormone (ACTH) from the pituitary. ACTH then acts to release the final hormone of the cascade, one of a family of hormones referred to as glucocorticoids (GCs), from the adrenal gland cortex. Note that both autonomic and endocrine systems act on the adrenal gland, but different parts of it; the cortex of the gland is an endocrine gland that makes and releases GCs, while the medulla, which is considered a modified sympathetic ganglion, makes epinephrine. The major GC in humans is cortisol, while in rodents it is corticosterone.

Like norepinephrine and epinephrine, GCs also prepare the body for action, but their time course is both slower and longer acting. This leg of the stress response steps in when the fight-or-flight response has died down, and its actions will be maintained for a longer time period. As their name suggests, one of the

---

14. Traditionally, only the HPA was referred to as the stress response and stress hormones meant only glucocorticoids (GCs). More recently, the stress response has come to encompass both systems, so epinephrine is now also known as a stress hormone.

major functions of GCs is to increase blood glucose. They do this differently than the sympathetic system, which simply breaks down the stored glucose—glycogen—in the liver. GCs increase blood glucose by converting the amino acids that make up proteins into glucose. Since the major source of proteins in the body is muscle, this is only meant as a short-term response. The stress response in general diverts energy from longer-term goals, such as reproduction, digestion, and immune function, to face the immediate threat. Over the longer term, however, this energy trade-off has a high cost; chronic stress can lead to significant muscle wasting, immune suppression, digestive disorders, and all the consequences posed by chronically high blood glucose—a significant risk of diabetes.

Hippocampal Regulation of GCs

Like all endocrine cascades, the HPA axis is regulated by negative feedback, such that high levels of blood GC inhibit the further release of GCs. For many years, this inhibitory feedback was thought to occur at the level of the hypothalamus and pituitary. It is now known, however, that the hippocampus also plays a critical role in regulating GC release. GC receptors found on hippocampal neurons regulate the inhibition of CRH secretion from the hypothalamus (for a review, see Saplosky, 2004). In a truly Machiavellian twist, this feedback system itself is vulnerable to chronic stress. High levels of GC can damage or destroy hippocampal neurons; the resulting impairment of negative feedback then initiates a vicious cycle: Less inhibition means more GCs will be released, further impairing negative feedback, and so forth. In chapter 8, we look at some of the consequences of this hippocampal disruption on memory, another major function of the hippocampus. Thus, the amygdala and the hippocampus play opposing roles in the stress response; the amygdala activates stress, which is inhibited by the hippocampus.

Box 4.2: Divisions of the Prefrontal Cortex

The **frontal cortex** is defined by the central and Sylvian fissures (see Figure 1.2); it refers to the whole area in front of where those major sulci divide the brain. The designation "prefrontal" as opposed to "frontal" excludes only the motor and premotor areas directly in front of the central fissure. **Prefrontal cortex (PFC)** is a large swath of important cortical real estate, especially in primates, and it has been subdivided in a number of ways. The terms that are most important for the level of analysis in this book are the directional terms that designate the three axes of the body: lateral/medial, ventral/dorsal, and anterior/posterior, which is sometimes designated as rostral/caudal.

Lateral/medial: *Lateral* refers to the sides and *medial* means toward the midline, or middle.

Ventral/dorsal: *Ventral* (from the Latin *venter*, meaning belly) refers to the front of the body, and *dorsal* (from the Latin *dorsum*, meaning spine or back) refers to the back of the body. Because of the orientation of the human brain that results from our upright posture, within the brain, *ventral* also refers to regions below, or *inferior*, and *dorsal* to those above, or *superior*.

Anterior/posterior: *Anterior/posterior* designates the head-to-tail axis.

Rostral/caudal: Anterior and posterior are also sometimes referred to as rostral and caudal. *Rostral* (from the Latin *rostrum*, meaning beak or nose) is toward the head, and caudal (from the Latin *cauda*, meaning tail) is toward the rear.

The surface regions of the PFC can be described using only the medial/lateral and dorsal/ventral terms, yielding four fundamental subdivisions of PFC:

Dorsolateral prefrontal cortex (dlPFC): The upper and outer area of PFC (see blue area of Figure 4.1 A). This region has been implicated in the executive functions needed for cognitive control, including working memory, response inhibition, task switching and task flexibility, reasoning, and high-level decision-making.

Ventrolateral prefrontal cortex (vlPFC): This refers to the undersurface or base of the PFC along the side (or away from the midline) (see yellow regions of Figure 4.1 A and B). Together with the dlPFC, the vlPFC has been

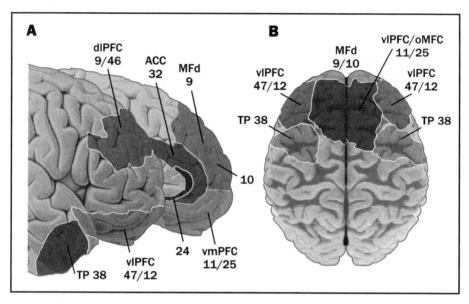

Figure 4.1 A) Separated medial and lateral views showing subdivisions of the frontal cortex. dlPFC: dorsolateral prefrontal cortex, vlPFC: ventrolateral prefrontal cortex, vmPFC/oMFC: ventromedial prefrontal cortex/orbitomedial prefrontal cortex, ACC: anterior cingulate cortex, dmPFC: dorsomedial prefrontal cortex. B) Basal view of the brain with some of the same frontal subdivisions marked.

Source: Adapted from Mobbs D., Lau H.C., Jones O.D. & Frith, C.D. (2007). Law, Responsibility and the Brain. PLoS Biology, 5(4): e103. doi: 10.1371/journal.pbio.0050103. CC-BY-2.5 (license: http://creativecommons.org/licenses/by/2.5/legalcode).

implicated in control mechanisms, especially the regulation of attention and inhibition of motor control, but also many other forms of control.

Ventromedial prefrontal cortex (vmPFC): The region of the undersurface toward the midline which lies above the eye sockets and olfactory bulbs, as shown in purple in Figure 4.1 A and B.

Dorsomedial prefrontal cortex (dmPFC): The upper and inner area of the cortex (see red area in Figure 4.1). This region is an important part of the **default mode network (DMN)**, the resting-state network of areas active when the brain is not presented with an external stimulus or task. It has been connected with autobiographical memory, the neural representation of self, and person judgments.

The terminology used to designate these regions of the PFC is sometimes used somewhat differently by different researchers. For example, some researchers restrict the vmPFC to above a region designated the medial orbitofrontal cortex, but others, such as Damasio, use the vmPFC to refer to a larger region that includes the orbitofrontal cortex at its base. The **orbitofrontal cortex (OFC)** refers to the region that lies above the orbits of the eyes; it overlaps both ventromedial and ventrolateral PFC, and is sometimes referred to synonymously with them. This creates some confusion about terminology, a common circumstance in neuroanatomy.

Box 4.3 Brain-Derived Neurotrophic Factor (BDNF)

Brain-derived neurotrophic factor, or BDNF, is one of a small number of neuro-chemicals referred to as neurotrophins, or neurotrophic (*trophic* is derived from the Latin term for "to feed") substances. Rather than acting to carry messages between brain structures as neurotransmitters do, they are instead substances required for neuron development and survival. BDNF is present in many brain structures but has been intensively studied for its role in the neuroplastic mechanisms required in both emotional learning in the amygdala and in context learning in the hippocampus, as well as for its role regulating neurogenesis, or the production of new neurons, in the hippocampus. Newly generated hippocampal neurons are thought to participate in the formation of new memories (Gould, Beylin, Tanapat, Reeves, & Shors, 1999), a function consistent with the role of the hippocampus in context-specific memories in both fear generalization and extinction context specificity. BDNF has also been linked to depression by the finding that the common action of antidepressant therapies, including psycho-therapy, is to increase neurogenesis (Malberg, Eisch, Nestler, & Duman, 2000). Hippocampal BDNF production increases during stress, which may increase the synaptic plasticity needed to successfully extinguish fears subsequent to the stressful event. A BDNF polymorphism, Val66Met, which reduces the regulated release of BDNF, has been implicated as a risk factor in PTSD. Met carriers in both mice and humans show slower suppression of learned fear, and the secre-tion and neuroplastic effects of BDNF are decreased. Even when healthy, Met carriers show a reduction in hippocampus volume compared to Val/Val homo-zygotes (Enoch, 2013), suggesting that reduced BDNF secretion and hippocam-pal volume may constitute a risk factor for the development of depression and PTSD.

5

The Role of the Body in Emotions and Decision Making

One September day in 1848, during the construction of railroad tracks in Vermont, an unfortunate foreman named Phineas Gage made a life-changing error. He and his gang were blasting rocks to clear a path for the tracks. While he was tamping down the gunpowder into a hole in the rock, something distracted him and he made the mistake of dropping his tamping rod onto the charge. The resulting explosion caused Gage's three-and-a-half-foot tamping iron to shoot violently out of the hole and straight through his head, then land several feet away. It entered his left cheek and exited from the middle of the top of his head. Remarkably, Gage was not killed or even rendered unconscious. Although he suffered from ongoing infections to the wound, in most ways he seemed to recover from the massive injury to his frontal cortex. He was still able to talk, walk, eat, and perform all the usual cognitive and bodily functions. But to most of the people who knew him, Gage never seemed the same after his injury. Before the accident, he had been considered reliable and upstanding, and according to John Harlow, the doctor who tended to him and wrote up his case for a medical journal, he had been in possession of "a well-balanced mind" and the ability to be "very energetic and persistent in executing all of his plans of operation" (J.M. Harlow, 1868, p. 340). After the accident, he became

> fitful, irreverent, indulging at times in the grossest profanity (which was not previously his custom) . . . at times pertinaciously obstinate, yet capri-

cious and vacillating, devising many plans of future operation, which are no sooner arranged than they are abandoned in turn for others appearing more feasible. (Harlow, 1868, p. 339)

As Harlow summarized, those who had known Gage formerly now considered him "no longer Gage" (1868, p.415).

Gage's devastating case has long captured the attention of neuroscientists and neurologists because the frontal lobes are the part of the brain that most clearly differentiates us from our closest primate relatives. The huge expansion of the frontal lobes of humans over evolutionary time had suggested to brain researchers that here would be housed the brain processes that were uniquely human: the elaborate cognitive functions that supported reason and rational thinking. Gage's case was puzzlingly inconsistent with these ideas: After losing a huge swath of this critical brain region, Gage's intellectual functions seemed intact; the only change that could be documented was his marked alteration in emotional functioning.

Interest in Gage's case has been reignited in contemporary times by the neurologist Antonio Damasio, who opened his influential 1994 book *Descartes' Error: Emotion, Reason, and the Human Brain* with this oft-told neurological tale. Using the case of Gage as well as his own research on Gage-like patients, Damasio makes the radical proposal that emotions depend on this highly evolved part of cortex because emotions are a critical component of reason and decision-making. He argued that this was particularly true for the kind of decisions that were most impaired in Gage and other Gage-like individuals: decisions in the personal realm and those that affect social interactions. For Damasio, it is the strict separation of reason and emotion in Descartes's dualistic philosophy, a philosophy that has permeated Western philosophical as well as neuroscientific thinking, that is the "error" of his book title. Much of Damasio's research is devoted to righting this error by demonstrating the deep interconnectedness of emotion and reason in cognitive functions.

In the course of his work linking emotion and reason, Damasio has also been instrumental in shifting attention back to the vital role of the body in feelings and emotion, the view championed by James in the 19th century. Damasio is now at the University of Southern California, but he spent much of his career after his medical training in his native Portugal, developing a post-Jamesian theory of emotion with his research group at the University of Iowa. The Iowa group, most prominently Antoine Bechara and Hanna

Damasio, together with Damasio have demonstrated that emotional reactions to situations or events provide a critical summary of past experience with similar events, a summary that is indispensable to complex decision-making. The bodily feelings generated by these emotional summaries function as signals or markers which are experienced as hunches and intuitions that guide and streamline the otherwise computationally complex decision-making process.

A Case Study of Damage to the Ventromedial Prefrontal Cortex

In *Descartes' Error*, Damasio presents an in-depth portrait of a modern-day Gage: the tragic Elliot, a patient who came to him after removal of a nonmalignant tumor that damaged his brain in the area directly above his eye sockets, a region known as the ventromedial prefrontal cortex (vmPFC).[1] This is also the region that is essential for learning that a previously fear-conditioned stimulus is now safe—the process of extinction that we discussed in the previous chapter. Before he developed the brain tumor, Elliot had a responsible job in business and a stable family life with his wife and children. After the operation to remove the tumor, he recovered well physically and showed no impairments in language, memory, or intelligence; importantly, his professional knowledge of business was intact when he returned to his job.

In spite of his excellent prognosis, Elliot seemed unable to carry out his day-to-day responsibilities. At work he would get stuck on a single task, such as reading or categorizing documents, and fail to progress in the organized and efficient way he had excelled at before the tumor. He had not lost the knowledge or reasoning needed to do any of the tasks required of him, but he could not coordinate and prioritize them to effectively perform his job, and he was finally fired. Unable to hold down any paying job, he became involved in a number of disastrous business schemes that ultimately resulted in personal bankruptcy. His personal life was equally tumultuous; he divorced, quickly remarried someone his friends and family considered highly inappropriate, and divorced again six months later. In his personal life as in his

---

1. The vmPFC is a broad term that can include other areas of interest in studies of emotion, such as the mesial part of the orbitofrontal cortex (OFC), and the subgenual anterior cingulate cortex (ACC). In later papers, Bechara and the Damasios often use the term OFC rather than vmPFC.

work, he seemed unable to use his knowledge of previous experiences and his intact reasoning skills to make advantageous decisions about his future.

Damasio was asked to assess Elliot's condition when his disability benefits were being questioned because of the discrepancy between his intact physical and intellectual capabilities and his consistent inability to use them to his own advantage. He was suspected of simply being lazy and malingering—of willfully not using his intact mental capacities. Damasio and his colleagues tried to find a neuropsychological measure that could demonstrate Elliot's impairment to the authorities withholding his disability pay.

Disappointingly, Damasio's initial testing simply confirmed the picture obtained from previous assessments; Elliot passed every test of cognitive function available. His intelligence, memory, language comprehension and production, visual perception, and attention were all average or superior. Given the location of Elliot's tumor, Damasio expected to find problems in the executive functions of the frontal lobe, such as the ability to switch between tasks when necessary, as it is normally assessed by tasks such as the Wisconsin card-sorting test,[2] or working memory, the ability to hold and manipulate information in mind; surprisingly, Elliot sailed through these tests as well. Confounded by these findings, Damasio turned to tests of personality, but again Elliot produced a normal performance.

Like Gage before him, most of Elliot's difficulties in day-to-day life seemed to be in the social and personal realm, so Damasio then wondered whether Elliot had selectively lost knowledge of social norms. In collaboration with his student Paul Eslinger and colleague Jeffrey Saver, Damasio presented Elliot with a series of tests that gauged his ability to generate solutions to hypothetical ethical dilemmas and social and financial problems, as well as his ability to understand consequences of actions. On these tests, as well as on Kohlberg's Standard-Issue Scoring Moral Judgment Interview and the means-end problem-solving procedure,[3] Elliot once again per-

---

2. The Wisconsin card-sorting test requires patients to be able to flexibly sort cards into categories such as color and shape. When the category-sorting principle is changed, patients with frontal lobe damage usually have difficulty switching categories, a phenomenon known as perseveration.

3. The Standard-Issue Scoring Moral Judgment Interview ranks individuals on Lawrence Kohlberg's scales of moral development, and involves giving opinions about difficult hypothetical moral dilemmas. The means-end problem-solving procedure tests subjects' ability to achieve desired social goals.

formed well. Elliot's poor judgment in his own life could not be attributed to a lack of knowledge of, or ability to analyze, social and moral codes.

Throughout the testing process, Damasio had noticed that Elliot was remarkably unflappable. In all of the many hours of tedious and taxing testing, Damasio had never seen him express any impatience, frustration, or sadness. Elliot's family had also noticed that after his surgery, and in spite of his many recent failures, he was surprisingly emotionally unperturbed. Elliot himself confirmed Damasio's suspicions about his lack of emotional experience during a debriefing following an experiment using emotionally charged images.[4] The most gruesome and gory of the images completely failed to move him. Elliot confided in Damasio that although he understood that the images should provoke feelings of distress, he could no longer feel anything strongly as he used to before the tumor. As Damasio suddenly realized, Elliot's problem seemed to be that he could "know but not feel" (Damasio, 1994, p. 45). It was at this point that Damasio began to suspect that the loss of emotional responses was a key contributor to Elliot's problems in decision-making, contrary to the long-standing view that emotions and reasoning are separate and distinct brain functions, and that emotions are located in subcortical structures that were not impacted by Elliot's disease.

To further test the emotional reactions of Elliot and other vmPFC patients, Damasio measured their ability to generate a skin conductance response (SCR), a measure of emotional arousal reflecting activation of the sympathetic branch of the autonomic nervous system to generate the flight-or-flight response. The SCR is a well-established physiological measurement that forms the basis of lie detector tests. When the sympathetic nervous system is activated, people perspire more, and even imperceptible increases in perspiration will lead to an increase in skin conductance that can be measured with sensors on the skin.

VmPFC patients can generate a normal SCR to a sudden loud noise or bright light, so are capable of becoming aroused. However, in spite of having a functioning arousal system, these patients show absolutely no SCR to gruesome images, such as the aftermath of a horrific accident, that normally evoke intense emotional reactions and correspondingly large SCRs. These

---

4. These were the IAPS (International Affective Picture Set) images that are used extensively in neuroimaging studies of emotion.

patients are capable of becoming aroused, but seem indifferent or unmoved by emotional situations that are usually seen as highly provocative. This is true in spite of their knowledge that the images represent emotional trage- dies, and in spite of their being able to articulate their understanding that they would have found these images emotionally disturbing before their injury.

Parsing the Prefrontal Cortex

Although Elliot's case was perplexing in terms of the inability to measure his deficit, Damasio was aware that his was not an isolated, idiosyncratic case. Elliot initially reminded him of the famous case of Phineas Gage that we recounted at the beginning of this chapter. In investigating the literature further, Damasio found a few other historical cases in which a disruption in emotional responses occurred together with severely compromised social functioning, and in spite of evidence that cognitive functions were intact. Putting together the pattern from the historical cases with observations of the locations of frontal lobe damage in other patients who came into their clinic, Damasio and colleagues proposed that this unusual set of symptoms following prefrontal damage occurred only when the damage was restricted to the inner and lower areas—the ventromedial frontal cortex. If the dam- age extended out further to the sides and toward the top of the frontal cor- tex—the dorsolateral prefrontal areas (dlPFC)—then the cognitive skills of attention and working memory that were more typically associated with prefrontal function were also affected.

The presence of a consistent pattern of symptoms with vmPFC damage confirmed Damasio's sense that Elliot's symptoms could be explained by damage to a region of the brain where emotional processing and reasoning come together in decision-making. He coined the term "Gage matrix" to refer to the constellation of symptoms observed in Gage and other cases of vmPFC damage: alterations in emotional reactivity that lead to great diffi- culties in making advantageous decisions in social and personal life despite intact cognitive and intellectual functions. He then wondered whether emotion and decision-making come together in other brain regions as well, and produce the Gage matrix of symptoms when damaged. If so, this would further strengthen his growing conviction that emotion and reason are deeply interconnected functions.

The Gage Matrix: Anosognosia

Reflecting on his experience as a neurologist, Damasio connected Elliot's case to another type of brain damage that, in addition to showing disrupted emotions and impaired decision-making, pointed to the idea that bodily feelings are also vital for decision-making. Damage to the right motor cortex, an area that lies directly in front of the central sulcus, leads to paralysis on the left side of the body. When that damage also encompasses the neural tissue of the right somatosensory cortices, the patients suffer from a peculiar condition known as *anosognosia*, which literally means a denial of disease. Damasio includes three areas in the umbrella term "somatosensory cortices": (a) primary somatosensory cortex, or SI, immediately behind the central sulcus; (b) association somatosensory cortex, or SII, in the upper cleft of the lateral sulcus, called the parietal operculum; and (c) the insula, an "island"[5] of lateral cortex buried beneath the frontal and temporal lobes (see Figure 5.1 for the locations of these areas). The insula will come up again in the next chapter on pleasure and motivation, and will be a major focus of chapter 7 on interoception. Its location is shown in Figure 7.1.

Damasio gives the example of one of his patients, D. J., who was completely unable to move the left side of her body, yet when Damasio first inquired about her paralysis, she resolutely denied its existence. It was only when he explicitly asked her to show him her left arm moving that she noticed, although only briefly, that "it doesn't seem to do much by itself" (1994, p. 63). Her knowledge of her paralysis was not automatic and readily available to her; it was only when she took note of it visually as she attempted to move her arm that she recognized its loss of movement. But that knowledge was fleeting, and disappeared as soon as her gaze was withdrawn.

What prompted Damasio to include anosognosics in his Gage matrix is that the emotions of these patients are profoundly altered together with disruption in their thinking and decisions about their life. They seem to be completely unconcerned about their physical condition, often dismissing it with humor or simply denying its existence, and are equally unconcerned about their future. This is in contrast to what is seen with a symmetrical left hemisphere lesion which results in an equally extensive right side paralysis

---

5. The Latin word *insula* means island. This brain area was originally called the Island of Reil after the person who first described it, Johann Christian Reil, but is now known simply as the insula.

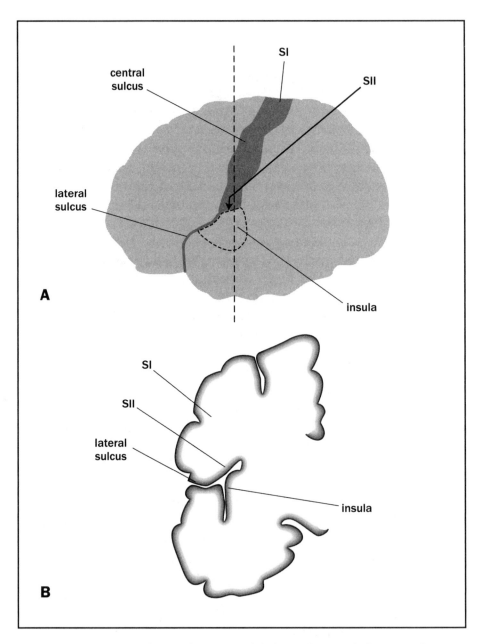

Figure 5.1 Lateral (A) and coronal (B) views of the brain showing the locations of primary somatosensory cortex (SI), secondary somatosensory cortex (SII) and the insula.

Source: Adapted from a drawing by Daniel Greenberg.

but does not produce anosognosia; such patients express acute distress about the devastating consequences to their life as they have known it. Although anosognosic patients have normal cognitive functions, their lack of emotions or awareness of their paralysis prevents them from actively engaging in rehabilitation therapy, so their prognosis is much worse than that of patients who care about their disability. Once again, the loss of emotional responses seems to lead to poor life choices, just as in the cases of Elliot and Gage.

The On-Line Body

As we described above, the damaged areas that lead to anosognosia include the right three somatosensory cortices—SI, SII, and the insula—as well as adjacent white matter linking these structures to other brain regions. This lateralized sector of the brain is unique in that it receives input from the full extent of the body, which Damasio refers to as "soma." This includes input both from external body sensors of the skin, such as touch, temperature, pressure, and pain, reflecting the impact of events in the external environment on the body, as well as from internal receptors that monitor the viscera and changes in the internal environment. Damasio argues that the right somatosensory cortices contain the most complete representation of the body. This representation is dynamic and ongoing, reflecting the moment-to-moment changes of the body as it responds to the challenges of the external world. Anosognosic patients have lost this ongoing representation of the state of their body; damage to right somatosensory cortices means that they have no body image of the present moment. Their only sense of themselves is a static, unchanging off-line image of their body as it was before their devastating stroke. The lack of these on-line bodily signals disrupted D. J.'s ability to make advantageous decisions, which require a realistic sense of the state of the body.

The Gage Matrix and S. M.

Patients with selective damage to the subcortical amygdala, a condition that arises much less frequently than anosognosia or vmPFC damage, also evinced the Gage matrix. Recall S. M., the patient of Damasio and colleagues discussed in our previous chapter; S. M. suffers from complete destruction of her amygdalae as a result of Urbach-Wiethe disease. In the wake of her amygdala loss, which was complete at about age 16, S. M. is always unperturbed and calm, even in the face of substantial loss and trauma. This lack of emotional response is also associated with poor decision-making and social difficulties. As we described in the previous chapter, S. M.'s inability to feel fear and her excessive and unjustified trust in others has landed her in a number of dangerous situations. How and why are emotions and bodily feelings tied to reason and decision-making?

Putting the Pieces Together: Emotions and Feelings

Damasio agrees with LeDoux that it is important to differentiate between emotions and feelings, and his view of emotions is largely consistent with that of LeDoux: Emotions are responses to salient, mainly external stimuli such as a threat (or recall of those stimuli). However, for Damasio, the key consequence of an emotional stimulus is its potential to disrupt the homeostatic state of the body. Emotional reactions are the response of the body to coordinate the necessary changes in the body and the brain needed to react successfully to the stimulus and re-establish homeostatic balance. Thus, for Damasio, emotions are intimately tied to the mechanisms of biological regulation. Damasio argues that feelings arise at the most basic level of emotional processing, and all emotions will be sensed as feelings by being encoded in somatosensory cortices. This is the neo-Jamesian component to Damasio's idea (although recall that, confusingly, James referred to these as emotions; he did not distinguish between emotions and feelings, and used the terms as synonyms). The difference in these models also has a consequence for questions of animal feelings; Damasio situates feelings well down the evolutionary scale, while LeDoux appears to restrict feelings to those animals with consciousness.

Background Feelings

Although all emotions produce feelings, Damasio argues that not all feelings are emotions. Background feelings refer to the ongoing sense of the state of the body. Although we are often unaware of these feelings, they are what we attend to when someone asks us how we are, and are essential to our sense of being. Damasio speculates that anosognosics, in addition to their loss of emotions, are missing what he calls "background feelings." When these feelings are disrupted by damage to the right somatosensory cortices, our core sense of self is affected, and the loss of this physical mooring sets our emotional vessel off course. As Damasio eloquently phrases it, "what does not come naturally and automatically through the primacy of feeling cannot be maintained in the mind" (1994, p. 154). Damasio cites the case of Supreme Court justice William O. Douglas, who suffered a right hemisphere stroke resulting in left side paralysis and accompanying anosognosia. Against the advice of his doctors, friends, and family, he discharged himself from the hospital and insisted on returning to the bench. His inability to update his body image resulted in an unrealistic understanding of the extent of his disability. Not only was he unaware of the extent of his paralysis, but he was also unable to do his job properly because his decision-making and social judgments were repeatedly off target. Sadly unaware of his physical and mental limitations, he refused to resign from the Court and had to be forced into retirement.

Thinking about his work with anosognosic patients led Damasio to a further insight about the relationship between awareness of the body and the person's concept of self. For most patients with brain damage, the injury is seen as profoundly affecting their self. They commonly say things such as, "My God, what is happening to me?" when discussing their impairment. The anosognosic patients, in contrast, never make comments like, "God, how bizarre it is that I no longer feel any part of my body and that all that is left of me is my mind" (Damasio, 1994, pp. 236–237). They do not refer their injury to their selves and contemplate how it affects them. Their injuries do not have an impact on their core sense of self and its well-being because they lack the ongoing representation of their now-paralyzed body.

The Embodied Mind: Reasoning and Decision-Making

Damasio argues that simple emotional responses, those that occur innately as well as those acquired as simple conditioned behaviors like those induced by fear conditioning, are examples of simple decisions: decisions to approach or avoid stimuli that have obvious survival value. Human reasoning and decision-making are obviously much more complex than these simple emotional responses. They rely mostly on learning and acquired cultural knowledge and traditions to deal with complex social and moral behaviors, and require the neocortex rather than survival circuits built into brain stem nuclei and associated limbic structures. Nonetheless, Damasio argues that complex social and personal decisions are equally crucial to survival, and so are equally tied to the bioregulatory mechanisms that ensure survival. As with more simple decisions, emotions are still used to establish the basic priorities that ensure making choices that will allow life to flourish. In Damasio's words, "Our experiences and responses to them must be evaluated and shaped by a fundamental set of preferences of the organism that consider survival paramount" (Damasio, 1994, p. 111). This requires that the brain has a continuous stream of information about the state of the body as well as knowledge about what is in the environment and how it might affect the body. Thus, for Damasio, another equally troublesome error of Descartes was his separation of the machinelike body and the ethereal mind. In Damasio's view, the biological regulation of the body is part and parcel of normal cognitive processes: "The mind is embodied in the full sense of the word" (Damasio, 1994, p. 118).

Damasio suggests that social and personal reasoning/decision-making is distinct and different from the "pure" reasoning that has been emphasized by philosophers and that we often associate with logical problem-solving. Social and personal decisions are notoriously complex and inherently uncertain; how to think about and plan for the future, or how to respond to someone we love and respect but whom we suspect has acted dishonorably, cannot be logically analyzed without reference to our emotions. There is no clear right or wrong response as there is in a logical inference. In addition, unlike finding a solution to a complex problem in number theory, decisions in the social realm can have life-or-death consequences; they are tied to survival, either directly or indirectly. The fact that Elliot and other vmPFC patients score well on measures of intellectual functions in standard neuropsychological exams yet fail spectacularly in their social and personal life is clear evidence that the social realm represents a discrete category of decision-making.

Secondary Emotions, the vmPFC, and Damasio's Somatic Marker Hypothesis

Damasio also differentiates between what he calls primary and secondary emotions. Primary emotions are innate or simple learned responses to salient features of an external stimulus mediated by the amygdala, and dominate our early life. Secondary emotions are acquired as we learn about the complex emotional consequences of our experiences. These secondary emotions can be activated by thoughts and memories or by any associations that have been made to the learned stimulus. For example, in the story of Elizabeth's walk in the potentially bear-infested woods in chapter 1, it wasn't necessary for her to have ever seen a bear in real life. Nonetheless, she had had many opportunities to learn from stories and from others that bears were extremely dangerous, and she could easily imagine how terrified she would feel if she were to see a bear. Her knowledge of bears and the emotional associations she had made with them were a learned secondary emotion, stored in a complex neural network activated by the vmPFC. Hearing from her neighbor that there might be a bear in the woods where she planned to walk triggered the stored image of the bear in visual cortex. This visual image in turn activated the vmPFC, triggering all her learned associations about bears, as well as activating the amygdala and related structures to provoke the changes in the body and the brain that would otherwise be activated by the actual sight of the bear. The bodily changes were in turn detected in somatosensory cortices, leading to the feelings of fear and anxiety that she experienced.

Because the stored secondary emotional associations in the vmPFC activate the body via the amygdala, Damasio also refers to this vmPFC representation as a somatic marker. The somatic changes that result provide a body marker about the goodness or badness of the situation. Elizabeth's body and brain were on high alert even without her actually seeing a bear; the feelings produced are a prediction or marker of potential danger. If she had in fact detected some sign that a bear was nearby, she wouldn't have had to spend much time deciding what to do; she was ready to run. In Damasio's hypothesis, somatic markers provide a summary of our past experience with a situation or stimulus, and that summary, experienced as a feeling, reduces the work that must be done in evaluating the stimulus or arriving at a decision in the event of a crisis.

Patients such as Elliot have primary emotions, as demonstrated by their ability to generate SCRs to loud noises. They can also have feelings about those primary emotions. However, without the vmPFC, they cannot have a secondary emotional response as measured by the SCR, and thus also lack feelings of distress when viewing gruesome images, which require the generation of a bodily response based on associations with the emotional consequences that might be experienced in the scenes depicted. Patients with amygdala damage, on the other hand, should lack both primary and secondary emotions (although S. M. had acquired some secondary emotions before her amygdala degenerated).

To further explore the role of primary and secondary emotions, Bechara, H. Damasio, and A. Damasio (2003) studied the ability of brain-damaged patients to reproduce the physiological and subjective experiential aspects of past emotional responses. They asked the patients to imagine a past time when they felt the emotions of happiness, sadness, fear, or anger intensely. The vmPFC patients were able to recall instances in which they felt those emotions but rated their subjective emotional experience at the time of recall as minimal. This was supported by the total absence of SCRs as measured during recall. In contrast, non-brain-damaged controls rated their emotion at recall at close to the maximum of the four-point scale and mounted a significant SCR in response to their memories. As seen in the response of these patients to gruesome images, vmPFC patients are unable to use stored representations to recreate emotional reactions at a later time.

In the same experiment, S. M., the patient with a pure case of amygdala damage, when recalling events that had occurred after destruction of her amygdala, behaved similarly to the vmPFC-damaged patients: She could recall emotional events, but doing so did not reevoke subjective feelings and her SCRs were unperturbed. In contrast, remembering events that she had experienced before the age of 16 led both to subjective feelings and SCR responses. Thus, the amygdala seems necessary for initially setting up the emotional response that the vmPFC can regenerate through the use of secondary emotions, but it is not necessary once the somatic markers have been established.

The Gage Matrix

Damasio has now identified three distinct brain regions where emotions and reasoning intersect: the vmPFC, a part of the brain crucial for decision-making and secondary emotions, which is near the output for behavior; the amygdala, involved in determining the salience or relevance of stimuli, which is on the input side of the brain; and the right somatosensory cortices, which provide an ongoing representation of the state of the body, including the impact of the environment on the outside of the body as well as the state of the viscera and the internal environment. What do these seemingly very different processes have in common?

Using Damasio's reasoning, the role of these Gage matrix structures becomes clearer. The amygdala instantiates the basic set of preferences of organisms, and can evaluate the goodness or badness of stimuli in terms of how they will affect the body and survival. The right somatosensory cortices provide a continuous map of the state of the body which is also important in establishing priorities; for example, when we are hungry, food stimuli will be preferred to other choices present. The vmPFC represents and stores the learned emotional associations that comprise secondary emotions, such that thoughts and memories, as well as immediate stimuli, provoke emotional feelings. These emotional feelings represent important summaries of past experience which are used to simplify and guide decisions.

Body Loops and "As-If" Body Loops

"Body loops" is the term that Damasio uses to describe the circle of connections from mind/brain to body and back to mind/brain. Thinking about past emotional experiences evokes sensory images that activate representations in the vmPFC. These stored representations in turn trigger bodily responses sensed as feelings by the right somatosensory cortices, providing critical markers of past experience.

In addition to the body loops, which actually recreate the feelings in the body, Damasio proposes that we also have the ability to generate "as-if" loops that directly activate brain representations of the body in somatosensory cortices without generating the full-fledged bodily responses. Thus, "somatic markers" don't always have to be expressed in the body proper; instead, the same brain processes can generate emotional signals without bodily expression of the emotions. In colloquial terms, somatic markers can be "all in the head." The "as-if" body loops are thought to be fainter than the actual body loops, but have the advantage of being much less energy intensive and are still useful for shaping complex decision landscapes.

The Iowa Gambling Task

Damasio's work with anosognosic, vmPFC-damaged, and amygdala-damaged patients led him to the realization that sensing of the state of the body is vital to the type of emotional signaling that aids decision-making in real life, forming the basis of his comprehensive, radically new model of brain function that he calls the "somatic marker hypothesis." He now needed a way to test this hypothesis. For this, he turned back to thinking about why laboratory tests were not able to pinpoint why Elliot was unable to make appropriate decisions in his life. The laboratory tests did not involve choices that had real consequences and so did not require any emotional engagement. In addition, in real life, choices often have to be made in the face of inherent uncertainty. To design a laboratory test that incorporated these real-life elements, Bechara came up with a gambling task in which participants are required to make choices between multiple options that result in rewards and punishments in an uncertain situation. In what has come to be called the Iowa gambling task (IGT), the participants were given $2,000 of pretend money, and their goal was to maximize their profit in a card-turning task.

In this task, participants turn over one card at a time from any one of four decks of cards for 100 turns, although they do not know in advance when the game will stop. Every card pays a reward of either $50 or $100, but occasionally, a variable penalty is also charged. Two of the decks are "good" decks that pay out more than they charge in penalties over time, and two are "bad" decks. The bad decks initially seem desirable because they pay out more than the good decks—$100 compared to $50—but ultimately they result in a net loss because they also penalize more. The size and timing of the losses initially seem unpredictable to the subject, but preprogrammed schedules are set up so that the total loss every 10 cards is $1,250 for the bad decks but only $250 for the good decks, and over time, subjects begin to realize this. Players are free to switch between decks at any point and usually do so after a loss occurs. As time goes on, normal players begin to make more selections from the good decks. In contrast, patients with vmPFC damage continue to make more selections from the bad decks than the good decks throughout the task. They never learn to avoid the bad decks and consequently lose money repeatedly. The IGT was the first neuropsychological test to successfully distinguish Elliot's behavior from that of normal controls. Bechara had succeeded in coming up with a laboratory test that could measure the real-life impact of vmPFC damage.

Damasio connected this test of vmPFC damage to his insight that loss of emotional experience is the core deficit in these patients. He proposed that the reason Elliot and other vmPFC-damaged patients fail the IGT is that they lack the somatic marker which over time represents the overall payout for each deck. Without the marker that represents the accumulated "goodness" or "badness" of decks, they behave as though they have no regard for the longer-term consequences of their actions. Bechara et al. describe these patients as having "myopia for the future" (Bechara, Damasio, Damasio, & Anderson, 1994, p. 14). Without the negative somatic marker to override the immediately desirable large reward of the bad decks, vmPFC-damaged patients keep making the wrong choices. Their rationality is compromised by the lack of emotional input to their decision-making process.

Connecting the Gambling Task with Somatic Markers

With an experimental test sensitive to the emotional guidance of decision-making in hand, Damasio now needed a way to measure the somatic markers that he proposed were needed for complex decision-making. His wife and longtime collaborator, Hanna Damasio, suggested monitoring skin conductance responses (SCRs) while patients and control subjects were performing the gambling task, as it had already been established that vmPFC-damaged patients could generate a startle response to a loud noise but were unable to generate the normal responses to emotionally distressing images.

Subjects' SCRs were measured both before and immediately after they turned each card. The SCR to a reward or penalty after turning over a card was the same for the non-brain-damaged control participants and the vmPFC-damaged patients, as expected. Where the vmPFC-damaged patients' SCRs differed markedly from the controls was in the few seconds leading up to their choice of card. Over time, after they had encountered several instances of reward and punishment, the control participants developed an anticipatory response: an increase in skin conductance that arose as they considered their choices (described in Damasio, 1994, pp. 219–222). The anticipatory SCR was larger before they chose from the bad decks, and it grew in magnitude as they gained more experience with the cumulative negative results of selecting from those decks. This was an unexpected finding; anticipatory SCRs had not been documented before. As the anticipatory SCR to the bad decks grew in size, control participants began to favor the good decks. In stark contrast, none of the patients with vmPFC damage developed these anticipatory SCRs, so they lacked the motivation to resist the large reward of the bad decks. They did not develop bodily signals that allowed them to predict the future value of their decisions in the gambling task.

Intriguingly, Bechara, Damasio, Tranel, and Damasio (1997) demonstrated that the anticipatory SCRs to the bad decks developed earlier in the experiment than the participants' ability to explicitly label the decks as good or bad. The researchers stopped the participants every 10 turns and asked them to describe what they thought was happening in the game. For the normal control subjects, there was a "hunch" period where subjects had a sense of which decks were riskier and so began choosing from the good decks, but could not articulate why. This was then followed by a "conceptual period" where subjects were able to explicitly describe the contingencies of the different decks.[6] In contrast, the vmPFC-damaged patients never developed hunches, yet 50% of them did reach the conceptual period where they could accurately describe the deck contingencies. Remarkably, the vmPFC-damaged patients continued choosing disadvantageously even after they consciously knew that the bad decks resulted in overall losses. Because the anticipatory signals that could override the response to immediate reward never developed, the vmPFC-damaged patients continued to select cards from the bad decks even once they became aware that those decks yielded much more severe punishments.

The results from the IGT were a resounding confirmation of Damasio's somatic marker hypothesis. Damasio likens the anticipatory SCRs to "gut feelings" that develop before people are able to explicitly explain the reasons for their decisions. What is remarkable is that the lack of hunches in the vmPFC-damaged patients cannot be compensated for the conscious knowledge of the deleterious consequences of selecting from the bad decks. This is consistent with Damasio's earlier observation that Elliot continued to make disadvantageous choices in his work and social life despite the fact that he could describe what constituted good moral and social behavior in hypothetical tests, and consistent with Damasio's sense that the social and personal realm represents a distinct form of decision-making. Just as with the anosognosic patients, "what does not come naturally and automatically through the primacy of feeling cannot be maintained in the mind" (Damasio, 1994, p. 154). The need for anticipatory SCR responses in order to perform well in the gambling task is a concrete experimental demonstration of the powerful role that emotions and bodily feelings play in decision-making.

Damasio contrasts the somatic marker hypothesis with another kind of decision-making that he calls the "high reason view." According to the high reason view associated with philosophers such as Plato, Descartes, and Kant, humans reach decisions by systematically considering the outcomes of all possible choices and computing a cost/benefit analysis for each option.

---

6. Interestingly, about 30% of the normal control subjects never reached the conceptual period but still performed normally on the gambling task.

The difficulty with such an approach is that even fairly simple decisions can generate a plethora of possibilities, so the process of deciding among them becomes slow and painstaking. Damasio conjectures that somatic markers evolved in order to make decisions faster and more effective by making use of past experience to quickly reduce the number of possibilities to be considered. In the gambling task, the development of anticipatory SCRs cuts the choices from four decks in total to only the two good decks quite early in the game. The somatic markers can be negative, as in the gambling task example where anticipatory SCRs serve as a warning signal that the high reward from the bad decks will eventually lead to even larger penalties. Somatic markers can also be positive, creating an incentive or approach response, moving the person toward certain choices rather than cutting out the potentially negative ones. In both cases, they bias and simplify decision-making when there are too many possible choices by providing good or bad "gut feelings" about some of the options.

Although both the amygdala and vmPFC are components of a brain network that is crucial for the influence of emotions on decision-making, the two structures play different roles within this network: The amygdala is part of an impulsive neural system that responds directly to immediate stimuli, whereas the vmPFC is part of a reflective neural system that works within a larger context that is more extended in time (Bechara, 2005). This system maintains a summary of past experience that can be used to modulate or over-ride the allure of the immediate stimulus. A dual-systems distinction between impulsive and reflective systems is a staple of the decision-making literature, and the components are often referred to as "System 1" and "System 2" (Sanfey & Chang, 2008).

Critiques of the Iowa Gambling Task as Evidence for the Somatic Marker Hypothesis

The somatic marker hypothesis is a wide-ranging theory that stresses the importance of the body in emotion, and in turn the overarching importance of emotion in decision-making. Damasio and colleagues have worked consistently over the last two decades to produce a comprehensive, coherent, and well-supported theory of emotional processing in the brain. It is a compelling story that furthers James's ideas by situating emotions, feelings, and the role of the body at the center of brain function. It is not without its critics, however. In particular, the adequacy of the gambling task as experimental support for the SMH has come under fire (for a review, see Dunn, Dalgleish, & Lawrence, 2006).

The first criticism is that participants in the IGT are more aware of the details of the different decks than Damasio et al. claimed—in other words, the reward/punishment schedule is more "cognitively penetrable" than the experimenters intended. This matters, because if somatic markers arise only after full conscious knowledge about a situation is available, it is unclear why people would use them rather than their explicit knowledge. However, Bechara et al.'s (1997) demonstration that vmPFC-damaged patients continue to select from the bad decks even after they are consciously aware that they result in net losses is compelling evidence that the felt record of the impact on the body of past decisions provides vital information for sound decision-making. It is this reminder of past homeostatic disruptions that provides the motivation needed to resist the allure of the immediate reward. Lacking this mechanism to 'feel' the bodily consequences of poor decisions in the past, vmPFC patients act as if they simply do not care enough about the future to forego the immediate reward.

A more significant criticism attacks the role of anticipatory SCRs as somatic markers in the gambling task on the grounds that skin conductance is not a particularly good way of discriminating between positive and negative valence. SCRs increase to positive as well as negative events; thus, this inherently ambiguous physiological measure may not be the best candidate for an emotion-based marker signal to indicate the goodness or badness of a decision. Perhaps it is not enough simply to focus on the existence of a somatic marker such as the anticipatory SCR; rather, because a single somatic marker is ambiguous, the larger context must be taken into account. This larger context includes appraisal processes that could well differ between individuals. For example, some people may appraise the arousal of anticipatory SCRs as exciting, whereas others may find them distressing and seek to avoid them. Damasio himself critiques James for omitting the concept of appraisal from his somatic theory of emotion (A. Damasio, 2010, p. 116). The IGT shows that somatic markers are necessary for effective decision-making, but in and of themselves they are not sufficient. There is more to emotional processing than registering bodily signals, and there is more to bodily signals than SCRs. As we will see in chapter 7, the work of Craig on interoception provides a more differentiated and more complete view of the range of bodily activations involved in emotions and their representation in the brain.

A Somatic Marker Theory of Addiction

Patients with brain damage to the vmPFC and amygdala are not the only people who experience difficulties with judgment and decision-making in everyday life. Many researchers have followed up on the Damasios' and Bechara's initial work by using the IGT with different groups of people. Patients with schizophrenia (Sevy et al., 2007), Huntington's disease (Stout, Rodawalt, & Siemers, 2001), and chronic pain (Apkarian et al., 2004) also show the same difficulty with advantageous decision-making in the IGT. However, not all who do poorly on the IGT have a primary somatic marker dysfunction. Impaired executive functions, such as working memory deficits as a result of damage to the dlPFC, will also result in faulty decision-making as assessed by the IGT; in this case the ability of the vmPFC to couple dlPFC with other key emotion processing regions such as the OFC and insula (these regions are discussed in more detail in chapters 6 and 7). So, impaired IGT performance is not always diagnostic of primary somatic marker dysfunction.

However, the impulsive behavior and lack of concern for consequences seen in substance abusers suggest that they do share some of the key features seen in vmPFC-damaged patients. Antoine Bechara and his colleagues Antonio Verdejo-García, Nasir Naqvi, Hanna Damasio and others have now developed a somatic marker hypothesis of addiction (Bechara & H. Damasio, 2002; Bechara, Dolan, & Hindes, 2002; Naqvi & Bechara, 2010; Verdejo-García & Bechara, 2009). In their model, the faulty decision-making that leads to addiction, relapse, and overdosing in drug-addicted individuals shares essential properties with the poor judgment shown by vmPFC-damaged patients: impulsive grasping at immediate rewards, as well as an inability to choose based on a prediction of future consequences or long-term outcomes. Both groups could be considered to suffer from a form of "myopia" for the future (Verdejo-García & Bechara, 2009, p. 49), which Bechara and colleagues propose can result from either a hyperactive, impulsive amygdala based system and/or a hypoactive reflective prefrontal system that acts to predict future consequences.

Bechara and Damasio (2002) compared the IGT performance of substance abusers, vmPFC-damaged patients, and healthy controls while measuring SCRs. This testing revealed two distinct groups of substance abusers: 37% performed normally, and the remaining 63% showed results similar to vmPFC-damaged patients, with poor performance on the IGT accompanied by a lack of anticipatory SCRs, yet with intact SCRs in response to wins or losses (although this measure showed some variability, which we will discuss below). The impaired group of substance abusers thus appear to have dysfunction in the vmPFC similar to that of patients like Elliot, so may lack the ability to generate somatic markers on the basis of past gambling decisions that act to steer them away from the high immediate rewards of the bad decks. However, because some substance abusers showed a decrease in the immediate SCR, and some substance abusers performed normally on the IGT, vmPFC dysfunction by itself did not fully explain the behavior of all substance abusers.

The abnormally large SCRs to wins and losses in some substance abusers suggested a defect in amygdala and related reward structures (recall that vmPFC damage results in the loss of the anticipatory SCR, whereas amygdala dysfunction alters the immediate SCRs to punishment and reward). To test for hypersensitivity to rewards in the substance abuse population, Bechara et al. (2002) compared performance on the normal IGT to a modified IGT in which the punishment and rewards schedules were reversed, so that punishment was immediate and occurred on every trial and reward was variable and accumulated over trials. The good decks had high immediate punishment, but over time paid out even larger rewards, whereas the bad decks had lower immediate punishment, but even lower accumulated rewards. Bechara et al. predicted that those who were oversensitive to reward would lose on the normal IGT because the high immediate rewards paid out by the bad decks would be irresistible, but would be more likely to win on the modified IGT because there were no high immediate rewards to cloud their judgment.

The addition of this modified IGT revealed a third subgroup of substance abusers that turns out to be the largest one (41%). In addition to the subgroup that was indistinguishable from the healthy population, and the one which was similar to the vmPFC-damaged patients and so failed both variants of the IGT, a third subgroup failed the normal IGT but did well on the modified form, indicating that they were hypersensitive to reward. This finding was consistent with the abnormally large immediate SCRs to reward seen in this group. This group retained an ability to anticipate future rewards, and even showed an exaggerated anticipatory SCR to rewards, which got larger over time for the good decks in the modified IGT. The group of substance abusers who failed both normal and modified IGT was, like vmPFC-damaged patients, unable to anticipate the future. Because they were able to predict the future large rewards in the good decks, the initial larger punishments deterred further choices from the good decks.

The behavioral and physiological similarities between patients with vmPFC damage and a subset of substance abusers suggest a shared neural deficit, a hypothesis that is supported by Franklin et al.'s (2002) structural imaging study that reported decreased gray matter in the vmPFC of cocaine-dependent patients relative to normal controls, a measure that likely would not be as evident as a difference in volume. The 5–11% decreases in grey matter in vmPFC and other prefrontal sites reported by Franklin et al. are much less extensive than the damage wrought to Elliot's brain by his tumor, so some differences in IGT performance between substance abusers and vmPFC patients would be expected. Notably, however, the degree of gray matter decreases seen by Franklin et al. was not related to the severity or length of time of the drug habit, a result now seen in other structural studies that identify abnormalities in substance abuser populations as well (Verdejo-Garcia & Bechara, 2009), and so could reflect a pre-existing dysfunction that serves as a risk factor. Indeed, deficits in IGT performance in drug-naïve individuals who were at high risk for drug abuse, such as having a family history, or those with externalizing behavior disorder (see Verdejo-Garcia & Bechara for references) also supports the idea of a pre-existing vulnerability to substance abuse. Bechara and Hanna Damasio (2002) noted that while 100% of their group of vmPFC patients failed the IGT, 64% of the substance-dependent group and, notably, 29% of the normal group were impaired on the task.

One group of Bechara et al.'s substance-dependent subjects performed normally on both the IGT and its modified form (36% of their sample). Because this group does not have a deficiency in decision-making, and because they are also functional in their real life, Bechara et al. suggest reclassifying them as "functional addicts" rather than true addicts (Verdejo-García & Bechara, 2009, p. 59). Because the gambling tests were performed on abstinent substance abusers, it's possible that this group shows disordered decision-making only when exposed to drugs. The group with a somatic marker disorder evident even when abstinent may have much greater difficulty overcoming their addiction compared to those with normal decision-making functions when sober. Finally, some individuals in the healthy control group did poorly on the IGT. Normal subjects who did poorly on the IGT showed a wide range of anticipatory SCRs. Those who did poorly but showed normal anticipatory SCRs tended to describe themselves as risk takers and gamblers, and it's likely that their decisions are being guided by cognitive and affective processes outside the somatic marker system. However, those of the healthy population who did poorly on the IGT and showed impaired anticipatory SCRs, and thus appeared to have faulty decision-making, might be a currently healthy population that is at risk for future substance abuse. Altogether, the somatic marker hypothesis for addiction seems supported, and helps identify differences within the substance abuse population that may be of value in determining the most effective treatments.

Concluding Comments

Damasio's paradigm-changing research on the role of the body and emotions in decision-making revived and updated James's neglected late-19th-century proposal that feelings arise from changes in the body as it reacts to an emotional stimulus. Based largely on brain lesion studies, Damasio argues that the ever-changing representation of the body as it senses and responds to changes in both the internal and external environment is most fully mapped in right somatosensory cortices, where it gives rise to a full representation of the self. Emotions and feelings as well as the sense of self in his model is fundamentally tied to the regulation of the body—homeostasis. At their most basic level, emotional stimuli represent potential disruption to the body and homeostatic balance, and emotional responses prepare the body to successfully meet that challenge and restore that balance. The *feeling* of pleasantness or unpleasantness associated with a body state provides the motivational imperative to restore homeostatic balance.

Damasio and colleagues' careful analysis of the puzzle posed by patients with damage to the vmPFC and other parts of the "Gage" network that has left cognitive functions intact but disrupted the system that provides a continuous and up-dated readout of the state of the body has conclusively demonstrated the importance of the emotional guidance of behavior. The somatic marker hypothesis based on these studies has provided one of the key scientific insights that has lead to the emotional revolution in brain sciences. No longer a poor cousin of cognition, emotions have now taken a front seat in the theater of the brain. In Chapter 7 we explore the next step in the science of the body, looking more closely at the anatomy and function of interoception, the feelings of the body.

Reward

Liking, Wanting, and Learning

Anthony Dickinson, now a neuroscientist at Cambridge University, relates a story that inspired some of his later work (Dickinson & Balleine, 2010). When he was a young student on holiday in Palermo, Sicily, he slaked his thirst with a big slice of watermelon on a boiling hot afternoon. Watermelon was not readily available in his native Britain at that time, so it was his first-ever taste of the delicious fruit, and he found it deeply pleasurable. Later that day, in what he describes as a "youthful overindulgence," he drank so much of the local red wine that he became violently sick. A few days later when he was once again hot, hungry, and thirsty, he thought of the delightfully thirst-quenching watermelon and made his way back to the square where he had first tasted it. Although he experienced a faint sense of queasiness when he first saw the ripe fruit, he quickly set it aside as he remembered the satisfying taste of the watermelon. This time, however, the watermelon tasted disgusting to him, bringing on a violent wave of nausea. He was struck by the realization that the same food could trigger such different reactions: great pleasure at one time and extreme disgust at another. Dickinson has assiduously avoided watermelon since that fateful day in Palermo.

Dickinson's unfortunate watermelon experience introduces key themes in the study of rewards and punishments, or how behavior is shaped by what's desired and avoided in our environment. Many of us have shared Dickinson's experience that the same food that is pleasurable in one circumstance can become intensely disliked if it becomes associated with illness.

The rewards obtained from food and many other pleasurable experiences are often dependent on our physiological state—watermelon is especially tasty when we're hot and thirsty, but may not be so appealing on a cold winter day, and the last bite of a huge slab of chocolate cake is usually not as satisfying as the first. French neuroscientist Michel Cabanac, now at Laval University in Canada, coined the term "alliesthesia" (from *allios*, meaning changed, and *esthesia*, meaning sensation) to describe how the internal state can modulate our responses to hedonic stimuli. Cabanac proposed that "pleasure occurs whenever a sensation indicates the presence of a stimulus which helps correct an internal trouble" (1971, p. 1004), a view of pleasure that coheres with Damasio's idea that emotions are intimately tied to homeostatic systems as discussed in the previous chapter.

As we've seen repeatedly in this book, affective reactions to a stimulus—whether it's liked it or not—powerfully modify behavior; based on their experience with a stimulus, animals learn to avoid or will work to obtain more of a stimulus. The rewarding feature of a stimulus, at least in humans, has a significant subjective component; it *feels* pleasurable. Contemporary neuroscientist Kent Berridge at the University of Michigan refers to this experience as the "hedonic gloss" that the brain "paints" on a stimulus (Berridge, 2004); it's a feature that is *added* to the sensory qualities of a stimulus.

Although the subjective experience of pleasure that comes from consuming tasty food or attaining other desirable stimuli may seem to be the primary feature that makes a stimulus rewarding, traditionally the study of reward has focused on its role in learning, primarily in terms of its ability to reinforce behavior. Animal learning research, originating with Pavlov and Skinner's exploration of associative and instrumental conditioning, has developed sophisticated computational models to describe the role of reward in shaping or reinforcing behavior. Thus, in much of neuroscience, the term *reward* has become synonymous with reinforcement, and the brain systems involved in reinforcement are referred to as the reward system. In this chapter we hope to integrate the study of hedonics with this more traditional view of reward as a reinforcer. We start by briefly summarizing what is currently understood about the brain basis of reward.

The Brain's Reward System

Olds and Milner's mid-20th-century self-stimulation studies, discussed earlier as a source of inspiration for Panksepp's work, laid the foundation for the study of reward and reinforcement learning. Recall from chapter 3 that Olds and Milner accidentally discovered that rats sought out areas of the cage where they had previously received stimulation in particular brain regions. They later showed that rats would not only voluntarily self-stimulate those same regions, but would perform work, such as pressing a lever, to obtain that stimulation. Their finding that brain stimulation was rewarding was unexpected, in part because at the time researchers thought that all brain stimulation was punishing. Furthermore, behavior was thought to be motivated only by the avoidance of negative states such as hunger, and not the pursuit of pleasurable states, such as the enjoyment expected from ingestion of a tasty morsel, a position known as the drive reduction hypothesis (Linden, 2011; Olds, 1958). Olds and Milner's work was the first to demonstrate the brain systems that mediate the powerful role of rewards in shaping behavior; rats are highly motivated to work for the reward of brain stimulation, and may even ignore naturally rewarding stimuli such as food and sex in favor of direct brain stimulation.

After their initial accidental discovery of the reinforcing effects of electrically stimulating the septal region, Olds and Milner systematically investigated which other brain areas would sustain self-stimulation. These consisted of a large swath of medial brain structures running from the hindbrain to the basal forebrain that are connected by a set of fibers known as the medial forebrain bundle (MFB) (see Box 6.1 for more details). One of Olds and Milner's interesting findings was that stimulating the outer and upper surface of the brain—the lateral neocortex—was simply not rewarding to their rats, an observation that makes sense in light of the earlier work of Papez distinguishing the roles of medial and lateral cortex in affective versus sensory and motor processing (see chapter 2).

Olds and Milner's identification of the motivational power of self-stimulation to certain brain regions quickly led to the idea that the brain contained a general, all-purpose brain *reward system* that, outside the lab, was normally activated by a variety of natural rewards. This idea—that there is a single system activated in similar ways by many different kinds of rewards—has been described as a mechanism to provide a "common currency" of reward, allowing very different kinds of rewarding stimuli, such as money, art, and food, to be compared when making a choice, and is consistent with a basic assumption underlying economic theories of decision-making (for a recent summary of these ideas, see Cabanac, 2010; Levy & Glimcher, 2012). Importantly, as shown by intensive studies in the wake of Olds and Milner's work, all drugs of abuse also activate this reward system, although with one significant difference. As we explore later in more detail, and consistent with Cabanac's concept of alliesthesia, the willingness to work to achieve natural rewards can normally be modulated by the environmental context or by a homeostatic state—hungry rats may ignore food in the presence of a receptive female, and sated rats are no longer motivated to work for a food reward. In contrast, drugs of abuse, and in some cases brain self-stimulation itself, do not prompt such modulation; animals will continue to press levers to self-administer drugs of abuse to the point of exhaustion or even death. With nothing to oppose the learned behavior to acquire the reward, the reinforcement provided by the drug each time it is consumed promotes more drug seeking. This learned behavior can be triggered by any drug-related cue, and is very long-lasting; sudden exposure to a drug-related cue such as a former drug-taking environment or drug paraphernalia can automatically trigger intense craving for the drug even in addicts who have been drug free for years.

The finding that the same sites that support self-stimulation also support the self-administration of drugs converged with other work that led to the identification of dopamine as the key neurotransmitter of reward and provided another way to identify brain systems that mediate reward. The brain reward system is now considered to consist most basically of the midbrain dopamine neurons and their major targets. These include the dopamine-containing neurons in the ventral tegmental area (VTA, see Figure 6.1) of the midbrain, which project to both subcortical limbic and cortical structures in what are known as the mesolimbic and mesocortical pathways, respectively. Mesolimbic dopamine targets include basal ganglia structures such as the ventral striatum, which contains an important reward-related region called the nucleus accumbens, as well as a ventral region of the globus pallidus, the ventral pallidum (VP) (see Box 6.1). The mesocortical dopamine targets include medial cortical structures, such as the anterior cingulate cortex (ACC), and medial prefrontal cortex (mPFC) structures (the orbitofrontal cortex, or OFC, and the ventromedial prefrontal cortex, or vmPFC), as well as the insula. As we will see, the mesolimbic projections from the VTA to basal ganglia structures, particularly the nucleus accumbens and ventral pallidum, have become major sites of investigation for Berridge and his collaborators. Although the nucleus accumbens has long been the focus of studies of reward, newer work by Berridge has identified the ventral pallidum, a region only relatively recently identified as a distinct anatomical structure, as a key, even unique, structure in reward function.

Indeed, Berridge now refers to the ventral pallidum, which is the major output target of the nucleus accumbens, as the "limbic final common pathway" (Smith, Tindell, Aldridge, & Berridge, 2009, p. 163). Together these structures have emerged as key subcortical components of the hedonic brain, while cortical structures of the reward system, particularly the OFC, may constitute the neural correlates of the conscious experience of pleasure or pain.

The finding that drugs of abuse, at least during the early stages of addiction, as well as natural rewards such as food and sex, increase the activity of dopamine neurons and dopamine release in the nucleus accumbens, led to the designation of dopamine as the "pleasure" neurotransmitter, a characterization that has resonated potently with popular culture. However, the role of dopamine in pleasure has since been contested in the scientific community, and work by Berridge that we discuss below has provided key arguments for that position. Furthermore, research on the role of dopamine in reinforcement, which measures the rewarding properties of stimuli by whether the animal will work to obtain them, had long avoided the use of this subjective "emotional" descriptor, particularly in reference to the most commonly used laboratory model for the experimental study of reward: the white rat.

This avoidance of referring to rewarding stimuli as "pleasurable" seemed justified when work beginning in the 1990s began to show that dopamine activity was not in fact tightly coupled to the subjective experience of pleasure. Instead, as first shown by Wolfram Schultz and his colleagues at Cambridge University in England, dopamine activity is best correlated with the occurrence of cues that predict a reward, and not the reward itself, and even occurs when an expected reward does not come about (Ljungberg, Apicella, & Schultz, 1992; Schultz, Dayan, & Montague, 1997; for a recent review of the role of dopamine in learning theory, see Glimcher, 2011). The finding that dopamine firing is correlated with reward cues, and not reward itself, in fact fit with the concept of a prediction signal that had been proposed as a feature essential to learning in computational models of reinforcement learning. Thus, dopamine's role as a learning signal has become the dominant model of dopamine function. As we will see, Berridge and his team have amassed considerable evidence that dopamine plays yet another role in reward: It carries a motivational signal that determines the desirability of a reward, or what Berridge refers to as *incentive salience*—how much the reward is wanted.

What Is Reward?

But what about the pleasure we experience in response to tasty food? Can reward be fully explained by its reinforcing properties without a component that captures the feeling of wanting commonly experienced for a desired reward? Early in his career, Berridge became convinced that psychological features of reward such as wanting had a biological substrate, and that the prevalent unitary concept of reward was too simplistic. We saw in chapter 3 that Panksepp's claims about the existence of subjective feelings in animals generated significant controversy. Subjective experiences are notoriously difficult to study scientifically because it is difficult to measure them in experimental organisms; we cannot ask nonhuman animals whether or not they are experiencing pleasure. To study subjective experience in animals, it needs to be operationalized by finding a correlate of the subjective experience that can be objectively and reliably measured. Berridge and his colleagues have now developed a way to operationalize hedonic responses in rats, and based on the findings from this research have described a classification system that divides reward into three separate components that can be dissociated both experimentally and behaviorally. In their scheme, reward consists of (a) reward-related *learning* that generates knowledge useful for predicting future rewards; (b) the motivation to seek out particular rewards, that is, the desire or *wanting* that we experience; and (c) the pleasure or *liking* that is derived from consuming rewards (Berridge & Robinson, 2003; Berridge, Robinson, & Aldridge, 2009). This three-way division of reward into learning, wanting, and liking recalls a trilogy of mind proposed by the philosopher Immanuel Kant, composed of cognition, conation, and affection. In Berridge's scheme, learning is akin to cognition; wanting can be equated with the less commonly used term *conation*, which means striving; and liking corresponds to affection (see LeDoux, 2002; chapter 7). Although this tripartite conception of mind was influential in early psychology, at the time that William James was writing, it was replaced during the reign of behaviorism with the single and "mindless" concept of reward, or the even more neutral term *reinforcement*. Note that Berridge's division of reward extends the usual division of mind into cognitive and emotional components by including a separate category for motivation.

To return to our opening example, these three components of reward can be identified in Dickinson's first experience of eating watermelon. The watermelon looked appealing, and because he was hot and thirsty, he was motivated to try it. He derived great pleasure from the watermelon while eating it—he liked it, and so the sight and smell of a watermelon became associated with a pleasurable experience. This first experience was recalled the next time he was hot, hungry, and thirsty, and the memory encouraged him to want it again, but this time his wanting and explicit memory were out of sync with his lack of liking of the taste. After being sick from overindulging in wine, he had implicitly learned to associate the novel taste of watermelon with nausea, but only became aware of the mismatch between wanting and liking when he actually retasted it. Wanting and liking became synchronized again: The new learning about the watermelon's nausea-inducing qualities prevented any future wanting of the fruit.

Behavioral Measures of "Liking" and "Wanting": Lip Licking and Eating

Berridge and colleagues, intrigued with the question of why rewards feel good, became interested in a more ecologically valid way of inducing and measuring this quality in animals. To do so, they made use of a taste reactivity test that had been developed to test reactions to taste solutions infused directly into the mouth of a rat. As parents of young children know well, human infants are readily able to express their liking or disliking of new foods: They show their liking for sweet tastes or highly palatable food with lip licking, tongue protrusions, and smiles, and their dislike of bitter tastes with grimaces and head shakes. Frijda (2010) supplied a charming term for the reactions to pleasing stimuli: "acceptance wriggles." Although first described in human newborns, nonhuman primates perform similar facial and bodily reactions, as do rats and mice,[1] so such affective responses appear to be highly conserved among mammals (see Richard, Castro, DiFeliceantonio, Robinson, & Berridge, 2013, for the history of this test). Berridge and colleagues used this taste reactivity test to measure "liking" responses to infused taste solutions and used the amount of the food actually consumed as a measure of "wanting." Although normally liking and wanting are strongly connected—we "like" what we "want" and vice versa—Berridge's work has been able to show that these two components of reward can become dissociated from each other, both experimentally in the lab and

---

1. Some great video illustrations of "liking" acceptance wriggles are available at the Berridge lab website: http://www.lsa.umich.edu/psych/research&labs/berridge/VideoIndex.htm.

possibly in pathological conditions such as drug addiction. Sometimes we may want what we don't actually like.

Unconscious Aspects of Reward

Berridge uses quotation marks around terms such as "liking" to indicate when he is referring to the objective measure of lip licking described above, and not the subjective experience of liking itself. He also assumes that the components of reward mediated by the subcortical structures he studies (described below) are an unconscious rather than a conscious aspect of these processes. We are used to thinking of pleasure as a conscious feeling, yet one of the major insights that emerges from the work of Berridge and colleagues is the extent and importance of largely unconscious aspects of all components of reward: "liking," "wanting," and "learning." He argues that it is useful to divide the components of reward into conscious and unconscious processes, just as has been done in work on emotions and feelings by researchers such as LeDoux. Unconscious "liking" consists of preferences the person is unaware of that nevertheless can guide his or her behavior, while unconscious "wanting" is the desire to approach a reward without the subjective awareness of that desire. The unconscious form of "learning" could be a type of conditioning; Dickinson's experience of not realizing that watermelon had become disgusting to him until he tasted it again illustrates that learning about the toxicity of a food can be unconscious. These unconscious components of reward are assumed to be widely shared among species, justifying the expectation that experimental work on animal behaviors that demonstrate "liking," "wanting," and "learning" can be applied to thinking about their role in humans.

Unconscious "Liking"

An experimental demonstration of unconscious "liking" in humans was devised by Piotr Winkielman, a Polish-born social psychologist who now directs a social cognition lab at the University of San Diego. Winkielman collaborated with Berridge on a study using subliminal presentation of faces with happy, angry, or neutral expressions (Berridge & Winkielman, 2003; Winkielman & Berridge, 2004). Participants who had been presented with happy faces drank twice as much of a novel fruit beverage at the end of the presentation, and rated it four times more highly than those subliminally presented with an angry expression. When questioned afterward, participants reported they had not seen the emotional face stimuli, and this was corroborated by their inability to pick the face they saw out of a lineup. Experiences that did not consciously register affected both people's consumption and their enjoyment of the drink. Other experiments have also shown that extensive processing of reward information can occur subconsciously. For example, the amount of effort exerted in a task is often determined by the value of the reward. To test whether this assessment can be made subconsciously, an image that depicted the total amount of money that could be earned by squeezing a handgrip was presented too quickly for conscious processing. Nonetheless, grip strength was stronger for higher potential rewards. Another test showed that pupil dilation, a well-documented correlate of the amount of mental effort exerted, was responsive both to the amount of effort required for the task (remembering sequences of either three or five digits) and to the value of what was gained, even when the amount of reward was presented subliminally; more effort was exerted in tasks that required more effort, but only if the unconsciously processed reward seemed "worth it" (Bijleveld, Custers, & Arrts, 2012). These experiments show that many of the components of reward can be processed and integrated unconsciously, and that this unconscious reward processing can have an effect on decision-making.

Dissecting Reward: "Wanting" and "Liking"

When Berridge and his coworkers first attempted to influence the pleasurable facial reactions to a sweet solution by manipulating dopamine, the "pleasure" neurotransmitter, they were unsuccessful. Surprisingly, not a single manipulation of dopamine function altered the rats' "liking" response (Berridge, 2007). Microinjections of dopamine-increasing substances such as amphetamine into brain reward structures such as the nucleus accumbens and ventral pallidum did not increase lip-licking behavior, and chemical suppression of dopamine did not diminish lip-licking. Even massive destruction of the ascending dopamine projections did not decrease lip-licking in response to sweet tastes. Likewise, enhancing dopamine transmission by genetic manipulation (a knockout of the dopamine transporter) did not alter the "liking" of a sucrose solution. Consistent with the finding that dopamine may not mediate subjective pleasure is the observation that patients with substantial loss of brain dopamine due to Parkinson's disease still rated the perceived pleasantness of chocolate milk similarly to people without Parkinson's (Sienkiewicz-Jarosz et al., 2005, as cited in Smith, Mahler, Pecina, & Berridge, 2010). Studies of drug-addicted subjects also confirm that dopamine is correlated with "wanting," but not "liking." Positron emission tomography (PET) scans measuring dopamine binding showed that subjective ratings of "want drug" better correlated with dopamine levels than did "like drug" ratings (Berridge, 2007).

In addition to measuring "liking" by counting instances of lip licking, Berridge and colleagues also measured the amount of liquid the rats voluntarily consumed as an index of "wanting." Although disruption of dopamine did not alter the rats' "liking" reaction—they continued to vigorously lip-lick to infused sugar solution—they no longer seemed interested in actually consuming the sugar; disrupting dopamine meant that "wanting" no longer went hand in hand with "liking." This result, showing that dopamine is associated with "wanting," although surprising at the time, was consistent with a large body of work showing that disruption of dopamine transmission by blocking receptors or lesioning dopamine-producing sites disrupts goal-directed behaviors and working for rewards, as seen in Parkinson's patients, as mentioned above. In fact, Berridge's dopamine-deficient rats would starve to death through lack of motivation to eat if they were not force-fed, although the rats continued to show "liking" reactions to the infused solutions. Berridge and his colleagues concluded that altering dopamine levels influences motivation to acquire the reward without affecting the "liking" reactions that typically occur to rewarding stimuli (Leyton, 2010).

As mentioned above, Berridge and colleagues suggest that the role of dopamine in the reward system is to modulate what they call the "incentive salience" of stimuli. Incentive salience is "the active assignment of salience and attractiveness to . . . stimuli that are themselves intrinsically neural" (Berridge, 2007, p. 408). Incentive salience for the same reward can vary, as we saw in our opening example; although the watermelon hadn't been altered, its incentive salience was transformed from a rewarding stimulus to an aversive stimulus. Hunger and satiety are thus key modulators of incentive salience as well as of "liking." Berridge's work suggests that the function of dopamine is to modulate the incentive value of a stimulus as a result of a change in physiological state or because of new learning. Stimuli with incentive salience are "wanted"—regardless of whether such stimuli are "liked." Berridge describes this component of reward as tagging a specific stimulus or action as an object of desire, and suggests that it has "evolved to add a visceral omph to mental desires" (2009, pp. 378–379). This concept overlaps substantially with Jaak Panksepp's concept of seeking discussed in chapter 3, an appetitive motivational neural system that generates curiosity and interest.

What mediates liking? Further work showed that the lip-licking responses to a sweet stimulus were disrupted by chemically blocking the endogenous opioid system. Previous work by Anne Kelley and her colleagues at Michigan had shown that opioid microinjections into the nucleus accumbens significantly increased the amount of food eaten. Intriguingly, this enhancement of eating was selective to foods that were highly palatable, such as those high in sugar or fat, so opioid stimulation did not seem to increase a general drive to eat, in contrast to dopamine which enhanced eating of all types of food. Kelley thus suggested that opioids act by enhancing the hedonic impact of palatable foods to increase their ingestion (for history of this work, see Richard et al., 2013). Opioids as well as cannabinoids had long been described as increasing eating by enhancing food palatability, and hunger is also known to increase food palatability. It is likely that endogenous opioid and cannabinoid systems that have now been shown to be integral to "liking" are how food palatability is enhanced.

Using the taste reactivity test, Berridge then showed that systemic opioid injections increased "liking" reactions to sugar solutions, and also decreased the aversive response to bitter tastes such as quinine. Animals injected with opioids also ate more, so opioids seemed to increase both "liking" and "wanting;" intriguingly, however, opioid blockers disrupted "liking" reactions but left the dopamine-dependent "wanting" reactions intact—the rats still drank the sweet solution. Thus, Berridge was now able to show that "liking" and "wanting," although normally functioning together, can be decomposed both behaviorally and pharmacologically.

Neural Bases of "Liking" and "Wanting"

The objective behavioral measures of lip licking and mouth gapes as indices of "liking" and "disliking" have been an important tool for Berridge and colleagues to precisely identify the brain substrates of hedonic responses. Using these behavioral indices, they identified the brain regions which when chemically manipulated by microinjections produced changes in lip licking provoked by a sweet taste[2] (Peciña & Berridge, 2005). Areas where opiates or other drugs increased the amount of lip-licking were called "hedonic hotspots." Not surprisingly, opiate hotspots were found in reward system structures, specifically the nucleus accumbens, the ventral pallidum, and the parabrachial nucleus in the pons, a deep brain stem area (see Figure 6.1 for the location of the nucleus accumbens, the ventral pallidum is close by but cannot be seen in this view). However, a key discovery is that the brain's "liking" mechanisms are quite restricted in extent; the hotspot in the rat's nucleus accumbens shell, for example, measures only 1 cubic millimeter (about a seventh of the whole structure), while the ventral pallidum hotspot is even smaller, about 0.8 cubic millimeters.

However, the effects of opiates on "liking" were complex; for instance, outside the hotspots, Berridge and colleagues encountered areas where opiates actually decreased the "liking" response, which they labeled "coldspots." Opiates also acted to reduce disliking, as measured by a decrease in the number of gapes to the bitter-tasting quinine, in areas that overlapped substantially with the hedonic coldspots (Peciña & Berridge, 2005), so in coldspots, opiates appeared to decrease hedonic reactions generally, both liking and disliking. Finally, in an even more limited region along the border between the hotspot and coldspot, opiates both increased "liking" and decreased "disliking."

Opioids also stimulate "wanting" in the hotspots, but opioid-stimulated "wanting" occurs throughout the entire nucleus accumbens, which explains why opioids increased eating when injected systemically. "Wanting" regions of the reward system, however, are defined by the areas in which dopamine and dopamine-enhancing drugs such as amphetamines increase eating. This includes essentially the full extent of the reward system (Berridge et al., 2009). Unlike the limited hedonic hotspots, the larger "wanting" areas are also more easily activated. Thus, there is an asymmetry in the dissociation of "wanting" and "liking"; dopamine increases "wanting" without a concomitant increase in "liking" in most regions of the reward system. Although opiates enhance "wanting" in those same areas, opiates alone enhance "liking," but only in the hotspots, and by also increasing "wanting," acts to

2. The drugs that are microinjected into the brain diffuse from the site of injection, so Peciña and Berridge (2000) had to come up with a technique to map more precisely where the brain was being affected by the drug. Based on the observation that several reward-related drugs trigger local production of the Fos protein, Berridge and colleagues developed a precise mapping tool that measures where neurons are producing more of this protein.

enhance the consumption of palatable food. Thus, large regions of the brain appear to represent wanting alone, but no regions appear to represent "liking" without "wanting."

The greater extent of "wanting" mechanisms in comparison to the more limited "liking" mechanisms helps make sense of the human brain stimulation experiments of Tulane research psychiatrist Robert Heath that were briefly described in chapter 3. Starting in 1950, Heath and his colleagues attempted to "cure" many psychiatric conditions (including homosexuality, which was classified as a psychopathology at the time) with stimulation of deep brain sites in the mesolimbic dopamine pathway. Like Olds and Milner's rats, Heath's patients furiously self-stimulated, suggesting that the electrodes were activating pleasure centers in their brains. Berridge (2003) revisited Heath's description of his patients' experiences with the "wanting"/"liking" distinction in mind. It was clear that electrical stimulation of areas like the septum and nucleus accumbens produced plenty of "wanting"—the patients wanted to press the button repeatedly, and they reported feelings of desire, sexual and otherwise. Yet when it came to "liking," as opposed to "wanting," Berridge could find little evidence of actual pleasure, no overt declarations of sheer delight. He described their statements as "rather murky, even when vaguely positive" (p. 116). Berridge (2004) also cited the case of another patient studied later by a different group of researchers who emphasized the displeasure caused by her excessive thirst and anxiety as much as the sexual arousal caused by stimulation of the electrodes. He speculated that Heath and the other researchers were activating the more widespread "wanting" mechanisms that motivate behavior rather than effectively targeting the brain regions that actually induce feelings of pleasure.

"Liking" in the nucleus accumbens hotspot is also activated by $GABA_A$-enhancing drugs (e.g., antianxiety drugs such as diazepam [Valium]) as well as by an endogenous marijuana compound, the endocannabinoid anandamide, which is well known to both enhance the palatability of food ("liking") and increase consumption. In Berridge and colleagues' experiments, microinjection of anadamide into a region of the nucleus accumbens that overlaps with the opioid hotspot doubled the amount of lip licking when the rats tasted sucrose, as well as increased "wanting" as measured by the amount of food consumed (Mahler, Smith, & Berridge, 2007). Although marijuana "drugs" are currently used to stimulate appetite in those suffering from the wasting that accompanies many major diseases, such as heart disease, cancer, and AIDS, marijuana-blocking drugs marketed as appetite suppressors have been removed from the market following the discovery that they produced a debilitating depression among many users. Knowledge that such drugs block reward signaling of both "liking" and "wanting" clearly helps us to understand the effect of such drugs. Anhedonia, a major feature of depression, is defined by the loss of pleasure.

From Desire to Dread: An Emotional Keyboard

A recent study from Berridge's lab dramatically demonstrated how incentive salience can be modulated by neurobiological states. In addition to the motivation of desire or "wanting," the nucleus accumbens also mediates fearful or dread motivations. The fear responses seen are an active form of antipredator defense, called *defensive treading*, that in the wild would result in kicking dirt or other debris at the threat, as well as distress vocalizations. Inputs to the nucleus accumbens are thought to carry cortical information that modulates local shell activity. Earlier work had shown that local inhibition of glutamate transmission (using either the glutamate antagonist DNQX or the GABA agonist muscimol) in the medial shell of the nucleus accumbens generated a rostrocaudal gradient of motivation that Berridge refers to as an emotional keyboard; rostral inhibition provoked intense eating behavior, which gradually declined and was slowly replaced by increasingly fearful responses as the inhibition proceeded more caudally. In 2008, Sheila Reynolds and Berridge explored whether the behavioral effects of inhibiting glutamate-related inputs to the nucleus accumbens can be influenced by the emotional state of the animal. To alter emotional state, the animals were tested in three environments: (a) a standard lab environment, (b) a familiar dark and quiet "home" environment that the rats preferred, and (c) a lab environment that was made extremely stressful by constant exposure to very bright lights and loud, unpredictable blasts of Iggy Pop music.

The remarkable finding in Reynolds and Berridge's study was that the home environment vastly expanded the area where inhibition provoked appetitive responses: Over 90% of the sites in the whole shell now increased eating, a significantly larger region than seen in the standard lab environment, while the fearful zone shrunk to a third of that in the lab environment. Conversely, being blasted with Iggy Pop and bright lights expanded the fearful zone so that almost 90% of the shell generated defensive treading behavior, with only sites in the far rostral tip producing some feeding behavior. The physiological state of the organism, in this case probably mediated by the level of stress experienced, dramatically altered the valence of the incentive salience attributed to environmental stimuli by retuning or "flipping" nucleus accumbens responsivity. Reynolds and Berridge describe this retuning as providing flexible "affective building blocks" for larger limbic circuits (2008, p. 425). The proposal that dopamine is responsible for assigning incentive salience was also supported in subsequent studies; blocking dopamine prevented the elicitation of either eating or fear behavior provoked by glutamate blockade (Faure, Reynolds, Richard, & Berridge, 2008; Faure, Richard, & Berridge, 2010).

The Ventral Pallidum

Although much early work focused on the role of the nucleus accumbens in reward, which had long been identified as the heart of the reward system, more recently Berridge's group has begun to reveal properties of the ventral pallidum that suggest it plays a unique role in regulating behavior, especially in terms of "liking" of rewards. Although the ventral pallidum is the main output target of the nucleus accumbens, this region had not often been included as part of the reward system. Instead, it was thought to be a ventral extension of another structure in the basal ganglia, the globus pallidus. As such, it was viewed as involved in regulating movements. As we described above, Berridge has now shown that the ventral pallidum contains a hotspot in its posterior section where opioids enhance "liking" reactions to sugar solution. Furthermore, it has emerged in more recent studies that lesioning or chemically disrupting the ventral pallidum not only eliminates normal "liking" reactions, but also converts "liking" to "disliking"— the lip licking and tongue protrusions normally provoked by sugar solutions are replaced by gapes. No other brain lesion is known to have this effect. This active aversion to food stimuli might account for the profound aphagia and adipsia (loss of eating and drinking) that occur in experimental animals with ventral pallidum lesions.

Hotspot neurons not only enhance the response to palatable food when activated, but they also appear to encode liking for foods. For example, these neurons normally fire rapidly to the taste of sugar, but not to a salt solution. However, when animals are made salt deficient, they begin to crave salt, and ventral pallidum hotspot neurons now fire to the salty solutions that previously did not activate them. Thus, they are not responding to the sensory features of the food, but whether the food is "liked," which will depend on physiological states such as satiety or need. Finally, lesion or inactivation of the ventral pallidum also impairs reward learning, and willingness to work; animals will shift their food choice from the preferred sugar to standard chow if it takes less work to acquire (Smith et al., 2009). Because these neurons not only encode liking but can also be activated to enhance "liking," Berridge now thinks that this hotspot may be where the hedonic pleasure "gloss" is actually painted onto tastes (Berridge, 2009).

Human Hot and Cold Spots

A neuroimaging study from a different group of researchers in Britain and the Netherlands provides evidence for hedonic hotspots in human brains. Calder et al. (2007) showed their participants pictures of appetizing foods, like delicious chocolate desserts, and found that a posterior region of the ventral pallidum was active, indicating a human hotspot in a location similar to those found in Berridge and colleagues' rat studies. In addition, when their participants were shown images of rotten food, a more anterior region of the ventral pallidum became more active, corresponding roughly to the location of the rats' hedonic coldspots. In humans, the hotspots and coldspots are a little larger than in the rats, scaling up for brain size, with centimeters replacing millimeters. Working with adult human subjects, Calder and colleagues replicated the anterior/posterior difference in valence of ventral pallidum response and the narrow localization of hotspots and coldspots first documented in Berridge and coworkers' rat studies.

Hotspots and coldspots appear to be unique brain regions mediating "liking." Evidence is just beginning to emerge that "liking" regions of the nucleus accumbens and ventral pallidum are anatomically as well as functionally distinct, and have neural connections that appear to make up a limbic circuit that stay segregated from other parts of these structures (Richard et al., 2013; Smith et al., 2009). "Liking" is clearly a functional and anatomical component of brain function that needs to be better understood.

Dissociating "Wanting," "Liking," and "Learning"

The dissociation of "wanting" and "liking" described above provided strong support for the proposal by Berridge and colleagues that reward can be decomposed into more basic elements, and that dopamine provides the incentive salience needed to "want" a reward. Nonetheless, the majority of research on the role of dopamine in reward suggested it served as a learning signal; dopamine neuron activity was correlated with the presence of the cue, not the reward, as postulated by models of reinforcement learning (Glimcher, 2011; Hart, Rutledge, Glimcher, & Phillips, 2014; Schultz, 2007; Steinberg et al., 2013).

Although Berridge acknowledges that dopamine neurons fire to the reward cue, he notes that cues not only have predictive value, but they also become invested with incentive salience. More significantly, he argues that information about learned associations alone is just that—information (see Berridge, 2012), and questions whether information alone is enough to guide behavior; instead, he argues, behavior must be motivated by something. This motivational component of reward is what he means by "wanting," or incentive salience. In his model, motivational properties are usually attached to rewards, but through learning, cues for rewards also become invested with incentive salience. Although the same cue also predicts the reward, the motivating property of the cue is separate from the predictive value of the cue. While the predictive property of the cue may stay the same, the motivational property attached to a cue can vary depending on other contingencies, in the same way that liking a particular food depends on our current appetite. He proposes that the levels of dopamine reflect these "fluctuations in temptation power" (Berridge, 2012, p. 1124) of an object rather than serving as a prediction cue.

Evidence that the "temptation power" of cues can act independently of the prediction value used in learning is seen when cues themselves begin to have "wanted" properties that make them "motivationally fascinating, a kind of 'motivational magnet'" (Berridge, Robinson, et al., 2009, p. 68). This motivational magnet effect is seen in a phenomenon called sign tracking. Sign tracking is often seen during conditioning experiments when some animals begin to react to the cue itself as if it were a reward. For example, animals trained to depress a metal lever to acquire a food reward begin to approach the lever, sniffing it and nibbling on it as though it were "wanted" even though it is clearly inedible. Such "wanted" cues can even be used as a reward for further conditioning or can be used to make an animal work harder for a reward than it will for the reward itself; the incentive salience of the cue appears to be added to that of the reward itself. Berridge points to the "ghost-chasing" behavior of crack addicts, who will scramble after any small white granule, even though they know it is not cocaine, as an example of when a neutral cue—the white granules—have acquired incentive salience and so can motivate behavior.

Neural studies on the ventral pallidum from Berridge and his collaborators have also been able to dissociate "wanting" from "learning" as well as from "liking." In the first of these studies, Amy Tindell, Berridge, and Wayne Aldridge (2004) recorded from neurons in the ventral pallidum after rats had been trained on a serial Pavlovian conditioning task that temporally dissociated the prediction component of reward from the "wanting" component. In serial conditioning, the first conditioned stimulus, a tone (T1), was paired with a sucrose solution, which thus came to predict the sweet reward; this single tone carried both the motivation information as well as the learning information. They then added a second conditioned stimulus, a different tone (T2), between T1 and the reward, to produce the sequence T1 → T2 → unconditioned stimulus (UCS). In this sequence, T1 predicts the rest of the sequence, so it has the highest information value (it predicts the reward with 100% certainty); thus, the second tone provides no more predictive information and is redundant for learning. However, Berridge argues that the second tone has the highest motivational value, or incentive salience, as it signals the reward is imminent. The third component, "liking," is associated with the actual delivery of the reward. Thus, neural activity associated with each element of the sequence encodes a separate element of reward: T1 encodes learning, T2 encodes "wanting," and the UCS, the reward, encodes "liking."

In Berridge's incentive salience model, dopamine-enhancing drugs such as amphetamines will selectively enhance "wanting" without increasing "liking." To show the selective effect of amphetamine on "wanting," the authors compared neural responses of ventral pallidum neurons to the three events—T1, T2, and the sugar reward itself—with and without amphetamine injection, in normal animals as well as in animals that had been repeatedly injected with amphetamines to create a drug-sensitized state. After conditioning, with no drugs present, ventral pallidum (VP) neurons showed the strongest response to T1, or the predictive signal. After amphetamine injection or sensitization, VP firing was robust at T2, the cue which had maximal incentive salience, with no change in the firing to T1. Importantly, this shift in T2 firing occurred without further learning, as would be required by learning theory. Activation of mesolimbic pathways by dopamine-enhancing drugs appeared to enhance the salience of T2 with no changes seen to either

T1 or to the reward (the UCS) itself. Mesolimbic reward system activity increased the incentive salience of the cue but had no effect on T1, the predictive signal, as required by reinforcement learning.

A later study (Smith, Berridge, & Aldridge, 2011) extended this finding. They used the same serial conditioning paradigm but this time tested the effects of both amphetamines and opiates microinjected into the nucleus accumbens while recording VP activity. After training, firing of VP neurons to T1 was preferentially enhanced, again suggesting dominance of the predictive cue T1 relative to T2 after training. Injection of either amphetamine or opiate into the nucleus accumbens had no effect on T1 firing rates, but shifted dominant firing to the T2 "wanting" signal. This increased "wanting" was also measured as increased consumption of M&Ms at the end of the test, consistent with the ability of both drugs to increase "wanting." However, only opiate injections increased firing to the hedonic UCS, confirming its function as enhancing "liking" as well as "wanting." As in the previous study, increased reward system activity, as represented by increased dopamine or opioid activity, promoted a shift in firing to the reward-proximal cue as predicted by incentive salience theory. Again, this change in incentive salience, or the motivation to acquire a reward, occurred in the face of no new learning.

This new work has documented the neural basis of the selective enhancement of "wanting" without changes in "liking." Why should "wanting" be amplified separately from "liking" or "learning"? Smith and colleagues speculate that the selective enhancement of "wanting" could be useful in encouraging animals to explore new food possibilities, increasing desire so that they will try things they have not already learned to like. Yet, this is exactly the mechanism that Berridge and Robinson (1995) identified as going awry in drug addiction—states where the excessive "wanting" or craving is out of line with the predictive value of rewards and the pleasure derived from them.

Addiction and Incentive Salience

In a 1993 paper, Berridge and his collaborator Terry Robinson first proposed that sensitization of dopamine-mediated incentive salience by addictive drugs is a vital and previously unappreciated component of drug addiction (Robinson & Berridge, 1993). This sensitization of incentive salience pathologically biases attention to drug-associated cues as well as pathologically heightening motivation to consume drugs. They argue that the basic features of addiction are not well explained by leading contemporary theories that explain it as a disorder of learning (Robinson & Berridge, 2008). This learning theory posits that repeated drug activation of a reward-mediated associative learning process will over time become frozen into an automatized and rigid stimulus–response "habit" that results in compulsive drug use whenever a drug cue is encountered. In keeping with their argument for the role of incentive salience in other forms of reward learning, Robinson and Berridge question whether learning alone can account for the key features of drug addiction. Other overlearned habits such as tying shoes, they argue, do not become compulsively performed. They claim that what is being left out of the learning model is the motivation that focuses the addict's attention on drug cues and drug taking.

The essence of Robinson and Berridge's alternative "incentive salience" theory is that sensitization of the dopamine system as a consequence of repeated drug use increases the "wanting" of drugs—their salience and desirability—far beyond the amount of subjective pleasure their consumption creates. The fact that sensitization of the dopamine system can be extremely long-lasting accounts for the persistence of cravings even after extended periods of abstinence. Evidence for Robinson and Berridge's theory has been building; for example, the serial-conditioning research by Tindell, Berridge, Zhang, Peciña, & Aldridge (2005) and Smith et al. (2009) demonstrated that sensitization by chronic amphetamine injection in rats persistently enhanced firing of ventral pallidum neurons to cues associated with incentive salience rather than predictive cues, even weeks after the drugs had been discontinued.

Paradoxically for most addiction theories, evidence from drug addicts suggests that the transition to drug addiction is marked by a decrease in drug liking, so the continued desire for drugs in addiction cannot be attributed to the pleasure they produce. Incentive salience theory can explain this finding by demonstrating that sensitization can produce an exaggerated form of "wanting" without an accompanying sensitization of "liking." Smith et al. (2011) also discussed the problem of relapse that frequently occurs even long after a seemingly successful drug treatment. The persistently sensitized system will be responsive to any event that activates the dopamine "wanting" system; for example, stressful situations, "taking just one," or encounters with previous drug-related cues boost craving and engender an exaggerated motivation to take drugs that is almost impossible to resist, despite a cognitive understanding of their adverse effects.

Affiliative Behavior and the Ventral Pallidum

Although the ventral pallidum is clearly important in reward behavior, only recently has its role in mediating social rewards such as affiliative behavior been explored. Early work that implicated the ventral pallidum in affiliation rewards came from the study of neurobiological differences mediating the mating systems of two species of voles. The prairie vole is monogamous, and after successful mating, males and females seem to bond for life. The closely related meadow vole is promiscuous, and the difference between the species has been related to a greater concentration of vasopressin receptors in the ventral pallidum of the male prairie vole. Incredibly, genetic manipulations that up-regulated vasopressin receptors in the ventral pallidum of the meadow mole switched its behavior from promiscuous to monogamous (Lim et al., 2004). Studies in human males have also shown that the ventral pallidum is activated during male sexual arousal (for further discussion, see Smith et al., 2009). This work highlighting the central role of the ventral pallidum should soon lead to many more intriguing discoveries of its functions.

Subjective Liking and the Orbitofrontal Cortex

In order to connect objective "liking" reactions with the subjective feelings that we more commonly associate with pleasure, we have to expand our consideration of mechanisms to "higher"-level processes involved in cognitive appraisal and conscious awareness of feelings (Berridge & Kringelbach, 2013). So far we have been discussing the subcortical brain mechanisms in the ventral pallidum and nucleus accumbens that are important for the generation of core pleasure, but cognitive processing and conscious awareness have typically been associated with areas higher up the neural axis, in cortical centers. The advent of neuroimaging has opened up new possibilities for studying the cortical basis of conscious or subjective liking in humans. An area that is frequently activated in imaging studies of a wide range of pleasurable stimuli is the orbitofrontal cortex (OFC). The OFC is located on the underside of the frontal cortex, the area that sits just above the orbits of the eyes (see Figure 4.1 for its location). Its medial, but not lateral, parts are included in the area that Damasio, Bechera, and colleagues refer to as ventromedial prefrontal cortex (see Kringelbach, 2005, and Box 6.1 for more details).

Edmund Rolls and his collaborators at the University of Oxford in England have intensively studied the properties of the OFC using macaque monkeys, whose cortex is more similar to that of humans than the rats studied by Berridge and colleagues (Rolls, 1999, 2000; Rolls & Grabenhorst, 2008). They have demonstrated that the OFC is a polymodal region that receives input from gustatory, olfactory, somatosensory, auditory, and visual cortices. Importantly, in primates, the OFC contains the secondary taste cortex plus the secondary and tertiary olfactory cortices, sensory areas that provide information that relates to the reward value of food, a primary reinforcer (Baylis, Rolls, & Baylis, 1995). Single neurons in the OFC respond to both gustatory and olfactory input, indicating that they provide the neural basis for the perception of flavor, a multimodal percept that we often mislabel simply as "taste" in everyday life. Rolls and his colleagues argue that the function of the OFC is to represent the reward values of multimodal sensory stimuli, and it does so in a flexible way that is updated depending on circumstances like the state of the body and the availability of potentially rewarding stimuli. By investigating the effects of lesioning the OFC on their monkeys' behaviors, Rolls and his coworkers discovered that the OFC was vital for "tasks that involve learning about which stimuli are rewarding and which are not" (Rolls & Grabenhorst, 2008, p. 219). Damage to the OFC resulted in the monkeys' experiencing difficulty with changes in what was rewarding. For example, in the reversal learning paradigm, where the experimenters switched which behavior would lead to a reward, the monkeys with OFC damage continued to respond with the previously rewarded behavior rather than adapting to the shift. Rolls and his coworkers also discovered that the responses of macaque OFC neurons depended on how hungry the animals were, and how much of that particular food they had already consumed.

Morton Kringelbach, another researcher at the University of Oxford[3] who has worked extensively on the brain mechanisms of reward, describes

---

3. Kringelbach now has a dual affiliation that includes Aarhus University in his native Denmark. He directs the Hedonia TrygFonden Research Group, whose goal is "to develop a better understanding of hedonic processing . . . in the human brain" in order to "more effectively treat affective disorders" (http://www.kringelbach.dk/science.html).

the primary role of the OFC as "linking food and other types of reward to hedonic experience" (2005, p. 691). In collaboration with Rolls, who was his doctoral mentor, Kringelbach prepared a large meta-analysis of neuroimaging studies on the OFC (Kringelbach & Rolls, 2004). In this paper, they reviewed 87 published studies that covered a wide-ranging list of pleasures and pains; facial beauty, chocolate, music, monetary reward, placebo analgesia, umami, odor sniffing and smelling, trustworthiness of faces, and ongoing neuropathic pain were some of the aspects of hedonics included. Kringelbach and Rolls found that they could organize the results into two groupings: activations of the medial OFC that correlated with the reward value of reinforcers, and activations of the lateral OFC that related to punishers. They also found that primary reinforcers like food activated regions toward the posterior of the OFC, whereas more abstract reinforcers like money activated more anterior regions, indicating a gradient of complexity across the OFC.

The linkage of hedonic experience with food rewards in the OFC is well illustrated by one of the studies that Kringelbach and Rolls review. Dana Small and her colleagues at Northwestern University and Montreal Neurological Institute investigated the brain processes involved in changing the hedonic gloss on chocolate (Small, Zatorre, Dagher, Evans, & Jones-Gotman, 2001). Their subjects were self-described chocoholics whose brains were scanned as they ate their favorite bittersweet or milk Lindt chocolate. Normally these people found the experience of eating Lindt chocolate deeply pleasurable, but the wily experimenters manipulated the hedonic gloss on chocolate by asking them to gorge themselves on it to the point of total fullness. Before they were full of chocolate, the caudomedial regions of the orbitofrontal cortex were more active, but the peak of activation shifted to the caudolateral OFC when they continued to eat past the point of satisfaction. Small and colleagues provided strong support for the idea that OFC activity represents the reward or punishment value of food, and, further, that there is a separation of the positive and negative glosses into medial and lateral regions of the OFC.

The variation in reward value of a food as a function of how much of it you have eaten, technically "sensory-specific satiety," was also manipulated in experiments conducted by Kringelbach, Rolls, and other colleagues at Oxford. These studies demonstrated how closely activation of a part of the OFC tracks with the subjective experience of pleasure. Sensory-specific satiety means that while one food can be eaten to the point of no longer giving pleasure, another distinct food will still be appetizing and readily consumed. Parents know this phenomenon well: The same stomach that cannot possibly fit another bite of the main course somehow has plenty of room for dessert. Elizabeth's younger son frequently claims that he has two stomachs: one for dessert and one for everything else. Sensory-specific satiety is a particularly helpful paradigm for studying pleasure because it provides a way to separate the reward value of food from its sensory qualities. The two substances that Kringelbach, O'Doherty, Rolls, and Andrews (2003) used in their sensory-specific satiety study were tomato juice and chocolate milk. The men[4] who participated all liked both drinks and had not eaten for at least six hours before the experiment. While they were in the scanner, they were fed chocolate milk, tomato juice, or a tasteless control solution through separate tubes in their mouths, and rated the beverage's pleasantness and intensity. After the initial scanning run, the participants were taken out of the scanner and told to drink as much as they possibly could of one of the liquid foods for their lunch[5] and then returned to the scanner. Kringelbach et al. found that the subjective pleasantness of the liquid food decreased strikingly after consumption of a heavy lunch of it, whereas the intensity ratings did not significantly change. For both chocolate milk and tomato juice, a number of the expected areas—ACC, insula, and OFC—were activated, but the one area that was significantly correlated with the subjects' pleasantness ratings for both substances was a region of the left OFC. For the chocolate milk, but not the tomato juice, sensory-specific satiety effects were also found for bilateral regions of the posterior insula and ventral striatum (recall that the nucleus accumbens is part of the ventral striatum). In their discussion of these findings, Kringelbach et al. theorize that sensory-specific satiety evolved to encourage the consumption of a varied diet that would better meet the body's nutritional needs.

Obesity: The OFC Run Amok?

The current obesity health crisis, however, indicates that many people are not managing to consume a varied, balanced, and healthy diet. In the United States, obesity rates have risen over the last three decades to reach epidemic proportions: In 2009, nearly one in four Americans were considered obese

---

4. Kringelbach et al. (2003) used only male participants because "female students are in some cases restrained eaters and eat little in a study of this type" (p. 1065).

5. As you might expect, those assigned to the tomato juice condition consumed less on average than those assigned chocolate milk—915 mL compared to 1160 mL.

(US government statistics cited in Berridge, Ho, Ricard, & DiFeliceantonio, 2010, p. 44). A breakdown in the normal mechanisms that devalue the rewarding properties of food when enough has been eaten could be a culprit. The food environment has changed drastically since the satiety mechanisms evolved: High-fat, high-carbohydrate, and sweet foods are much more readily available. A dysregulation of the OFC could potentially play a role in the increasing difficulties that people have in regulating their food intake in this environment of abundance. The potential involvement of the OFC in obesity is bolstered by the finding that patients suffering from frontotemporal dementia, which attacks the OFC as well as other frontal structures, often put on enormous amounts of weight.

The OFC is not the only aspect of the brain's reward system that could be dysregulated in obesity. Berridge and colleagues (2010) posit that small individual differences in the reactivity of the "liking" and "wanting" systems could be a factor in the incremental weight gain that leads to obesity. Modern foods can intensely trigger both "liking" and "wanting" mechanisms. Overactivation of the hedonic hotspots in nucleus accumbens and ventral pallidum could lead to too much liking. Another possibility is that in obesity, as Robinson and Berridge (1993) proposed for drug addiction, "wanting" mechanisms could somehow have become hyperactive, causing increased consumption that is out of alignment with the pleasure derived from the food. In this case, dopamine-based incentive salience could enhance food cues and prompt a compulsive urge to eat. The largely unconscious nature of these mechanisms makes it difficult to change problematic eating habits. Neuroscientific analyses of the cortical processes involved in subjective experience and their interactions with unconscious aspects of reward are important and could yield therapeutic applications. As Berridge et al. (2010) state, the mostly "go" brain systems that evolved in environments of scarcity now need to be tempered with some regulatory "stop" mechanisms that require more prefrontal involvement.

Social Rewards

The same brain regions that have been identified as crucial components in the network that assigns value to delicious foods like chocolate have also been implicated in studies of social rewards. A basic factor in social interactions, something that acts as social glue, is the perception of fairness. Social neuroscientist Matthew Lieberman from the University of California, Los Angeles, has written about this in his accessible new book, *Social*. In an aptly titled chapter, "Fairness Tastes Like Chocolate," he describes work conducted with Golnaz Tabibnia that demonstrates the common brain currency of social and food rewards (Lieberman, 2013). They used a version of a well-known economic bargaining game to investigate the brain's response to fairness. In the Ultimatum Game, two players are tasked with splitting a sum of money. The person playing the role of proposer decides on a split that the other player, the responder, can either accept or refuse. The twist is that if the responder refuses the proposer's split, neither participant gets any money. The key finding from this paradigm is that often people will choose to get nothing rather than accept an offer that they perceive as unfair. Offers of less than 20% are quite likely to be rejected; below this threshold, punishing perceived unfairness usually trumps personal monetary gain.[6] Tabibnia, Satpute, and Lieberman (2008) measured brain responses while people were playing the Ultimatum Game and found that fair offers activated components of the reward network, specifically the ventral striatum, vmPFC, OFC, amygdala, and a midbrain region near the substantia nigra. Fairness is indeed like brain chocolate.

Other studies have demonstrated that positive social regard, such as praise from others, also activates the same reward system. Not only is receiving praise from others rewarding, but the other side of the interaction—giving praise, helping others, cooperating—also activates brain areas associated with reward. A different economic game has been used to demonstrate the effects of prosocial behavior on brain activity. In a 2002 study, James Rilling and his colleagues at Emory University measured the neural activation of female participants playing the Prisoner's Dilemma game. In this game, the players also split a sum of money, but in this task the decision they make is whether or not to cooperate with their partner. If both players choose to cooperate, they split the sum of money evenly. If both choose to defect, then both receive smaller, and equal, amounts of money. If one player cooperates and the other defects, however, the defector gets the whole sum of money. Rilling and colleagues' most notable finding was that activity in areas that have been linked with reward[7] was greater when both players cooperated than it was in the condition where the person received a

---

6. The Ultimatum Game is a social task whose results vary widely in different cultures (Henrich, Heine, & Norenzayan, 2010). In their studies with small-scale nonindustrialized human societies, Henrich and colleagues found that very low offers were frequently made and *not* rejected.

7. The areas Rilling et al. (2002) list are the nucleus accumbens, the caudate nucleus, the ventromedial frontal/orbitofrontal cortex, and the rostral anterior cingulate cortex.

larger sum of money by defecting when the other player cooperated. Further, the women in Rilling et al.'s study chose mutual cooperation more frequently than defection. These results give credence to the idea that our brains are wired to take pleasure in being cooperative and helping others.

Concluding Comments

Following Darwin's lead, Berridge and his many colleagues used the externally visible reactions of emotional expression that are widely shared among species as a tool that enabled them to approach study of the brain processes of affect objectively. Their extensive work also expands Panksepp's vision of affective neuroscience and comes closer to realizing the goal of understanding how affect is created by brain mechanisms. The study of hedonics has added significantly to our picture of the feeling brain. We now know more of the specifics of how brain systems add a hedonic gloss to sensations, including which parts connect to which areas and some of the neurotransmitters involved. Parsing reward into the three components of liking, wanting, and learning, a categorization with a long-standing theoretical foundation, has been highly productive in terms of providing insight into how the normally adaptive overlapping brain mechanisms of reward can become maladaptive through their dissociation.

Understanding of the subjective aspects of reward has also progressed in the last few decades. Neuroimaging work with humans confirms the finding from nonhuman primate studies that the orbitofrontal cortex is a vital component of hedonic brain systems. The feelings of pleasure obtained from food and other rewards have been extensively investigated, demonstrating that the OFC represents the value of rewards in a contextually sensitive way that takes account of homeostatic factors and the history of experience with that stimulus. In the previous chapter, we discussed Damasio and Bechara's work with patients suffering medial OFC damage, which shows that these types of value judgments are important for decision-making processes that we have been used to thinking of as more rational and less emotional. In the following chapter, we will continue our exploration of how subjective feelings are related to brain mechanisms, but our focus will initially be on the painful end of the affect continuum.

Box 6.1: Structures of the Reward System

Ventral tegmental area (VTA): A nucleus in the midbrain that contains the cell bodies of dopamine producing neurons.

Medial forebrain bundle (MFB): A massive fiber bundle that connects the medial brain stem with the basal forebrain. It has been described as the "brainstem's main artery for monoamine traffic" (Lautin, 2001, p. 66). Along with many other neurotransmitter pathways, it contains the **dopamine axons** that run from the VTA to limbic structures such as the nucleus accumbens and amygdala. Its anatomy was well described in rodents in the early 20th century, but the more recent development of the diffusion tensor imaging technique (DTI) for mapping brain connectivity has allowed contemporary researchers to explore it in living human brains (Coenen, Panksepp, Hurwitz, Urbach, & Madler, 2012).

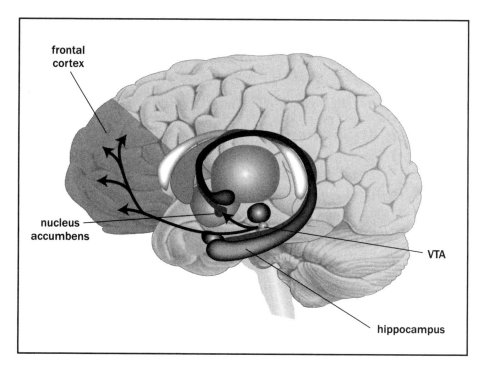

Figure 6.1 Important reward system structures: the ventral tegmental area (VTA), and nucleus accumbens. The dopamine pathways running from VTA to the nucleus accumbens and frontal cortex are shown.

Source: Image created by Daniel Greenberg. Used with permission.

Nucleus accumbens (NAc): The nucleus accumbens, a forebrain nucleus in the ventral region of the striatum of the basal ganglia, is one of the major targets of VTA dopamine neurons. The VTA and the nucleus accumbens together are often considered to be the heart of the reward system. All drugs of abuse have as a common action an increased release of VTA dopamine from their terminals in the nucleus accumbens. The nucleus accumbens sends output to the basolateral amygdala and the **ventral pallidum**.

Ventral pallidum (VP): The ventral region of the **globus pallidus**, a basal ganglia structure that has been linked with control of movement. The VP, which gets input from the nucleus accumbens as well as dopamine from the VTA, is now considered to be part of the reward system. Destruction of the VP leads to severe anorexia and adipsia. The VP sends output to the medial dorsal nucleus of the thalamus, which then projects forward to the prefrontal cortex.

Septum: This set of nuclei that lies below the rostral corpus callosum is the area where Olds and Milner originally discovered self-stimulation. It projects to parts of the hypothalamus and thalamus, the hippocampus, amygdala, and cingulate among other structures.

Orbitofrontal cortex (OFC): The area at the base of the prefrontal cortex directly above the orbits of the eyes (see Figure 4.1). The term OFC is used in different ways by different researchers. It is a polymodal sensory integration region that receives and integrates input from the classical five external senses of sight, sound, touch, taste, and smell, as well as information from the viscera and plays a role in associating reward or value to sensory stimuli in a way that can be continuously updated. For example, OFC neurons can exhibit sensory specific satiety: The activity of a neuron to a specific taste will decline with satiety.

The OFC overlaps with the vmPFC, as described by Damasio, Bechara, and colleagues, but extends further laterally.

7

Body and Mind

The Linkage of Interoception and Emotion

Feelings, Damasio argued, are "mental experiences of body states" (A. Damasio & Carvalho, 2013, p. 143). The neuroanatomist A. D. (Bud) Craig, using modern techniques for tracing neural pathways, extends Damasio's idea with his discovery of a previously unknown pathway conveying sensory information from the body to the brain. In lower animals and most mammals, this new bodily pathway joins with sensory inputs from viscera in brain stem nuclei that then initiate the basic autonomic and endocrine reflexes needed to regulate the body. In primates, however, the pathway evolved to include cortical targets, primarily the insula, that buried "island" of cortex that lies below the frontal, temporal, and parietal opercula (Latin for "little lids"), allowing homeostatic information to be integrated with higher-level brain processes and functions (see Figure 7.1 for the location of the insula). In humans, the evolution of this body representation culminates in a final integrated map of the body located in the front end of the insula, a cortical region not present in even our close primate relatives. Craig argues that this region, the anterior insula, underpins our subjective awareness of *all* feelings—and engenders what he calls the uniquely human "sentient self." In this chapter we look more closely at the role of interoception and how it is mapped in the insula, a formerly hidden island in the brain that has emerged as a central structure representing the body, feelings, and the self.

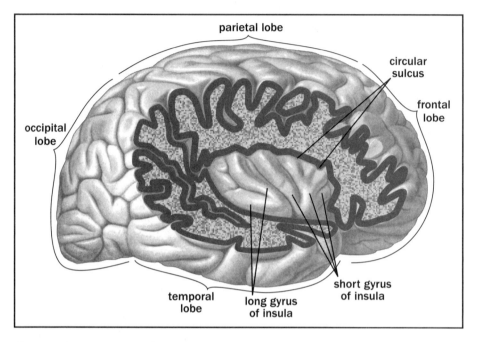

Figure 7.1 Brain image with the opercula cut away to show the insula.

Source: Reprinted from *Atlas and Text-Book of Human Anatomy* by Dr. Johannes Sobotta, © 1908, W. B. Saunders Co.

Why Pain Hurts

The story begins as Craig, the director of the Atkinson Pain Research Laboratory at the Barrow Neurological Institute in Arizona, was struggling to better understand how pain fibers project into the spinal cord and then on to the brain. Pain is one of the most puzzling of body senses, both in terms of its neurobiology and as a sensation. Unlike nonpainful touch or other innocuous stimuli, pain is much more than a simple sensation. At times pain can so utterly hijack one's sense of self that no other stimuli can break through. Yet, at other times, a similar painful stimulus may be tolerated or even ignored; soldiers with horrific battlefield injuries have been able to help themselves or others to safety, seemingly unaware of a level of pain that would in other circumstances be crippling. The pain during voluntary body piercing or while acquiring a desired tattoo may even add to the excitement of the event. It is this dissociation of the *affective* component of pain—its ability to cause emotional distress—from pain as a sensation that differentiates it from other sensory experiences. What is it that makes pain hurt emotionally? As we will see below, an answer to this question emerged as Craig tried to more carefully dissect the anatomy of the pain system. These studies have prompted Craig to propose a radical re-classification of pain from a sensory system responding to external events, to one reporting instead on internal homeostatic processes. Consistent with the conceptual model proposed by Damasio, a primary function of such a homeostatic report is to provoke feelings.

What Is Pain?

The complexity of pain is evident in the ongoing debates about how pain is encoded and which neurons encode pain information (Craig, 2003) as well as the confusing and sometimes conflicting models of pain pathways. It had long been assumed that the sensory features of pain, such as its location, intensity, and type, were mapped along with other body senses such as touch in the topographic map in primary somatosensory cortex, SI, in the area of the parietal lobe that lies immediately behind the central sulcus at the top of the brain. In the course of investigations of brain activity in epileptic patients at the Montreal Neurological Institute, Wilder Penfield and colleagues demonstrated that SI contains an orderly mapping of the whole body (Penfield & Boldrey, 1937). He called this the somatosensory homunculus (i.e., little man; see the arresting 3-D rendering in Figure 7.2), and it was widely viewed as the common neural basis underlying the ability to discriminate and localize both innocuous touch and peripheral pain.

But while the sensory features of pain, such as its location and intensity, were thought to be processed with other exteroceptive somatosenses, pain's affective features were explained in terms of additional projections of pain fibers to a whole suite of limbic structures, including the brain stem, amygdala, insula, and other targets in the prefrontal cortex.

In fact, pain and temperature diverge from other somatosenses even in the spinal cord, a separation that allowed a useful surgical treatment for intractable pain; lesions to pain pathways in the lateral spinal cord prevent pain stimuli from reaching the brain while not disrupting other somatosenses (unfortunately, this treatment is often only temporarily effective, for reasons that are still mysterious).[1] This was the understanding of the pain system when Craig began work that gradually led him to reconceive the

---

1. In the spinal cord, pain and temperature project through the lateral spinothalamic tract, which projects to the contralateral spinal cord, while other skin senses project through the ipsilateral dorsal column/medial lemniscus pathway.

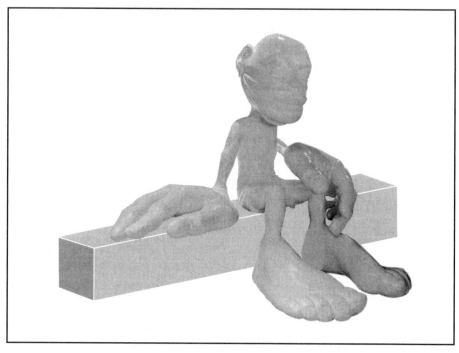

Figure 7.2 A rendering of Penfield's somatosensory homunculus based on a model on display at the Glasgow Science Museum, Ibrox, Glasgow, Scotland. The sizes of the body parts reflect the amount of cortical area devoted to them in the somatosensory strip (SI).

Source: Based on a photograph taken by Son of Groucho, CC-BY-2.0 (license: https://creativecommons.org/licenses/by/2.0/legalcode).

pain system as one part of a newly discovered interoceptive sensory system.

It's Not Just Pain

Pain and temperature were known to be carried by a system of slowly conducting nerve fibers,[2] which are easily distinguished from the larger and faster fibers that carry information from other skin senses such as touch and proprioception. In single-cell recordings from pain fibers, Craig began to realize that many of the so-called "nociceptors" (*nociception* was a term coined by the early physiologist Sherrington for the detection of *noxious* or painful stimuli by *nociceptors*) showed ongoing activity regardless of the

---

2. The unmyelinated C fibers and the small, myelinated A delta fibers.

presence of a painful stimulus. Over time he was able to relate this activity to a diverse range of nonpainful stimuli, such as innocuous temperatures (warm and cool), or signals providing information about the ongoing state of local metabolism (pH, hypoglycemia), muscle function (hypoxia, lactic acid), and many other aspects of body function, including activity of the joints and bones as well as immune and hormonal activity.

One compelling example of a non-pain related stimulus now known to be conveyed to the brain by these so-called nociceptors is the slow, gentle stroking that has come to be called "affective touch." Affective touch has only recently been identified as a system anatomically and functionally distinct from other forms of touch (Olausson et al., 2002). It provokes a pleasurable, calming, sensuous experience that triggers emotional responses typically associated with a variety of affiliative behaviors, including cuddling, grooming, and sexual behaviors.

In light of the wide range of stimuli activating this afferent sensory system, it was clear that it could no longer be described as a pain system, but it did seem to represent a *system*. What kind of system would include pain together with affiliative touch and information about the homeostatic state of body tissues? To Craig, this system appeared to be broadly concerned with information about the physiological status of the body—it was an interoceptive system.

Interoception

Interoception has been described informally as "how the body talks to the brain" (Cameron, 2001, p. 698). When he first defined the term, Sherrington distinguished two types of body senses based on whether they processed information from the internal or external environment. The *interoceptive* signals arose from the internal organs, the viscera, whereas the *exteroceptive* signals came from the outside environment. The cutaneous sensation of touch arising from contact with the externally accessible body was classified as exteroceptive, whereas sensations from the gut were interoceptive. Sherrington devised the alliterative moniker the "material me" to refer to the interoceptive body representation.

In contrast to the precise topographic mapping of the body documented by Penfield in SI, ideas about how the brain represented interoceptive information were fairly limited. Penfield and colleagues had shown that stimulation of the insula provoked feelings of nausea, disgusting tastes, and disturbing stomach sensations, and later work identified the insula as primary gustatory cortex. Interoceptive information was known to be conveyed to the brain through parasympathetic nerves, primarily the vagus nerve that innervates much of the body.[3] This interoceptive sensory input was not thought to form the kind of topographic map that Penfield demonstrated for the exteroceptive sense of touch. Topographic maps are needed to precisely identify and localize stimuli, so their absence explained why visceral sensations, which are mostly unconscious, are often difficult to discriminate and identify even when they do reach conscious awareness, usually during distress or times of pain. The viscera, and by association the insula, just did not seem all that interesting to neuroscientists working to understand the brain and its functions. Unconscious homeostatic reflexes were all that were needed to attend to the prosaic needs of the body.

The Lamina I Interoceptive System and Homeostatic Emotions

As a result of his studies, Craig realized that the system previously described as a pain system might in fact represent a previously unknown sympathetic sensory correlate of the parasympathetic visceral sensory system which conveys additional information about the homeostatic state of the body. Because these interoceptive afferents first project to lamina I of the spinal cord, this is now known as the Lamina I system. The Lamina I system provides information, such as muscle ache and affective touch, as well as pain and temperature, to produce a much richer representation of the body than that provided by the parasympathetic sensory afferents alone. From his work tracing the brain pathways of this interoceptive system, Craig argues that it makes sense to consider the signals that travel in this system—pain, temperature, and affective touch—as interoceptive rather than exteroceptive, because of their primary concern with the homeostatic state of the body. To explain this idea, Craig asks us to consider what happens when a homeostatic imbalance or need is detected. Interoceptive signals that energy reserves are low (e.g., hypoglycemia), or that there is a water imbalance in our body, generate the well-known "feelings" of hunger and thirst, which

---

3. Parasympathetic afferents from the head travel in cranial nerves IX and VII (the glossopharyngeal and facial nerves), while the parasympathetic nerve (cranial nerve X) collects afferent information from the rest of the body.

act as powerful motivators to take actions to offset the imbalance and thus restore homeostasis—in this case, to eat or drink. Such homeostatic motivations become all consuming when survival is at stake. Temperature provides a clear example of this kind of interoceptive "feeling" that motivates action to achieve homeostatic balance; an object that is pleasingly cool when one is overheated can become painful when one is chilled. Although the temperature is the same, the affective reaction is opposite because the needs of the body are different. Pain, Craig argues, is another such homeostatic emotion; its affective features depend critically on the state of the body. Thus, feelings from the body represent a homeostatic readout that can induce motivations to achieve homeostatic balance when needed. The hurt of pain motivates withdrawal from the source of distress.

The Anatomy of Feelings

In lower mammals such as rodents, Lamina I sympathetic afferents come together with parasympathetic afferents in brain stem autonomic centers that coordinate the behavioral and homeostatic reflexes needed to maintain homeostatic balance. In primates, however, these interoceptive afferents continue upward, making separate projections to three major cortical targets—the insula, the anterior cingulate cortex (ACC), and region 3a of SI (a region thought to be more closely allied with the insula that with other regions of SI)—where they form the kind of precise, topographic maps described for SI. Single-cell recordings in monkeys and functional magnetic resonance imaging (fMRI) in humans conducted by Craig and his coworkers have documented separate somatotopic maps of pain, temperature, and itch in the posterior regions of the insular cortex (Brooks, Zambreanu, Godinez, Craig, & Tracey, 2005; Hua, Strigo, Baxter, Johnson, & Craig 2005; Craig, Chen, Bandy, & Reiman, 2000; summarized in Craig, 2010). Craig proposes that there are individual sensory maps for all of the distinct bodily sensations; pain, itch, thirst, hunger, temperature, air hunger, muscle ache, and affective touch are each transmitted in specific "labeled lines" to a topographical map at the posterior end of the insula.

The interoceptive topographic maps in the insula thus give rise to all the distinctive affective bodily "feelings," such as warmth, hunger, visceral fullness, and illness, that we can perceive. Craig refers to these as homeostatic emotions, which he argues are composed of both a sensation, or a feeling, and a motivation. Although feelings are thus grounded in an awareness of the needs of the body, they can also lead to the more general sense we may have of ourselves; we can feel energetic, stressed, or have a sense of well-being based on interoceptive signals about the state of the body. Craig argues that feelings about the body give rise to all forms of feelings; the "pain" of social exclusion or the "chills" experienced when listening to a moving piece of music are also grounded in homeostatic signals from the body. Craig has thus expanded the range of interoception, from the coarsely mapped parasympathetic vagal afferents, which only occasionally give rise to poorly localizable and vague feelings of distress, to detailed maps of a broad variety of homeostatic sensations from throughout the body that constitute the foundation of our ability to "feel."

Craig's demonstration that a rich system of sympathetic sensory afferents map to the posterior insula, which had previously been shown to be a target only for parasympathetic afferents, suggests a much more complete representation of the physiological condition of the body: Sherrington's "material me." Furthermore, the extension of modality-specific representations of the body to the cortex in primates extends the level of representation of homeostatic information, conceivably providing primates with conscious access to bodily feelings, and opening up the possibility of voluntarily modifying them.

The Sentient Self

Interoceptive afferents take up the whole extent of the insula in nonhuman primates, but in humans the insula extends significantly beyond the initial receptive region (Craig, 2011), forming three cytoarchitectonically distinct regions: the posterior, mid, and anterior insula, the last of which may be unique to humans. Craig argues that the interoceptive information that first projects to the posterior insula represents affective feelings of the body which provide a template that becomes successively re-represented, in the midinsula and then again in the anterior insula, where it leads to the awareness of all types of subjective feelings, not only bodily and emotional, but also cognitive types of feelings such as moments of insight. The dense interconnection of the insula with many widely dispersed brain areas ideally positions it anatomically to link the homeostatic condition of the body with sensory, motivational, emotional, and social aspects of the environment (Critchley, 2005). Important emotion-related brain structures that we have discussed so far—the amygdala, nucleus accumbens, orbitofrontal cortex (OFC), and ACC—are among the regions that are bidirectionally connected to the insula (Craig, 2009b; Singer, Critchley, & Preuschoff, 2009). The idea of a successive representation of homeostatic information in the insula has recently been supported in an fMRI neuroimaging study on temperature, which showed that posterior insula activation correlated with the objective temperature of a probe, while activity in the more anterior sections correlated instead to a subjective assessment that depends on the current homeostatic state of the body (Craig et al., 2000).

From this and related work, Craig proposes that the final metarepresentation in the anterior insula provides the basis for the subjective "feeling" of the material self. Here the integration of salience from both the external and internal worlds which has occurred in the midinsula comes together with neural activity from yet higher regions. This massive integration leads to a metarepresentation of the combined internal and external environments at each moment in time, which Craig calls the "global emotional moment." A succession of these global emotional moments forms the "sentient self"—a complete representation of how the person feels at the present time—in the area where the anterior region of the insula and the frontal operculum meet. Craig sees support for this model in the demonstration that the strength of a representation of memory accessibility or familiarity expressed as a "feeling of knowing" is linearly related to activity in the insula and neighboring frontal operculum. Over the course of the human insula, the material me in posterior insula is transformed into the sentient self in the anterior insula. In Craig's model of the insula, "subjective feelings are directly based on homeostatic sensory integration" (Craig, 2011, p. 74); sentience emerges when subjective feelings become associated with Sherrington's material me.

Since the first demonstration that activation of the anterior insula is correlated with the subjective assessment of temperature, insula activity has been shown to be associated with subjective feelings of many kinds, including subjective pain; subjective judgments of trust, disgust, anger, and happiness; sexual arousal; romantic love; and enjoyment of music. In addition, the anterior insula activates to "task-related and attention related aspects of behavior, including subjective time estimation, music appreciation, mental effort and behavior salience" (Craig, 2011, p. 74). Indeed, as work on the insula has expanded, activity in the anterior insula appears to be associated with *all* subjective feelings.

The AI/ACC Salience Network

Conjoint activation of the anterior insula (AI) and ACC occurs in virtually all neuroimaging studies of emotions—both primary emotions, such as anger, sadness, fear, and disgust, and secondary and social emotions, such as empathy and trust (Craig, 2009a). In considering the respective roles of these two structures, Craig cites Edmund Rolls's definition of an emotion as composed of both a feeling and a motivation, and aligns feeling with insular activity—the sensory limbic cortex, culminating in the AI sentient self—and the motivational, action-oriented element with the ACC, which Craig terms the limbic motor cortex. Consideration of the long list of different emotion-related stimuli and tasks associated with AI and ACC activation is one of the pieces of evidence that led to the idea that together they constitute components of an emotional "salience network" network that engenders human awareness (Seeley et al., 2007).

The AI and ACC uniquely contain a special class of large spindle-shaped neurons known as von Economo neurons (VENs), which could be responsible for fast interconnections between them (Allman et al., 2010; Craig, 2008). Their loss in the behavioral variant of frontotemporal dementia (bvFTD) is thought to underlie its devastating symptoms of poor judgment; lack of empathy, tact, and caring; loss of self-control; loss of initiative; and compulsive behavior (Seeley, 2010; Seeley et al., 2006). John Allman and his colleagues at Caltech have proposed that VENs are crucial for making fast intuitive judgments in complex social situations, and that their dysfunction may contribute to the difficulties in social interactions experienced by people with autism (Allman, Watson, Tetrault, & Hakeem, 2005). Their importance in self-awareness is supported by the observation that VENs have been found only in species that pass the mirror test of self-recognition, a group that includes humans, gorillas, bonobos, chimpanzees, elephants, and whales (Craig, 2009a).

The Sentient Self in Time

In Craig's model, the anterior insula provides "a cinemascopic view of the sentient self" (2009b, p. 1933). The word *cinemascopic* captures his idea that our awareness consists of a series of "frames"—the global emotional moments—that represent all feelings at one moment in time, providing a sort of feeling working memory. Craig proposes that the ticking by of these global moments could form the basis for our sense of time. Interestingly, subjective time is not identical to objective time—it varies with our emotional state, as anyone who has ever anxiously waited for test results in a doctor's office for what seems like an endless interval can attest. When something of great significance, such as a car accident, happens, people often report a drastic slowing down of time, a kind of suspension of the normal flow of subjective events. Craig attributes this subjective time dilation to the large amount of relevant sensation from the body that the brain must process in such instances (2009a, 2009b). Each global emotional moment has a limited information capacity, so that when there are many more highly salient events to attend to, more global emotional moments are needed to represent highly emotional circumstances, thus speeding up the endogenous time base so that subjective time appears to slow down.

Craig points out that the "global emotional moments" model of subjective awareness could provide the means of marking temporal progression. This in turn would connect emotional feelings to rhythm, and thus music, which he defines as "the rhythmic temporal progression of emotionally laden moments" (2008, p. 283). Music is deeply moving to people, and the loss of emotional response to music as a result of brain damage, a condition known as amusia, is devastating. Griffiths, Warren, Dean, and Howard (2007) described the case of a 52-year-old man who suffered a stroke that destroyed his left insula and surrounding structures and as a result lost the sense of intense pleasure that listening to Rachmaninov preludes had always given him. Anne Blood and Robert Zatorre (2001) had previously correlated musical "chills" or "shivers-down-the-spine" with increased and decreased activity in areas that related to "reward/motivation, emotion, and arousal" (p. 11818), which included the insula bilaterally. The intense response to music is another of the feelings that depends upon the neuroanatomical basis of the sentient self: the anterior insula.

Intriguingly, the use of rhythm in communication is shared by species with VENs that allow rapid communication between the ACC and AI. For example, bonobos signal agreement with synchronous rhythms and disagreement with contrapuntal rhythms, whales identify themselves to each other with characteristic "songs," and Thai elephants have been recorded making group music (Craig [2009a] cites a film on the National Geographic website as evidence [http://ngm.nationalgeographic.com/ngm/0510/feature5/video.html]).

Hemispheric Asymmetry and Balancing

In the recently evolved interoceptive system in primates, sympathetic and parasympathetic afferents remain separate, rather than becoming integrated in brain stem control centers as in nonprimates, and then become lateralized in the anterior insula. This hemispheric separation of the two opponent autonomic nervous system pathways may aid in the efficient balancing of energy in the brain, an important functional consideration given the massive energy demands of brain processing: The brain accounts for about 25% of total energy consumption in adults (Craig, 2008). The "calm and connect" restorative functions of parasympathetic activity target the left AI, and fight-or-flight-activating sympathetic activity is predominantly channeled to the right AI (see Figure 1 in Craig, 2005). Observations in humans support this idea that the autonomic nervous system is lateralized at the level of the anterior insula; for example, taste, which is clearly important for restoring energy (parasympathetic), is left lateralized, while arousing (sympathetic) stimuli that evoke pain, feelings of warmth and coolness, muscle ache, and sexual arousal all selectively activate the right AI (Craig, 2002, 2005). A study of the cardiovascular effects of electrical stimulation of the insula in human temporal lobe epilepsy patients supports the idea that autonomic activity is lateralized; slowing of heart rate (bradycardia) was more frequently found in response to left insular stimulation, whereas a rapid heart rate (tachycardia) was more frequently induced in response to right insular stimulation (Oppenheimer, Gelb, Girvin, & Hachinski, 1992). An important consequence of the evolution of distinct sympathetic and parasympathetic cortical pathways is that it may be possible to become more conscious of the opponent processing involved in balancing the two systems. Craig has produced a specific neurobiological model of the processes involved in coping with stress: Purposeful engagement of calming, energy-restoring parasympathetic processes can offset the arousing and taxing activity, particularly chronic activity, of the sympathetic nervous system. Behaviors that stimulate the parasympathetic system, such as some of the breathing exercises involved in yoga and meditation, can be useful in the treatment of psychological disorders.

Expansion of Craig's Sentient Self Model

In 2009, a group of scientists from diverse subfields of neuroscience pooled their talents to extend Craig's ideas of insular function into the domains of social neuroscience and neuroeconomics, or the study of motivated decision-making. Tania Singer, a social neuroscience researcher at the University of Zurich who has extensively investigated the neural bases of empathy; her colleague at Zurich, Kerstin Preuschoff, an expert in the field of neuroeconomics; and Hugo Critchley, who works on the autonomic nervous system and interoceptive awareness, have each identified the importance of insular activity in the distinct types of behavior they study. The remainder of this chapter is devoted to work that expands the concept of the sentient self, further enriching an embodied view of the feeling brain in ways that can provide significant clinical insights.

Pain and Empathy

Empathy is broadly defined as "an interaction between any two individuals, with one experiencing and sharing the feeling of the other" (Decety & Jackson, 2006, p. 54). In 2004, Tania Singer, who was then at University College, London, was the lead author on an important study that she and her colleagues conducted to explore the brain activations caused by pain-related empathic responses (Singer et al., 2004). They scanned the brains of the female half of 16 heterosexual couples while their male partners sat beside the MRI machine. Pain was applied to the hands of both partners successively during the study, and a mirror setup enabled the woman to see her own and her partner's hand. Singer et al. found that self and close-other pain both activated parts of the pain matrix,[4] including the middle and anterior insula, the ACC, the brain stem, and the cerebellum, while self pain also generated activity in regions of the pain matrix responding to the sensory characteristics of pain, such as the posterior insula. Intriguingly, women's scores on self-rating empathy scales correlated highly with activity in the ACC and left (but not right) AI.

Singer et al.'s results suggest that empathy for pain is correlated with conjoint activity in the AI and ACC, which had previously been correlated with subjective ratings of the unpleasantness of pain as well as the anticipation of pain (Ploghaus et al., 1999). Placebo and opioid analgesia were also known to activate rostral ACC and right AI. These studies support Singer et al.'s

---

4. Singer et al. list the components of the pain matrix as "the secondary somatosensory cortex (SII), insular regions, the anterior cingulate cortex (ACC), the movement-related areas such as the cerebellum and supplementary motor areas and, less robustly, the thalamus and the primary somatosensory cortex (SI)" (2004, p. 1158).

conclusion that "rostral ACC and AI appear to reflect the emotional experience that evokes our reactions to pain and constitutes the neural basis for our understanding of the feelings of others and ourselves" (2004, p. 1160).

The overlap in neural activation of regions activated in subjective pain and when observing a loved one's distress is a form of "neural resonance" that may undergird the ability to empathize with other people's distress. The same neural resonance occurs when the pain is only imaginary. Jackson, Brunet, Meltzoff, and Decety (2006) showed their participants images of other people's hands and feet in either painful or nonpainful situations and found that imagining either oneself or another person experiencing those situations resulted in partially overlapping patterns of brain activation. Paralleling Singer et al.'s study of actual pain, both self and other imagined pain activated the ACC and anterior insula.[5] However, participants rated their own imagined pain more highly than that of imagined others, and imagined self pain also activated more of the pain matrix, including posterior insula and SII. The more extensive activation for own versus other imagined pain may represent the neural differentiation between self and other.

Empathy for emotions other than pain has also been connected to insular activation. In 2003, a group of European researchers published a paper with the catchy title "Both of Us Disgusted in My Insula," reporting on brain activity while their human participants either inhaled disgusting or pleasant odorants or viewed movies of actors smelling a glass of disgusting, pleasant, or neutral liquid (Wicker et al., 2003). Their key finding was that both self and other disgust generated activity in the same area of the anterior insula. In 2007, Mbemba Jabbi and his colleagues in the Netherlands found that people who scored higher on a self-rating empathy scale also showed more activation of the anterior insula and adjacent frontal operculum when viewing actors expressing both disgust in response to citric acid and pleasure in drinking orange juice (Jabbi, Swart, & Keysers, 2007).

The activation of the insula in both self and others' disgust and pain is reminiscent of the much discussed and much publicized phenomenon of "mirror neurons,"[6] motor neurons that are activated to initiate specific movements or when viewing those same movements made by others (Rizzolatti & Craighero, 2004). In fact, two of the authors of the Wicker et al.

---

5. Jackson et al. (2006) also listed the parietal operculum.
6. The mirror neuron concept has also been vigorously criticized, especially as it pertains to humans (see, for example, Gregory Hickok's recent book, *The Myth of Mirror Neurons*).

study, Giacomo Rizzolatti and Vittorio Gallese from the University of Parma in Italy, were involved in the initial discovery of mirror neurons in monkey premotor cortex (Rizzolatti, Fadiga, Gallese, & Fogassi, 1996), which led to their proposal that mirror neurons are the neural substrate of simulation (Gallese, 2003; Gallese & Goldman, 1998). Simulation theory posits that the feelings of others are understood by resonance with the neural systems that represent our own mental states. The work of Singer et al. and others on shared self and other pain and disgust representations in the anterior insula suggests a dual function for insular representations of the physiological state of the body; they are the basis of subjective feeling states as described extensively in this chapter, but they also play a role in simulating how others will feel when they encounter emotional stimuli (Singer et al., 2009).

Shared Physical and Social Pain Networks

The subjective feeling states processed by the insula go beyond responses to physical sensations. In 2003, Naomi Eisenberger and Matthew Lieberman, a married couple who work in social neuroscience at the University of California, Los Angeles, collaborated with Kipling Williams of Macquarie University in Sydney to produce a fascinating study of the neural basis of pain created by social rather than physical distress. To produce the experience of social pain in the scanner, they used a computer game that Williams had created to study social exclusion. In Cyberball, the participant plays a game of virtual catch with two computer-generated players; at first, the ball is passed freely among all players, and then the two other players start systematically excluding the participant. The newsworthy finding was that some of the same brain areas noted in imaging studies of bodily pain were activated in response to the social pain of exclusion from a fairly meaningless game. The researchers discovered that the brain processes involved in social pain are more similar to those involved in physical pain than many scientists originally thought. The ACC is a key part of these shared brain networks, and the anterior insula is also activated, albeit less vigorously.

Anxiety and the Insula

The neural basis of anxiety has been investigated using a heartbeat detection task that psychophysiologists devised for measuring interoceptive sensitivity (Wiens, 2005; Wiens, Mezzacappa, & Katkin, 2000). Hugo Critchley and colleagues found that activity in the right anterior insula and the neigh-boring opercular cortex correlated with an individual's ability to perform a challenging heartbeat detection task (Critchley, Wiens, Rothstein, Öhman, & Dolan, 2004). Participants were asked to introspectively monitor the beating of their heart and judge whether it was either synchronized with a series of notes or delayed by half a second.[7] They found that people's ability to do this accurately varied widely, from chance levels of performance to 83% correct. Importantly, Critchley et al. also documented a positive cor-relation between participants' scores on a standard measure of anxiety, the Hamilton anxiety scale, and their heartbeat detection performance. This finding fits with clinical observations that enhanced somatic symptoms and attention to interoceptive states characterize anxiety disorders and suggests that reducing activity in the right insular cortex should be a target of thera-peutic interventions. The anxiety–insula connection is confirmed by symp-tom provocation studies with a variety of anxiety disorders including phobias, posttraumatic stress disorder (PTSD), and obsessive-compulsive disorder (OCD), which show significantly increased insula activity (Rauch, Savage, Alpert, Fischman, & Jenike, 1997). In his commentary on Critchley et al., Craig (2004b) emphasized that the most exciting implication of the study was the correlations the researchers found among individual mea-sures of heartbeat awareness, anxiety, and right anterior insular activity, providing a physical substrate for individual differences in emotional expe-rience.

Critchley and colleagues linked anxiety proneness with individual sensi-tivity to interoceptive signals about the current state of the body. Work in neuroeconomics has gone on to link insula activity to predicting or antici-pating aversive body states in addition to registering the current body state (Kuhnen & Knutson, 2005). Thus, another function of the insula is to gen-erate signals about predicted body states that are useful for decision-making and learning, particularly in situations of uncertainty or ambiguity (Singer et al., 2009). Martin Paulus and Murray Stein, who work in the Depart-ments of Psychiatry and Family and Preventative Medicine at the Univer-sity of California, San Diego, integrated these insights about interoception from neuroeconomics and psychophysiology to develop a more detailed

---

7. This is considered a more reliable measurement than simply asking people to count their heartbeats, because in that case they could easily rely on preconceived ideas about the rate of their heartbeat rather than actual sensations. In other words, they could use educated guesses about their typical heart rate.

theory of the connection between anxiety and predictive interoceptive signaling in the insula.

Anxiety is characterized by worry about aversive future events, a process known as "catastrophizing"; in chapter 4, we mentioned that this pathological process is the potential cost of being able to speculate about and predict the consequences of future choices. Paulus and Stein (2006) proposed that anxiety-prone individuals have altered interoception that results in an exaggerated anterior insula signal when anticipating aversive future events. In response to signals about the salience of anticipated aversive stimuli coming from structures such as the amygdala and the nucleus accumbens, the insula generates an inflated prediction signal that anticipates a highly aversive body state out of keeping with the current situation, which then brings that distressing bodily state into being. Further, Paulus and Stein (2010) emphasized that not only are the predictive signals exaggerated for anxiety-prone individuals, but they are also noisy, so that normal ongoing fluctuations in the body state are interpreted as aversive signals. Paulus and Stein view these alterations in interoceptive signaling as primary in initiating the anxiety state. The elevated insular activity creates a subjective sense of distress that is difficult to tolerate and creates the desire to avoid future situations that could evoke it, such as parties or other social gatherings if the person suffers from social anxiety disorder. The enhanced insula prediction signal also engages cognitive "worry" processes to try to solve the problem indicated by the aversive body state.

Some pharmacological evidence for Critchley et al. and Paulus and Stein's linkage of heightened insula responses with anxiety comes from studies showing decreased insula activation after treatment with the anxiolytics lorazepam and citalopram (Paulus & Stein, 2006). Experimental support for their theory comes from their neuroimaging study of risk-taking (Paulus, Rogalsky, Simmons, Feinstein, & Stein, 2003). In the "risky gains" task, their participants had to select between a safe option and two risky higher-paying options that could result in losses. Activity in the right insula was higher overall for the risky than for the safe choices, and scores on harm avoidance and neuroticism measures, personality factors previously linked with anxiety, were correlated with the degree of insula activation. Further, larger responses in the right anterior insula during punished risky trials predicted safe responses in subsequent trials. For more anxious individuals, the exaggerated insula response to punishment leads them to anticipate more aversive bodily sensations in upcoming trials and initiates avoidance of the risky options in the future. Thus, the pathology of anxiety arises from an exaggeration of otherwise adaptive risk avoidance learning mechanisms.

A later neuroeconomics study by Samanez-Larkin, Hollon, Carstensen, and Knutson (2008) provided more support for Paulus and Stein's theory linking altered interoceptive signaling to avoidance behaviors in anxiety. Samanez-Larkin et al. found that the level of activity in the insula when anticipating gains or losses in a timed behavioral task predicted individual ability to learn to avoid losses in a test given 8 to 10 months later. They conclude their discussion with the argument that anxiety-related traits have persisted as part of our genetic makeup because they are based in adaptive avoidance learning.

Critchley's group produced another innovative experimental study that fits with Paulus and Stein's emphasis on the role of elevated insular aversive bodily signals in anxiety (Gray, Harrison, Weins, & Critchley, 2007). Based on studies in the 1960s that had shown that falsely representing auditory heart rate feedback as elevated increased the attractiveness ratings of photographs of nude females by male college students, Gray et al. measured the effects of false feedback on the perceived emotionality of faces during brain imaging. False feedback about elevated heart rate increased the intensity ratings for neutral, but not happy or angry, faces, and right anterior insula was more active in the false compared to the true feedback conditions. This suggested that a heightened response to the mismatch between elevated bodily signals and neutral stimuli in the environment could be the neural basis of the perceptions of nonthreatening stimuli as threatening that plague anxious people.

Studies with the Iowa gambling task (IGT) devised by Bechara, Damasio, and colleagues that we discussed in chapter 5 provide additional support for the idea that anxiety-prone individuals are more sensitive to insular bodily signals that indicate aversive future outcomes. An fMRI study of the IGT by Lin, Chiu, Cheng, and Hsieh (2008) demonstrated the importance of the insula in the anticipatory phase of the task, and Werner, Duschek, and Schandry (2009) found that student participants with higher levels of trait anxiety generated larger anticipatory skin conductance responses and learned to avoid the bad decks more effectively than less anxious students.[8]

---

8. Miu, Heilman, and Houser (2008) reported the opposite result: In their study, students with high trait anxiety scores performed more poorly than those at the low end of the trait anxiety distribution. Werner et al. point out that Miu et al. used a very small number of participants

Paulus and Stein argue that the anticipation of a highly aversive future body state is the trigger for a full-fledged anxiety response that includes deeply worrying thoughts and maladaptive avoidance behaviors. Mindfulness-based therapies, with their focus on present-moment rather than past or future experience, can be helpful in breaking the cycle of anxiety, with its excessive focus on anticipated aversive body states (Greeson & Brantley, 2009; Kabat-Zinn, 2003; Linehan, 1993).

In addition to the well-documented altered functioning of the amygdala in anxiety that we have already discussed in connection with LeDoux's work on fear conditioning, Paulus and Stein draw attention to anterior insular dysfunction as a key component of the anxiety circuitry. The insula and amygdala are bidirectionally connected and form part of a larger network, which includes other areas of the prefrontal cortex, that is altered in anxiety disorders. This expanded view of the anxiety circuitry, with its inclusion of more complex cortical processing, makes sense in terms of the nature of the disorder, which as we saw can also be based in dysfunction of the prefrontal circuits that modulate the fear conditioning in the amygdala.

Paulus and his collaborators have noted that a high level of interoceptive sensitivity and awareness can also be a key neural component of optimal performance in extreme environments, such as elite athletic competitions and complex combat operations (Paulus et al., 2009). Individuals who are able to utilize a finely "contextualized" body state resulting from the insular integration of body representations with other ongoing affective, cognitive, or experiential information about the salience and value of the events in the environment may be better placed to act appropriately in highly demanding conditions. Although the corticalization of interoception and the ability to anticipate the consequences of future events on the body can facilitate anxiety, it clearly has significant adaptive value.

Distortions in Body Awareness

Insula dysfunction has been implicated in a number of clinical syndromes that include a dysfunctional sense of the body. Recall from chapter 5 that Damasio linked anosognosia, the perplexing denial of body dysfunctions such as paralysis, with insular damage (Jones, Ward, & Critchley, 2010). A

---

and only studied those at the extremes of the distribution whose extreme sensitivity to somatic signals could have overwhelmed their ability to use them effectively in decision-making.

related disorder which involves denial of ownership of specific body parts such as the arm, somatoparaphrenia, has also been documented in a patient with insula damage (Cereda, Ghika, Maeder, & Bougousslavsky, 2002).

A striking demonstration of the role of the insula in body awareness is seen in the rubber hand illusion. When a visible rubber hand is stroked simultaneously and in exactly the same way as a person's out-of-sight hand, the individual begins to experience the rubber hand as his or her own. Remarkably, evidence that the rubber hand has actually replaced the (unseen) real hand is seen by a selective decrease in skin temperature of the out-of-sight hand, indicating that body ownership and temperature regulation go hand-in-hand (pun intended); the illusory body perception actually drives homeostatic processes. During the illusion, the right posterior insula is highly active, and patients with posterior insula damage were reported to be less susceptible to the illusion (Jones et al., 2010; Tsakiris, Hesse, Boy, Haggard, & Fink, 2007). Those with low interoceptive sensitivity as measured with a heartbeat detection task were also seen to be more susceptible to the rubber hand illusion (Tsakiris, Tajadura-Jimenez, & Costantini, 2011) and showed a higher decrease in skin temperature of the replaced own hand than controls. Together, these studies suggest that individual differences in interoceptive awareness could contribute to variations in susceptibility to distorted body perception.

Dysregulated interoception has recently been linked to other clinical conditions in which body perception is distorted (Kaye, Wierenga, Bailer, Simmons, & Bischoff-Grethe, 2013). Those with anorexia nervosa (AN) fail to respond to sensations of hunger, perhaps as a result of decreased awareness of the bodily sensations. Indeed, Pollatos and colleagues (2008) showed that AN participants were much worse at a heartbeat detection task than controls. Functional MRI scans of recovered anorexics[9] (REC AN) found significantly less left insula response to sweetened water than controls, and insula activity in controls but not REC AN participants was positively correlated with pleasure ratings to the sugar water, suggesting an enduring alteration in brain taste responses (Wagner et al., 2008). Notably, several research groups have documented alexithymia (difficulty in identifying one's own emotions) in people with AN (Sexton, Sunday, Hurt, & Halmi, 1998; Speranza et al., 2005). It is possible that the decreased interoceptive

---

9. Women who had recovered from AN were used to avoid the possible confounding effects of starvation and emaciation.

awareness and enduring differences in insular activity seen in AN are related to the emotional and self-concept struggles faced by people with this devastating and often fatal disorder.

A recent neuroimaging study has shown a connection between the processing of pain, AN, and alexithymia (Strigo et al., 2013). The right posterior insula responses of REC AN patients to heat pain were lower than those of controls, in keeping with the reduced interoceptive responsiveness in AN. In contrast, these patients had higher activity in the right anterior insula in anticipation of heat pain. Further, the REC AN participants who had the most difficulty identifying emotions also had the highest levels of anticipatory pain activity in the right anterior insula. This difference in sensitivity to anticipated and actual experience of pain for the REC AN participants is reminiscent of the mismatch between anticipated future aversive states and the current body state that Paulus and Stein noted in anxiety. In fact, there is high comorbidity of anxiety and AN (Kaye et al., 2013); Strigo et al.'s study lends support to the idea that they may share a common neural substrate that should be a key neural target for treatment.

The Effects of Insula Damage on Craving

In anorexia, people suffer from insensitivity to insular body signals, but in drug addiction, the reverse occurs: People are too sensitive to the bodily signals produced by the drug and crave the sensations it evokes. In craving, the usual linkage between the state of the body and motivation appears to be disrupted such that addicted individuals do not reach a state of satiety— they continue to crave the drug (Goldstein et al., 2009). An intriguing example of the insula's crucial role in craving comes from a study connecting insula lesions and smoking behavior. Naqvi, Rudrauf, H. Damasio, and Bechara (2007) reported that patients with insula damage found it much easier to give up smoking than patients with lesions in other areas of the brain. The insula-damaged patients reported that they no longer felt the urge to smoke; the craving that makes quitting so difficult simply did not plague them. Naqvi et al. relate the reduction of craving to a loss of interoceptive function. In addition to its well-known psychotropic effects, they argue, smoking is also associated with a number of bodily changes, such as airway stimulation. Smokers may come to experience these bodily changes as pleasurable, and these effects of smoking may also come to be craved. The lack of airway stimulation with nicotine patches and gum could contribute to the lack of effectiveness of nicotine replacement therapies. Treatments that stimulate the airways without nicotine, such as irritant inhalers, have been developed, and may help in preventing smoking relapse (Westman et al., 1995, as cited in Naqvi & Bechara, 2009). Interestingly, some of these airway stimulation alternatives have been shown to increase insula activation (Mazzone, 2007, as cited in Naqvi & Bechara, 2009). Perhaps the lack of awareness of airway sensations as a result of AI damage is what enables insula-damaged patients to so readily give up smoking. Although there is not yet a substantial body of research on disruptions in interoceptive processing in addicted populations, the potential for translation of findings from this research into more effective treatments means that this area is likely to grow in coming years (Verdejo-García, Clark, & Dunn, 2012).

Positive Social Emotions: Love and Compassion

Although insular activation is often associated with aversive experiences such as disgust (e.g., Ochsner, Silvers, & Buhle, 2012), it has also been implicated in more positive experiences. For example, we have already discussed how the insula processes affective touch that mediates comfort and bonding, and the role of the insula in the pleasurable response to music. Neuroimaging work has also shown activation of the insula in affiliative responses. For example, the insula and amygdala were more active when mothers viewed pictures of their own children in comparison to pictures of other familiar children[10] (Bartels & Zeki, 2004; Leibenluft, Gobbini, Harrison, & Haxby, 2004). In addition, Bartels and Zeki (2004) noted substantial overlap between areas activated in this study on maternal love with regions activated in earlier studies in which participants viewed pictures of romantic partners.

The cultivation of positive emotions is the explicit aim of *metta* or loving-kindness meditation (LKM). Richard Davidson, Antoine Lutz, and their colleagues at University of Wisconsin, Madison, have collaborated with Buddhist monks who have logged thousands of hours of mediation. Compared to the brains of novices, during LKM, experts' brains showed stron-

---

10. The researchers also found increased activation in areas previously associated with theory of mind processing: the anterior paracingulate cortex and the posterior superior temporal sulcus (STS).

ger responses in the insula, ACC, and amygdala to emotional sounds, such as laughter or crying (Lutz, Brefczynski-Lewis, Johnstone, & Davidson, 2008), and the researchers conclude that extensive practice in the cultivation of compassion changes how the brain responds to emotional stimuli. As they express it, "concern for others cultivated during this form of meditation enhances affective processing" (p. 1).

Concluding Comments

Craig's detailed journey through the neuroanatomy of interoception has brought him to the study of the nature of human consciousness. For Craig, the foundation of self-awareness is the integration of multiple representations of the state of the body with higher neural systems, including those processing salience, value, memory, and learning. He argues that our consciousness depends on brain representations of the body, which form the blueprint for our sense of self in time and space. Some contemporary researchers have criticized Craig for his exclusive focus on the insula at the expense of the many other cortical and subcortical regions that have also been shown to be involved in emotions and consciousness. Most models of consciousness focus on the synchronization of firing in widely distributed and shifting brain networks, so it is understandable that their proponents would be skeptical of the localization of self-awareness to a small portion of the cortex at the junction of the anterior insula and frontal operculum.

Damasio and his colleagues recently provided clinical evidence that Craig's identification of the anterior insula as the "sole platform" and "critical provider of human awareness" (A. Damasio, Damasio, & Tranel, 2013, p. 147) may be simplistic. To argue this point, they used the example of Patient B., who contracted encephalitis in his late forties, which resulted in the destruction of a large area that included the ACC, orbitofrontal cortex, hippocampus, entorhinal cortex, and amygdala, as well as his entire insula on both sides. Although he was densely amnesic as a result of the hippocampal damage, Damasio et al. argue that Patient B. was aware of his own bodily and emotional feelings, as well as those of others, something that should be impossible without his insula, according to Craig. It is difficult to assess the extent of Patient B.'s explicit emotional awareness because of his inability to reflect on and recall much of his personal life, but Damasio and colleagues were able to show that he experienced pleasure and displeasure in the moment (his global emotional moments appeared to be intact). Patient B.'s case presents a different picture than Seeley et al.'s work with frontotemporal dementia patients who have sustained widespread insular and anterior cingulate damage that seems to have had a larger impact on their emotional awareness.[11]

Damasio et al. further contest the idea that "feelings" are uniquely associated with the insula. Like Panksepp, whose work we discussed in chapter 3, Damasio argues that rudimentary feelings first emerge from upper brain stem structures, such as the periaqueductal gray (PAG) and parabrachial nucleus (PBN), where incoming sensory information first forms somatotopic maps of the body. This is supported by studies showing that these structures are activated in neuroimaging studies of induced emotional feelings (Buhle et al., 2012; Damasio et al., 2000), and high-frequency electrical stimulation of the upper brain stem in humans can induce feelings of deep sadness (Bejani et al., 1999). Damasio and Panksepp also cite the unfortunate and unusual case of hydranencephalic children who are born without any cortex, yet express pleasure and displeasure and emotional engagement (A. Damasio, 2010; Panksepp & Biven, 2012).

However, Damasio agrees with Craig's characterization of the insula as a vital integrative site in the human brain that brings together interoceptive and exteroceptive information for the purpose of survival-related life regulation: homeostasis. While the insula is not absolutely necessary for the experience of basic or core feelings, its extensive connectivity to other cortical regions serves to connect feelings to memories, language, and reasoning, providing a richer context and the opportunity for integration of cognition and emotion. Without this cortical communication, the conscious control of drives and emotions is more difficult, as can be seen in Patient B's case; he is at the mercy of his feeling states and is not able to monitor and regulate his emotions as he could before he contracted encephalitis, consistent with Craig's conception that the corticalization of homeostatic regulation processes in primates gave rise to the ability to exert more conscious and effortful control of our feelings.

In primates, especially human ones, new neural pathways have evolved that enable the brain to create what Damasio describes as "a composite and

---

11. Damasio et al.'s recent paper also seems at odds with an earlier statement that Damasio made about the effect of insular lesions: "Lesions which compromise the ability to experience emotional feelings and to sense the body are often located on the right side of the somatosensory complex, including, and in particular to the right insular cortex. The patients so affected have a compromised sense of self as well." (A. Damasio, 2003, p. 260).

continuous map of the body state" (2003, p. 261). Craig situates this composite map in a particular cortical location, but recognizes that it is densely interconnected with many other brain regions. Ironically, the most important feature of the insula could be that it is not an island. The foundation for self-awareness may be present in the neural mappings of the material me, but it is vital to connect those ongoing mappings to a larger sense of the self in time, a more extended autobiographical past and projection further forward than the next few global emotional moments. In the next chapter, we turn to studies of emotion and memory that provide some of that larger context.

8

Emotion and Memory

One of us (EBJ) remembers the evening of December 21, 1988, and the following morning vividly and in much greater detail than any other days around that time. That afternoon I had completed the oral defense of my doctoral thesis in front of two intimidating experts and was filled with relief and joy. After the intense culmination of such a long, arduous process I thoroughly enjoyed the celebration dinner with my husband and two other British-American couples. Thinking about it now I can envision the restaurant—the Cherwell Boathouse in Oxford, where we sat— how all the people there looked, how much we all loved the food, and the feeling of being on an incredible emotional high. It makes me happy just to think of it. But that happiness is always tempered as I quickly connect it to what happened next. The following morning we awoke to a radio announcement of the bombing of Pan Am 103. This flight, scheduled to fly from London to New York, exploded over Lockerbie, Scotland, killing all 243 passengers, 16 crew members, and 11 people on the ground. Many of the passengers were American students from Syracuse University flying home from a study abroad program. This was deeply shocking to us and close to home in many ways. I am from near Edinburgh in Scotland, and we were about to travel up there for Christmas with my family, passing through Lockerbie. My husband is American, and we were scheduled to fly on Pan AM 103 the next week to visit his family. I can revisit that period of time at will, mentally traveling back in time to go through the events and feel the emotions with an intensity matched by few other periods in my past, excepting the births of my two sons.

Why do some memories, such as this memory about an intensely emotional experience, seem to persist in vivid detail for years, while others seem much less detailed and fade over time? William James in an oft-quoted statement claimed that "an experience may be so exciting as to almost leave a scar on the cerebral tissue" (1890, p. 670). Although the notion that extremely emotional memories are in a special class that are more vividly and completely recorded than less emotionally intense events has long been part of psychologists' thinking, contemporary research from many kinds of studies—diary studies of memory in everyday life, laboratory list-learning tasks, and more recent neuroimaging work (see Kensinger & Schacter, 2008, for a review)—has shown that a normal function of emotion is to enhance memory in order to improve recall of experiences that have importance or relevance for our lives. Neuroscientists now understand more about the neural processes that underlie the emotional enhancement of memory. We saw in chapter 4 that the amygdala contributes to the formation of a persistent form of implicit memory that LeDoux refers to as emotional memory. Although the implicit emotional memory stored in the amygdala is a very different form of memory than the explicit memory that can be accessed by conscious recall (see Box 8.1 for more on the implicit/explicit memory distinction), common neurochemical processes are involved in both types of memory. As we saw in chapter 4, emotionally salient events are arousing, and activation of the stress hormones norepinephrine and cortisol by the amygdala plays an important role in modulating emotional memories.

Emotion can effectively turn up the volume dial on memory, a function that makes evolutionary sense when you think about the need to remember life-threatening events in order to avoid those events in the future. Bombings of planes such as Pan Am 103 are calculated to create this sort of terror in people. Another metaphor that is frequently used is emotion as a highlighter pen that accentuates certain aspects of experiences to make them more memorable (Levine & Pizarro, 2004). We see this effect in the opening example, where some of the central details of the post-thesis exam restaurant visit are vividly recalled despite the long time that has elapsed since that one experience. A photographic metaphor, likening memories of extremely emotional events to taking flashbulb images, is also used to describe the effect of emotion on memory (Brown & Kulik, 1977). Memory for the circumstances of hearing about the Pan Am bombing in the opening anecdote is a paradigmatic example of such a flashbulb memory. As we will see later in the chapter, such emotionally charged memories seem to be distinguished from run-of-the-mill memories by the subjective sense of vividness they convey. Elizabeth can mentally revisit December 21 and 22, 1988, in a way that is simply not possible for other days around that time because of the vividness and coherence of her emotionally enhanced memory.

Although most often emotions facilitate the formation of memories, in some circumstances emotions can selectively facilitate some forms of memory while simultaneously impairing others. For example, in posttraumatic stress disorder (PTSD), emotionally devastating images of the traumatic event burst unbidden into awareness, showing a strong memory for the event, yet simultaneously the person can have great difficulty with memory recall in everyday life. This paradoxical mix of excesses and deficits in memory caused by severe emotional stress illustrates some of the complexities of the interactions between emotions and memory.

The Multiplicity of Memory

Part of that complexity arises because of the multiplicity of forms of memory. As we already learned from chapter 4, memory is not a single process; different forms of memory are carried out in different brain regions. We saw that fear conditioning was learned and stored in the amygdala as an implicit memory, while the explicit memory of the context in which the fear learning occurred was a hippocampus-dependent process. One unfortunate person, known in the literature as H. M., was instrumental in establishing the multiplicity of memory types and their brain bases. In order to control his otherwise intractable epilepsy, the hippocampus, amygdala, and some of the medial temporal cortex that sits around these structures were surgically removed from both sides of the 26-year-old H. M.'s brain in 1953 (see Figure 2.1 for the location of these structures).

While the operation substantially reduced the severity and frequency of his seizures, it had devastating effects on his long-term memory. H. M.'s immediate or working memory, his ability to hold information in consciousness and manipulate it (see Box 8.1), was not damaged by the operation, so he was able to converse normally from the time of his recovery. Unfortunately, he did not recall the content of any of these conversations later because of his inability to form explicit long-term memories. For example, each time he met the researcher, Dr. Suzanne Corkin, who interacted with him regularly for 46 years, she had to reintroduce herself as someone studying his memory.[1] H. M. could initially register that he was meeting a researcher, but he could not consolidate that event into an explicit enduring memory of Dr. Corkin and her relationship to him. Eventually she did become familiar to him, but he explained that feeling of familiarity by saying that she was someone he'd known in high school.[2] He had a severe case of anterograde amnesia,[3] or an almost complete inability to form new memories. What entered into his working memory could not be converted into longer-term memories; H. M. was almost completely lacking the *consolidation* mechanisms responsible for the creation of memories that last more than a few minutes.

At first the doctors and researchers thought that H. M.'s anterograde amnesia was complete, but through extensive testing they learned that if a task did not require explicit knowledge, H. M.'s performance on it would improve over time. This put him in the peculiar position of becoming highly skilled on perceptual and motor tasks like mirror drawing without having any recall of ever having done them before. The formation of new explicit memories depends on the hippocampus, whereas other areas that were not damaged in H. M.'s brain are responsible for implicit memories. This recalls the distinction made by LeDoux between implicit "emotional memory" of fear conditioning in the amygdala and explicit memory of the emotion involving the hippocampus.

In addition to being unable to consolidate new explicit memories, H. M. suffered from retrograde amnesia: He was unable to recall past experiences for some time leading up to the surgery. The temporal extent of this memory loss was difficult to establish; early on, researchers estimated that it was about two years, but in later papers estimates rose to as much as 11 years (Corkin, 2013; Milner, Corkin, & Teuber, 1968). However, different kinds of memories may require more or less time for consolidation to become complete. Yet the fact that H. M. could recall earlier periods of his life shows that access to much older memories no longer requires the hippocampus. Later studies of H. M.'s remote memories of experiences, however, revealed that

---

1. This is described in a 2007 radio program that has rare excerpts from interviews with H. M. *The Weekend Edition* segment by Brian Newhouse is available at: http://www.npr.org/templates/story/story.php?storyId=7584970.
2. Oddly, Corkin did know William Beecher Scoville, the neurosurgeon who operated on H. M., while she was in school; he was the father of a close friend (Corkin, 2013, p. xiv).
3. Anterograde amnesia refers to the ability to make new memories, whereas retrograde amnesia is the term used for the inability to recall previously established memories.

these were mostly stereotyped and schematic accounts that probably did not have the dynamic and vivid phenomenological qualities that we associate with autobiographical recall; they were unlikely to create the experience of "mental time travel" that we described for the memories of our opening anecdote (Corkin, 2002, 2013).

The pattern of preserved abilities and deficits in H. M. shows us that memory consists of many more types of recall than we originally thought. His well-studied case is one of the linchpins in the current neuroscientific taxonomy of memory, which identifies multiple types of memory with distinct neural bases and different time courses (Squire, 2004). In this chapter, we focus primarily on the role of emotion in modulating explicit long-term memories. The formation of memories is often described as consisting of distinct stages, which can be separately modulated by emotion. The initial representation of an event in working memory is referred to as *encoding*, a process that, as we'll see below, is highly dependent on attention. Information encoded in working memory then undergoes a variable period of *consolidation*, which requires the hippocampus. During consolidation, memories are slowly converted into a permanent form which is thought to be stored in neocortex. Finally, stored memories are recalled by the process of *retrieval*. Although retrieval of memories initially depends on the hippocampus, over time it also becomes independent of that structure, as indicated by H. M.'s ability to retrieve information about his more remote past. Emotion could potentially affect the encoding, consolidation and storage, and retrieval of memories differently, so we will consider studies of emotional modulation of each phase of memory in turn.

Encoding

When we look at the world, we often feel as if we are taking everything in, but this is an illusion. Numerous psychological studies have shown that we are aware of only a small amount of the visual information present at any moment in time. What we become aware of is what we attend to. Attention thus functions to select what's most relevant for more extensive processing, and only a few items can be processed at any time. Daniel Simons and Christopher Chabris at the University of Illinois produced a stunning demonstration of the importance of attention in our ability to register or encode information (Simons & Chabris, 1999). They prepared a video of two intermixed teams of players, one in black shirts and the other in white, throwing balls to their teammates. Participants were asked to count the number of throws between the players in white shirts only, and to ignore the black-shirted players. Halfway through, someone dressed in a big black gorilla suit sauntered through the two groups of players and even stopped to beat its chest dramatically. When the participants were asked about it afterward, many of them were shocked to hear about the gorilla; they simply had not seen it even though it was right in front of them, because they were only attending to the white shirts. The limited capacity of attention can act as a sort of bottleneck that cuts down the possibilities for encoding information.

As we learned in chapter 4, activation of the amygdala by an emotional stimulus increases arousal and by directing attention to that stimulus selectively facilitates its processing, thus acting as an attentional highlighter. This was tested directly by a study that New York University researcher Elizabeth Phelps conducted with her postdoctoral student Adam Anderson using the "attentional blink" task, a task that illustrates the limited processing capacity of attention (Anderson & Phelps, 2001). Participants viewed a rapidly presented stream of words that were mostly in black type and were asked to identify only the target green words that occasionally appeared. In the standard form of the attentional blink task, if two target words are presented close together in time (within about 500 milliseconds), the observer typically misses the second one; it is as though his or her attention had "blinked." Anderson and Phelps tested whether the duration of the blink is modulated by the emotional content of a stimulus, by comparing the duration of the blink when the second word was an emotionally evocative negative word, such as *bastard*, to the duration of the blink following a neutral word like *broom*. They found that strongly negative words reduced the duration of the blink, suggesting that emotional words are better able to capture limited attentional resources. The role of the amygdala in enhancing attention to emotional words was confirmed by a study on a patient, S. P. with bilateral amygdala damage, who showed no reduction in the blink duration with emotional words.

Although attention usually acts adaptively to guide our focus to the most salient stimulus, during times of extreme stress it may be so narrowly focused that little else can be remembered. This idea was first proposed by Easterbrook (1959), who suggested that high levels of emotional arousal act to narrow the scope of attention so that a few central cues are emphasized at the expense of many peripheral cues; he called this the cue utilization hypothesis. This is thought to be the basis of the weapon focus effect reported by victims or observers of violent crimes—identification of the perpetrator is difficult because the person's attention was captured by the weapon. Just as the gorilla was filtered out by the selective focus on the white shirts in Simons and Chabris's experiment, details of the perpetrator's appearance are not attended to and therefore not encoded. While the selective focus on salient or emotional stimuli is clearly adaptive, there are circumstances when the narrowing of focus turns out to be a disadvantage.

Consolidation and Storage:
McGaugh's Studies of Consolidation and Stress

So information strongly activating the amygdala will be attended to, and thus have a better chance of being encoded, but does it also have a better chance of being consolidated into a longer-lasting memory? This question has inspired the long and productive career of psychologist James McGaugh, based at the University of California, Irvine. McGaugh and his many collaborators have demonstrated that emotional events that activate the amygdala trigger neural and hormonal mechanisms that enhance memory consolidation processes in the hippocampus and other brain areas. Like the work of LeDoux and colleagues discussed in chapter 4, the work of McGaugh's group shows that emotional and nonemotional stimuli are processed somewhat differently in the brain.

In a long series of studies that date back to his doctoral work in the 1950s, McGaugh has demonstrated that rats injected with stimulant drugs to mimic the effects of arousal show enhanced memory for tasks such as maze learning and avoidance of footshock (McGaugh, 2003). Most important, in McGaugh's experimental setup, the drugs were injected into the rats *after* they had completed their training rather than during encoding. Thus, the drugs were improving the consolidation of memory rather than simply heightening the rats' sensory, motor, or attentional processes during the initial learning trials. Further, there seems to be a window of time during which arousal enhances consolidation: If McGaugh waited for two hours or more after training to inject the drug, it no longer enhanced memory the next day. In further studies McGaugh also showed that memories can be disrupted in this same window by injections of drugs such as those that block adrenergic receptors. Work from several groups has shown that protein synthesis inhibitors, such as anisomycin, prevent the consolidation of memories when given during this time period, but not when given at the time of learning itself (see McGaugh (2003) for a description of these studies). This suggests that, unlike other phases of learning or memory, consolidation requires new protein synthesis in order to actively modulate the physical features of synapses involved in learning (see Davis & Squire (1984) for a review, and Gold (2008) for a critique). McGaugh sees the time between the initial learning or encoding and the successful formation of long-term memory as a window of instability during which memory can be either consolidated or lost. He argues that this period of instability after initial encoding means that long-term memories are not formed instantaneously, as suggested by the flashbulb metaphor. Rather, memories can be modified by what happens for a period of time subsequent to encoding. He suggests that this serves the adaptive function of "enabling the significance of an experience to regulate the strength of the memory of the experience" (2000, p. 248) as it unfolds over time. Thus, arousal affects these two features of memory independently: Arousal at the time of encoding allows significant events to selectively capture attention to facilitate initial learning, while arousal that persists beyond initial learning selects those events to be retained in a more permanent form.

The drugs used by McGaugh and colleagues to enhance memory mimicked those occurring naturally during stress, such as the norepinephrine and epinephrine released by the sympathetic fight-or-flight response, as well as the classic stress hormone, cortisol, normally released from the adrenal cortex by activation of the HPA[4] axis (see Box 4.1 for more on this term). In fact, peripheral injections of epinephrine or glucocorticoids after footshock avoidance learning further enhanced the learning already enhanced by the footshock, but again, only if they were administered within two hours of the training.

The amygdala itself is an important target for stress hormones. Although peripheral adrenaline cannot enter the brain, it can stimulate autonomic vagal afferents that project into the brain and trigger the release of brain norepinephrine from sites in the brain that in turn project to the amygdala. Propranolol, a drug commonly used for treating hypertension and heart arrhythmias, blocks β-adrenoreceptors (hence its common name "beta-blocker") and prevents the memory enhancing effects of peripheral arousal when injected directly into the amygdala. Thus, amygdala adrenorecep-

---

4. The "classic" stress response refers to the activation of the hypothalamic-pituitary-adrenal axis (HPA), resulting in the release of glucocorticoids like cortisol (corticosterone in rats).

tors proved to be essential for the memory boosting effects of stress hormones.

The amygdala is thought to play a modulatory role in many different types of memory tasks. It has extensive projections to many other brain areas that also play a role in memory consolidation. The hippocampus is a clear target for the consolidation of explicit memory tasks, and is at play in the footshock avoidance task used by McGaugh and colleagues. The hippocampus is also required for spatial learning tasks such as the Morris water maze, where rats use spatial cues to learn the location of a platform that allows them to escape from a pool of murky water (Morris, 1984). Later performance on the spatial water maze task improves if amphetamine is injected directly into the hippocampus after initial training. The same boosting of consolidation in this hippocampus-dependent spatial task occurs when the amphetamine is injected into the amygdala, indicating that the amygdala can modulate the consolidation of spatial memory in the hippocampus (Packard, Cahill, & McGaugh, 1994). In the same study, Packard et al. showed that learning of a visually cued form of the water maze task that has been shown to be dependent on the caudate nucleus, part of the striatum that is important for implicit learning, can also be enhanced by amphetamine injections either directly into the caudate nucleus or into the amygdala. Other work has documented amygdala enhancement of memory consolidation in the insular cortex, anterior cingulate cortex, and prefrontal cortex (Roozendaal, McEwen, & Chattarji, 2009). Although the manner in which the amygdala influences all of these other brain sites is not yet completely understood, it is clear that it is a facilitator of a wide range of memory processes in a diverse set of brain areas.

Human Studies of Emotional Boosting of Memory Consolidation

While the rat studies of footshock avoidance allowed McGaugh and his colleagues to effectively dissect the neurochemistry of the memory consolidation process, the question was still open as to whether the same type of mechanism is at work in the more complex and varied process of human remembering. In collaboration with one of his graduate students, Larry Cahill, McGaugh devised a task for human use that replaced electric shocks and the injection of stimulant drugs with images and stories. Cahill and McGaugh (1995) adapted a task originally reported by Friderike Heuer and Daniel Reisberg (1990), which used stories accompanied by visual slide shows to manipulate the emotionality of the material to be recalled. Cahill and McGaugh's clever variant of the experimental task was to use the same set of 12 slides for both the emotional and the nonemotional stories. Both stories began the same way, with a boy and his mother on their way to the hospital where the boy's father worked. In the crucial middle section of the story, the "neutral" group heard an unexciting tale of the mother and son visiting the hospital to watch disaster-drill procedures. In the alternative "emotional" narrative, the same slides were accompanied by a much more traumatic story: The boy was critically injured in an accident and rushed to the hospital, where surgeons reattached his severed feet. Both stories ended the same way, with the mother going home alone and the boy staying in the hospital with his father. Two weeks later, the participants were tested on their memory of specific details of the visual slides that accompanied the narratives. The key finding was that the emotional group demonstrated enhanced memory for the middle sequence of slides, where the story became traumatic, whereas the neutral group showed no memory advantage for any part of the slide sequence. In the emotional narrative condition, it was as if the traumatic middle section had been marked by a mental highlighter. Cahill and McGaugh's study supports the view that emotion serves to accentuate salient events.

In subsequent studies, McGaugh and Cahill demonstrated that the amygdala is crucial for the emotional enhancement of memory in their story experiment. Patients with amygdala damage did not show any boosting of memory for the emotional middle of the story (Cahill, Babinsky, Markowitsch, & McGaugh, 1995). Further, when the researchers blocked the norepinephrine receptors of normal subjects with propranolol,[5] thus preventing enhancement of consolidation, their data looked just like that of the patients with amygdala damage: There was no enhancement of their memories of the emotional part of the story (McGaugh, 2003).

Adolphs, Tranel, and Buchanan (2005) conducted a similar study by presenting "intrinsically neutral" images and embedding them in either an emotional or a neutral story context by reading out different accompanying narratives. For example, one of the images was a simple shot of two people in a car; the neutral narrative was about a relaxing drive in the country, whereas the emotional narrative was that the couple's children had been

---

5. They did not have to inject propranolol directly into their human subjects' amygdalae! Propranolol crosses the blood-brain barrier, so it can be injected peripherally.

killed in a car crash and they were on their way to collect their remains. Thus, the neutral images became emotionally salient or not depending on the narrative context. A day after presenting the narrated images, Adolphs et al. assessed their participants' memory for two different aspects of the images: details that were central to the story, such as the main characters, and those that were irrelevant, such as the shape of the clouds. Consistent with Easterbrook's hypothesis that emotional arousal focuses processing resources on the most salient information, embedding the images in an emotional context had the effect of enhancing memory for their central but not their peripheral details. The researchers also tested patients with amygdala damage, including S. M., the person suffering from Urbach-Wiethe disease discussed in chapter 4, and found that for these people, embedding the images in an emotional narrative did not make the central details more memorable. They concluded that the amygdala is a necessary structure for the arousal-induced focusing of processing resources.

Neuroimaging studies have also implicated the amygdala in emotional processing that leads to the enhancement of memory. For example, Canli, Zhao, Brewer, Gabrieli, and Cahill (2000) used functional magnetic resonance imaging (fMRI) to measure the level of activity in the amygdala while participants rated the emotional intensity of negative and neutral pictures. Three weeks later, the participants were given a surprise recognition test where they were asked to distinguish previously seen pictures from new pictures. Pictures that were rated as more emotionally intense were better remembered than those with low ratings of emotional intensity. Further, for the most emotionally intense pictures, activity in the left amygdala at the time of encoding predicted subsequent memory. The images that generated more amygdala activity at the time of encoding were better remembered.

Florin Dolcos, Roberto Cabeza, and Kevin LaBar from Duke University furthered the neural investigation of the emotional enhancement of memory effect for human subjects in an fMRI study using negative, positive, and neutral IAPS (International Affective Picture Set) images. The ability to measure brain activity while human subjects were engaged in a memory task enabled them to devise a new measure of the neural basis of emotional memory enhancement. Dolcos, LaBar, and Cabeza (2004) developed the subsequent memory paradigm where brain activity during initial encoding is correlated with whether or not an item is subsequently remembered on a later test. Activity in the amygdala and medial temporal lobe memory system structures (MTL), including the hippocampus and surrounding cortex, was monitored while presenting the IAPS images, then separately computed for the images remembered and forgotten on a later cued-recall test. The difference in localized brain activity for remembered versus forgotten images yields a measure known as the Dm (difference due to memory). The researchers found that Dm was higher for emotional (both positive and negative) images than for neutral images in both the amygdala and MTL. Furthermore, activity in the amygdala and MTL was higher and more correlated with emotional images than neutral images, suggesting that it is the interactions between these regions that underlie the emotional memory enhancement effect.

In a follow-up study a year later, Dolcos, LaBar, and Cabeza (2005) gave 9 of their original 16 subjects a recognition test that mixed the IAPS images they had viewed in the original study with some foils that were not previously presented. Visual recognition memory is amazingly strong and enduring, something that had been documented by earlier memory researchers (e.g., Standing, 1973). Dolcos et al.'s participants correctly recognized over half of the emotional images that they had seen for only three seconds each a year earlier, whereas they recognized only about 33% of the neutral images. The Dm was significantly higher in the amygdala and MTL for the emotional than for the neutral images, indicating that even a whole year later, emotional enhancement of memory is subserved by coordinated activity in these brain regions.

The human studies accord well with the results of McGaugh's work on the consolidation of rats' memories of aversive experiences. Images that humans perceive as emotional are better retained over time, so are more successfully consolidated. The amygdala proves to be a crucial structure for the emotional enhancement of consolidation of memories in human as well as rat brains; for both, an emotional stimulus increases activity in the amygdala, leading to increased arousal and/or a stress response. The stress hormones, epinephrine and cortisol, play a key role in the enhancement of consolidation by enhancing the release of norepinephrine in the amygdala. The amygdala then facilitates consolidation of memory processes in a wide range of brain areas.

Retrieval

What about the third stage of memory processing—the retrieval of memories? Is retrieval affected by the emotional impact of the material or event to be remembered? This aspect of memory processing has been less intensively investigated, but there are some relevant human data on the effects of stress on retrieval. So far we have discussed the memory-enhancing effects of the emotional arousal that can result from stress, yet the common experience of mentally blanking during a high-pressure examination or interview, or forgetting essential items like keys when under a lot of stress, alerts us to the possibility of deleterious effects of stress on memory retrieval. An old theory based on avoidance learning experiments is often put forward to describe the relationship between arousal (particularly the negative arousal that arises from stress) and learning: the Yerkes-Dodson law. In a 1908 rat study, Robert Yerkes and John Dodson demonstrated that as they increased the level of footshock in an avoidance learning task, the rats initially became better at the task, but then reached a peak, after which increasing the strength of the shock proportionately impaired learning of the task.[6] The inverted-U-shape relationship that describes the effect of arousal on how well a task can be learned has been generalized to describe the effect of the level of arousal on how well the task will be remembered as well. Another way of characterizing this relationship is what Elizabeth's yoga teacher calls the Goldilocks principle—not too little, not too much—the amount of stress has to be "just right" for optimal memory. Throughout this chapter, we have been largely focused on the ascending limb of the inverted U-shape curve, where increasing arousal results in memory enhancement, but thinking about the memory impairments during stressful retrieval circumstances now draws our attention to the downside of the curve.

Another collaborator of McGaugh's, Benno Roozendaal, has shown that glucocorticoids can impair the retrieval of well-established memories (Roozendaal, 2002). This is in direct contrast to the enhancing role they play in memory consolidation processes. The researchers tested this effect using the Morris spatial location task mentioned above—finding a submerged platform in a water maze. Normally, rats showed clear evidence of recall when given a retrieval test on the day following training; however, if they were subjected to a stressful footshock 30 minutes before the test, retrieval of the memory of the maze was blocked. Further testing demonstrated that the memory was still there: If the retrieval test was delayed until four hours

---

6. D. M. Diamond, Campbell, Park, Halonen, and Zoladz (2007) pointed out that this is a simplification of Yerkes and Dodson's findings. If the learning task was easy, then increasing the level of footshock continued to improve performance on it; only when the task was more challenging did Yerkes and Dodson find the classic inverted-U-shape function.

after the shock, then the rats again demonstrated recall of the maze. Blocking corticosterone pharmacologically prevented the impairment of retrieval, demonstrating that glucocorticoids are an essential part of the mechanism. By injecting drugs that activate glucocorticoid receptors directly into the hippocampus and amygdala, Roozendaal and his collaborators were able to show that the hippocampus, but not the amygdala, is a crucial site for the retrieval impairment effects.

Roozendaal suggests that far from being contradictory, the amygdala-dependent memory consolidation enhancing effects and the hippocampal-dependent memory retrieval impairing effects are complementary parts of a synergistic process. During a stressful experience, the release of stress hormones and neurotransmitters activates the amygdala, switching the brain into a state where consolidation of new material is readily achieved. At the same time, retrieval of older information may be blocked to prevent it from interfering with the new learning. Thus, the retrieval impairment is recast as an adaptive process.

Human studies of recall under stressful conditions are generally in agreement with Roozendaal's theory. The majority of laboratory studies of memory retrieval under conditions of stress induced by the experimenters show that people are less able to recall previously learned information than control participants (Wolf, 2009). The stress-induced retrieval deficit occurs when the stress is induced psychologically using techniques such as the Trier social stress test (TSST), which involves challenges like public speaking and mental arithmetic in front of a panel of judges, and when physiological stress induction techniques such as hydrocortisone injections or exposure to painfully cold temperatures (cold pressor stress, or CPS) are used. The type of material studied makes a difference—the retrieval deficit is larger for emotional than for neutral material, and in fact some studies show no stress effect with the neutral material. Het, Ramlow, and Wolf's 2005 meta-analysis of 16 studies that involved cortisol administration showed that overall, cortisol significantly impaired retrieval. Interestingly, the natural diurnal variations in cortisol levels had an effect: Cortisol treatment in the morning, when cortisol levels are naturally higher, was consistently linked to significant retrieval deficits, whereas cortisol treatment in the afternoon, when natural levels are lower, actually resulted in a small but significant enhancement of retrieval. Oei et al. (2007) used fMRI to connect cortisol-induced retrieval deficits to reduced activity in the hippocampus and prefrontal cortex. The human and rodent studies both point to the importance of the effects of cortisol on the hippocampus during memory retrieval.

The human studies showing retrieval deficits under conditions of stress have important implications for educational testing. Variations in the location and time of day of testing and other factors that can influence cortisol levels could have substantial impacts on people's ability to recall previously learned information. It is also possible that stress can enhance people's ability to retrieve information in testing situations. Hupbach and Fieman (2012) recently reported an intriguing study of memory enhancement under conditions of moderate stress—but only for their male participants. They subjected people to painful cold stimulation for two minutes to induce stress, then immediately tested their recall of a neutral scientific prose passage they had attempted to memorize the previous day. All of their testing took place between 11 a.m. and 4:30 p.m. in order to avoid the natural periods of high and low cortisol. Only the male participants showed a significant increase in cortisol levels as a result of stress and recalled significantly more in the cold versus the warm water control condition. Hupbach and Fieman speculate that the lack of retrieval enhancement in their female participants could be due to the prevalence of oral contraceptive use in their sample; birth control pills elevate cortisol levels, so there could be a ceiling effect at play. The memory enhancement effect in males was contrary to Hupbach and Fieman's predictions, and they explain it in terms of an inverted-U-shape Yerkes-Dodson-like function: Very low and very high levels of cortisol impair retrieval, but moderate levels can have the reverse effect of increasing recall. This research adds to the argument that individuals' physiologies can interact with test-taking conditions in ways that create either systematic memory advantages or disadvantages, something that should be taken into consideration in educational settings.

Flashbulb Memories

Some memories are so highly emotional that they seem to be in a class of their own; as James observed, they seem to scar the brain. In the later 1970s, Harvard psychologists Roger Brown and James Kulik introduced the term "flashbulb memories" to describe this seemingly unique class of particularly intense emotional memories. Their observations of how well people recalled their own experiences of finding out about the shocking and highly consequential 1963 assassination of President John F. Kennedy prompted their investigations. In their seminal study, Brown and Kulik interviewed participants about their memories of hearing the news about JFK, plus the assassinations of Robert Kennedy, Martin Luther King, Malcolm X., and Medgar Evers; the attempted assassinations of George Wallace and Gerald Ford; and the death of Spanish dictator General Franco. Because the researchers suspected that the emotional significance of some of the events might vary between African-American and Caucasian-American groups, they collected data from 40 black and 40 white participants. Accounts were scored as flashbulb memories if their respondents claimed to remember their personal circumstances at the time they first learned about the event and their narrative contained information about one or more of the following six "canonical" categories of information: where they were, who informed them, what they were doing just beforehand, how they felt, how other people present felt, and the aftermath. Of course, many of the accounts contained more than one of these pieces of information. Only one of their 80 participants failed to have a flashbulb memory of Kennedy's assassination; the numbers were lower for the other events and tended to vary between the African-American and Caucasian-American groups.

Brown and Kulik argued for a special brain mechanism for flashbulb memories. They linked their findings to a speculative physiological theory devised in the late 1960s by Robert Livingston, with the evocative name "'Now Print." Livingston postulated that a loop from the reticular activating system[7] to the limbic system and back recognizes novelty and biological meaning, whereupon diffuse reticular projections[8] to the cortex issue a "Now print!" order to record the details of the event. Despite the fact that their own data demonstrated that there was not a full and literal recording of personal circumstances upon hearing of a shocking and consequential event, Brown and Kulik effectively put forward an *indelibility hypothesis* for a select class of memories.

The special status of flashbulb memories generated a lively debate in cognitive psychology. One of the major players, Ulric Neisser, a founding

---

7. *Reticular activating system* is an older term for the modulatory neurotransmitter systems in the brain stem which project through the thalamus to the cortex. It is involved in alertness and sleep-wake cycles.

8. This refers to what we now recognize as the locus coeruleus, which is the main noradrenaline input to the basolateral complex (BLA), as well as many cortical regions, that mediates brain arousal, so Livingston was referring to similar mechanisms to those more intensively studied later by McGaugh and colleagues.

cognitive psychologist, illustrated the issues with a personal example (well described in Fancher & Rutherford, 2011). Neisser had immigrated to the US from Germany with his parents as a young child, and he reported in his autobiography that his great enthusiasm for America's national pastime of baseball was an important part of "fitting in" in his new country. He vividly recalled being in his family's living room listening to a baseball game between the Giants and the Dodgers, and being shocked when the announcement about the bombing of Pearl Harbor broke into the game. It was only years later, after he had become a memory researcher, that Neisser realized the impossibility of this memory: Pearl Harbor was bombed on December 7, 1941, at a time of year well outside the baseball season (Neisser, 1982). Other psychologists were able to find a plausible explanation for Neisser's false flashbulb by discovering that a *football* game between the Giants and Dodgers was played on December 7, 1941 (Thompson & Cowan, 1986); Neisser's stronger personal identification with baseball made him misremember the sport. This category error provided a vivid anecdotal report of the fallibility of the supposedly indelible flashbulbs.

When the Challenger shuttle exploded on January 28, 1986, Neisser and his collaborator Nicole Harsch realized that they had the opportunity to collect systematic data to address the malleability of flashbulbs. Working quickly, they devised a questionnaire and administered it to their class at Emory University the next morning, asking them to recount where they were, what they were doing, how they found out, the time of day, and whether there were others present when they heard the news. Two and a half years later, Neisser and Harsch were able to contact 44 of the original 106 participants to ask them the same questions. Only 3 participants showed complete consistency between the two accounts, while 11 of the 44 were completely discrepant. Overall, the consistency ratings between the first and second survey averaged only 42%. The types of errors that their participants made were reminiscent of Neisser's baseball/football "time-slice" error, where events that occurred at two distinct points in time are confused at the time of remembering. For example, a number of their participants exhibited a phenomenon that they labeled "TV priority"; although only 21% initially reported hearing the news on television, two and a half years later, 45% believed that they first heard of the disaster from a television report. As Daniel Schacter (1996) pointed out in his lucid review of flashbulb memory studies, this is a form of source amnesia. Clearly, flashbulb memories were not fixed at the time of the precipitating event but were affected by later experience, such as watching news coverage on TV.

One criticism of Neisser and Harsch's study was that while the Challenger explosion was tragic and shocking, it did not have the same long-term national consequentiality as the JFK assassination. When the September 11 attacks on the World Trade Center and the Pentagon happened in 2001, many psychologists realized that they were in the midst of a powerful flashbulb-producing event. Mobilizing quickly, a large group of researchers pooled their talents to form the 9/11 Memory Consortium with the aim of conducting an extensive national interview study (Hirst et al., 2009). Hirst et al. employed the same test-retest methodology as Neisser and Harsch, but increased the frequency of retests, collecting data at 1-week, 11-month, and 35-month retention intervals. They produced the largest-scale flashbulb memory study to date, with over 2,000 respondents and complete three-survey data for 391 participants. Hirst and colleagues have recently completed their analysis of a further 10-year follow-up that is about to be published.

Eleven months after the attacks, the average overall consistency was 63%, two years later the consistency dropped only slightly to 57%, and, notably, almost ten years later it was still around 60% (Hirst et al., 2009; Hirst et al., 2014). These consistency ratings are substantially higher than Neisser and Harsch's finding of 42% after two and a half years, plus the much smaller drop in consistency at the later retest times indicates that such memories are more stable after the first year. In fact, Hirst et al. (2014) liken flashbulb memories to the "permastore" concept introduced by Harry Bahrick for semantic memories (Bahrick, 1984, see Box 8.1 for the definition of semantic memory). Collective remembering processes could have contributed to increased memorability of personal circumstances when hearing of 9/11 in comparison to the Challenger: The events of 9/11 and their aftermath have received much more media attention, providing more occasions for the reinstatement of memories of personal circumstances. Also, the participants in Hirst and colleagues' work had more opportunities to consolidate their memories as a result of the study itself with four recalls, rather than only two for Neisser and Harsch's participants.

Another major factor that emerges when considering the 9/11 studies is the role of personal experience. A large percentage of Hirst et al.'s participants were categorized as experiencing personal loss or inconvenience—40.4%. There is a major difference between hearing about a national tragedy and actually being there. This discrepancy had already been noted by Neisser and colleagues in their reporting of the results of a study of flashbulb memories of the 1989 Loma Prieta earthquake in California (Neisser et al., 1996). Their respondents in Santa Cruz and Berkeley who felt the effects of the earthquake had much higher consistency ratings (99% and 96%) over a period of a year and a half than their respondents in Atlanta, whose consistency ratings were only 55%. Hirst et al. (2009, 2014) found that their measure of personal loss did not relate to the consistency of the flashbulb memories, but it did affect the accuracy for memory of the details of the 9/11 events themselves and the participants' motivation to complete later surveys.

A neuroimaging study by Elizabeth Phelps and colleagues comparing New Yorkers' memories of 9/11 with autobiographical memories from the summer before sheds more light on the brain mechanisms involved (Sharot, Martorella, Delgado, & Phelps, 2007). Three years after the 9/11 attacks, Phelps and colleagues asked people who had been in Manhattan that day to remember either events of 9/11 or events from the summer months before in response to 60 cue words,[9] as they monitored their brain activity. The researchers compared the level of activity in the amygdala for the two conditions, September and summer, for two groups of participants—those who had been closer to the World Trade Center, the Downtown group, and those who had been further away in Midtown. Activation of the left amygdala was greater during the 9/11 trials than it was during the summer trials for the Downtown group, but not for the Midtown group. Participants' ratings of their feelings about the memories were consistent with this finding; the Downtown group also gave higher ratings of the power and negativity of their experiences.

Note that nothing can be said about the accuracy or consistency of the recall of the participants in Sharot et al.'s neuroimaging study, since those were not measured. Instead, the researchers' focus was on the subjective quality and strength of recall that result from emotional highlighting of memory. In an earlier study, Sharot, Delgado, and Phelps (2004) studied

---

9. Examples of the cue words are *family, transportation, thought,* and *New York City.* All of the cue words are listed at www.pnas.org/cgi/content/full/0609230103/DC1.

brain responses to emotional and neutral images using the know/remember task. In this experimental paradigm, participants are asked to judge whether they "remember" the particular time when a previously presented image was shown, or if it is simply familiar or "known" to them without their being able to remember the context of presentation; the remember/know distinction is related to the semantic/episodic distinction described in Box 8.1—in the "remember" case, the episode of that particular stimulus presentation is recalled. The researchers found that emotional images were much more likely to be "remembered" the next day, rather than just seeming familiar or "known." In contrast, neutral images were equally likely to be designated "remembered" and "known." Brain activation corresponded to the differences between emotional and neutral images. The right amygdala was more active when participants "remembered" the emotional images than when they "remembered" the neutral ones, and it showed the opposite pattern for "know" responses. Sharot et al. speculated that the enhanced amygdala activity was related to a greater sense of arousal and perceptual fluency that resulted in an increased feeling of remembering an emotional event.

Indeed, it seems to be the experience of remembering—people's confidence in their flashbulb memories and their high ratings of believability—that distinguish flashbulbs from other memories. The 9/11 Memory Consortium found that recall of the details of flashbulbs was not always accurate, as had been found in some earlier studies as well; nevertheless, their participants rated their confidence in their memories very highly at all of the testing times. Another study by a separate group compared individuals' recall of 9/11 memories with control memories of "everyday" events from anytime in the three days leading up to September 11 (Talarico & Rubin, 2003). Everyday and 9/11 memories showed a very similar decline in consistency over time. The difference lay in the feeling of belief, or conviction about the memory's veracity, that the participants attributed to the two types of memory. Their ratings of belief dropped substantially for the everyday memories at the later testing times, but the believability of their 9/11 memories remained high at all of the testing intervals.

Why do accuracy and confidence differ, and what does this mean for the function of declarative memories of events and their emotional enhancement? Perhaps the focus on accuracy and indelibility engendered by the flashbulb metaphor has led researchers astray. It is counter to a view of memory as dynamic and constructive that has a long experimental history.

Frederic Bartlett's[10] well-known early studies of repeated reproduction of folktales led to his characterization of memory as constructive, schema driven, and motivated by people's interests and habits (Bartlett, 1932/1995). He described the constructive nature of memory as follows:

> Remembering is not the re-excitation of innumerable, fixed, lifeless and fragmentary traces. It is an imaginative reconstruction, or construction, built out of the relation of our attitude towards a whole active mass of organized past reactions or experiences, and to a little outstanding detail which commonly appears in image or language terms. It is thus hardly ever really exact, even in the most rudimentary cases of rote recapitulation, and it is not at all important that it should be so. (1932, p. 213)

Bartlett's insight that accuracy is not the most important aspect of remembering is confirmed by Phelps and Sharot's (2008) functional account of emotionally enhanced memory. Bartlett, Phelps, and Sharot agree that the function of memory, even highly emotional memory, is not to record every detail of an experience in a "Now print" manner; that level of detail is just not needed to make use of past experience in the future. Instead, emotional highlighting provides a means of picking out the important aspects of an experience to hold onto because they could prove important for future survival. Phelps and Sharot propose that the enhancement of the subjective sense of recollection brought about by strong emotional arousal aids in the speed and clarity of decision-making. When we are very confident in our memories because of a strong sense of recollection, then we act quickly rather than taking extra time to search further through our memory. The subjective power of memories of highly emotional events—their "time travel" quality—also has an impact on their ability to evoke emotions when they are recalled later. The believability of the imagery, particularly visual imagery, is connected to the emotional impact of remembering.

The Default Mode Network and Autobiographical Recall

The linkage of autobiographical remembering with other aspects of mental function, such as prospection or future planning and imagination, has

---

10. Sir Frederic Charles Bartlett (1886–1969) was the first professor of experimental psychology at Cambridge University in England. His 1932 text *Remembering: A Study in Experimental and Social Psychology* was highly influential.

recently cohered in a newly discovered brain system called the default mode network (DMN). The "mental time travel" described by Tulving and his colleagues has been linked to a set of brain regions that seem to become active by default when the brain is not otherwise engaged in externally oriented tasks. Just as with Olds and Milner's fortuitous discovery of the reward system, the discovery of the DMN was an accidental by-product of studies designed for other purposes. Neuroimaging researchers realized that the brain was highly active during the so-called rest periods between assigned tasks, and, even further, that some brain areas actually became *less* rather than more active when engaged in externally oriented experimenter-defined activities.

These areas in the medial prefrontal cortex (both ventral and dorsal)—the posterior cingulate and retrosplenial cortex behind it, the inferior parietal lobule, the lateral temporal cortex, and the hippocampal formation—have been shown to be tightly interconnected and coactivated in a wide variety of tasks in meta-analytic studies (Gusnard, Akbudak, Shulman, & Raichle, 2001; Raichle, MacLeod, Snyder, Powers, & Gusnard, 2001; Shulman et al., 1997; Spreng, Mar, & Kim, 2009). Brain activity patterns when engaged in reminiscing about the personal past turn out to overlap extensively with characteristic patterns of activity in other sorts of tasks, like the mind reading involved in theory of mind tasks asking participants to take other people's perspectives, contemplating possible happenings in the personal future, solving moral conundrums, and imagining navigating familiar environments. Thinking about what links these diverse tasks led to a reconception of autobiographical memory as part of a larger set of mental simulation processes that activate the DMN. As Buckner, Andrews-Hanna, and Schacter state in their comprehensive 2008 review, an important function of "the default mode network is to facilitate flexible, self-relevant mental exploration—simulations—that provide a means to anticipate and evaluate upcoming events before they happen" (p. 2). These "simulations" or "self-projections" (Buckner & Carroll, 2008) that encompass autobiographical remembering and future planning are a crucial part of emotional life, enabling us to more flexibly respond to and contemplate situations that arise in our everyday lives. As memory researchers Daniel Schacter and Donna Rose Addis (2007) point out, this view of episodic memory (see Box 8.1) as only one of the outputs of a simulation system that is also active in future thinking, helps make more sense of its constructive rather than literal nature. Occasional errors in autobiographical remembering are part and parcel of the adaptive recently cohered in a newly discovered brain system called the default mode network (DMN). The "mental time travel" described by Tulving and his colleagues has been linked to a set of brain regions that seem to become active by default when the brain is not otherwise engaged in externally oriented tasks. Just as with Olds and Milner's fortuitous discovery of the reward system, the discovery of the DMN was an accidental by-product of studies designed for other purposes. Neuroimaging researchers realized that the brain was highly active during the so-called rest periods between assigned tasks, and, even further, that some brain areas actually became *less* rather than more active when engaged in externally oriented experimenter-defined activities.

These areas in the medial prefrontal cortex (both ventral and dorsal)—the posterior cingulate and retrosplenial cortex behind it, the inferior parietal lobule, the lateral temporal cortex, and the hippocampal formation—have been shown to be tightly interconnected and coactivated in a wide variety of tasks in meta-analytic studies (Gusnard, Akbudak, Shulman, & Raichle, 2001; Raichle, MacLeod, Snyder, Powers, & Gusnard, 2001; Shulman et al., 1997; Spreng, Mar, & Kim, 2009). Brain activity patterns when engaged in reminiscing about the personal past turn out to overlap extensively with characteristic patterns of activity in other sorts of tasks, like the mind reading involved in theory of mind tasks asking participants to take other people's perspectives, contemplating possible happenings in the personal future, solving moral conundrums, and imagining navigating familiar environments. Thinking about what links these diverse tasks led to a reconception of autobiographical memory as part of a larger set of mental simulation processes that activate the DMN. As Buckner, Andrews-Hanna, and Schacter state in their comprehensive 2008 review, an important function of "the default mode network is to facilitate flexible, self-relevant mental exploration—simulations—that provide a means to anticipate and evaluate upcoming events before they happen" (p. 2). These "simulations" or "self-projections" (Buckner & Carroll, 2008) that encompass autobiographical remembering and future planning are a crucial part of emotional life, enabling us to more flexibly respond to and contemplate situations that arise in our everyday lives. As memory researchers Daniel Schacter and Donna Rose Addis (2007) point out, this view of episodic memory (see Box 8.1) as only one of the outputs of a simulation system that is also active in future thinking, helps make more sense of its constructive rather than literal nature. Occasional errors in autobiographical remembering are part and parcel of the adaptive

pants were categorized as experiencing personal loss or inconvenience—40.4%. There is a major difference between hearing about a national tragedy and actually being there. This discrepancy had already been noted by Neisser and colleagues in their reporting of the results of a study of flashbulb memories of the 1989 Loma Prieta earthquake in California (Neisser et al., 1996). Their respondents in Santa Cruz and Berkeley who felt the effects of the earthquake had much higher consistency ratings (99% and 96%) over a period of a year and a half than their respondents in Atlanta, whose consistency ratings were only 55%. Hirst et al. (2009, 2014) found that their measure of personal loss did not relate to the consistency of the flashbulb memories, but it did affect the accuracy for memory of the details of the 9/11 events themselves and the participants' motivation to complete later surveys.

A neuroimaging study by Elizabeth Phelps and colleagues comparing New Yorkers' memories of 9/11 with autobiographical memories from the summer before sheds more light on the brain mechanisms involved (Sharot, Martorella, Delgado, & Phelps, 2007). Three years after the 9/11 attacks, Phelps and colleagues asked people who had been in Manhattan that day to remember either events of 9/11 or events from the summer months before in response to 60 cue words,[9] as they monitored their brain activity. The researchers compared the level of activity in the amygdala for the two conditions, September and summer, for two groups of participants—those who had been closer to the World Trade Center, the Downtown group, and those who had been further away in Midtown. Activation of the left amygdala was greater during the 9/11 trials than it was during the summer trials for the Downtown group, but not for the Midtown group. Participants' ratings of their feelings about the memories were consistent with this finding; the Downtown group also gave higher ratings of the power and negativity of their experiences.

Note that nothing can be said about the accuracy or consistency of the recall of the participants in Sharot et al.'s neuroimaging study, since those were not measured. Instead, the researchers' focus was on the subjective quality and strength of recall that result from emotional highlighting of memory. In an earlier study, Sharot, Delgado, and Phelps (2004) studied

---

9. Examples of the cue words are *family, transportation, thought,* and *New York City.* All of the cue words are listed at www.pnas.org/cgi/content/full/0609230103/DC1.

brain responses to emotional and neutral images using the know/remember task. In this experimental paradigm, participants are asked to judge whether they "remember" the particular time when a previously presented image was shown, or if it is simply familiar or "known" to them without their being able to remember the context of presentation; the remember/ know distinction is related to the semantic/episodic distinction described in Box 8.1—in the "remember" case, the episode of that particular stimulus presentation is recalled. The researchers found that emotional images were much more likely to be "remembered" the next day, rather than just seeming familiar or "known." In contrast, neutral images were equally likely to be designated "remembered" and "known." Brain activation corresponded to the differences between emotional and neutral images. The right amygdala was more active when participants "remembered" the emotional images than when they "remembered" the neutral ones, and it showed the opposite pattern for "know" responses. Sharot et al. speculated that the enhanced amygdala activity was related to a greater sense of arousal and perceptual fluency that resulted in an increased feeling of remembering an emotional event.

Indeed, it seems to be the experience of remembering—people's confidence in their flashbulb memories and their high ratings of believability —that distinguish flashbulbs from other memories. The 9/11 Memory Consortium found that recall of the details of flashbulbs was not always accurate, as had been found in some earlier studies as well; nevertheless, their participants rated their confidence in their memories very highly at all of the testing times. Another study by a separate group compared individuals' recall of 9/11 memories with control memories of "everyday" events from anytime in the three days leading up to September 11 (Talarico & Rubin, 2003). Everyday and 9/11 memories showed a very similar decline in consistency over time. The difference lay in the feeling of belief, or conviction about the memory's veracity, that the participants attributed to the two types of memory. Their ratings of belief dropped substantially for the everyday memories at the later testing times, but the believability of their 9/11 memories remained high at all of the testing intervals.

Why do accuracy and confidence differ, and what does this mean for the function of declarative memories of events and their emotional enhancement? Perhaps the focus on accuracy and indelibility engendered by the flashbulb metaphor has led researchers astray. It is counter to a view of memory as dynamic and constructive that has a long experimental history.

Frederic Bartlett's[10] well-known early studies of repeated reprodu[c]e folktales led to his characterization of memory as constructive, driven, and motivated by people's interests and habits (Bartlett, 1932 He described the constructive nature of memory as follows:

> Remembering is not the re-excitation of innumerable, fixed, lifeless [and] fragmentary traces. It is an imaginative reconstruction, or construct[ion] built out of the relation of our attitude towards a whole active mas[s of] organized past reactions or experiences, and to a little outstanding de[tail] which commonly appears in image or language terms. It is thus har[dly] ever really exact, even in the most rudimentary cases of rote recapitu[la]tion, and it is not at all important that it should be so. (1932, p. 213)

Bartlett's insight that accuracy is not the most important aspect of r[emem]bering is confirmed by Phelps and Sharot's (2008) functional acc[ount of] emotionally enhanced memory. Bartlett, Phelps, and Sharot agree th[at the] function of memory, even highly emotional memory, is not to recor[d the] detail of an experience in a "Now print" manner; that level of detail [is] not needed to make use of past experience in the future. Instead, emo[tional] highlighting provides a means of picking out the important aspects [of an] experience to hold onto because they could prove important for futu[re sur]vival. Phelps and Sharot propose that the enhancement of the subj[ective] sense of recollection brought about by strong emotional arousal aids [the] speed and clarity of decision-making. When we are very confident [in our] memories because of a strong sense of recollection, then we act q[uickly] rather than taking extra time to search further through our memor[ies. The] subjective power of memories of highly emotional events—their ["time] travel" quality—also has an impact on their ability to evoke emotions [when] they are recalled later. The believability of the imagery, particularly [visual] imagery, is connected to the emotional impact of remembering.

The Default Mode Network and Autobiographical Recall

The linkage of autobiographical remembering with other aspects of m[ental] function, such as prospection or future planning and imagination[is]

---

10. Sir Frederic Charles Bartlett (1886–1969) was the first professor of experimental ps[ychol]ogy at Cambridge University in England. His 1932 text *Remembering: A Study in Experi[mental] and Social Psychology* was highly influential.

system that helps us navigate the complex social world and manage our emotional reactions to what arises.

Posttraumatic Stress Disorder: A Malady of Memory

With PTSD, the stress-induced memory impairment is troublesome and extreme, and as we discussed in chapter 4 it can be difficult to treat. PTSD is a chronic response to a traumatic event that is characterized by a triad of symptoms: (a) flashbacks of the traumatic event, (b) avoidance of situations associated with the trauma, and (c) hyperarousal. People who suffer from PTSD are plagued with recurring memories of the originating traumatic event that are easily triggered. These vivid memories often seem so real that people feel as though they are reexperiencing the trauma. The stress induced by the recurring traumatic memories severely interferes with the retrieval of other non-trauma-related information. A hyperactivation of automatically retrieved, disturbing, and often fragmented memories is paired with memory difficulties for ongoing events in everyday life and an inability to remember other autobiographical events in a specific and detailed way (Kuyken & Brewin, 1995; Williams et al., 2007). A person suffering from PTSD often feels stuck in the past, unable to control the recurrence of the traumatic memories.

The Amygdalocentric Neurocircuitry Model of PTSD

The neural model that we briefly described in chapter 4 attributes the pattern of memory impairments and activation seen in PTSD to the differential effects of traumatic stress on three brain structures that we have already discussed at some length: the amygdala, the hippocampus, and the ventromedial prefrontal cortex (vmPFC). The amygdala is thought to be highly activated, accounting for the heightened emotionality and hyperarousal experienced by PTSD sufferers. In contrast, the hippocampus, a structure that we have seen to be crucial for consolidating declarative memories, is underactive, which could be a factor in difficulties with forming new specific memories.[11] In addition, the hippocampus can inhibit the amygdala, so

---

11. However, Patel, Spreng, Shin, and Girard (2012) found *hyper*activity of the right hippocampus in their more recent meta-analytic study of PTSD neuroimaging work, which they suggest could contribute to the intrusive nature of 'flashback' traumatic memories.

hippocampal down-regulation could result in up-regulation of amygdala activity. The vmPFC is also less active and therefore less able to inhibit the overactive amygdala, accounting for the hyperreactivity to any reminders of the traumatic event. Neuroimaging studies of PTSD patients whose brains are scanned after a reminder of the traumatic event confirm this pattern: increased amygdala activity, decreased hippocampal activity, and lower vmPFC response (Rauch, Shin, & Phelps, 2006, but see Patel et al. (2012) for a different view of hippocampal involvement).

Studies with rodents have been able to document structural changes in neurons that account for the increased amygdala activity in response to stress. When rats are exposed to stressful experiences like inescapable foot-shocks or long periods of immobilization, dendrites proliferate on BLA neurons and the density of their spines increases (Roozendaal, McEwen, & Chattarji, 2009). These neuronal changes are correlated with increases in anxiety like behaviors, such as avoiding the open arms of a maze, and only forms of stress that trigger dendrite growth result in greater anxiety behavior. Chronic treatment with glucocorticoids leads to the same changes in dendrites of BLA neurons. Stress has the effect of making the amygdala hyperresponsive.

The rodent work on extinction discussed in chapter 4 is relevant to the out-of-control amygdala hypothesis. There we noted that the vmPFC is vital for the new learning involved in extinguishing fear responses that are no longer relevant and useful. The flashbacks of PTSD are in dire need of extinction, a process that depends on a fully functional vmPFC. The activation of vmPFC is correlated with the magnitude of extinction recall in healthy humans (Phelps, Delgado, Nearing, & LeDoux, 2004). The up-regulation of the amygdala paired with the down-regulation of the vmPFC tips the balance away from the new learning that puts the brakes on the no-longer-appropriate fear response of PTSD.

What role does the hippocampus play in these interactions? The vmPFC is not the only area that down-regulates amygdala activity; one of the functions of the hippocampus is to regulate the stress system by inhibiting amygdala output. In addition, the hippocampus responds to increases in glucocorticoids by inhibiting the HPA axis, which in turn down-regulates the amygdala (see Box 4.1 for more details). Thus, damage to the hippocampus may result in hyperactivity of the amygdala, amplifying the stress response. Recall the unfortunate H. M. who was unable to form new memories but could retrieve much older ones. In PTSD patients, the hippocampus is not absent as it was for H. M., but there is evidence of significant damage to it. Structural imaging studies using MRI technology have documented reduced hippocampal volume in PTSD patients in comparison to trauma-exposed people who did not develop PTSD (Bremner et al., 1995, 1997, 2003a; Gurvits et al., 1996). A few groups have failed to replicate this finding, but a meta-analysis of all published studies concluded that adults with PTSD have significantly smaller hippocampi than comparison groups (Kitayama, Vaccarino, Kutner, Weiss, & Bremner, 2005). In an elegant twin study with Vietnam veterans, Gilbertson et al. (2002) found that the non-combat-exposed monozygotic twins of veterans with PTSD also had smaller hippocampi. Nonetheless, work by Rockefeller University researcher Bruce McEwen has shown that chronic stress is damaging to the hippocampus. This suggests that smaller initial hippocampal volume was an underlying risk factor that made some soldiers' hippocampi more vulnerable to the damages wrought by stress.

McEwen's Studies of the Effects of Chronic Stress on the Hippocampus

To create stress in their rats, McEwen and his colleagues restrained them so that they could not move for long periods of time, as much as six hours a day. When this restraint stress was repeated daily for three weeks, it had deleterious effects on spatial memory, a function that requires the hippocampus. They measured the memory impact using a radial arm maze with food rewards placed at the end of each of the eight arms. This task was challenging because the rats had only eight minutes to collect all of the food. The rats exposed to repeated stress had more difficulty remembering which arms of the maze they had already visited to collect their peanut reward and thus wasted time running down the arms they had already emptied (Luine, Villegas, Martinez, & McEwen, 1994). In PTSD, the stress is also chronically repeated because flashbacks constantly recreate the traumatic experience, and this chronic stress could impact memory in similar ways.

McEwen and his research group have made a lot of headway in documenting the physiological changes in the hippocampus that bring about the chronically stressed rats' memory difficulties. Both the stress induced behaviorally by restraint and the pharmacological mimicking of its effects by the injection of glucocorticoids result in changes in the structure of neurons in the hippocampus. The dendrites in a region of the hippocampus called CA3 shrink; neurogenesis, the growth of new neurons, is curtailed;

and cell death can occur (McEwen, 2000). Chronic stress—through restraint or injection of glucocorticoids—has also been shown to disrupt a process known as long-term potentiation that is thought to be the basis of memory formation in the hippocampus. Brief episodes of stress can be arousing and thus aid memory, but extended periods of stress actually bring about structural changes in the brain that impair memory.

The hippocampal damage could underlie many of the memory deficits seen in PTSD. Patients report a variety of difficulties with memory for ongoing events in their lives—difficulties in recalling information they need, and trouble forming coherent autobiographical memories that are not related to their trauma. Behavioral tests confirm that PTSD sufferers have deficits in a range of memory tasks, and neuroimaging studies relate these memory difficulties to reduced activity in the hippocampus. For example, Douglas Bremner and colleagues at Emory University School of Medicine found reduced blood flow in the hippocampus (and other areas) of abuse survivors with PTSD compared to controls who did not suffer from abuse or PTSD while they were performing memory tasks with narrative passages and pairs of emotional words (Bremner et al., 2003a, 2003b).

Distinguishing between Flashbulbs and Flashbacks

The flashbacks of PTSD seem to be an excess of memory, a hypermnesia, rather than memory failure. How does this relate to the hippocampal damage and impairments of memory? A closer consideration of the nature of these memories reveals that there is a striking difference between the stress-enhanced flashbulb memories of circumstances of hearing tragic news and the fragmented flashbacks of PTSD. Flashbulbs possess narrative coherence; they are stories that people often want to tell that allow them to place themselves in the context of larger, historically significant events. The types of distortion that arise in accounts of flashbulb memories are often in the service of producing coherent, believable stories. In contrast, PTSD flashbacks are often confused, piecemeal, and profoundly sensory in nature; they involve a reexperiencing of horrific sights, sounds, and smells. They are especially difficult to integrate with the person's life story prior to the trauma and very disruptive to an integrated autobiographical narrative (Dalgleish, Hauer, & Kuyken, 2008). Hippocampal damage could contribute to the often nonverbal, only partly explicit, nature of flashbacks. Part of the task of therapy for PTSD, particularly cognitive therapy, is to consciously remember the traumatic event in a controlled rather than automatic and disruptive way. Further work is then needed to integrate the traumatic memories in the hope of loosening their grip on the patient's ongoing experience.

Plasticity and Potential Treatments for PTSD

A vital aspect of McEwen's group's findings is that the effect of stress on memory does not last forever. Their rats were impaired on the maze task if they were tested the day after the restraint stress stopped, but not if the researchers waited 18 days, indicating that the brain changes that result from stress can be reversed—that there is some degree of plasticity. A neuroimaging study by Bremner's group suggests that human hippocampal damage resulting from PTSD can also be reversed to some extent. Vermetten, Vythilingam, Southwick, Charney, and Bremner (2003) studied a group of patients with PTSD arising from a variety of causes who were participating in a drug trial for the SSRI antidepressant paroxetine (Paxil). At the end of the 9 to 12 months of treatment, their hippocampal volume had increased by an average of 4.6%. This possible effect of Paxil on PTSD patients' hippocampal volume is consistent with earlier studies showing that a number of different types of antidepressants may increase the growth of new neurons in the hippocampus of rats (e.g., Duman, Nakagawa, & Malberg, 2001). The PTSD patients' scores on verbal declarative memory tests also substantially improved, confirming the linkage between hippocampal damage and memory impairment in PTSD.

One of the chief tasks facing clinicians treating PTSD is to find a way to change the person's relationship to the traumatic memory in order to prevent it from constantly intruding and taking over awareness in a reexperiencing fashion. Some recent rodent work that came out of Joseph LeDoux's lab provided a surprising new clue to a means of altering established fear memories.

Reconsolidation

One of LeDoux's postdoctoral researchers, Karim Nader, came to him with an idea about altering fear memories that have already been consolidated. As we discussed in chapter 4, LeDoux believed that fear-conditioned memories are permanent. Nader suggested instead that the fear memory could be altered if it was recalled under conditions that make consolidation itself less likely. Schafe and LeDoux (2000) had already demonstrated that they could prevent fear conditioning from being established in the first place by injecting the rat's amygdala with a drug that blocks the synthesis of proteins. It had previously been discovered that long-term, but not short-term, memory depends on the synthesis of new proteins, presumably because proteins are needed to construct the cellular changes required for long-term memory. Nader proposed that he could go a step further and erase an already established fear memory by administering protein synthesis blockers at the same time as triggering the memory. To LeDoux's amazement, Nader's experiment worked: When he simultaneously injected protein synthesis blockers and played the tone to reevoke the fear memory established the day before, the rats did not freeze (Nader, 2003; Nader & Einarsson, 2010; Nader, Schafe, & LeDoux, 2000). The fact that memories can be removed at the time of reconsolidation means that they are much more labile than neuroscientists previously thought: Consolidated fear memories are not unalterable. Instead, they revert to the instability that characterized the consolidation phase of new learning studied by McGaugh.

Nader has uncovered a means of erasing fear memories in rats, but his studies cannot be repeated exactly in humans because it would be dangerous to give humans protein synthesis blockers. It was possible, however, to put together Nader's insight about the malleability of established memories at the time of recall with McGaugh and Cahill's pharmacological technique for manipulating human emotional memory. As described above, Cahill and McGaugh (1995) demonstrated that giving humans the beta-blocker propranolol could prevent the enhancement of emotional memories. Nader and his new collaborator at McGill University, psychiatric researcher Alain Brunet, reasoned that giving propranolol at the time of recall could open up the possibility of transforming the overlearned traumatic memory when it is reconsolidated, thereby providing a "window of opportunity" for change. They joined forces with Harvard Medical School psychiatrist Roger Pitman, who had already demonstrated that crash victims treated with propranolol within the six hours following the accident are significantly less likely to develop PTSD (Pitman et al., 2002). In Nader, Brunet, Pitman, and coworkers' collaboration, 19 patients with chronic PTSD participated in a new study of the effects of propranolol on much later recall of the traumatic event (Brunet et al., 2008). Patients were given either propranolol or a look-alike placebo and asked to recall the traumatic event in writing. One week later, the experimenters read them a short "script" portraying their traumatic experiences while monitoring their physiological responses. The patients given propranolol at the time of the initial recall session had significantly lower heart rates and skin conductance responses during the second session than those given a placebo. Brunet et al. argued that these reduced responses during subsequent recall in the propranolol group show that the drug affected the reconsolidation of the traumatic memory. The effectiveness of propranolol in this small research study holds out the promise of using it as a therapeutic tool by incorporating it into other methods of treatment.

Brunet and his colleagues continued their study of the effects of propranolol on the severity of PTSD symptoms by having patients recall their trauma after taking beta-blockers in six separate sessions (Brunet et al., 2011). Some of their patients reported that the course of treatment enabled them to live more comfortably with their traumatic memories, not by forgetting them, but by reducing their emotional impact. As we saw earlier in our chapter 4 discussion of LeDoux's studies of fear conditioning, the capacity to separate emotional aspects of the memory from the facts of what happened is a key insight into the organization of memory in the brain. Memories are not unitary and unchangeable packages that can be retrieved only as intact bundles; rather, the process of remembering has many components that are normally integrated but can be teased apart. The emotional response to the memory can be altered while other aspects of it are retained. Yet, the multiplicity of memory also means that there is no simple solution for the memory problems of PTSD. Despite fictional variants of Nader's idea of fear erasure—such as the movie *Eternal Sunshine of the Spotless Mind*, where memories are wiped wholesale from characters' minds—the notion of being able to extract a whole traumatic memory is not tenable given the complex and distributed nature of brain processes involved in memory. A specific memory of fear may be altered by reconsolidation processes, but many other aspects of the experience are retained in explicit memory and can restart the cycle of memories evoking emotional arousal, which in turn enhances those memories until they are an overwhelming presence in the person's life. More is involved in regulation of the emotions evoked by memories of trauma than inhibiting a specific fear memory, yet it gives an entry into altering those processes that can be built upon in therapy.

Behavioral Modifications of Memory

Other work by Israeli scientist Daniela Schiller, now at the Mount Sinai School of Medicine in New York, explores a means of altering traumatic memories that also has clinical implications but does not rely on pharmacological interventions. When Schiller moved from Israel to New York University, she had initially intended to study memory alteration during reconsolidation in humans using propranolol, but was waiting for permission to conduct such a study (Specter, 2014). In the interim, a chance remark about behavioral modifications of fear conditioning in rats by her colleague Marie Monfils led Schiller to an "aha!" moment: Behavioral means of opening the window of opportunity on memory during reconsolidation had never been tested. Monfils ran the experiment with rats (Monfils, Cowansage, Klann, & LeDoux, 2009) while Schiller conducted a study with humans (Schiller et al., 2010). Their findings were remarkable and have generated a lot of interest and controversy.

Recall from our discussion in chapter 4 that conditioned fears can be extinguished by repeatedly presenting the conditioned stimulus (e.g., a tone) without the unconditioned stimulus (e.g., a shock), but that this new extinction learning does not erase the original fear conditioning, which is apt to reassert itself in other contexts, particularly when the individual is under stress. Schiller and Monfils' clever variation on this experimental protocol was to introduce a reminder of the fear conditioning prior to extinction training. In Schiller's human studies, she achieved this with a single presentation of a colored square (the unconditioned stimulus) in order to reactivate the fear memory and potentially make it open to change during reconsolidation. Schiller and colleagues found that if the extinction training was carried out within 10 minutes of the reminder, then the fear response (measured using skin conductance responses) did not spontaneously recur the next day. However, if they waited six hours after the reminder or never gave a reminder before extinction training, the fear response returned the next day. Monfils et al. (2009) reported the same finding with rats, although Chan, Leung, Westbrook, and McNally (2010) reported that they could not replicate the rat study.

The impact of a carefully timed reminder before extinction on the longevity of the effects of the training is a stunning result. Schiller and colleagues retested their participants one year later and found that those in the 10-minute group still retained their extinction training; timing the extinction training to take place within the reconsolidation window after a reminder led to long-lasting changes. In a later fMRI study, Schiller, Kanen, LeDoux, Monfils, and Phelps (2013) found that the extinction training conducted during the reconsolidation period seems to use different brain mechanisms than the usual process of extinction. VmPFC activity during extinction training increased in the nonreminded group, and was strongly coupled with amygdala activity, while that in the reminded group did not. Schiller et al. (2013) suggest that during reconsolidation, extinction actually changes the amygdala's representation of the fear memory rather than only temporarily dampening the amygdala's activity through vmPFC inhibition as in the usual extinction process. Extinction during reconsolidation does not seem to engage the same vmPFC-amygdala inhibitory mechanisms used in conventional extinction and is more enduring.

The behavioral memory retrieval-extinction procedure has also been effectively applied in a recent study of drug addiction (Xue et al., 2012). As we discussed in chapter 6, relapse is a major issue in drug addiction, and memories play an important role in triggering craving when former addicts are exposed to drugs and drug-taking equipment, or even the thoughts of these. A group of Chinese and American researchers led by Yan-Xue Xue recently explored the effectiveness of the memory retrieval-extinction paradigm with a group of currently abstinent heroin addicts. A short video with scenes of drug use was used to remind them of heroin cues. If the reminder was given 10 minutes before extinction training, both their blood pressure increases and self-reported cravings in response to drug cues were reduced the next day. In contrast, for the group given the reminder six hours before the extinction training, cravings were not reduced, indicating that it was outside the reconsolidation window. Further, follow-up tests 30 days and 180 days later showed that the reminder 10 minutes before extinction training resulted in an enduring reduction in cue-induced cravings. However, it's important to note that the cravings were only weakened and not completely eliminated, so the behavioral measures cannot be said to erase memories.

This is an early study, and much remains to be discovered about the effectiveness of the memory retrieval-extinction procedure for treatment of drug addiction. For example, little is known about individual differences in responsiveness to the procedure, and how well it can ultimately inoculate against future relapse. Some other research groups have recently found that they were unable to erase fears by opening up the reconsolidation window

(Golkar, Bellander, Olsson, & Öhman, 2012; Kindt & Soeter, 2013), and the same difficulties with replication may arise with drug addiction applications in the future. Despite the criticisms in the current literature, memory reconsolidation is an active research area with great potential for clinical translation; finding a way to open up the reconsolidation window in therapy holds the promise of achieving more long-lasting amelioration of PTSD, other anxiety-related symptoms, and drug addiction (Schwabe, Nader, & Pruessner, 2014).

Concluding Comments

Memory and emotion interact with each other on many levels. The arousal that is part of the experience of emotions can boost memory to make emotional events stand out in our minds more vividly and for longer periods of time. Arousal acts to select what is important by focusing attention and processing resources on salient events so that they will be encoded in the first place; then arousal post-encoding enhances the consolidation of those memories in long-term storage. The work of James McGaugh and his many collaborators has elucidated the brain mechanisms involved in the emotional enhancement of memory by proving conclusively that activation of the amygdala is vital for the process. Increasing the activation of noradrenergic receptors in the amygdala enhances memory, whereas blocking the same receptors with drugs like propranolol eliminates the memory enhancement effects of stress hormones. Studies with humans have confirmed that the same arousal-based enhancement of memory occurs and that the amygdala is a crucial brain structure for this effect. Emotion functions to highlight salient events and relevant information and increases their memorability. Flashbulb memories are an extreme example of memory enhancement processes at work. Shocking public events like the 9/11 attacks align in particular and sometimes strange ways with personal circumstances to make them stand out as enduring mnemonic landmarks.

Although the enhancement of memory by emotion is usually adaptive and functional, it can become pathological in conditions like PTSD. The overactive intrusive traumatic memories of PTSD are deeply disturbing. At the level of functional brain networks, this imbalance is manifested as an overactive amygdala response that automatically triggers traumatic memories combined with weaker-than-normal activity in the hippocampus and vmPFC that lessens the control that the person has over his or her memories. Psychologists, psychiatrists, and neuroscientists are currently collaborating to apply to clinical practice the insights gained from studies of the brain processes involved in reshaping memories during the window of opportunity provided by reconsolidation. Although the jury is still out on the extent of the malleability of memories during reconsolidation, the shift to a more dynamic, adaptive view of memory has opened up new possibilities for the treatment of anxiety disorders like PTSD, making it an exciting area of research to watch for future developments.

The psychological and neural study of flashbulb memories has revealed that emotion does not interact with memory to etch every detail upon the person's brain, as James implied with his brain-scarring analogy. What is special about highly emotional memories is the subjective sense of vividness and believability that they convey. The ability to mentally "time travel" back to these events means that the memories themselves can be used to control and alter our emotional states. One example connected to our opening anecdote is Elizabeth's use of her vivid recall of the elation she felt upon the completion of her thesis exam to motivate herself when she is discouraged by the difficulty of writing projects. The voluntary regulation of emotional states through consciously accessing emotional memories is a vital part of the emotional regulation work that we will discuss in more depth in a later chapter.

Box 8.1: Subdivisions of Memory

The first major division made between types of memory is between **short-term memory** and **long-term memory**. Short-term memory is a very limited immediate memory storage system that allows you to hold things in consciousness. It is what you use when you are trying to keep a phone number that you have heard in mind long enough to find your phone and make a call. It has traditionally been tested with the digit span task—how many digits can you hear read out, then immediately repeat back? In 1956, George Miller published a famous paper, titled *The Magical Number Seven Plus or Minus Two*, about the span of short-term or "immediate" memory. Sometimes the computer metaphor is used to explain the distinction between short- and long-term memory: Short-term memory is a limited but easily accessible storage system, like computer RAM, whereas long-term memory is much more extensive, like hard drive storage.

George Miller, Galanter, and Pribram (1960) coined the term **working memory** that is now the term of choice for immediate memory in the research literature. Working memory refers to the active maintenance and manipulation of material in immediate memory. It includes, but goes beyond, the notion of short-term storage. To contrast it with short-term memory, Corkin (2013) asks us to imagine performing mental arithmetic—say multiplying 68 and 73 in your head. This involves more active mental work than just repeating digits, and working memory provides the mental workspace for these types of mental activity. Alan Baddeley and his colleagues in England pioneered work on the differentiation of components of working memory (Baddeley, 2007). In this model, so called "slave systems"—the phonological loop and the visuospatial sketchpad—are the short-term storage components, and these are connected to a "central executive" that is responsible for the active working with material of short-term memory. Corkin described working memory as "short term memory on overdrive" (2013, p. 65).

Long-term memory is further subdivided into implicit and explicit memory. **Implicit memories** are acquired automatically through experience, such as learning skills or procedures; the paradigmatic case is learning to ride a bicycle. Implicit or **procedural** memories are not consciously brought to mind, instead, they are accessed by the performance of the procedure or task. They involve knowing how without knowing what. Conditioning is a form of implicit memory. Priming is another form of implicit memory that can be measured with a word completion task: Prior reading of a list of words makes it more likely that word fragments will be completed by words from the list rather than other possible solutions, even when the whole list cannot be explicitly recalled. **Explicit or declarative memory**, in contrast, is the conscious remembering of the details and facts associated with what was learned, such as where and how we learned to ride a bike or who presented the list of words to us. The case of H. M. was instrumental in demonstrating that explicit memory is hippocampus dependent and implicit memory is not. Implicit memories reside within brain structures engaged during learning itself, such as the conditioned fear circuit in the amygdala.

Explicit memory is further subdivided into semantic and episodic memory, a distinction pioneered by Endel Tulving (1972). **Semantic memory** taps into our vast knowledge stores. Our vocabulary and knowledge of facts depend on this type of memory. Some of our autobiographical memory is semantic—who we are, where we live, what we typically like to do, and so on. This type of memory does not require knowledge of where you first learned the information; it is general in form. In contrast, **episodic memory** is memory of particular events that took place in a specified location at a particular point in time. For many years, Tulving and colleagues have studied a patient known as K. C., who in an accident suffered brain damage that includes both sides of his hippocampus; K. C. retains his access to semantic memory but has no episodic memory recall to speak of (Rosenbaum et al., 2005). For example, he can recall that his family owns a summer house, but he cannot recall any particular visit or incident that occurred there.

In 1985, Tulving introduced the concept of **mental time travel** to refer to the subjective experience of episodic memory. Only in episodic (not semantic or procedural) memory does the rememberer recall the context for the event recalled, mentally recreating the time and place of the event. Tulving's emphasis in making this distinction is on the different forms of consciousness or phenomenal relationship to the memories entailed in the three types of remembering. The terminology he coined for this distinction uses the root *noetic*, meaning "knowing": Episodic memory is **autonoetic** or "self-knowing," semantic memory is **noetic** or "knowing," and procedural memory is **anoetic** or "non-knowing."

9

Feelings-as-Information

How Affect Influences Thought and Judgment

The weather is a frequent topic of everyday casual conversation, and is often used dramatically to set the emotional tone in films and novels. We intuitively understand that how we feel can be affected by changing weather conditions, but are not always aware of the extent of its effects on our mood. In 1983, two social psychology researchers, Norbert Schwarz and Gerald Clore, made clever experimental use of this common observation. They called students at their home institution of University of Illinois, Urbana-Champaign, and asked them to participate in a survey about well-being and life satisfaction. Half of the students were called on one of the first warm and sunny days of spring, and the other half received their calls on a more seasonal cold and rainy day. Not surprisingly, those called on the bad-weather days felt considerably less positive about their lives. The twist in Schwarz and Clore's experiment was that they found that they could counteract the depressing effect of the rainy weather by asking how the weather was before conducting the survey. If the students' attention had been explicitly drawn to the bad weather, they did not attribute how they felt to this passing circumstance. With this creative experiment, Schwarz and Clore devised a means of investigating what they term "feelings as information": how our feelings inform our thoughts, judgments, and decisions, thus opening up a topic that had been relatively ignored in psychology for many years.

The interaction of emotion and cognition is the subject of the next three chapters. In this chapter, we begin by reviewing behavioral research spearheaded by the experiment of Schwarz and Clore (1983) described above, which has since compiled an impressive body of work demonstrating that affective states affect even the highest cognitive functions. Previous chapters have focused primarily on the rapid short-term responses provoked by a specific stimulus, or what we call an emotion. In this chapter, we explore other affective states as well, especially the low-intensity but continuous *moods* that permeate our day-to-day life, even though they may have been provoked by something as seemingly irrelevant as the weather. Why should these affective states that are sometimes so subtle that they escape our attention infuse a seemingly unrelated judgment on life satisfaction into our daily living? Do these affective states also have an adaptive function?

In the following chapter, we move into the brain to take up the neuroscience research beginning to map the neural substrates of the emotion–cognition interaction explored in this chapter. This research importantly includes work from the emerging field of neuroeconomics, a field that is beginning to make important contributions to an understanding of the role of emotions in judgments and decision-making. Finally, in chapter 11, we explore how cognition in turn affects emotion, focusing specifically on the role of cognition in emotion regulation.

What Is the Meaning of an Affective Experience?

The beginning of an answer to this question came from the ingenious twist in the experiment by Schwarz and Clore described above. These researchers used the already well-known effects of weather on mood to test their new hypothesis about how affective states influence cognitive processes such as judgments and decisions. Their now-influential *feelings-as-information* hypothesis posits that like emotions, the often-subtle affective feelings represent a continuous evaluation of ongoing events. They mark our response to those events as good or bad, and this affective tag can then be used as information as we judge an object or evaluate a situation. We in effect ask ourselves, "How do I feel about this?"

Schwarz and Clore developed the feelings-as-information hypothesis as an alternative to the prevalent model of how mood or emotions affect cognition, a model known as affective congruency, or priming. This theory posits that affect is an important category which is used to organize information; for example, memories of good times would become linked together because of their shared affect, forming an associative network (a model attributed to Gordon Bower; see Forgas, 2008). In affective congruency, a good mood acts as a prime, activating the recall of other good memories in the network. The increased life satisfaction on sunny days seen in Schwarz and Clore's study could thus be explained by assuming that the good mood induced by the weather primed the recall of other positive memories. The memory of all those positive experiences must mean life is good.

Although Schwarz and Clore's initial findings about the effect of weather on mood seemed consistent with the affective priming model, something just didn't seem "quite right" to Schwarz introspectively, as he has since reflected (Schwarz, 2012, p. 3). On sunny days, he just felt good; it didn't seem to depend on recalling good memories (also see Schwarz & Clore, 2003, for a more detailed history of this field). Searching for other ways to think about the role of affect in cognitive functions, he was drawn to researchers who were beginning to think about the information content of emotion. Emotions-as-information were first proposed by Wyer and Carlston in 1979 (see Schwarz, 2012), who argued that a pleasant interaction with someone will be experienced as "liking" the next time you meet that person. The feeling of liking is thus information about your past experience with that individual. This way of thinking about affect just "felt" more right to Schwarz than affective congruency, but more importantly, it also suggested a nonintrospective test of the idea that moods are a reflection of one's current situation, an idea first proposed by the early Gestalt psychologists.

Misattributing Mood

Borrowing a technique from appraisal psychology, Schwarz and Clore came up with a test of the idea that the decrease in life-satisfaction judgment on a rainy day was due to affect being used as information. Recall that appraisal theory, first proposed by Arnold and experimentally tested by Stanley Schachter and Singer (1962) (see chapter 1), posits that although emotional stimuli will automatically activate the sympathetic nervous system to increase arousal, the identification of *which* emotion is occurring can only take place after a cognitive *appraisal* of the situation. This was supported by showing that artificially induced arousal (by an injection of adrenaline) was attributed to whatever cues were present at the time; in Schachter and Singer's experiment, participants felt anger or excitement depending on whether they were exposed to a happy or mad confederate. Other experiments, such as Dutton and Aron's "attractive experimenter at the end of the bridge" effect described in chapter 1, also showed that arousal is sometimes misattributed to wrong events. Schwarz and Clore wondered whether something similar was happening on rainy days; maybe the decreased-life-satisfaction ratings on a rainy day were due to a mistaken attribution of the cause of the bad mood. To test this, the interviewer posed as an out-of-towner, and in half of the experiments began by asking the seemingly irrelevant question: "By the way, how's the weather down there?"

The striking finding that this weather question eliminated the previously measured decrease in life-satisfaction ratings seen on rainy days provided resounding support for Schwarz and Clore's new hypothesis. How does a simple question about the weather eliminate the effect of current mood on judgment? The authors proposed that those called on rainy days did not realize that their mood was being "dampened" by the weather, so assumed that it reflected a more general dissatisfaction with life. When the interviewer's question drew attention to the weather, an alternative explanation for their bad mood was suggested, correcting the previous *misattribution*. Because priming would be expected to occur regardless of the question, the change in life satisfaction on rainy days demonstrated by this *misattribution paradigm* was clearly proof against the affective congruency theory; instead, feelings must be being used as experiential information.

Editing Our Moods

It's important to note that once people were reminded of an alternative reason for feeling bad, the value of mood as information for judging life satisfaction was eliminated, suggesting that how affective information is used is subject to the same rules of reasoning that guide the use of cognitive processes. Misattributions occur because, as evidenced by the first rainy day survey, affective experiences tend to be experienced as being about the current situation (Clore & Huntsinger, 2009). Clore and colleagues have referred to this as the affective immediacy principle; affective feelings will be experienced as reactions to current mental contents, which are referred to as *integral* feelings. Misattributions occur when the mood is *incidental* to the situation being judged, but is mistakenly judged as integral to it. The affective immediacy principle is probably why a bad day at work makes us feel critical of those around us when we return home; although the bad mood is incidental to events at home, it can appear to be integral to the behavior of one's partner or children.

Clore and Huntsinger (2009) have mused that the impact of an emotional experience, like the impact of movies, depends on good editing. Wisdom lies in being able to identify the appropriate object or target of our affective reactions—which is sometimes much harder than it might seem. The assumption that mood is integral to the present situation is automatic, but is sometimes wrong, and misattributions can have significant consequences for our judgments and decisions and our personal interactions. One of the goals of cognitive behavioral therapy is to educate patients about their habitual mood misattributions.

Although feeling bad usually generates a negative judgment and feeling good a positive assessment, it's important to emphasize that the answer to the question "How do I feel about it?" will depend on the context. Feeling sad while watching a sad movie or reading a sad book is likely to produce a *positive* evaluation of the work, because feeling sad is evidence it has achieved its intended goals. Another important point to emphasize about this research is that although Schwarz and Clore focus on misattribution of incidental feelings as a way of demonstrating the information value of affect, normally the use of feelings as information takes place with integral rather than incidental feelings. Most often, attribution is correctly assigned to integral feelings. In subsequent work, the role of integral feelings, as well as the misattribution of incidental feelings, has also been researched.

Feelings-as-Information and the Somatic Marker Hypothesis

The idea of an emotional experience as an evaluation of the value or relevance of a situation or stimulus to the individual should sound familiar by now. A primary function of the amygdala, as we saw in the work reviewed in chapter 4, is to draw attention to salient or relevant stimuli in the environment so they can be prioritized for processing. The identification of emotionally salient events by the amygdala acts to "separate the significant from the mundane" (Lim, Padmala, & Pessoa, 2009, p. 16841). Schwarz and Clore see the same function for these longer-term affective states. Importantly, however, they add that an emotion or affective state can be useful information in its own right, to be processed together with other information about a situation. This concept of feelings-as-information is largely equivalent to Damasio's somatic marker theory discussed in chapter 5, which posited that an evaluation of all one's past experience with a particular situation is expressed as a bodily experience to be used during ongoing decisions.

Surprisingly, these two almost identical ways of thinking about the role of affect and emotions in decision-making were generated independently. The work by Schwarz and Clore on feelings-as-information was published in the disciplines of social, personality, and consumer psychology, whereas the work of Damasio and colleagues appeared in neuroscience journals and texts, and unfortunately, different academic subdisciplines can exist in relative isolation from each other. Only recently have some of the remarkably parallel findings in the fields of consumer and personality psychology begun to cross-fertilize with those of affective neuroscience.

Why Do We Need Affective Information?

One question that has been asked about the feelings-as-information hypothesis is why affective feelings are needed. Clore and Storbeck (2006) have emphasized that their paradigm makes the assumption that the majority of affective processes take place outside of consciousness, as we've learned is true of many emotional processes. The conscious "feeling" thus provides a mechanism for us to learn about the underlying implicit judgments that have been made. Kent Harber has pithily summarized this idea: "Feelings act as persuasive messages from the self to the self" (2005, p. 276). In addition, affective reactions are much more rapid than the effortful and time-consuming cognitive assessments, and have the ability to summarize a number of different events into a single affective feeling. As Schwarz has stated, feelings are "an integrative expression of the general state of the organism" (Schwarz, Strack, Kommer, & Wagner, 1987, p. 70), a definition almost identical to that Damasio has given for feelings.

Thinking about Affective Information

Prior to Schwarz and Clore's work, judgments and decision-making were thought to be based only on the beliefs, attributes, traits, stereotypes, and so forth that make up our declarative knowledge store. Since that seminal experiment, the misattribution paradigm has generated a wealth of evidence showing that, contrary to the traditional view that judgments are based only on the *content* of what is being judged, affect plays a critically important role in judgment. Affect has been shown to influence judgments and decisions in contexts ranging from jury trials to the stock market, as well as consumer behavior, political attitudes, and how we judge other people; in fact, it's hard to find an example in which mood hasn't been shown to alter judgments of objects or events. Given the ubiquitous role of affect in judgments and decisions, a better understanding of the rules guiding how and when affective information is used as well as how and when misattributions are likely to occur is critical.

Michel Pham, a researcher based at Columbia University's Business School, and his coworkers recently reviewed the field to determine the conditions that modify how and when affective information is used (Griefeneder, Bless, & Pham, 2011). They identified five categories that act to moderate reliance on affective information. First, only the most salient feelings, those which "stand out" relative to other information, are selected to be used as information. Salience is often determined by the context in which the feelings occur, but personality variables have also been shown to modify how and if salient feelings are used. For example, those who focus more on their feelings, who score higher on an openness-to-emotions scale, who are visualizers as compared to verbalizers, or who are more impulsive, tend to use integral affects more than others, presumably due to the increased salience of feelings in these groups.

Second is the *representativeness* of the affect, which is a metacognitive judgment about the degree to which the affect is assumed to be an essential characteristic of the target. This is essentially how Schwarz and Clore tested their hypothesis; by drawing attention to the possibility that mood was due to the weather, and not a consideration of life satisfaction, the representativeness of the information was called into question. When multiple targets are evaluated, an induced incidental mood usually affects only the first target, since it's judged unlikely to be representative of other targets as well.

A third metacognitive modifier is whether the affect is considered *relevant to the judgment* (rather than *representative of the target*). For example, induced mood was found to affect the decisions of subjects to go to a movie if they were given the motive of having a good time but not if they were given the motive of qualifying for a study, presumably because mood was not thought to be relevant to the goal of qualifying for an experimental study. Interestingly, affective influences are greater in those who have higher self-esteem, either dispositionally or through experimental manipulation, possibly because they have greater trust in their insights, and so are more likely to assume their feelings are relevant in their judgments.

Affective information is also more likely to be used when judgments are considered *malleable*, or when judgments are open to extraneous influences. Some judgments, such as judging the trustworthiness of someone, are inherently more malleable than others, such as gender judgments. Likewise, some targets may be more malleable. An early demonstration of this was seen in work showing that mood has a stronger impact on the judging of neutral slides, which could be viewed as either positive or negative, than on the judging of clearly positive or negative slides. Targets that have not been judged previously or for which only little or ambiguous information is available are also malleable.

The fifth and final category moderating the use of affective information is *processing intensity*. Mood has a larger effect when a judgment has been made with low processing intensity or with low motivation for processing, such as when people are asked to judge a consumer product that has little self-relevance. If there is a paucity of relevant information about, or interest in, the target being evaluated, then letting our initial affective reaction guide us is probably the best we can do.

Given the ubiquitous use of feelings in day-to-day judgments, the finding that affective information is subjected to a cognitive, rational assessment of when and how it is useful is reassuring. Although the immediacy principle, or the attribution of affective responses to what is present at the moment, is seen by some as the Achilles' heel of affective guidance, it should be remembered that in Schwarz and Clore's initial experiment, subjects were called by a stranger and asked to provide an answer to a complex assessment on a moment's notice. It is likely that with more time for reflection, a metacognitive assessment of the relevance and representativeness of the mood would modify the rainy day influence. However, these studies are important in emphasizing the kinds of situations in which we might become overly reliant on feelings or when we tend to neglect a more careful and effortful analysis. The work on feelings-as-information draws our attention to the significant and often underappreciated role that affect plays in cognitive assessments and documents the specifics of how cognition and emotion interact, raising our awareness of these integrative processes.

A Privileged Window

Consistent with Damasio's conclusion that emotions are most essential in complex situations, when there are too many permutations to be handled efficiently by conscious stepwise reasoning, Schwarz and Clore hypothesize that the value of affect is its ability to summarize a large amount of information. As explained by Griefeneder et al. (2011), feelings act as *metasummaries* of the value of events around us. As such, they provide a mapping of the world—what the authors refer to as *a privileged window*—that is more efficient and ecologically valid than an analysis of content only, since content specific to a single event is encountered and assessed less frequently. This privileged window can signal when something is wrong in much the same way that an unusual or incorrect grammatical structure just "sounds wrong." Although such feelings may not specify exactly what is wrong, they identify the presence of a problem and then initiate the appropriate cognitive processes needed to analyze the problem in more detail.

Extracting the Emotional Gist

An intriguing example of the metasummary function of feelings was recently provided by Haberman and Whitney (2009). For their experiment, they constructed sets of face images that ranged on a continuum between two strongly expressed emotions, such as happiness and sadness. A computer program was used to generate images with expressions that systematically varied between the two extremes. Subjects viewed a grid of images composed of 4 to 16 faces selected from one of the sets, balanced around a mean expression that was not one of the faces shown. Immediately following viewing of the grid of face images, subjects were shown a test face and asked to decide whether or not it was a member of the preceding set. Although subjects were not explicitly told to attend to the emotional expressions on the faces, their subsequent judgment about membership in the set was found to be influenced by how closely the test face expression matched the mean expression of the set. Assessment of mean expression was found with set exposures as short as 50 milliseconds, and subjects were able to judge whether a test face was happier or sadder than the mean of the sets as easily as they could determine which of two faces was happier—a discrimination that can be done quite easily. Accurate affective information, in this case the mean emotional expression of a set of systematically varying faces, appears to be extracted quickly and automatically and regardless of instruction to attend to a different kind of information. A quick glance was enough to provide an accurate summary of a large amount of information and, as this experiment demonstrates, our brains seem designed to acquire the emotional "gist" of a situation automatically.

Trust in Feelings

Given the validity of feelings due to their basis in extensive experience, Pham and coworkers wondered why they are not used more frequently and why there is so much individual variation in their use (Pham, Lee, & Stephen, 2012). Some people trust their feelings more than others, depending on factors like self-esteem and emotional intelligence (Clore & Colcombe, 2003; Gohm & Clore, 2002). Pham et al. manipulated people's trust in their feelings experimentally by asking them to recall either 2 or 10 situations where they had made a decision that turned out well and in which they had trusted their feelings. Simply because it is much more difficult to come up with 10 situations, people in the larger number or "low-trust" condition subsequently placed less trust in their feelings than the people in the "high-trust" condition who were asked to recall only 2 situations.

Those with the high-trust manipulation better predicted eight different future events, including the 2008 Democratic presidential primary, Dow Jones movements, movie box office performances, American Idol winners, college football outcomes, and even future weather conditions. Results averaged over three similar studies showed that participants in the high induced trust conditions had prediction accuracies of 53.2%, while those in the low induced trust group had only 31.9%, against the baseline of 34.4%. The increased accuracy in predictions when feelings are trusted is clearly significant.

Pham and coworkers have dubbed the ability of feelings to improve predictions of the future the *emotional oracle effect*, which they showed was due to increased trust in feelings, whether natural or induced, and not to a decrease in performance due to lack of trust in the low-induced trust group. They hypothesize that having trust-in-feelings may facilitate access to the privileged window of affect rather than forcing reliance on the necessarily more limited input that has been selected by logical analysis. The authors stress that those with higher trust who made better predictions took just as long over their deliberations as did the low-trust group, which argues against the idea that feelings simply provoke a rapid "gut" or "blink" response. Instead, reflective cognitive inferences are used to determine the value of these feelings.

This study also identified some important boundary conditions; only those with high trust *and* sufficient background knowledge about the prediction domain made more successful predictions. High trust could *not* improve the results of those with more limited knowledge. Thus, the opinions of others should be valued only if those individuals have confidence in their feelings *and* significant proven experience in what is being judged. Unfortunately, too often confidence is mistaken for expertise, by individuals themselves as well as by those who might place their trust in them.

The Affect Heuristic

The use of feelings-as-information has been called an *affect heuristic* (Slovic, Finucane, Peters, & MacGregor, 2002). Heuristics are simple rules of thumb that are acquired based on extended learning about a situation. The affect heuristic represents the affective consequences of our past experiences. The use of heuristics in thinking and decision-making was long thought to involve a sometimes necessary trade-off; although heuristics were simple and quick, and thus might be needed when time was limited, they lacked the accuracy of cognitive deliberation, which was clearly superior. The recent work of Gerd Gigerenzer and colleagues at the Max Planck Institute for Human Development in Berlin (e.g., Gigerenzer & Gaissmaier, 2011), however, has been instrumental in showing that heuristics can also result in optimal decision-making. For example, how well or quickly a stimulus is recognized is likely to reflect its environmental frequency, which is an important metasummary of its ecological validity. Thus, a simple recognition heuristic may allow accurate decision-making, as has been seen in experiments showing that the recognition of Wimbledon players' names by amateur tennis players was a better predictor of their success in the tournament than the ATP rankings; a simple name recognition heuristic trumped seeding, which is based on a complex statistical calculation. Recognition-based stock portfolios have been shown to outperform those of managed funds, and the name recognition of candidates was more accurate than information gained by interviewing the voters in predicting German election outcomes. Heuristics can be both a valid and an accurate representation of experienced events that even outperforms other forecasting methods.

What about Sunny Days?

The careful reader may have wondered about the effect of drawing attention to the weather on a sunny day in Schwarz and Clore's experiment; life satisfaction ratings were not reduced once they were reminded of an alternative explanation for their good mood. Why were sunny days immune from misattribution? The answer to this question led to the expansion of the feelings-as-information hypothesis from feelings having an influence on *what* we think to their influencing *how* we think.

Schwarz (2012) began by noting that research has shown repeatedly that a mildly good mood is the baseline for most people (we will talk more about this so-called optimism bias later). If a good mood is the expected state, being sad signals a problem that demands an explanation. Note that if at the moment an interviewer happens to ask about our life satisfaction and we are feeling low for any reason, our sad mood may be attributed to a lack of life satisfaction.

Cognitive functions such as attention, working memory, and general cognitive control processes are often conceptualized as resources that have limited capacity. Thus, Schwarz reasoned that if cognitive resources are needed in negative moods, fewer resources will be available for other kinds of cognitive activity. To test this, participants who were first induced to be in a good or bad mood were asked to evaluate the sufficiency of strong and weak persuasive arguments (Bless, Bohner, Schwarz, & Strack, 1990). If being sad consumes cognitive resources, sad participants should be more willing to accept a weak argument than those in a good mood, who have more resources available to evaluate arguments. Surprisingly, however, the study showed the opposite: Those in the sad mood were more likely to reject the weak argument, while those in the happy mood found weak and strong arguments equally persuasive.[1] This was the first of a now substantial literature showing that mood not only affects judgments of objects or situations, but even affects *how* we think. Although this study suggested that sad moods enhance analytical thinking while good moods make one less discriminating, further work has modified thinking about how mood alters information processing and cognitive style, as we discuss below. Interestingly, this first study suggests that the persuasion practice of putting those we want to influence in a good mood will work best with weak arguments, and might even be counterproductive when strong arguments are available.

---

1. The conceptualization of negative moods as bad and positive moods as good has a long history and a persistent grip on psychology. However, research in this field is beginning to challenge the hegemony of positive moods.

Cognitive Tuning

The finding that mood affects how we think prompted a rethinking of how the information function of mood is used. Schwarz and Clore now suggest that mood may serve as a cue to activate or "tune" a cognitive processing style that is appropriate to the needs of the environment that triggered the mood. A bad mood results when a problem is detected or when an expected positive outcome does not occur, and activates a problem-solving program focused on the local details of the situation. A good mood means all is well, so the need to focus on the local environment can be relaxed. Because the immediate environment doesn't demand attention, time can be spent exploring, trying out new ideas, or making unusual but potentially interesting connections between ideas. Rather than focusing on an analysis of a specific stimulus, this kind of cognitive processing instead associates incoming stimuli with contextual information as well as with concepts in memory, a relational style that is often described as being cognitively flexible because of the many potential connections that can be associated with the stimulus. This global relational style of processing is also thought to facilitate play and has frequently been linked with creativity, which we discuss in more detail below.

Stereotypes, Scripts, and Schemas

Another type of distinction frequently made between types of information processing contrasts stimulus-focused, or "bottom-up," processing with more relational "top-down" processing. The fear response to a threat—driven by the amygdala, as described in chapter 4—is a good example of bottom-up processing; attention is narrowed and focused on the specific threat. Top-down processing is characterized as more cognitive in style, meaning that already-existing information such as schemas or scripts are used to characterize the situation. Drawing on work by the great Swiss developmental theorist Jean Piaget (1896–1980), these two styles can be equated with *assimilation* of incoming information with existing schemas or the *accommodation* of new information by changing existing schemas. Although everyday information processing relies on the interplay of both kinds of processing, work on affect has suggested that positive moods tend to privilege top-down, assimilative, or theory-driven processing, whereas negative affect leads to detailed, stimulus-bound or "referential" processing.

The reliance on general knowledge structures in top-down processing can lead to quick and easy rule-of-thumb processing of incoming information, with less attention being given to the individual details of a situation. This kind of processing can result in stereotyping, whereby people are judged only by the group to which they belong rather than by consideration of their individual characteristics. Several studies have shown an increase in racial and ethnic stereotyping when good moods are induced, a finding consistent with Schwarz's cognitive-tuning hypothesis that links good moods with schematic top-down processing.

The well-known social and psychological consequences of stereotyping, together with the finding that those in a positive mood are more willing to accept a weak argument, gave rise to the suggestion that this kind of processing is superficial or simplistic. Bless and coworkers, including Schwarz and Clore (Bless et al., 1996), tested the extent of processing in good versus sad moods using a going-out-to-dinner story, a scenario with a well-established script. Those induced to be happy made more intrusion errors—falsely recalling information that was not presented but could easily have been part of the typical dinner script, indicating that they were more reliant on the script and paying less attention to individuating details. However, happy and sad groups did equally well on recall of information atypical of the script, contradicting the idea that the happy group were generally lacking in processing resources. Thus, those in a happy mood did not seem to engage in more superficial or simplistic processing overall; they were able and willing to elaborate on information that was not part of the script. This result was also consistent with other work by Schwarz on how mood affects the processing of weak and strong arguments described above; happy participants who were willing to accept weak arguments were able to differentiate between the weak and strong arguments just as well as those in a sad mood once they were asked to pay attention to argument quality.

Bless et al. (1996) proposed that their findings could be best explained by the feelings-as-information model. When a problematic environment cues avoidance of available scripts, attention can be directed to a detailed analysis of specific items; in contrast, a happy mood encourages use of the general knowledge base that usually serves well. This does not mean that those in a happy mood are unable or unwilling to engage in analytical tasks; it just suggests that a detailed analysis is not required in a benign situation. Instead, processing effort can be put into top-down, relational processing, favoring exploration and discovery of new information.

Thus, moods will influence the degree to which general knowledge is relied on. Negative moods lead to placing less confidence on acquired scripts and schemas, and positive moods, increase confidence in the use of acquired knowledge that has been tested over time. Relying on ready-made scripts frees up resources that can instead be used for extending the knowledge base, and going beyond the inferences available from present information may over time lead to new or creative ideas. The affective state selects the processing style that is most appropriate, given the present environment.

The Forest and the Trees

The use of heuristics such as schemas or scripts in top-down processing also suggests that attention is centered on global features, or the forest, as opposed to local features, or the trees. The idea that attention or information processing can focus on the trees or the forest has been studied using test materials such as Navon or Kimchi figures. Navon figures are made of nested letters, such as a large letter H composed of different smaller letters, for example, many smaller Ss. Most people have a natural bias to "see" the global features, so that the H will be detected more quickly than the local Ss, even if the subject is directed to attend to the local features. Kimchi figures have a similar nested structure, but use basic geometric shapes rather than letters to vary the local and global features. The preference for global processing or categorization in these tests shows variation, both culturally and with age; while some cultures exhibit a slight preference for local processing, others have a significant global preference (Gasper & Clore, 2002). In general, children begin with a local preference that becomes more global with age.

Stable personality traits related to optimism and happiness or to anxiety and depression have been shown to be correlated with global and local preferences, respectively. Given the research suggesting that good moods foster reliance on heuristics, Gasper and Clore (2002) proposed that mood might also cue either global or local processing. They reasoned that if global processing is usually dominant, and a positive mood promotes reliance on what is accessible, positive feelings should cue selection of global processing while a sad mood should signal that local processing is required. They tested this "level of focus" hypothesis in two experiments.

In the first experiment, mood was induced before presenting subjects with the classic visual memory experiment first reported by Bartlett in 1932 (see Gasper & Clore, 2002). After viewing a drawing of an African shield that contained abstract facelike features and carried the label "Portrait of a Man," participants were asked to redraw the image from memory. This first reproduction was then shown to a second participant, who was given the same task, and so on for several reproductions. Bartlett found that on the whole, his participants' drawings became more facelike with successive reproductions, which he attributed to their reliance on a holistic face schema. Gasper and Clore manipulated the mood of their participants by having them recall either happy or sad experiences prior to the drawing task and found that the reproductions from the happy group became more facelike than those of the sad group. However, those in the sad mood did not have better recall of the picture or produce more complex drawings, suggesting that they had not engaged in more extensive processing. Instead, negative mood seemed to inhibit a global focus.

In their second test, happy participants were more likely to categorize Kimchi figures based on global features, while those in a negative mood were more likely to use local features. Together, these results show that a good mood promotes a global processing focus while a bad mood fosters local processing, consistent with findings that a good mood increases the use of heuristics such as stereotypes. In addition, because chronic or trait affect also shows a similar relationship with global or local processing, situational moods may influence level of focus by a similar mechanism.

Cognitive Flexibility

Alice Isen (1942–2012), a long-term professor of marketing and psychology at Cornell University, and her colleagues have argued that positive moods increase cognitive flexibility and creativity. Over many years, she and her colleagues (for a review, see Isen, 2008) used a range of cognitive tasks, such as puzzles and simulations of complex life situations, to demonstrate that positive affect is associated with thought patterns that are described as unusual, flexible and inclusive, creative, integrative, open-to-information, and efficient. For example, while in a positive mood, people are more likely to include fringe exemplars in a category, find creative solutions to puzzles, provide more diverse word associations, exhibit a preference for variety, and accept a broader range of options than those in a negative mood. More integration of information was found in medical decision-making tasks, and a positive mood increased the ability to work against strong habitual tendencies. This work thus suggests that rather than facilitating global processing, positive mood facilitates an open, flexible, and efficient mode of processing.

Some evidence for increased flexibility in good moods was provided by Baumann and Kuhl (2005). They measured their participants' default bias for local or global processing of Kimchi letters, then manipulated their mood. Those put into a positive mood were able to more readily overcome their default preference and respond more rapidly to nonpreferred features if the task demanded it, even if that meant shifting to a local focus. This experiment again demonstrates that a good mood does not preclude the capability to process locally if the task requires it.

The Dopamine–Creativity Link

Isen (2008) proposed that positive affect increases flexible and creative thinking by increasing the release of dopamine in frontal brain regions involved in higher cognitive functions. These so-called executive functions include the ability to switch attention quickly and to quickly identify and resolve any processing conflict. In support of this idea, Panksepp's SEEKING system has been claimed to be dependent on dopamine (see chapter 3), which is also related to creativity (Chermahini & Hommel, 2012).

Over a series of studies, Chermahini and Hommel have obtained experimental evidence linking dopamine with mood and divergent thinking (another measure of creative thinking) using the eye blink rate (EBR), an established clinical marker of dopamine levels. Although they initially reported linear correlations between positive mood, EBR, and creativity, subsequent research found that the relationship between EBR and creativity is more accurately described by an inverted-U-shape function. That is, those with a medium EBR performed better on a test of creativity than those with either high or low rates. Those with a low baseline EBR showed the expected increase in divergent thinking with positive mood induction, while those with a high baseline EBR were pushed over the peak of the inverted U by the positive mood induction and actually became worse at the divergent thinking task. Thus, a better mood might increase, have no effect on, or even decrease creativity in different individuals, depending on their initial dopamine levels. No effect was found for negative mood on either EBR or divergent thinking. This result cautions that the demonstration of a benefit for one mood should not be taken to mean that the other mood will be associated with a converse effect. Instead, positive and negative moods may be mediated by different mechanisms; one mood should not be seen as the opposite of the other mood.

Flourishing through Broadening and Building

Barbara Fredrickson, a psychologist at the University of North Carolina and one of the leaders of the positive psychology movement, has expanded these findings to suggest that positive affect is not only a signal that all is well in our environment, but that, by acting to broaden interactions with the environment, positive mood has a significant impact on overall happiness and physical wellness, or what she calls *flourishing*—living in an optimal range of human functioning (Fredrickson, 2001; Fredrickson & Branigan, 2005). She argues that whereas narrowing of attention and perception by negative emotions is adaptive for short-term threats, positive emotions enhance long-term survival through a complementary broadening of attention (Fredrickson & Losada, 2005; Johnson, Waugh, & Fredrickson, 2010).

In addition to the role of affect in processing style, Fredrickson's work also considers the role of emotions and affect in what she calls *thought-action tendencies*, the automatic, coordinated responses, including changes in thoughts, actions, and physiological processes, that are activated by a stimulus. Specific emotions such as fear or anger provoke specific thought-action tendencies in response to specific environmental challenges. The sight of a predator provokes fear, expressed as an urge to flee, while an unfair distribution of resources may provoke anger, expressed as an urge to approach and confront. The majority of work on action tendencies has focused on negative emotions, yet it is usually assumed that positive emotions, such as joy and contentment, also provoke specific action tendencies. Fredrickson argues that this expansion of specific action tendencies to positive emotions is incorrect. Although it's easy to describe the action tendency of fear as an urge to escape, or of anger as an urge to attack, it's difficult to describe a specific response associated with a positive emotion such as joy. As she points out, descriptions of positive action tendencies are very vague; the specific action tendency for joy has been described as aimless activation, while contentment is described as an urge for inactivity.

If positive emotions do not function to coordinate specific action programs, then what are their functions? Fredrickson argues that while negative emotions require specific action tendencies to allow quick actions tailored to specific environmental challenges, positive emotions typically signal the absence of a specific challenge, indicating that vigilance can be relaxed. She proposes that all positive emotions have the common function of facilitating a nonspecific motivation to approach and explore. This "urge" to engage with the environment as well as other individuals ensures that productive activity, which can lead to the discovery of new and valuable information, occurs whenever no critical survival response is needed. The new information gained with this nonspecific engagement and activity allows information about the environment to be updated, encouraging the expansion of existing action programs or the development of new ones. Positive emotions will thus expand, rather than narrow, the potential repertoire of action choices.

Fredrickson has argued that many of the documented effects of positive mood on cognition might be the consequence of this broadening function. Working with Branigan (Fredrickson & Branigan, 2005), she demonstrated that two different specific positive emotions broadened perceptual or attentional scope, as seen with the Kimchi figures, compared to both neutral and negative emotions. Positive emotions also increased conceptual or representational breadth, as demonstrated by more and more-varied answers on the Twenty Statements Test, which asks participants to imagine experiencing the emotion portrayed in the inducing film and then list the potential behaviors that emotion might provoke in them. Those who saw films portraying positive emotions not only came up with more "actions," but the actions were less specific, such as playing, being outside, or being social. Together, this work suggests that positive affect increases both perceptual and conceptual breadth.

Experimental studies reported by Rowe, Hirsh, and Anderson (2006) provide further support for Fredrickson's suggestion that a single broadening mechanism can explain many of the effects of positive mood on diverse aspects of cognition. They first showed that positive mood impaired selective attention in the Eriksen flanker task. In this task, observers are asked to press the right button for certain letters and the left button for other letters. The target letter is flanked by letters that are either congruent (same button press) or incongruent (opposite button press). Attending to the incongruent flanking letters slows performance on the task, something that happens more frequently in positive moods, indicating that attention has been broadened to include the flanking letters. This test suggests that increased attentional breadth actually alters the scope of what is seen; more is seen in a positive mood.

The researchers next confirmed an earlier finding that positive mood increases conceptual scope as measured by improved completion of remote associations in the Remote Associates Test (RAT), then correlated individuals' RAT results with their performance on the Eriksen flanker task. They found that the increase in the number of remote associations identified in the RAT was correlated with slower responses on incompatible flankers in the Eriksen task, suggesting that both effects are due to the common mechanism whereby positive mood relaxes the central inhibitory control that normally acts to filter or limit the amount of information in the focus of attention. This common mechanism expands both internal conceptual and external perceptual information processing, providing a unifying framework that helps explain the interaction between attention and creativity.

From this work, Fredrickson and colleagues have developed the *broaden-and-build* theory, which asserts that positive mental states will not only *broaden* the array of thoughts and actions that come to mind, but also lead to behaviors that over time result in *building* enduring personal resources. Fredrickson uses play behavior, which she conceives of as an urge in response to joy, as an example of long-term resource building. Play is seen in the young of many species, and it extends throughout adulthood in humans. We saw in chapter 3 that Panksepp includes PLAY as one of his core affect systems. Although the exuberant behavior seen in play may seem arbitrary and nondirected, research in nonhumans has shown that play allows the development of skills and behaviors that will be used by adults in response to very specific challenges, such as escape behavior. In humans, play is also associated with cognitive creativity as well as building experience with social interaction.

The broaden-and-build hypothesis holds that positive affect encourages the kinds of interactions and exploratory behaviors that build enduring resources for the future. Thus, in addition to being a response to environmental conditions, signaling current well-being, positive affect lays the foundation for future health and well-being. As Fredrickson indicates, prospective studies have linked frequent positive affect to resilience to adversity, psychological growth, reduced inflammation and lower levels of cortisol, increased resistance to colds, reductions in strokes, and finally, as might be expected from the links with better overall health, longevity (see Fredrickson & Losada [2005] for references; Kok et al., 2013).

But It's Also OK to Feel Sad

Recently, Joseph Forgas has argued that the benefits of good moods have come to dominate both academic and popular culture, and suggests that not only are they exaggerated, but the risks of relying on heuristics at the expense of more systematic, analytical thinking is often discounted. In a recent review, he highlights a number of benefits of negative mood, or the "up-side of feeling down" (Forgas, 2013). For example, because negative moods recruit more accommodative and externally focused processing, they improve attention and facilitate encoding of memories. In one study, shoppers remembered significantly more information about the interior of a shop on rainy, cold days, which induced worse moods, than on sunny warm days. Negative mood has also been shown to increase accurate recall. For example, subjects who were induced into a sad mood before witnessing a staged but realistic altercation between a professor and female intruder were less likely to incorporate false or misleading details into their memories than the happy participants.

False Memories

False memories can be experimentally induced by the Deese-Roediger-McDermott paradigm (DRM) in which participants are deliberately "lured" into recalling words that were never presented. In this experiment, subjects study a list of close associates of a word that is not included on the list, referred to as the "critical lure." For example, words such as *bed, pillow, rest,* and *snore* are clearly related to the lure word *sleep* (Roediger & McDermott, 1995). A happy mood induced before list presentation increases misremembering of the critical lure as belonging to the list (Storbeck & Clore, 2005. These false memories are assumed to be created by the automatic activation of related concepts during encoding, which is facilitated by the relational, global processing style promoted by a good mood.

Many studies have now shown that being in a sad mood facilitates more accurate eyewitness memories, which may be related to the increased risk of false memories with global processing privileged by a good mood (Storbeck & Clore, 2011). Indeed, when both sad and happy subjects were asked to list both words on the list and any other words which came to mind, those in the negative mood group produced fewer associated words (Storbeck & Clore, 2011). The ability to bring to mind more associated words is also a demonstration of the increased cognitive flexibility that underlies the kind of creativity promoted by positive mood. The downside is that it may become difficult to remember which words were on the list and which simply came to mind while reading the list, creating a source memory issue.

In addition to enhancing accurate recall, negative moods also improved judgmental accuracy. Subjects were asked to form an impression about a person after reading two sequential paragraphs, one describing the individual as an extrovert and the other as an introvert. The order of the two paragraphs was varied, and the one presented first had a disproportionate effect on the overall impression, a phenomenon known as the primacy effect. Negative mood induction eliminated the distorting primacy effect. Negative mood also reduces another bias, the so-called halo effect, in which a good-looking person is judged as having more desirable qualities.

Negative moods also reduce gullibility and increase skepticism, and because they increase attention to details, increase the ability to detect deception. Bad moods can also reduce the tendency to stereotype, as shown in a startling shooter game experiment that used Islamic headdress to indicate Muslim targets (Unkelbach, Forgas, & Denson, 2008). Australian undergraduate subjects were instructed to shoot at an image of a target only when the target carried a gun. Those in a negative induced mood were less likely to shoot at targets in Islamic headdress not holding a gun, while those in a good mood shot more at gunless Muslim-appearing targets than those in either neutral or negative moods. Unkelbach et al. nicknamed this finding "the turban effect," and proposed that it is a sensitive measure of unconscious bias that can be potentiated by positive moods.

Somewhat surprisingly, there are also motivational benefits of a negative mood (Forgas, 2013). Subjects in a sad as opposed to a happy mood persevered longer on a demanding cognitive task with no time limit, attempted to answer more of the questions posed, and were more successful on the task. Finally, again somewhat counterintuitively, there are interpersonal benefits to a negative mood. A negative mood promotes more polite and attentive behavior in interpersonal interactions. During the Ultimatum Game, where one person decides how to split a reward with another participant, people in negative moods give more resources to their partner on average. They are also more likely to reject unfair offers when they are the recipient. Thus, negative moods seem to increase concern for others as well as attention to fairness.

Clearly, neither positive nor negative affect is universally desirable, and each also has its strengths. Forgas (2013) suggests that "the unrelenting pursuit of happiness may be self-defeating" because of a reduced ability to adapt to situational needs and concludes that a "more balanced assessment of the costs and benefits of positive and negative affect is long overdue in professional practice and in popular culture as well" (p. 230).

Cognitive Feelings

Schwarz and Clore very deliberately focus attention on "feeling" rather than moods in the naming of their theory. The feelings-as-information research includes a variety of "feelings" beyond affect that have been shown to influence cognitive functions. These "feelings" include bodily feelings such as warmth or cold or the feeling of the body when exhausted or activated during emotional arousal. The somatic marker theory of Damasio provides a dramatic example of a bodily experience that affects decision-making and behavior. Finally, there are also cognitive feelings. Cognitive feelings are the experiential feelings of the effort associated with information processing.

The Body Speaks

The research reviewed above includes work on both easily identifiable specific emotions such as joy or fear, as well as the more diffuse and subtle moods that may not always be explicitly identified. However, affect takes place in the body as well as the brain, and some researchers have explored whether bodily information associated with approach or withdrawal action tendencies may also provide information useful in the selection of appropriate cognitive processing strategies. Arm flexor contraction, or pulling the arm toward the body, occurs during approach behaviors, such as acquiring desired food or objects, and is also associated with pain offset (e.g., withdrawing a hand from the hot stove). Arm extensor contraction, on the other hand, acts to push the arm away from the body, as when distasteful or disgusting objects are rejected. The habitual association of these movements with positive or negative events suggests that the movements themselves might facilitate the corresponding affective or cognitive processes.

R. S. Friedman and Förster (2010) suggest that arm flexion can signal a benign environment while arm extension is more likely to be associated with a problematic environment, and their work provides an extensive body of research in support of this. Arm flexion or extension has now been shown to affect judgments as well as how information is processed. In one intriguing study, subjects were asked to push or pull on a lever as quickly as possible when a word occurred on the screen. The content of the words was irrelevant to the task, but subjects pulled the lever toward them more quickly after good words, such as *peace*, than after bad words, and vice versa. In another study, the researchers found that appetizing foods were both judged more favorably or unfavorably and consumed in greater or smaller quantities when the arm was flexed or extended, respectively. Other studies demonstrated that arm extension increased holistic processing in perceptual tasks, such as the snowy pictures test, which requires identification of familiar objects obscured by visual noise (snow), and the Gestalt completion task, which tests people's ability to perceptually "close" and identify fragmented images.

Other kinds of bodily feelings have also been shown to affect cognitive processing. Work by Dennis Proffitt and colleagues showed that feelings of physical tiredness induced by wearing a heavy backpack or previous exercise led to the same overestimation of the slope of an incline as the sadness created by listening to gloomy music (Proffitt, Bhalla, Gossweiler, & Midgett, 1995; Reiner, Stefanucci, Proffitt & Clore, 2011). Intriguingly, the effect disappeared if subjects were asked to indicate the angle of the slope using a haptic measure of tilting an unseen board instead of verbalizing their response or using a visible protractor. The haptic measure is thought to reflect unconscious perceptual processing in the dorsal "where" pathway, which requires accuracy because it is used to localize a stimulus or for placement of the body in space during action. In contrast, the more conscious ventral "what" pathway takes energy resources into account in determining the amount of work needed to get up the hill. This work illustrates the multiplicity of effects of feelings on cognitive processing that are task dependent and vary in their level of conscious accessibility.

The Forest or the Trees? It Depends on the Context

Recently there have been further findings about the role of affect in processing style that recast our understanding of that relationship. Researchers are now questioning the assumption that the relationship between affect and processing style is invariant; that is, that positive moods always facilitate global processing and negative moods are always associated with local processing. The ongoing context influences which thinking style is favored; thus, the same affective state can trigger different cognitive approaches.

If affective information is taken to be "about" whatever is present (as postulated in the immediacy principle), Gerald Clore and his colleagues (Clore & Huntsinger, 2007, 2009; Huntsinger, Isbell, & Clore, 2012) recently suggested that "what is present" should include the current cognitive processing style. A good mood not only signals a benign environment, but it also signals that the current processing strategy is appropriate for that environment. A sad mood, on the other hand, signals that the current processing style is not getting the job done. Thus, rather than triggering a specific processing style, affect acts to confirm or reject the mode currently being used. Exploration of this question has led to the articulation of the *malleable mood effects hypothesis*, which posits that positive affect says "go" to those cognitive tendencies most accessible at the time, while negative affect is a "stop" signal, and promotes a switch from ongoing processing. What seemed to be an invariant link between positive affect and relational or heuristic processing only appeared so because relational processing is the naturally dominant style for many people much of the time (Huntsinger et al., 2012).

To test the malleable mood effects hypothesis, Huntsinger and colleagues manipulated the style of processing that was dominant and investigated whether it was prolonged by positive moods and switched to another style by negative moods. Crucially, could they show that negative moods will switch people away from local processing to a more global focus, breaking the exclusive linkage between negative affect and local processing? They made local processing dominant by first asking their participants questions about their current feelings or by scenting their questionnaires with a "subtle but pleasant" odorant, reasoning that unexplained odors trigger a focus on the immediate environment. Then participants engaged in an impression formation task where they were given a descriptive paragraph about a hypothetical person, "Carol," and asked to rate how introverted or extroverted she seemed to be. Reliance on categorical information about her occupation (introverted librarian or extroverted salesperson) was taken as evidence of a global focus, whereas reliance on the descriptions of specific behaviors indicated a local focus. Consistent with the malleable mood effects hypothesis, Huntsinger and colleagues found that the local focus was maintained in happy moods, but that their participants switched to a more global focus if they were in sadder moods. Thus, the relationship between affect and processing style depends upon the initial level of focus; it is context dependent, rather than happiness always inducing a global focus and sadness always inducing a local focus.

The tight linkage between positive affect and global focus has also been questioned by Philip Gable and Eddie Harmon-Jones (2009, 2010a, 2010b). They point out that an exclusive focus on the effects of valence led Clore and colleagues to ignore the other key emotional dimension of arousal. Highly arousing positive moods are much more motivating than the low-arousal, mild affective states that are usually induced in experimental tests of feelings-as-information. Gable and Harmon-Jones argue that the lack of motivational intensity in experimental protocols for inducing positive moods, such as watching amusing video clips, listening to pleasant music, receiving small gifts, or recalling pleasant memories, rather than the valence per se, is what leads to heuristic and superficial processing; the participants simply don't find the tasks particularly engaging or motivating and invest little effort because their approach motivation is low. Harmon-Jones, Gable, and colleagues supported this argument experimentally by using video clips of delicious-looking desserts to create higher-intensity approach motivation.[2] In comparison to participants who watched amusing videos of cats, those viewing the delectable and therefore highly desirable desserts showed evidence of a more focused, attentionally narrow cognitive scope on the Kimchi and Navon local/global tasks (Harmon-Jones, Gable, & Price, 2013). Local focus was increased even further when subjects were told they could later consume what was shown. Thus, by increasing the appetitive power of their stimuli, Harmon-Jones and colleagues got results that resembled those of Clore and colleagues' for negative, sadness-inducing stimuli.

Further, Price and Harmon-Jones (2010) found that simply manipulating body position could significantly alter cognitive scope. Leaning back led to a more inclusive (forest) approach to a categorization task, whereas leaning forward lessened the tendency to include borderline items in the category (trees). This intriguing result is reminiscent of James's advice to change body position as a way to initiate changes in emotional experience.

---

2. Gable and Harmon-Jones did not increase approach motivation by ensuring that their participants were hungry before viewing the dessert images, as in some of the hedonic studies discussed in chapter 6, but they did sometimes specify that the participants could take any of the desserts they wished at the end of the experiment, and they did find that their participants rated the desirability of the dessert clips highly.

In addition to casting doubt on the invariant linkage of positive affect with global cognitive scope, other follow-up research has led investigators to question the uniformity of the effects of negative emotions. Lerner and Tiedens (2006) made the case that anger has distinct effects in judgment and decision-making because, unlike other emotions that are considered negative like fear and sadness, it encourages approach motivation and a feeling of confidence in the person experiencing it. When they evoked anger in some of the experiments traditionally used in the feelings-as-information literature to investigate whether processing follows heuristic "rules of thumb" or is more systematic, they found that the sense of certainty evoked by righteous anger had important effects. People in experimentally induced angry states of mind focused more on stereotypes and relied more on readily accessible preexisting schemas than people in sad or fearful states; their results more closely resembled those of people encouraged to feel happy. Further, both happiness and anger resulted in estimating a higher proportion of positive events in the future, an increased optimism. Overall, Lerner and Tiedens found that the effects of anger on risk-taking and decision-making were more akin to those of happiness than those of other "negative" emotions of fear and sadness. They argued that the dominant left prefrontal activation during anger provides neurobiological support for its grouping with approach emotions that are usually considered positive. Note that Lerner and Tiedens' finding that the approach emotion of anger leads to more global processing does not square with Gable and Harmon-Jones's alignment of high approach motivation with local processing. Simple formulae equating "positive" or "approach" in general with "global" and "negative" or "avoid" with "local" do not pan out. Lerner and Tiedens' work adds to the growing sense that it is not enough to consider only the valence dimension when considering the effects of mood and emotion on cognitive mode. They add "certainty" or confidence to the list of other factors that must be taken into consideration in more complete accounts of the integration of emotion and cognition.

Concluding Comments

The study of emotions, as well as our individual relationships with emotions, has traditionally been fraught with contradictory notions. Emotions are seen as the source of our most elevated experiences, such as love and joy as well as religious and aesthetic ecstasy, but are also seen as the source of our most base and animalistic impulses, such as selfishness, envy, jealousy, and behavior motivated by hatred. Emotions have thus been both vilified and elevated, as can be seen by consulting the synonyms given for emotions in different thesauruses: "effusive, fervid, maudlin, and mawkish" in one text contrasted with "moving, touching, poignant, exciting, and arousing" in another (Gohm & Clore, 2002, p. 90). Until the development of the feelings-as-information model, the dominant view of emotion in the study of judgment and decision-making in behavioral economics was as a source of unwanted biases, while in social psychology the focus was on the need for emotion regulation.

The long-standing view of emotions as disruptive to reason, something to be discounted to achieve rational objectivity, was fueled by scientific work that concentrated on arresting urgent emotions such as fear and panic. By refocusing our attention on milder, more everyday, ongoing variations in affective state, the pervasive "feelings" that we experience continuously, the feelings-as-information approach has redressed the balance. Now, the commonsense view that our thoughts, memories, imaginations, judgments, and decisions are influenced by our emotions in *both* productive and unproductive ways has scientific backing. Neuroanthropologist Terrence Deacon at the University of California, Berkeley, vividly expressed this point: "Emotion is not distinct from cognition. Emotion cannot be dissociated from cognition. It is the attached index of attention relevance in every percept, memory or stored motor subroutine" (2006, p. 37).

The feelings-as-information hypothesis posits that emotions are routinely used in making judgments and decisions. It takes the view that emotions are neither good nor bad, but instead provide information that reflects a personal assessment of the relevance of a particular situation; emotions can be seen as the common currency used to assign value to all decision options (Suri, Sheppes, & Gross, 2012). Decisions are made by comparing the anticipated affects associated with various decision options, then choosing the most favorable anticipated affective state. In just a few years, we have moved from allowing no role of affect in decision-making theories to recognizing that emotions are needed to explain the mechanisms behind all decisions, which are made by affective comparisons.

The mostly behavioral accounts covered in this chapter represent an impressive body of work demonstrating the role of affect in cognitive function. There is no longer any question that affective variables alter judgments, cognitive strategies, and decision-making. However, only limited work in this field has attempted to ground these findings in brain functions. In a review of affective influence on judgments and decisions, Winkielman and colleagues argue that some questions about the interactions of emotion and cognition can only be answered in reference to a biopsychological model (Winkielman, Knutson, Paulus, & Trujillo, 2007). For example, what is the neural coding for the "value" that affective states represent and that gives rise to subsequent feelings? How does affect influence the neural functions involved in information processing, such as attention, perception, memory, and decision-making? What is the neural basis of feelings, and where and how is the affective information brought together with the cognitive evaluation to form a judgment or decision? Answers to these questions are beginning to emerge in the vibrant and growing interdisciplinary field of neuroeconomics, work that we will take up in detail in the next chapter.

10

Emotion–Cognition Interactions

Attention, Perception, and Neuroeconomics

Trying to find my son among the throng of commuters at Grand Central Station at 5 o'clock always seems surprisingly effortless to me (LO). As I quickly scan the streaming crowd, my eyes seem almost pulled to the tall male with short blond hair and earphones. How do I so readily pick his image out of the mass of visual information? This common yet noteworthy experience of the ease of an apparently complex visual search introduces a key theme of this chapter: how our perceptions and attention can be guided and focused by our emotions.

As seen in the previous chapter, the feelings-as-information paradigm spearheaded by Schwarz and Clore has conclusively established that affective states influence cognitive processes, including high-level processes such as judgment and decision-making. The elegant work of Joseph LeDoux described in chapter 4 showed that emotional stimuli are processed differently than neutral stimuli, in part because they activate the amygdala. In this chapter, we look at the related question of how the emotional stimulus or affective state alters information processing in the brain. A number of researchers are currently exploring the effects of affective stimuli on information processing, beginning from the earliest levels of perception and attention and progressing to the use of that information to make choices or decisions. Work in affective neuroscience is beginning to more clearly outline how emotional systems function in the brain to shape behavior. We begin by looking at the brain processes that alter attention to affective stimuli, and conclude with a brief introduction to the emerging field variously called decision neuroscience or neuroeconomics.

Attention: Spotlights and Zoom Lenses

As we saw in the chapter on emotions and memory, we become aware of only a limited set of the vast array of sensory information reaching our senses (and remember even less). What and how information is selected for processing has traditionally been seen as the function of attention. As is often the case in psychology, the nature of attention was coherently captured by William James:

> Everyone knows what attention is. It is the taking possession by the mind, in clear and vivid form, of one out of what seem several simultaneously possibly objects. Focalization, concentration, of consciousness are of its essence. It implies withdrawal from some things in order to deal effectively with others. (1890, p. 403)

The metaphor commonly used to capture the ability of attention to make sensory information "clear and vivid" is a spotlight, although recently it has also been compared to the zoom lens of a camera. The attentional beam illuminates the scene, and then zooms in on objects of interest, which seem magnified and more vivid relative to the rest of the visual field (Muller, Bartelt, Donner, Villringer, & Brandt, 2003). Objects within the spotlight of attention are processed more quickly or efficiently, often at the expense of information at other locations, as pointed out by James above, and so dramatically demonstrated by the invisible gorilla example described in chapter 8. Functional magnetic resonance imaging (fMRI) studies support the sense that attention is necessary for sensory processing; if attention is occupied by an absorbing task, stimuli may fail to activate visual processing areas in the midtemporal lobe (Rees, Frith, & Lavie, 1999, as cited in Pessoa, McKenna, Gutierrez, & Ungerleider, 2002). Attention can thus also act as a gate or filter to limit the awareness of stimuli not selected for processing.

The spotlight and zoom lens metaphors turn out to accurately capture what is happening in the brain. In an fMRI study, Brefzynski and DeYoe (1999) measured the neural effects of attention independently of eye movements by making use of our remarkable ability to direct attention to a particular area of visual space *without* actually moving our eyes to focus on that spot. They found that activity increased in visual areas responding to the covertly attended regions, just as the spotlight metaphor predicts. This modulation by attention begins in the earliest visual cortical regions, again supporting the idea that attention acts to gate what gets processed. Furthermore, Muller et al. (2003) found that zooming in on objects by contracting attentional focus allows them to be identified more quickly and accurately than objects in an expanded attentional focus. Consistent with this behavioral evidence, the level of activity in visual cortex decreased when attention covered a larger region and increased as attention contracted. As we'll see, other recent findings further confirm the aptness of these attention metaphors.

As a limited capacity system, the attentional system can only fully and carefully process what is most relevant, so how and which stimuli receive attention has been a major question in cognitive psychology. Current models of selective attention include two basic processes, referred to as top-down and bottom-up (for recent reviews, see Knudsen, 2007; Petersen & Posner, 2012). Top-down regulation, or endogenous attention (for a brief review, see Wolfe, 2010), is what was used to activate a search image for the tall blond male in the opening example. An internally generated representation is used to gate sensory processing, which is now known to be mediated by the dorsal frontoparietal attention network. Top-down attention is often described using the well-known "cocktail party effect"; it's what allows attention to be focused on the conversation of a friend by "tuning out" all other conversations at the party. Endogenous top-down attention is under volitional control, thus reflecting a prioritization of information processing based on what is deemed to be of relevance or interest.

Bottom-up, or exogenous, processing, on the other hand, is driven by low-level features of the stimulus itself; this is what occurs when we immediately notice a red box among an array of black boxes. Stimuli that differ from others in the array along a single, basic element of vision such as color, size, or intensity, seem to "pop out" of the background and enter awareness independently of the will of the individual (this paradigm was pioneered by Princeton psychologist Anne Treisman; for a review, see Treisman, 1986). "Pop-out" stimuli are identified quickly and automatically regardless of the number of other objects, or distractors, in a visual array. Targets that do not automatically activate attentional focus, such as a red 5 in a field of red 2's, can only be identified after a sequential inspection of each item. With stimuli that do not pop out, adding more distractors increases looking time, as each item has to be inspected in turn. Bottom-up processing of stimuli is thought to occur by simultaneous parallel processing of the entire sensory field. However, although parallel processing is fast and efficient, it cannot provide a full evaluation of a stimulus at this unconscious, preattentive stage. Objects in the parallel streams subsequently compete for attentional resources, and built-in wiring or previously learned characteristics ensure that novel, unexpected, or biologically significant stimuli pop out automatically, reflexively capturing the focus of attention. The selection of attended bottom-up features is also thought to be under the control of a frontoparietal attention network, although it is attributed to a different subregion than that which guides top-down regulation—the ventral as opposed to the dorsal stream. Although bottom-up processing is often described as automatic and reflexive, it can be modulated by top-down goals or expectations. For example, if a previous target was red, attention will be drawn to a red item in the next task even if it is now irrelevant (Wolfe, 2010). Likewise, top-down goals can be diverted due to sudden and compelling bottom-up events, and even unconscious goals have recently been shown to modulate conscious top-down goals automatically (Dijksterhuis & Aarts, 2010). Thus, most of the time, attentional processing results from an interplay of bottom-up and top-down effects, and recent models of attention tend to emphasize the need to understand the interplay of these two systems during perceptual processing (see Pourtois, Schettino, &Vuilleumier, 2012). Regardless of the source, attentional regulation modulates activity in the sensory pathways activated by the attended stimulus, from as early as primary sensory cortex (Padmala & Pessoa, 2008) to higher object-specific regions such as the fusiform face area (Phan, Wager, Taylor, & Liberzon, 2002).

Emotion and the Regulation of Attention

Emotionally salient stimuli always demand attention; indeed, a primary function of emotion is the regulation of attention (Öhman, 2005), ensuring that what is salient and meaningful has privileged access to attentional resources. If the crowd Leah was scanning for her son had included something unexpected, such as a sudden movement, a loud noise, or someone with a gun, her attention would have been "grabbed" in spite of its top-down directive. As described in chapter 4, Öhman and Mineka (2001) showed that threat stimuli and emotional faces take less time to identify than do similar neutral targets in a visual array. These stimuli are able to activate the amygdala even when they are presented subliminally by masking (Whalen et al., 1998). As we'll see below, many researchers now propose that emotional modulation of attention is mediated by the amygdala.

This effect of emotion on attention has been cogently demonstrated in another version of the cocktail party effect. In this version, hearing one's name mentioned elsewhere in the room will instantly grab one's attention even when one is intently attending to an engrossing conversation. This has been explored experimentally using a dichotic listening experiment in which a listeners hear a different stream of verbal information in each ear. The subjects' attention is directed to the information in one ear by asking them to repeat what they hear there, a process called shadowing. Although subjects are usually unable to decode semantic information in the unattended channel, they pick out their own name, even when it's embedded in a stream of other unattended words (reviewed in Phelps, 2006).

In addition to the visual search and dichotic listening tasks mentioned above, a number of other tasks are used to explore the effects of emotion on attention. Work using the attentional blink paradigm introduced in the chapter on memory showed that the detection of an emotional second target (T2) in a stream of distractors is less affected by its proximity to the first target (T1) than a neutral T2. Thus, emotional items are able to grab attention even if it is already occupied, and may also be able to access attention earlier than neutral stimuli. In fact, emotional stimuli produce their own blink; when a negative arousing picture is shown at T1, the subsequent attentional blink is longer, presumably because attentional resources remain engaged with the emotionally salient stimulus (A. K. Anderson, 2005; A. K. Anderson & Phelps, 2001). Because emotional stimuli demand and require more attentional resources, they interfere with processing of other, non-emotional stimuli; for example, a simple task, such as determining the orientation of a visual stimulus, is slower following viewing of emotional pictures (Pereira et al., 2006), and participants perform a word discrimination auditory task more slowly when simultaneously viewing unpleasant pictures. In the emotional Stroop paradigm, which replaces the color names of the original version with emotional stimuli, people take longer to name the color of the ink if the word is emotional as opposed to neutral, also demonstrating the ability of emotion to grab and retain attention.

In the dot probe task, the time participants take to detect a simple dot stimulus in the peripheral visual field is reduced if the dot's location was previously cued by an emotional face, demonstrating that an emotional stimulus can bias attention to its location. Attentional bias has also been shown using a subliminal stimulus, such as a rapidly presented masked face. A neuroimaging study performed by Patrik Vuilleumier and his colleagues in London found that emotional face stimuli activated the left amygdala regardless of whether or not they were the target of attention (Vuilleumier, Armony, Driver, & Dolan, 2001). Together, these and many other experimental tasks have shown that emotional stimuli are selected for preattentional processing and so have privileged access to attentional resources, even when those resources are limited (for recent reviews, see Pourtois et al., 2012; Vuilleumier & Huang, 2009).

Traditionally, however, attention and attentional regulation have been studied as cognitive processes, so until recently the effect of emotion on attention was scarcely investigated. As a consequence, numerous controversies and debates have emerged as emotion researchers have attempted to incorporate the role of emotion into the traditional attention models described above (Pessoa, 2005; Pessoa, Kastner, & Ungerleider, 2002; Pourtois et al., 2012; Vuilleumier, 2005; Vuilleumier & Huang, 2009).

Does the privileged processing of emotional stimuli mean that they don't require attentional resources? Luiz Pessoa and his colleagues at the National Institute of Mental Health and Princeton tested this by varying the attentional load of a competing task; they reasoned that if processing of emotional stimuli is not dependent on attention, then even concurrent tasks that demand a lot of attention will not interfere with emotional processing. The results of such studies are currently mixed. Some research has shown that high attentional load eliminates the increased activation of the amygdala by emotional stimuli, even when using highly arousing emotional stimuli such as mutilation pictures (Pessoa et al., 2002; Pessoa, Oliverira & Pereira, 2010). These results indicate that attentional resources are needed for emotional processing. Furthermore, researchers now agree that the identification of emotional stimuli is not fully independent of the number of distractors in a visual array (Pessoa, 2008), so it is not equivalent to the preattentive pop-out described for bottom-up processing using simple salient visual stimuli .

However, other work supports Vuilleumier and colleagues' position that emotional stimuli have privileged access to processing resources even under attentionally demanding conditions. For example, Attar and Müller (2012) recorded neural responses and demonstrated that task-irrelevant, emotionally distressing IAPS (International Affective Picture Set) pictures withdrew processing resources from the task stimuli, and, importantly, this occurred even when participants performed a high-attentional-load visual discrimination task. Another recent study by Beatrice de Gelder and colleagues (Pichon, de Gelder, & Grèzes, 2012) using short video clips of actors performing threatening and neutral bodily actions adds to the evidence that threat stimuli are automatically processed. The researchers asked their participants to either attend to emotional aspects of the stimuli by identifying the emotion expressed as fear, anger, or neutral, or to attend to nonemotional aspects of the stimulus by identifying the color of a small, briefly presented patch on the actor's chest. The responses were significantly slower for the nonemotional color naming when the clips depicted threat rather than neutral stimuli, suggesting that threat stimuli were accessing processing resources despite the high attentional load created by the concurrent task and the fact that attention was not directed to the emotional aspects of the stimulus. Some of de Gelder and colleagues' neuroimaging results also support the idea that threat stimuli are automatically processed regardless of other attentional demands. They found that brain regions involved in regulating defensive bodily movements, namely, the periaqueductal gray region (PAG), hypothalamus, and the premotor cortex, were active in response to threatening conditions in both the emotion and the color-naming tasks. In contrast, activation in the amygdala and regions of the temporal cortex did depend on explicitly directing attention to the emotional expression: The activations were larger to threat than to neutral stimuli during emotion labeling, but not during the color-naming task. Thus, de Gelder and colleagues found that some brain regions are automatically triggered by threat stimuli, specifically those involved in activating a threat response, whereas others, surprisingly including the amygdala, are affected by whether or not the focus is explicitly directed to emotional aspects of the stimuli.

Thus, the role of attention in the prioritization of emotional stimuli remains unresolved; some studies support Vuilleumier's position that emotional stimuli have privileged and automatic access to attention, whereas others provide evidence for Pessoa's claim that emotional stimuli require attentional processing resources, and discrepancies in results may in some cases be due to task differences or differing levels of attentional load. Bishop (2007) has made the intriguing suggestion that individual differences may also need to be considered; for example, anxious individuals show greater interference from threat-related stimuli, and so seem more resistant to the effect of attentional load.

Emotion Determines What We Smell and Hear

In addition to, or possibly as a result of, the regulation of attention by emotion, emotions and affective states can alter the processing of sensory stimuli in a way that actually changes how we experience the world. One of the earliest experiments to demonstrate this used the fear-conditioning paradigm described in chapter 4. Monkeys were fear-conditioned using an auditory tone that before conditioning was relatively ineffective at activating the auditory neurons being recorded (Weinberger, 2004). Fear conditioning shifted the preferred frequency response of cells to the conditioned frequency, a change that persisted for weeks. Although only frequencies within an octave of the initially preferred frequency were effective at switching the frequency preference, this was sufficient to retune the system, such that the previously unstimulating frequencies could now be "heard" and thus activate the necessary survival behaviors. Later work showed that this plasticity depended on the amygdala and its ability to activate the forebrain acetylcholine system. An even more dramatic modification of sensory processing has now been shown in humans (Li, Howard, Parrish, & Gottfried, 2008). In this study, pairs of odor enantiomers[1] that could not be discriminated before aversive conditioning were easily distinguished after fear conditioning to one of the pair. The ability to discriminate between these formerly indistinguishable odors was correlated with the development of distinct signaling patterns in primary olfactory cortex. Emotional experience reshaped neural pathways to represent the now-relevant distinction between the odors.

In a final related study (Siegel & Stefanucci, 2011), the mood of subjects was manipulated by asking them to write about a frightening or neutral experience before having them rate a series of short tones for loudness. Those who wrote about a frightening experience rated the tones as significantly louder than those in a neutral mood. Thus, both emotional experiences and affective state can alter sensory processing so that sensory sensitivity is optimally tuned to the needs of the experienced environment.

---

1. Enantiomers are mirror-image molecules that have nonsuperimposable structures, akin to the left and right hands.

In a real sense, the world that is seen, heard, and smelled is shaped by emotional experience.

Emotional Awareness

A recent study by Eric Anderson and his colleagues at Northeastern University provides compelling evidence for the idea that emotional affect may actually alter what we see. This study used the classic binocular rivalry paradigm to explore how affective state influences what contents reach visual awareness (Anderson, Siegel, & Barrett, 2011). To create binocular rivalry, they presented a different image to each eye using special goggles, resulting in the two eyes' images competing for perceptual dominance. A smiling, scowling, or neutral face shown to one eye competed with a house stimulus presented to the other eye. Prior to the binocular rivalry task, positive or negative affective state was induced by presenting a series of five congruent IAPS images. Faces always dominated visual awareness over houses, but scowling faces had the strongest effect when subjects were in an unpleasant mood, while smiling faces dominated most strongly when subjects were in a pleasant state. Thus, preexisting affect is able to influence which stimuli enter awareness.

A further question that can be asked is whether emotional stimuli typically impair or enhance attention. Although early studies, such as the emotional Stroop or the attentional blink, showed that emotional stimuli interfere with the perception of immediately subsequent stimuli, an emotional event may also sharpen the senses and so facilitate the processing even of nonemotional objects present in the same environment. The ability of emotions to enhance perceptual function was also seen in an experiment by Elizabeth Phelps and colleagues (Phelps, Ling, & Carrasco, 2006), who showed that briefly flashing a fearful emotional face decreased the contrast needed to detect the orientation of a grating subsequently presented in the peripheral visual field. Viewing fearful faces actually lowered a basic perceptual threshold. This effect did not occur using nonemotional faces or inverted emotional faces (which prevents the recognition of emotional expression). Importantly, contrast sensitivity was further increased if the fearful face was used to direct attention to the location of the subsequent grating. Thus, emotional and nonemotional directing of attention appeared to have additive effects, a point we'll return to later in the chapter.

Bocanegra and Zeelenberg (2009) recently extended this result by showing that although an emotional stimulus may enhance the perception of some features of the environment, it may simultaneously impair the processing of other features. In their study, they found that briefly presented fearful faces did enhance the processing of subsequent low-spatial-frequency (LSF) gratings, confirming the findings of Phelps, et al. (2006). In contrast, brief presentation of fearful faces before high-spatial-frequency (HSF) gratings actually impaired their subjects' detection of the orientation of the gratings. The visual system is known to decompose stimuli into low- and high-spatial-frequency features that are separately processed in distinct pathways. Coarse-grained LSF features of a stimulus travel quickly through the magnocellular visual pathway, whereas fine-grained HSF features are processed in the more slowly conducting parvocellular pathway. Bocanegra and Zeelenberg found that emotional stimuli selectively enhance processing in the rapid, magnocellular pathway, which is tuned to detect visual features such as motion, depth, direction, and global configuration that help identify a potential threat. This makes adaptive sense, as even the hint of a threat needs to be detected quickly, whereas a more detailed analysis can begin once the threat is known.

Thus, in addition to producing attentional biases to cued locations as seen in the classic dot-probe studies, emotional stimuli also produce a perceptual bias toward the coarser, lower-frequency aspects of stimuli that provide a rapid assessment of the threat. Importantly, in a follow-up study, Bocanegra, Huijding, and Zeelenberg (2012) showed that, unlike the perceptual enhancement effect of emotional threat stimuli, the preferential biasing of attention to locations cued by threat stimuli is not selective for spatial frequency, suggesting that perceptual and attentional modulation by emotion are distinct processes that could rely on different neural pathways. Interestingly, in their later study, Bocanegra et al. also measured their participants' social anxiety, and found that the spatial frequency effect occurred only in the group that scored above the median on their anxiety measures. The biasing of attention to locations cued by threat stimuli was also higher in the greater-social-anxiety group, suggesting that anxiety heightens both perceptual and attentional responses to threats.

Whether an emotional stimulus enhances or impairs a subsequent or contiguous stimulus depends on timing. In the version of attentional blink studies where T1 is emotional, this emotional stimulus impairs the processing of an immediately subsequent stimulus. However, the fearful faces/contrast sensitivity study by Phelps and colleagues described above showed that if time is provided for disengagement from the emotional stimulus, the processing of subsequent stimuli close in time will be enhanced. This has also been shown using the visual search paradigm, where fear stimuli can enhance search for subsequent nonthreatening stimuli in the larger environment (Becker, 2009). In Becker's study, participants needed to determine whether a house was present in a complex scene. The presence of a fear face just preceding the search scene produced a faster search rate compared to preceding happy or neutral faces. Becker argues that there are two stages in the threat detection process: For a short time immediately after presentation of a threat stimulus (under 600 milliseconds), processing of other stimuli is impaired, but that inhibition is followed by a generalized increase in processing of all stimuli that might help in fight or flight.

Ciesielski, Armstrong, Zald, and Olatunji (2010) further examined the temporal characteristics of emotion's effects on attention. Using a rapid serial visual stream paradigm similar to that used in attentional blink studies, the authors varied the timing between an emotional image and a subsequent target image (a rotated image) over four intervals ranging from 200 to 800 milliseconds, comparing fear, disgust, and erotic images to neutral images. All emotional stimuli impaired subjects' target detection rates compared to neutral images up to 600 milliseconds, suggesting that attention had been captured by the emotional stimuli. However, consistent with Becker's two-phase theory, at 800 milliseconds emotional stimuli actually enhanced rather than suppressed target detection compared to neutral images. These findings also support the idea that emotional attention consists of two separate mechanisms acting at different times. Emotional stimuli first capture attention, and so impair attention to other nearby stimuli. Subsequently, the stimulus is disengaged, and processing of other features of the environment, which may be of relevance to the emotional event, is then enhanced.

As we discuss in more detail later, it is likely that both enhancement and impairment of early vision are due to the activation of the amygdala by emotional stimuli, and importantly, projections from the amygdala to early visual cortex are primarily magnocellular. Magnocellular and parvocellular pathways are thought to mutually inhibit each other, so the facilitation of the LSF pathway from the amygdala to visual cortex might act to inhibit the competing HSF pathway. Indeed, it is LSF information in emotional faces that is critical for activating the amygdala (see Pourtois et al., 2012, for a review).

Emotion-Enhanced Vividness

Emotional experiences and memories are often described as uniquely vivid. In an ingenious experiment, Adam Anderson and his colleagues (Todd, Talmi, Schmitz, Susskind, & Anderson, 2012) produced evidence suggesting that this subjective vividness is due to enhancements of neural signaling provoked by the emotional event, which they call emotion-enhanced vividness (EEV). It is this vivid quality of emotional events that may allow them to be more easily detected and encoded for subsequent memory.

Vividness was measured by having participants estimate the amount of physical visual noise overlaid on an image. An emotional image was judged as having less noise than a neutral image with the same noise, and the difference between these measurements was used to calculate EEV. EEV was found to predict measures of both recognition memory and vividness of recall one week later. Visual signals measured as event-related potentials (ERPs) that correlated with EEV were found over the lateral occipital cortex, a region involved in object recognition, showing that subjective vividness of emotional images was based on a perceptual process. A mediation analysis further determined that the increased sensitivity to emotional images as measured by EEV was mediated by the amygdala. Thus, emotional objects have increased visual clarity, which may allow them to be more rapidly discriminated, and endows them with special salience that enhances their memorability.

Emotional Attention

How is the regulation of emotional attention integrated with other known attentional regulation mechanisms? Recently, Vuilleumier and colleagues (Pourtois et al., 2012; Vuilleumier & Huang, 2009) have argued that emotional attention should be considered a separate process, independent from either top-down or bottom-up mechanisms. They argue that the activation of the amygdala by emotional stimuli is what distinguishes the effects of emotional attention independent of the frontoparietal attention networks. However, although the source of emotional attention regulation is distinct from top-down or bottom-up mechanisms, it nonetheless acts to modulate the same sensory processes and in much the same way (although not exactly the same, as we just saw for the distinctive effect of emotion on subjective vividness). One piece of evidence that the amygdala plays a central role in facilitating the processing of emotionally salient stimuli is the finding that the attenuation of the attentional blink by emotionally salient stimuli does not occur in patients with amygdala lesions (Anderson & Phelps, 2001).

Recall from chapter 4 that the amygdala, which acts as a central neural hub, is massively interconnected to other brain regions, and is thus potentially able to modulate sensory systems from the very earliest stages of processing. In addition to having direct inputs to sensory regions, the amygdala can also influence these systems indirectly by activating nonspecific nuclei[2] that mediate arousal, as has been described in its enhancement of memory processes. Recent neuroimaging studies have shown that the emotional enhancement of activation in many visual regions, from primary visual cortex to object recognition regions in the temporal lobe, is mediated by amygdala activity (Pessoa et al., 2010).

Further evidence comes from studies of humans with damage to the right frontoparietal attentional network. Such patients appear oblivious to information in contralateral left hemispace in the face of intact perceptual function, an attentional disorder called hemispatial neglect. Although they will be able to "see" an object in this neglected space if explicitly asked to attend to it, at other times they act as if the left half of the world simply doesn't exist. The effects of spatial neglect can be profound; if asked to draw a clock, for example, patients may draw only half the clock, or will try to fit all 12 hours into the right half. They may use only the right half of a piece of paper to write on, and patients have been known to shave or put makeup on only half their face.

Although hemineglect results in great difficulties with visual search when the targets are in the left visual field, emotional stimuli such as images of fearful faces or spiders are less severely neglected than neutral images. The advantage of emotional stimuli in breaking through the neglect is accompanied by increased activity in the visual cortex as well as the orbitofrontal cortex (OFC) and anterior cingulate cortex (ACC) (Pourtois et al., 2012; Vuilleumier, 2005). Thus, visual sensory pathways appear to be enhanced in

---

2. These include the nucleus basalis of Meynert, which uses the neurotransmitter acetylcholine (ACh), and the locus coeruleus, which use norepinephrine. Both of these nuclei are activated by the amygdala and distribute their axons widely throughout the brain to mediate arousal.

spite of the destruction of the crucial parietal component of frontoparietal attentional networks, suggesting that a separate amygdala network can act to enhance the perception of emotional stimuli. Conversely, those with lesions of the amygdala still show enhanced signaling of face processing in the fusiform face area during spatial attention, but will show no increased enhancement to emotional as opposed to neutral faces. Thus, although spatial attention and emotional attention act to enhance sensory processes in similar ways, they appear to be dissociable.

Anxiety and Attention

Attention clearly plays a role in modulating anxiety: Top-down control of attention to lessen the impact of threat-related stimuli is an important regulatory strategy. Models of anxiety discussed in chapter 4 emphasize hypersensitivity to threats as well as impaired attentional regulation in response to potential threats, such as impaired extinction of fear. Sonia Bishop and her coworkers at the University of California, Berkeley, propose that a more general attentional deficit is an additional contributor to the development of pathological anxiety. Bishop (2009) proposes that when demands on attention are otherwise low, people with anxiety disorders are less able to regulate how their attention is allocated to ignore distractors, but in circumstances when attention is fully occupied by a task, anxious people are no more distractible than those without an anxiety disorder. This attentional deficit is not specific to threatening stimuli; rather, it is a general attentional style that leads to great difficulties and ongoing discomfort in day-to-day life.

To test her hypothesis about the existence of a general attentional deficit in trait (rather than state) anxiety, Bishop devised an experiment with non-threatening stimuli, using a task that varied attentional load as well as the amount of conflict between the target and the distractors. She divided her participants into anxious and nonanxious groups using a standard self-report anxiety scale that measures both trait and state anxiety, then asked participants to notice either Xs or Ns in briefly presented strings of six letters (see Figure 10.1 for example stimuli). The task was made more difficult (high perceptual load) by embedding only one of the target letters in the string and easier (low perceptual load) by presenting strings consisting of only Xs or only Ns. To test distractibility, an irrelevant and larger letter appeared below the letter string, which could be either the same as the tar-

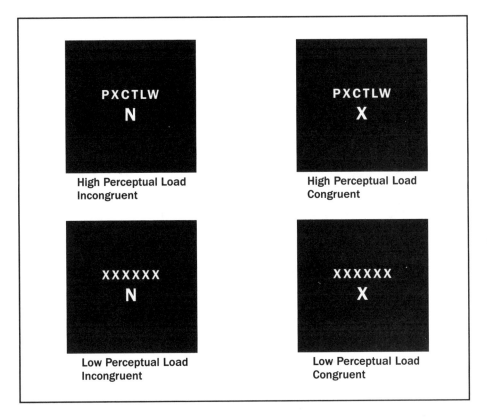

Figure 10.1 Example stimuli used in Bishop's (2008) experiments on attention and anxiety.

Source: Adapted from *Nature Neuroscience*, Volume 12, Sonia J. Bishop, "Trait anxiety and impoverished prefrontal control of attention," pages 92-98. copyright © December 2008, with permission from Nature Publishing Group.

get letter present in the current string (congruent), the target letter (X or N) not presented in the current string (noncongruent), or a letter other than X or N (neutral). The conflict between the target and distractors is much greater in the congruent than in the noncongruent conditions, and thus these distracting stimuli make more demands on response conflict attentional mechanisms. Under the high-load conditions, anxious participants were just as good at ignoring the distractor letter as those with lower anxiety scores, which contradicts the "processing efficiency" theory that proposes generally less efficient attentional mechanisms in anxious individuals. Where the anxious and nonanxious groups differed was in their responses in the low-load condition: Anxious participants were more distracted by the irrelevant letters, as measured by greater slowing of reaction times in the incongruent versus congruent distractor condition. This finding provides experimental support for the idea that an important component of anxiety is an inability to regulate attention in situations when it is not fully occupied by a demanding task.

Using fMRI with regions of interest in prefrontal cortex, Bishop and colleagues found higher levels of activity in dorsolateral prefrontal cortex (dlPFC) for the incongruent than the congruent distractors because of the need to resolve conflict between the target and distractor. Importantly, the increased dlPFC activity occurred *only* for the low- and not for the high-anxiety group, suggesting that the anxious participants lacked an important attentional mechanism for response conflict.

Bishop has identified a specific attentional deficit that contributes to the development of anxiety disorders, in combination with the several other variations in brain systems that relate to anxiety that we have discussed in previous chapters. The high sensitivity to threatening stimuli and overactivation and responsiveness of the amygdala, plus the deficits in extinction of fear correlated with lower ventromedial prefrontal cortex (vmPFC) activity discussed in chapters 4 and 8, probably interact with the decrement in attentional regulation under low-load conditions to increase the effect of perceived threats. In addition, other mechanisms of body awareness and homeostatic regulation dependent on the insula, discussed in chapter 7, may also amplify the effects of distracting stimuli, adding to the "perfect storm" of variations in brain systems that predispose people to anxiety and make this condition difficult to treat effectively.

Bishop (2009) suggests an approach that we have already discussed for the management of anxiety: mindfulness. Her experimental work provides a new rationale for the potential power of the attention-training techniques developed through the practice of meditation. The idea is that the ongoing monitoring of and disengagement from distracting thoughts, feelings, and sensations in order to return to the object of focus in meditation (e.g., the breath, the body, an image) can give anxious individuals practice in disengaging their attention from distractors under low-load conditions.

Emotional stimuli thus appear to use specialized pathways, primarily featuring the amygdala with its unique ability to alter and direct information processing throughout the brain, to ensure that emotional signals have priority access to necessary processing and attentional resources. This not only allows emotional stimuli to alter processing of other stimuli in the broader environment, which may contain information relevant to elaborating a well-integrated behavioral response, but it allows them to tune sensory systems based on relevant emotional experience. Emotional stimuli are thus key in adapting individuals to their environments, as they have also been key in shaping the more general features of a species. We next turn to looking at how these emotional signals affect decisions and choices.

The Human Decision-Maker

Together with research actively exploring the role of affect in judgments and decision-making, discussed in the previous chapter, work in economics is beginning to show that emotion and affective state have a significant influence on decision-making. Although some early economic theorists (e.g., Adam Smith) considered the role of emotions or "passions" like fear and anger in economic behavior (see discussion in Wu, Sacchet, & Knutson, 2012), classical economic models of choice and decision-making were based on the assumption that humans are rational "actors" who, after assessing all available information, make decisions that maximize utility (the economic term for value or benefit). This implies that the context in which a choice is presented should have no effect on decision-making, a concept referred to as invariance. The rational decision-maker need consider only information affecting the overall cost and gain of his or her choices.

Beginning in the 1970s, psychologists Daniel Kahneman and Amos Tversky began to test the theoretical assumptions of classical economic models by looking at real-life human decision-making and choice. Their work has compiled impressive evidence showing that human choices are subject to a number of seemingly irrelevant—and, by the criteria of classical economic models, irrational—yet predictable influences that result in deviations from maximum utility theory. They have identified over 20 different errors of reasoning or thinking they call "cognitive biases," although some of these biases clearly arise from emotional influences that "distort" rational thinking. These biases highlight the "psychological processes that underlie perception and judgment" (Kahneman & Tversky, 1996, p. 582) that were thought to be due to various mechanisms, from inherent limitations in brain function to the tendency of humans to operate in a subjective reality informed by emotional or moral motivations, such as the desire for a positive self-image, that can seem impermeable to objective reasoning. One example of such an emotional or "hot" bias is the well-known optimism bias that leads individuals to think that they are less likely than others to experience negative outcomes, such as a car accident or getting lung cancer from smoking. Other biases are more cognitive, or "cold," in form, such as the tendency to ignore relevant information such as probability, which may reflect inherent biases in how the brain works.

One disconcerting example of a cognitive bias is called the anchoring effect, in which a reference point or anchor is used as a guide for reaching a decision. This anchor can be implicit, and decisions have been shown to be influenced by totally irrelevant, unconscious anchors. Kahneman (2011) provides an example in his recent book titled *Thinking: Fast and Slow*. Experienced judges were asked to throw a pair of dice that had been secretly loaded to roll only three or nine before making a sentencing decision on a shoplifting offense. They were then asked whether the prison sentence should be more or less than the number they rolled before deciding on an exact sentence. Although the long experience of these judges meant they would normally arrive at very similar sentences in the two cases, those who rolled a nine proposed an average of eight months, while those who rolled the three proposed an average of five months. Their decision had been "anchored" unconsciously to the number that randomly came up on the dice.

Based on their research, Kahneman and Tversky developed an alternative model of decision-making under risk, called prospect theory, that reflects the role of psychological functions in decisions and choices. Psychologist Daniel Kahneman was awarded a Nobel Prize in Economics in 2002 for this work, which has been expanded into a whole subfield of economics called behavioral economics (Amos Tversky had died four years earlier at age 59, and the prize is not awarded posthumously[3]). More recently, the nascent field of neuroeconomics has begun to establish the neural substrates for how and why humans make the choices they do. The study of neuroeconomics has grown explosively in the last decade, and in this chapter we focus on only a small subset of work being done in this field.

---

3. Kahneman told the *New York Times* in an interview, "I feel it is a joint prize. We were twinned for more than a decade" (Goode, 2002). Kahneman is married to psychologist Anne Treisman, whose work on visual search we mentioned earlier in this chapter.

Heuristics

We introduced the concept of a heuristic, or the use of a rule of thumb in decisions, in the last chapter through the affect heuristics of the feelings-as-information hypothesis. Kahneman and Tversky also proposed that the deviations from rational thinking produced by cognitive biases often result from the reliance on heuristics. These mental shortcuts, based on general-ized schematics for arriving at a rapid decision, rather than taking time to engage in slower, more effortful reasoning based on the facts at hand, can result in reasoning errors. The idea that decision-making can be guided by two separate processes, one fast but sometimes faulty and the other more accurate but effortful, led Kahneman and Tversky to propose the existence of two separate human brain systems that carry out these different pro-cesses. System 1 is the fast, automatic intuitive system that relies on heu-ristics, while System 2 uses slow and deliberate analytical reasoning that requires conscious attention to reach decisions.

The idea that the brain is organized into two separate operating modes or systems has a long history in both psychology and philosophy, and in some ways overlaps with the emotion/cognition duality we have already discussed. In Kahneman's scheme, System 2 should serve as a check for the quick first impression provided by System 1, but he proposes that it sometimes suffers from its own emotional shortcomings, such as the tendency to be lazy, and so often accepts the quick-and-dirty decision of System 1 without question. This is partly justified because System 1, based on accumulated experiential evidence, *is* often right; in addition, it takes effort to analyze the situation more carefully. Intriguingly, System 2 is more likely to accept the response of System 1 when energy reserves are low, which can be measured by some-thing as simple as levels of blood sugar, or when available information is incomplete or overly complex. As Damasio found with his patient Elliot, complex decisions can overwhelm the analytical processing capacity of the brain, and relying on a rapid, affective summary of our past experience is sometimes the best that can be done.

Loss Aversion

To better model the complex decisions humans face in real life, Kahneman and Tversky focused their work on decision-making under risk or uncertainty, although their results have been found to extend to other kinds of decision-making as well. One of their first results challenged the classical economic assumption of invariance, that context should not influence decision-making, by showing that how a choice is *framed* significantly influences choice. For example, people are more likely to choose to bet if the odds are expressed as having a 50% chance of winning than if they are described as having a 50% chance of losing, in spite of the obvious fact that the risks of the two bets are equal. The tendency to prefer a choice expressed as a gain, or to prefer avoiding losses over acquiring gains, is a common cognitive bias called *loss aversion*, and in some cases the size of this effect is astonishing. For example, people will take a bet that gives them a 50% chance of winning $100 only if the potential loss of the bet is under $50, about half the gain. Thus, the hedonic impact of a loss of $50 appears to be experienced as equal to the hedonic impact of a gain of $100; people feel twice as bad about the possibility of losing something as they feel good about the possibility of gaining it. In betting scenarios, the point at which the hedonic impact of losing and gaining is equal, or when individuals are equally like to choose to bet or not bet, is referred to as the *risk premium*.

Loss aversion also leads to the related phenomenon of *risk aversion*, or the tendency to prefer a certain gain over a potentially larger but uncertain gain. Together, loss and risk aversion have been found to explain many "irrational" risky decision-making phenomena (e.g., the preference to invest in safer bonds rather than the riskier but better-performing stocks), and has been seen in trading behavior in both children as young as five and capuchin monkeys (Tom, Fox, Poldrak, & Trepel, 2007).

Framed by the Amygdala

Benedetto De Martino, Kumaran, and Dolan (2006) explored the neural substrates of loss aversion using fMRI. Subjects were imaged while they made a choice to either take a "sure" outcome by keeping $20 of the $50 stake they were given at the beginning of the experiment or to take an all-or-nothing gamble whose odds of winning were presented in the form of a pie chart. The odds were constructed so that over time, they would gain the same amount ($20) as those who took the sure choice. However, in half the trials, the sure choice was framed as "keeping" $20 of the original $50, while in the other half it was posed as a "loss" of $30. Thus, the loss frame was expressed in terms that would provoke the loss aversion bias.

Because earlier studies had shown that people were risk-averse when they expect to gain but risk-seeking when facing a loss, De Martino et al. predicted that they would see more risk-taking behavior in the loss than in the gain frames. Lending support to the idea that the framing effect is mediated by an emotional response, or an affect heuristic, amygdala activity was correlated with susceptibility to the frame, that is, taking the sure option in the gain frame and the gamble option in the loss frame. However, a preference for choices counter to this general behavioral tendency (choosing to gamble in the gain frame or take the sure option in the loss frame) was correlated with ACC activity, which possibly represented the detection of a conflict between an analytical response to ignore the frame and the emotional response mediated by the amygdala to be loss-averse. Resolution of the conflict was required to successfully ignore the frame, and this appeared to be mediated by the ACC.

The Rationality Index in Prefrontal Cortex

The findings described above were based on group results, but because of significant intersubject variability, the authors also used individual susceptibility to the frame to construct what they called a "rationality index." Those who were less susceptible to the frame (a higher rationality index) showed enhanced activity in the right OFC and ventromedial prefrontal cortex (vmPFC) associated with the frame. This is the same region lesioned in Elliot and similar patients whose brain damage led to decision-making impairments, such as the inability to use the consequences of behavior to guide future decisions, as shown by outcomes in the Iowa gambling task. The OFC, which includes the vmPFC, has strong reciprocal connections with the amygdala, providing further support for a role for the amygdala and emotional systems in decision-making. It also suggests that the OFC acts to evaluate and integrate emotional and cognitive information, and the authors suggest that higher activity in this region allows the more "rational" individuals to better represent their own emotional biases, protecting them from suboptimal decisions.

One System or Two?

Later work by De Martino, Camerer, and Adolphs (2010) more directly implicated the amygdala in loss aversion, using a paradigm that allowed a direct quantification of loss aversion. The subjects in this study, S. M. and A. P., were the two patients with amygdala lesions caused by a rare genetic disease introduced in chapter 4. In this behavioral test, participants could accept or reject a series of gambles; each gamble carried an equal probability of winning or losing, but the amount gained or lost varied from $20 to $50 in $2 increments. Both subjects were dramatically *less* loss-averse than the controls in this experiment and typical subjects in many other studies, demonstrating a much higher willingness to accept gambles, although this was more marked in S. M. than in A. P. Both subjects also showed a significantly lower risk premium than controls; in other words, the point at which they were equally likely to choose to bet or not was lower, so the hedonic value of losses and gains tended to be more equal. However, both amygdala-damaged participants responded normally to reward, so the change in behavior appears to be due to the significant reduction in loss aversion, which was about half that of the matched controls, rather than a change in reward sensitivity. The finding that reward and loss were dissociated in these participants suggests that losses and gains are computed by different brain structures.

However, the results of a study by Sabrina Tom and colleagues on people without brain damage (2007) do not seem to implicate the amygdala in loss aversion, and instead point to a single system that calculates both losses and gains. The authors used a similar behavioral choice study, but in addition imaged the participants' brains while they made choices about the gambles. Their study found a level of loss aversion very similar to that of the control subjects in De Martino et al.'s 2010 study, and consistent with that study, individual differences in behavioral loss aversion could be directly correlated to an increased sensitivity of the brain to losses. However, they saw no changes in amygdala activity with either losses or gains. Instead, activity was detected in brain regions that encompassed midbrain dopamine nuclei and their targets, such as the nucleus accumbens (part of the ventral striatum and discussed at length in chapter 6; see Box 6.1 and Figure 6.1). The activity in this region both increased with gains and decreased with losses, thus suggesting a single system that can represent both losses and gains. It's unclear how to explain the differences in these two studies. One suggestion by De Martino et al. is that the decreased range of potential losses in the Tom et al. study (losses varied from $5 to $20 compared to $20 to $50 in the De Martino et al. study) accompanied by larger potential gains (from $10 to $40) resulted in the larger gain signals swamping the weaker amygdala signal. It is also possible that the amygdala signal, which is known to provide input to the striatum, is better measured by its ability to decrease the striatal signal than in terms of increased amygdala activity (recall that the De Martino et al. study looked only at behavior; it did not include imaging). The lesions to the amygdala clearly had a significant consequence on risky decision-making, so further studies should help refine the role of these structures in loss aversion. Nonetheless, together these studies firmly establish the role of emotional brain systems in decision-making.

Thinking Like a Trader

A recent study has explored the physiological correlates of loss aversion, as well as whether these correlates could be modulated by intentional regulation of the emotional response to loss (Sokol-Hessner et al., 2009). Investment companies, knowing that loss aversion may reduce the kind of risk-taking that pays off over the long run, deliberately remind inexperienced traders to focus on their investments as a whole rather than on the risky individual return. Experienced traders show lower physiological reactions, as measured by skin conductance, heart rate, and so forth, to periods of market volatility than do less experienced traders (Wu et al., 2012). Thus, Sokol-Hessner et al. instructed their subjects to use the strategy presumably used by experienced traders to decrease their loss aversion. Subjects were given a $30 stake and told they could keep winnings of 10% of the trials, which would be selected at random. Although they could potentially lose the whole $30 stake, the potential payoff could be much larger (the maximum possible win was $572). Each choice was between a gamble and a guaranteed amount, and gambles were paid immediately. Skin conductance responses were measured during the payoff. Each subject completed two sets of 140 choices. In one set, subjects were instructed to think of each gamble as the only one, while in the other they were told to consider the whole portfolio in the way that experienced traders do. Included in the instructions were phrases such as "Imagine yourself as a trader" and "You do this all the time" (p. 5039).

Not surprisingly, there was considerable individual variation in risk sensitivity; about half of the subjects showed risk aversion (14/30), while the others were either risk-neutral (7/30) or risk-seeking (9/30). As hypothesized, skin conductance responses were significantly larger for dollars lost compared to dollars gained in the uninstructed gambles. Intriguingly, however, 28 of the 30 participants showed a decrease in loss aversion when adopting the instructed cognitive strategy of "thinking like a trader," and their physiological arousal in response to losses decreased as a result of this cognitive strategy.

This study was one of the first to record a physiological correlate of loss aversion, as well as to suggest that loss aversion is due to the hedonic impact of the anticipated loss. Importantly, however, this study showed that the hedonic reaction can be modulated by intentional regulation strategies. Thus, by regulating how we feel, we may also be able to change how we decide.

Is Framing Irrational?

Are the framing effect and cognitive biases such as loss aversion irrational, providing examples of how emotions mislead rational decision-making, as generally posited by the work of Kahneman and Tversky? Being more concerned about the loss of what one already has compared to the potential gain of something new seems sensible. What one does not have may not be needed, and certainly its real value is hard to determine without direct experience.

Although De Martino and colleagues suggested that more "rational" individuals—those who were less susceptible to the frame—may better represent their emotional biases, and thus are better at detecting when such biases will lead to suboptimal decisions, note that in that study there was no "optimal" choice; the decision outcome was designed to be the same.

Most of the time choices do matter, of course, and evidence from individuals such as Elliot suggest that emotional heuristics, which represent a summary or assessment of a large body of information, can often enhance decision-making. As Kahneman has noted,

> A theory of choice that completely ignores feelings such as the pain of losses and the regret of mistakes is not just descriptively unrealistic. It also leads to prescriptions that do not maximize the utility of outcomes as they *are actually experienced*. (2003, p.706; italics added)

That is, the "utility" of our choices should include a measure of the pleasure or pain experienced as associated with decisions. A better understanding of emotional heuristics may allow us to use them more wisely.

The Pain of Waiting for Pain

Kahneman's caution to attend to the hedonics associated with the circumstances of decision-making was brought home by an intriguing experiment by Berns et al. (2006; also discussed in Loewenstein, 2006) that challenged another assumption of classical economics. This theory considered how decisions are made when the outcome occurs at some point in the future— what is referred to as intertemporal choice. Since humans tend to value a future reward less than an immediate reward, standard economic theory discounts the value or utility of a future reward by the amount of delay to calculate the overall expected utility. This "intertemporal discounting" theory predicts that people should expedite rewarding outcomes and delay undesirable outcomes. However, the opposite is often seen in real life: People frequently choose to delay positive outcomes and speed up unpleasant outcomes. One explanation for why people tend to get unpleasant events out of the way quickly is that the "dread" that occurs during waiting itself has a cost. Alternatively, in the case of painful stimuli, it is possible that sensitization, a common neurological phenomenon in pain, consisting of an increase in the neural response to the actual painful stimulus, is responsible for people's desire to get pain over with rapidly. Berns et al. (2006) tested these alternatives by looking at brain activity during the delay period after informing individuals of when they would be receiving a painful shock. At the beginning of each fMRI trial, a cue indicated both the level of voltage to be applied and the amount of time until the shock would occur. Subjects were then forced to make a choice between two alternatives—for example, to endure a shock 90% of that expected but occurring after only 3 seconds, or a lesser shock at 60% of that scheduled, but with a longer wait time of 27 seconds. Their choice represented the value, or utility, of each option to that subject. With a choice of equal shocks, most subjects chose the shorter delay, but some subjects were even willing to sustain a larger shock to have it over more quickly.

Based on their choices, subjects were then divided into extreme dreaders, those who preferred higher shocks to waiting, and mild dreaders, who chose a shorter delay but not if they had to sustain a higher shock. Anticipation of the shock was shown to activate some parts of the pain matrix activated by the shock itself, but primarily in the posterior regions, such as somatosensory cortices SI and SII and the posterior insula, which encode the sensory features of pain; however, activity was also seen in the caudal ACC. As the time of the shock drew nearer, activity in these regions of the posterior pain matrix increased, and the extreme dreaders showed significantly larger increases. Recall from our earlier description of Singer et al.'s (2004) empathy-for-pain experiment in chapter 7 that these are the regions activated during the physical experience of pain. The more anterior regions, including the anterior insula and rostral ACC that represent emotional aspects of pain, such as anticipatory anxiety, did not show increased activity. This pattern of activity suggests that dread is associated neurally with excessive attention to the expected location of the physical response and not simply a result of the emotional reactions of fear or anxiety. Berns et al.'s fMRI results favor the "cost of dread" explanation over the sensitization explanation, because waiting did not alter the neural response to the shock itself; rather, the increased physical pain–related responses in extreme dreaders occurred during the waiting period.

These results provide important insights into models of intertemporal choice, as they show that whether or not an outcome will be postponed depends on whether the waiting is itself pleasurable or painful. When waiting for a painful event is also painful, subjects should want to reduce waiting time as much as possible. Indeed, contrary to the prediction of economic theory that negative events should be postponed as long as possible, when the shocks were equal in intensity, approximately 79% of Berns et al.'s participants preferred getting the shock as soon as possible. If the waiting is pleasurable, however, as in the case of anticipation of a positive event, then waiting might actually be preferred.

Anticipatory Affect

Brian Knutson and colleagues at Stanford University (Knutson & Greer, 2008; Wu et al., 2012) have proposed that anticipatory affect explains many human choices in financial risk-taking, including those that deviate from predictions of optimum models. His model, the anticipatory affect model, draws on behavioral studies which used self-reported affect to show that anticipation of uncertain gains elicits positive arousal, while anticipation of uncertain loss triggers negative arousal. From this work, Knutson's group has been able to link these anticipatory affective responses to uncertain gains and losses to activation of specific brain systems that can be used to predict choice. Knutson was a postdoctoral student of Jaak Panksepp, whose work we reviewed in chapter 3, and Panksepp's influence is evident in Knutson's emphasis on the role of affect in motivating approach or avoidance behaviors when making choices. The anticipatory affect hypothesis is also clearly consistent with Damasio's somatic marker hypothesis, although it does not require a bodily response, as well as the feelings-as-information hypothesis, which posits that risky choices will be assessed by the feelings experienced in anticipation of the outcome.

Through a meta-analytic study of their own and other groups' work in this field, Knutson and Greer (2008) have been able to show that the level of activity in the nucleus accumbens indexes positive anticipatory affect, while insula activity is associated with negative anticipatory affect. The level of activity in these structures also correlates with behavioral reports of the degree of anticipatory excitement or anxiety in participants. Indeed, work from Knutson's lab has shown that activity in these regions can predict choice in a shopping task performed during imaging. Nucleus accumbens activity during the presentation of a product predicted that participants were more likely to make a purchase, whereas increased activity in the insula together with a decrease in activity in the medial prefrontal cortex (mPFC) correlated with later reports that the price was higher than participants were willing to pay (Knutson & Greer, 2008). Brain activation variables were found to predict purchases with about 67% accuracy, significantly greater than chance (50%). While Knutson and Greer's neural monitoring certainly does better than chance at predicting purchases, Panksepp somewhat overstates their results when he claims that Knutson is able to "identify when a person is going to buy something" (Panksepp, 2010a, p. 28). Translating this to more general financial decisions, Knutson's work has shown that increased activity in the nucleus accumbens predicts a switch to high-risk options, while an increase in anterior insula activity is correlated with a tendency to avoid risks or a switch to low-risk choices. This is reminiscent of the correlation between insula activity and anticipatory anxiety in Paulus and Stein's model, discussed in chapter 7.

Finally, drawing on the misattribution paradigm, another study (Knutson & Greer, 2008) tested whether irrelevant affective stimuli can influence risk-taking by influencing anticipatory affective brain activation. Heterosexual males viewed either positive pictures (erotic heterosexual couples), negative pictures (snakes or spiders), or neutral pictures before each trial where their choice was between a high-risk gamble (50% chance of gaining or losing $1) or low-risk gamble (50% chance of gaining or losing $0.10).

Positive pictures, by generating as anticipatory positive arousal, should promote a preference for potential gains, while negative pictures should reduce risky choices. Consistent with this hypothesis, positive images did increase selection of the high-risk gamble, and this effect was shown to be mediated by increased nucleus accumbens activity. Kuhnen and Knutson (2005) suggested that gambling casinos deliberately make use of the role of anticipatory affect by inundating guests with reward cues such as free food, gifts, and other incentives. By activating positive anticipatory activity, these rewards may shift guests from being risk-averse to risk-seeking.

Evidence of neural markers of anticipatory affect, and the ability of anticipatory affect to correctly model choices in a variety of settings, suggests that "affect stands at the centre rather than the periphery of decision making" (Knutson & Greer, 2008, p. 12).[4] Moreover, Knutson and colleagues argue that the anticipatory affect model is a better predictor of human choice than current economic models, which are based on statistical models derived from expected utility. His work has shown that the model of anticipatory affect and analysis of brain activity preceding choice both encompasses and transcends current economic models, and can predict both optimal decisions (conforming to expected utility) and suboptimal decisions (deviating from expected utility). The idea that affective responses can explain why attitudes to risk differ explains a wide range of choice behaviors, such as why stock market traders hold losing stocks for too long (risk seeking) and sell gaining stocks too early (risk aversion). Knutson and colleagues argue that affect provides a single "common currency" to compare different options, an idea that we also explored in chapter 6 on the reward system.

The Ultimatum Game

Another canonical example that challenges the rational decision-making model of classical economics is the Ultimatum Game described in chapter 6 and briefly in the previous chapter. Recall that in this game, one subject,

---

4. In attempts to correlate activation with affective self-reports, a meta-analysis showed that the nucleus accumbens is correlated with positive arousal, but the anterior insula is correlated with both positive and negative arousal. This asymmetry of markers for anticipation of gain versus loss seems contrary to the findings from behavioral economics, which finds that "losses loom larger than gains" (Kahneman & Tversky, 1984). These findings may reflect the current limits of imaging technology.

the proposer, is asked to split a sum of money, for example, $10. The responder then chooses whether to accept the offered split or refuse it, but if the offer is refused, both players get nothing. If the subjects acted as rational deciders, the proposer would offer the smallest sum allowable, 1 cent, which would be gladly accepted by the responder. After all, 1 cent is better than nothing. Instead, most responders refuse the 1-cent offer, and 50% of responders in industrialized cultures[5] will even reject offers of 20% (Sanfey, Rilling, Aronson, Nystrom, & Cohen, 2003). Indeed, proposers seem to understand that low offers will be refused, and across many studies, the modal offer has been found to be about 50%.

Questioning the players has revealed that responders reject low offers because of their perceived unfairness, and this sense of being unfairly treated provokes an angry rejection of the offer, even if it means losing what was offered. Thus, as we discussed in chapter 6, people appear to be motivated by a sense of fairness, or by an aversion to inequity, and objecting to unfairness is thought to be a primary mechanism for establishing and maintaining a social reputation. In an fMRI study, Sanfey et al. (2003) showed that unfair offers activated the bilateral anterior insula, dlPFC, and ACC more than fair offers. Intriguingly, when responders thought they were playing against a computer rather than a human, they were more likely to accept offers that they would otherwise deem unfair. Subjects had a stronger emotional reaction to human partners, and activation in emotion-related brain regions was also significantly higher. Thus, the activation of these structures is sensitive to the context of the offer—who it comes from—and is not simply a response to the magnitude of the offer itself.

Some regions of the anterior insula systematically increased in activity as perceived unfairness increased, and thus index the degree of unfairness. Those participants who showed higher levels of anterior insula activation also rejected a higher percentage of unfair offers. Sanfey and colleagues draw attention to the links that we discussed in depth in chapter 7 between insula activity and negative emotions, such as disgust and anger as well as pain and distress. As the level of insula activity predicted which offers would be rejected, these neural representations of emotional state appear to be guiding choice behavior. Activity of other regions, such as the dlPFC and

---

5. Recall that in chapter 6 we mentioned that Henrich, Heine, and Norenzayan (2010) found that very low offers were frequently made and *not* rejected in their studies with small-scale nonindustrialized human societies.

ACC, did not correlate with acceptance of offers. The dlPFC, a region implicated in working memory and cognitive control, appeared to be in competition with the anterior insula, since unfair offers that were later rejected showed more anterior insula activity than dlPFC activity, while those that were later accepted showed the reverse pattern. As expected, ACC activation appeared to represent the detection of conflict between emotional and cognitive processes.

The results of the Ultimatum Game and other games of trust have resulted in models of *social utility* to explain how players respond not only to their own payoff, but to what others are getting as well. Theories of social utility have been able to explain decisions and choices involving other emotions as well, including guilt from getting more than others and envy from getting less. For example, Henrich et al. (2010) reported that in nonstudent samples in a variety of countries, including Sweden, Russia, China, Germany, and the Netherlands, people also rejected offers that were *too high* in the Ultimatum Game. These results show that the brain is designed to respond to signals that are required for humans to exist in a social environment, and that social emotions are the primary means by which that information is shared. Clearly, a full understanding of social utility will be necessary to be able to fully understand decisions and choice.

Social emotions can often be expected to stimulate feelings and behaviors that may appear to be in conflict with those that are motivated by individual self-interest. In the Ultimatum Game, we began to see the participation of brain systems such as the dlPFC, or the region of frontal cortex lateral to the more medial regions involved more directly in determining emotional value. As mentioned above, the lateral PFC includes regions that regulate executive functions, such as inhibition of impulsive behavior, switching of behavior when a current plan or goal is not working, and self-control. The dlPFC is thought to carry out these functions by inhibiting lower, more emotional regions of the brain. Although we will argue for a more nuanced view of dlPFC function, these regions are required to regulate the conflict between self-interest and social utility provoked by the social interactions in the Ultimatum Game. In the next chapter, we look more closely at how emotion is regulated as emotion and cognition become integrated to provide maximally flexible behavior.

Emotion Regulation

Wait one sec, let me finish.
Wait one sec, let me think.
Wait one sec, I need to do this.
Wait one sec, I'm not ready.
Wait one sec, I'm almost done.
Wait one sec, ok, ok, I'll come.
Wait one sec, let me turn it off.
Wait one sec, DINNER'S COLD?!!
by Cameron Cagenello

This poem, by one of our young sons, captures a situation that is all too familiar to parents and their children. Breaking away from engrossing play to do something necessary for life but much less interesting to a child can lead to emotional conflict between the child and his or her caregivers. This is especially the case with interactive computer games that just never seem to have a good stopping point. These situations require a lot of control of emotions on both the child's part and the parent's part. Young children's self-control abilities are very much under development, and it can be one of the most challenging tasks of parenting to help children gain control over strong emotions while keeping their own frustrations from erupting and providing poor models of the very thing they are trying to encourage: good emotion regulation.

James Gross, a leader in the field based at Stanford University, defines emotion regulation (ER) as "the processes by which individuals influence which emotions they have, when they have them, and how they experience and express these emotions" (Gross, 1998a, p. 275). We frequently need to

275

regulate our emotions, but do not always do so effectively. Dysregulated emotions are the hallmark of psychological disorders like depression and anxiety, and regulation strategies are explicitly targeted in modern psychotherapies like dialectical behavioral therapy and emotion regulation therapy (e.g., Fresco, Mennin, Heimberg, & Ritter, 2013; Linehan, 1993). However, a diagnosed clinical disorder is not necessary to experience the need for improved ER. Parents often have to exert control over their emotions to prevent themselves from "losing their cool," particularly if they are tired or under a lot of stress. The need to tamp down, or at least not express, other emotions, comes up frequently in all sorts of social situations, such as masking sadness in the face of loss in a game or disappointment at receiving a well-intended but unappealing gift. Emotions are powerful attention-grabbing mechanisms that can rise up suddenly and consume all of our cognitive resources, a power that makes sense in terms of their survival value as discussed earlier, particularly in relation to LeDoux's work on fear. Control over and the ability to voluntarily change the experience of emotions and their outward expression is a vital social skill that can require a lot of effort.

Neuroscientists have modeled their concepts of the brain networks involved in emotion regulation in terms of general control mechanisms. A broad-strokes description of what has become the standard ER brain model depicts the prefrontal and cingulate cortical regions as inhibiting cortical and subcortical regions involved in generating emotional responses, such as the amygdala and the insula. A temperature metaphor is frequently used to capture this model: "Hot," emotion-generating processes are cooled down by "cold" cognitive control mechanisms. Young children have less fully developed prefrontal areas and can therefore need more support in using the cold to temper the hot. Some means of cooling or, in other cases, heating up emotions are explicitly taught, by parents, at school, and sometimes in the course of therapy. Others are more automatic responses, such as turning away from distressing sights. There is a huge amount of variation in people's ability to regulate their emotions both deliberately and automatically; the temperature metaphor is at play again in the adjectives we use to describe this variation in emotion regulation tendencies—for example, we describe people whose emotional flare-ups are not well controlled as "hotheads."

The experimental field of emotion regulation grew out of the developmental literature in the late 1980s (Campos, Campos, & Barrett, 1989). In the 1990s, the study of adult emotion regulation took hold and expanded rapidly, an effort that was spearheaded by Gross, who concisely described the meteoric rise of the field in his preface to the 2007 *Handbook of Emotion Regulation*. In that same handbook, Gross and Ross Thompson, a prominent social development researcher, set out the conceptual foundations for the ER field. While acknowledging the difficulty of defining emotions because the "term was lifted from common language, and refers to an astonishing array of happenings" (2007, p. 4), Gross and Thompson described three essential characteristics of prototypical emotions: They are goal directed, multifaceted, and, most importantly for the field of ER, malleable. The multifaceted nature of emotions means that there are many possible ways that ER can operate. Gross developed a standard way of identifying ER strategies based on the stage of the emotion generation process in which they take effect, earning it the name "process model." Starting in the early 2000s, much progress has been made in charting the brain regions and networks involved in implementing emotion regulation strategies (e.g., Ochsner, Bunge, Gross, & Gabrieli, 2002; Ochsner et al., 2004). Much of the neuroimaging work is based on Gross's characterization of how emotions unfold over time and how they can be altered at different points in that process.

Gross's Process Model of Emotion Generation and Regulation

Gross characterizes the generation of emotion as a dynamic process with several stages and components that provide multiple potential targets for regulation (1998a). He breaks the process of emotion generation into four stages: situation, attention, appraisal, and response (see lower line of Figure 11.1), and stipulates how emotions can be regulated using different strategies at each stage (upper line of Figure 11.1). Although Gross cleanly separates emotion generation and regulation in this model, it is sometimes difficult to disentangle the two, as when emotions are regulated by generating opposing emotions (Gross & Barrett, 2011). People often prepare in advance for emotionally challenging situations so that their emotion regulation is in fact a way of generating different emotional responses to the same situation. Nevertheless, Gross's process model provides a means of organizing the multiple aspects of emotions that clearly delineates the many points at which they can be altered.

Gross describes emotion regulation processes as "antecedent focused" if they take effect before the emotional response is fully formed; they do this by altering the situation, attention, or appraisal in some way as the emotional response is unfolding. In contrast, if emotion regulation processes

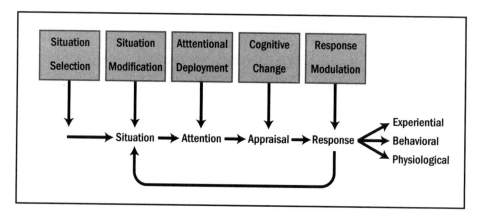

Figure 11.1 A diagram of the Gross and Thompson's (2007) process model of emotion regulation showing the five families of strategies.

Source: *Adapted from* Gross, J. J. (Ed.). (2007). *Handbook of emotion regulation*. New York, NY: Guilford Press, Figure 1.5. Used with permission of Guilford.

come into play once the emotion has been fully generated, they are described as "response focused." As Richards and Gross put it, "response-focused modulation mops up one's emotions; antecedent-focused regulation keeps them from spilling in the first place" (2000, p. 411). Because an emotional response is multifaceted, consisting of how we think and feel about it (the experiential component), the action urges it causes (the behavioral component), and its bodily effects (the physiological component), emotion regulation strategies can act on any of these three components to alter the nature of the response. The linear model shown in Figure 11.1 depicts just one cycle of the emotion generation process, but in reality it is an ongoing process: Emotional responses lead to changes in the situations which initiated them, which in turn changes how subsequent emotions unfold. The feedback arrow from response to situation in Figure 11.1 is intended to capture the dynamic nature of emotion generation and regulation. This iterative, dynamic process means that strategies initially characterized as antecedent can act to change aspects of the response once an emotion is already under way.

Five Families of Emotion Regulation Strategies

Many different strategies can be used to alter our emotional responses. Gross organizes them into five families, grouping them by the stage of the emotion generation process where they take effect. Although his tempo-rally based process model is not the only one put forward in the research literature (see Koole, 2009, for an alternative view), it has been extremely influential and has driven the explosion of behavioral, neuroimaging, and clinical ER studies.

Situation Selection

The earliest group of strategies, *situation selection*, is put in place even before an emotional response is initiated by choosing situations that are emotion-ally comfortable and avoiding those that provoke emotions that are difficult to handle. In the case of children having difficulty limiting their computer game playing, parents can help by providing plenty of opportunities for other kinds of play—like outdoor play. Or they can avoid the emotionally challenging situation by putting the machine away for a while or by limiting computer access to particular situations, such as the library. A less drastic form of situation selection would be to choose a game that would allow for easier breaking-off points, such as building games that are less time sensi-tive.

Situation Modification

If the situation cannot be avoided, it can often be *modified* to alter its emo-tional impact, a strategy frequently used by parents attempting to regulate their own and their children's emotions. For example, parents' mounting frustration in the face of ignored requests to get off the computer to come to dinner or to do homework can be circumvented by modifying the situa-tion by, for example, allowing access only after homework and dinner and for a set amount of time. Routines for mealtimes, bedtime, homework, and so forth are ways of modifying children's situations to make them less emo-tionally taxing and therefore less in need of effortful regulation.

Attentional Deployment

The third family of ER strategies, *attentional deployment*, involves diverting attention from an emotional situation, and is one of the earliest to appear in development. Even very young children are able to avert their eyes from troubling sights in order to lessen their impact.[1] This is well illustrated in Walter Mischel's classic "marshmallow study" (Mischel, Ebbesen, & Zeiss, 1972). Mischel and colleagues put a marshmallow in front of young children (three to five years old) and told them that if they were able to wait to eat it for 15 minutes, they could have a second marshmallow. Some of the children were unable to resist the overwhelming temptation of the tasty marshmallow and gobbled it up immediately, but others were able to distract themselves by looking away, talking or singing to themselves, or sitting on their hands. Focusing their attention on something other than the delicious marshmallow helped children to gain the self-control needed to resist eating it. Footage of children performing this task[2] shows how difficult it can be for some as they squirm in their seats and grimace; their body language conveys the great effort involved. Great effort can also be involved in tearing yourself away from an absorbing task like a computer game, but distraction can be helped by other strong attentional magnets, such as a favorite dinner.

Cognitive Change

The fourth family of strategies, *cognitive change*, operates at the level of appraisals to change how an emotion-provoking stimulus or situation is evaluated. In other words, changing how you think about or "frame" a situation can alter your emotional response to it. This strategy is more commonly known in the research literature as *reappraisal*, and is introduced as an antecedent-focused strategy by Gross and colleagues because the new ways of appraising the emotions that people learn become habitual and thus take effect prior to the response. At the time of initial learning, reappraisal could be more appropriately described as response focused because the response occurs first and then the person thinks about it differently, and in fact it is usually used in this way in the experimental literature.

Reappraisal is a major target of cognitive psychotherapy. Therapists often encourage their clients to reframe or reappraise their thoughts about difficult situations in order to change how they feel about them. Although reappraisal became widely discussed only after Aaron Beck's cognitive therapy

---

1. You could also think of this as a form of situation modification, showing that the lines demarcating the different families of strategies are not always clear-cut.
2. Videos are available at http://www.youtube.com/watch?v=QX_oy9614HQ.

broke away from the more strictly action-oriented behavioral therapies, the concept was present early on in W. H. R. Rivers's treatment of shell-shocked soldiers during World War I. In a 1918 paper, Rivers recounted the case of a soldier haunted by the nightmare of looking for a close friend's body and finding pieces of it widely dispersed as a result of an explosion. In casting about for something that would make the recurring image tolerable to the soldier, Rivers came up with the following:

> The aspect to which I drew his attention was that the mangled state of the body of his friend was conclusive evidence that he had been killed outright and had been spared the long and lingering illness and suffering which is too often the fate of those who sustain mortal wounds. (Rivers, 1918, p. 6)

The soldier had never thought of the disturbing image in this way before, and found that doing so helped him to come to terms with it and to grieve for his friend without reigniting the same trauma. Rivers changed how the soldier felt about the image by changing how he thought about it.

Reappraisal can be highly effective, but it takes more cognitive effort than the previous strategies because it involves more interpretation and reworking through language. In the case of child–parent disputes about breaking off from an absorbing computer game, a reappraisal that could lessen the negative emotions involved would focus on reframing the game as something that can be picked up again at will and recasting the meaning of a good stopping point. This type of more consciously thought through reinterpretation can be hard to come up with while in the midst of a fast-paced, attention-grabbing game, so it's a strategy that requires more reflection and advance planning. The hope is to make the reappraisal a habit, so that the new appraisal automatically occurs in the potentially frustrating situation.

Response Modulation

The last family of ER strategies, *response modulation*, acts to alter some aspect of the emotional response. Each of the three components of the emotional response—behavioral, experiential, and physiological—can be targeted for regulation. Direct *suppression* of the behavioral indicators of emotion, such as facial or bodily expressions or tone of voice, is one of the most common response-focused strategies. This can be helpful in smoothing social interactions, such as when a parent wants to calmly convey the importance of doing something like coming to dinner even though he or she is frustrated. More positive feelings can also be induced by regulating the behavioral response; one example is James's opposite-action strategy of smoothing the brow and adopting an upright posture even when you feel despondent (1884, p. 198).

The second component of the emotional response, its experiential aspects, can be altered through relaxation techniques, such as visualizing a calming scene or the successful completion of an anxiety-provoking task. The strategies of reappraisal and attentional deployment that were described above as antecedent focused can also act to change the experience of emotional responses that have already formed. For example, people can catch themselves already feeling anger and decide to think about the situation differently or to distract themselves in order to stop the escalation of the response into the behavioral expression of shouting or lashing out.

The third aspect of the response that can be altered is physiological. Taking some slow, deep breaths when you are angry or anxious activates the parasympathetic nervous system to counteract the fight-or-flight response of the sympathetic nervous system. Drugs such as beta-blockers effectively reduce anxiety because they block the activation of bodily responses by the sympathetic nervous system. Many response-modulation strategies work on multiple aspects of the response simultaneously; for example, taking deep breaths changes the experiential as well as the physiological response, acting as a form of attentional deployment, and reappraising the situation can calm the bodily responses at the same time as it changes how you think about it.

Are Some ER Strategies Better Than Others? Early Studies of Reappraisal and Expressive Suppression

The five families of ER strategies give people many options, but the earliest efficacy studies focused on two in particular: reappraisal and expressive suppression. The emotion investigated in these early studies was most often disgust, due to the ease of evoking a strong response to images and films, usually of bodily mutilation. In the 1960s, appraisal theorist Richard Lazarus and his coworker Elizabeth Alfert presented subjects with a film of ritual circumcision accompanied by a "reappraisal" soundtrack. The soundtrack drew attention to the celebratory aspects of the ritual at the same time that it downplayed the pain caused by the incision in order to put a more positive slant on the graphically depicted experience. The participants who heard the reappraisal soundtrack rated their moods more positively and had lower skin conductance levels and heart rates than the control participants who watched the same film in silence (Lazarus & Alfert, 1964). Further, Lazarus and Alfert found that if the participants were given the celebratory narrative in advance of viewing the film, they were even less affected by it experientially and physiologically, suggesting that they could prepare their reappraisal strategy in advance.

Inspired by Lazarus and Alfert's demonstration that the emotional impact of disturbing images can be altered in an experimental setting, Gross (1998b) designed his own study using short films of an arm amputation and the treatment of burn victims to elicit disgust of the body-boundary-violation type. He decided to pit reappraisal against one of the most commonly used and instructed strategies: expressive suppression, or simply not letting emotions show. Before viewing the films, subjects were told that they could be distressing[3] and given one of three sets of instructions: (a) reappraise: "Try to think about what you are seeing in such a way that you don't feel anything at all" (p. 227); (b) suppress: "Behave in such a way that someone watching you would not know you are feeling anything at all" (pp. 227–228); or (c) control: simply "Watch the film" (p. 224). He measured the effects of reappraisal and suppression on the three aspects of the response: subjective experience of the emotion, physiological measures of arousal,[4] and the behavioral measure of emotional expression obtained from ratings of facial and upper body movements by coders blind to the participant's instruction set. While suppression did have the largest effect on tamping down external expression of the subjects' disgust, the other two response measures—how the participants felt and their physiological responses—were more effectively reduced by reappraisal. In fact, Gross found that expressive suppression did not significantly reduce the subjective emotional experience—the suppression participants reported that they felt just as disgusted on average as those in the control group. Further, measures of sympathetic activation like skin conductance were actually significantly higher in the suppress

---

3. Specifically, they were told, "It is important to us that you watch the film clip carefully, but if you find the film too distressing, just say 'stop.'" (Gross, 1998b, p. 227)

4. The physiological measures were finger pulse amplitude, finger temperature, and skin conductance response. These were monitored as the participants were viewing the disgusting films.

condition than in the control condition. Although suppression is a widely used ER strategy, it is not highly effective, especially over the long term. Suppression is costly because the effort involved in preventing expression exacts a physiological toll, plus the subjective experience of the emotion is not cognitively processed and can give rise to later difficulties. This experimental demonstration of the superior effectiveness of reappraisal made it a prime candidate for neuroimaging studies of its brain basis.

Brain Mechanisms of Reappraisal

The lead author on one of the earliest neuroimaging studies of emotion regulation was Kevin Ochsner, then a postdoctoral researcher in Gross's lab and now the director of his own thriving Social Cognitive Neuroscience Lab at Columbia University. Ochsner et al. (2002) began by determining which brain regions were activated during reappraisal of negative images, many of which evoked disgust.[5] Participants were asked in advance of viewing the images either to simply attend to them or to "interpret photos so that they no longer felt negative in response to them" (p. 1217). People were able to reappraise successfully in the somewhat challenging and artificial environment of the scanner; they reported feeling significantly less negative emotion when they reappraised than when they just watched the images.

The researchers predicted that the brain mechanisms activated during reappraisal would be similar to those already discovered for other forms of cognitive control. Previous work on control had emphasized the vital role of the prefrontal cortex in regulating behaviors (E. K. Miller & Cohen, 2001). By analogy with control of attention and other cognitive processes, such as the control demonstrated in the Stroop test, where automatic reading of the word has to be inhibited in favor of naming the ink color, Ochsner et al. hypothesized that the higher-level prefrontal regions would moderate the reactivity of emotion generation systems at a lower, often subcortical, level (particularly the amygdala). In its simplest terms, this is a model of "top-down" cognitive control of "bottom-up" emotional processes.

More specifically, Ochsner et al. predicted that successful reappraisal would draw upon three different cognitive processes that depend upon activity in the lateral and medial prefrontal cortex. First, generating a

---

5. The images were taken from the standardized International Affective Picture Set (IAPS) database of normed emotional images already described in earlier chapters.

reframe to diminish the emotionality of the image and then keeping that reframe in mind are both activities that depend on working memory, which is associated with dorsolateral prefrontal cortex (dlPFC). In addition, the ventrolateral prefrontal cortex (vlPFC, see Box 4.2 and Figure 4.1 for the location of this region) has been linked with people's ability to access appropriate information in semantic memory (Badre & Wagner, 2007) and therefore is likely to play a role in selecting a good reappraisal strategy on the basis of what has worked in the past. Second, the process of monitoring the conflict between the top-down reframe and the continuing bottom-up emotional response in order to assess whether further reappraisal is needed was expected to depend on the dorsal anterior cingulate cortex (dACC) because it had previously been associated with overriding prepotent response tendencies and cognitive error detection and correction (Bush, Luu, & Posner, 2000). Third, the process of monitoring changes in one's own subjective state was expected to involve dorsomedial PFC (dmPFC), an important component of the default mode network discussed in earlier chapters. Ochsner and colleagues' predictions held true: The left dlPFC and vlPFC, the dmPFC, and a part of the ACC[6] were significantly more active in the reappraise than in the attend trials. The increased activity in prefrontal cortex found by Ochsner and colleagues is consistent with that seen in earlier studies of cognitive control in tasks with nonemotional stimuli, suggesting that the same set of prefrontal regions is involved in both cases.

The increased prefrontal regulatory control activity was accompanied by decreased activity in regions linked to emotion processing. As we would expect from the many studies showing the importance of the amygdala in emotional processes, this "rock star" structure was one of the regions that was less active in the reappraise as opposed to the attend trials. Reappraisal was also associated with down-regulation of the medial orbitofrontal cortex (mOFC), an area where the affective value of a stimulus is represented in a more flexible way that is sensitive to contextual changes. Recall Damasio's patient Elliot, whose tumor in this region led to an inability to make sound emotionally informed decisions. The amount of prefrontal "top-down" activity was related to the size of decreases in "bottom-up" emotion processing

---

6. Although Ochsner et al. (2002) actually state that the ACC was not differentially activated, they do list Brodmann's area 32 (which is usually included in the ACC) as one of the areas more active in reappraisal than in the control condition (see Table 1 of Ochsner et al., 2002). Many later studies have found increased ACC activation in reappraisal, particularly of the dorsal ACC (e.g., Ochsner et al., 2004; Kim & Hamann, 2007).

regions, suggesting that prefrontal control processes inhibit activity in the amygdala and mOFC related to evaluating the affective salience and contextual relevance of an image. Ochsner and colleagues' findings are important, because this was one of the first studies to demonstrate the neural substrate of the behavioral finding that thinking differently about the same image changes its emotional impact.

To date, there have been several follow-up functional magnetic resonance imaging (fMRI) studies of reappraisal by Ochsner's and Gross's groups (Goldin, McRae, Ramel, & Gross, 2008; Giuliani & Gross, 2009 Ochsner et al., 2004), but also by other US labs (Kim & Hamann, 2007; Urry et al., 2006) and in different cultures such as China (Mak, Hu, Zhang, Xiao, & Lee, 2009) and Switzerland (Vrtička, Sander, & Vuilleumier, 2011). Ochsner and two colleagues recently reviewed 43 different studies of reappraisal (Ochsner, Silvers, & Buhle, 2012). In general, these studies have supported the basic finding that reappraisal increases activity in the prefrontal and cingulate regions implicated in cognitive control and decreases activity in structures which have been implicated in emotional responding. In support of Ochsner et al.'s initial findings, and consistent with the large body of work on the amygdala's importance in detecting arousing stimuli decreases in amygdala activity have been noted in the overwhelming majority of reappraisal studies. Down-regulation of the other structure Ochsner et al. (2002) noted, the mOFC, is reported in some but not all reappraisal studies.

Over the course of these many studies, additional brain regions have been identified as being regulated during reappraisal. Later work has shown decreased activity in the insula with reappraisal, a finding consistent with Craig's and others' extensive work on its importance for the generation of feelings (e.g., Grecucci, Giorgetta, van't Wout, Bonini, & Sanfey, 2013; Ochsner & Gross, 2008; Ray & Zald, 2012). Another area associated with emotion generation, the ventral striatum, is also modulated by reappraisal (Ochsner et al., 2012). As we discussed in the earlier chapter on hedonics, this structure is important for associating cues with reward or reinforcement, so it makes sense that it comes into play in ER studies.

Varieties of Reappraisal

The numerous subsequent studies of brain activity during reappraisal have explored the effects of several different variables. Researchers have asked if the pattern of brain activity depends on whether the emotions are positive or negative, whether the emotion is increased or decreased, and what kind of reappraisal strategy is used.

Up- versus Down-Regulation

Ochsner et al. (2004) expanded their original study to include increasing as well as decreasing the emotion evoked by negative images. It may seem odd to ask people to increase negative feelings, but there are circumstances where it is adaptive to be able to do so. We are used to thinking of emotions like anxiety and anger as negative, yet they are adaptive emotions that can serve as powerful motivators for action. For example, too little anxiety about an upcoming test or work deadline might lead to a lack of preparation. Ochsner et al. (2004) found that when people voluntarily up-regulated negative emotion using reappraisal, many of the same areas involved in down-regulation of emotion were activated. There were some important differences, too: While up- and down-regulation activated regions of the PFC on the left side fairly equally, regions on the right side of the PFC were more active when decreasing than when increasing the negativity of the emotion. Ochsner et al. (2012) explained the greater recruitment of right PFC during down-regulation in two ways: First, the greater difficulty of down-regulating could result in more recruitment of the PFC overall, and, second, the right vlPFC has been associated with inhibiting existent responses (Lieberman, 2009), something that is needed for down- but not up-regulation. Another difference noted by Ochsner et al. (2004) was the direction of amygdala modulation. It increased during up-regulation and decreased in down-regulation of negative emotions, suggesting that the prefrontal cortex both inhibits and excites amygdala activity, depending on the direction of regulation. In their 2012 review, Ochsner et al. noted different regional modulation of the amygdala in up- and down-regulation. While both up- and down-regulation affect the central nucleus and adjacent regions that mediate the behavioral response, only down-regulation seems to affect the basal and lateral nuclei that receive sensory information. Ochsner et al. (2012) speculated that down-regulation relies on altering perceptual and semantic input in addition to altering the behavioral response. Again, down-regulating seems to be more demanding of neural resources than up-regulating.

Valence Effects

Most studies of reappraisal have been done on negative emotions, an approach that makes sense given the need to understand possible changes in the brain mechanisms that underlie the severe dysregulation of negative emotions in clinical disorders like depression and anxiety. There are some neuroimaging studies, however, that do include regulation of positive emotions, and these could illuminate how best to boost good feelings in both clinical and nonclinical settings. Studies that include positive emotions, such as one reported by Sang Hee Kim and Stephan Hamann of Emory University, generally show that it is easier for people to regulate positive than negative emotions. Kim and Hamann (2007) presented positive, negative, and neutral IAPS images to their participants and asked them to both up- and down-regulate their emotional response to the pictures. The changes in amygdala activity were larger overall for positive than for negative stimuli, indicating a neural basis for their greater malleability. The pattern of amygdala activation in Kim and Hamann's various conditions was complex, and differed between the two sides. It did not follow a straightforward pattern of tracking with the perceived negativity of the image, possibly because different conditions activated different areas of the amygdala. In addition to the strong amygdala modulation, Kim and Hamann also reported increases in activation of the ventral striatum when their participants up-regulated positive emotions, consistent with its important role in reward.

Different Forms of Reappraisal

Two distinct flavors of reappraisal have been investigated in neuroimaging studies: situation-focused and self-focused. To illustrate the differences between the two, Ochsner and colleagues (2004) ask you to imagine viewing a picture of a sick person in a hospital. Using situation-focused reappraisal, you could more positively reinterpret the situation by thinking that the person is going to recover quickly because he or she has a disease that will respond well to treatment. Using the second type of reappraisal, self-focused reappraisal, you might instead focus on your relationship to the depicted person, imagining him or her as a stranger rather than a close loved one to decrease the negative feelings. Ochsner et al. (2004) found that self- and situation-focused forms of reappraisal were equally effective at regulating negative emotions both upward and downward. Further, there were extensive overlaps in activated brain areas: the dlPFC, vlPFC, dmPFC, ACC, temporoparietal junction, middle temporal gyrus, subcortical caudate, thalamus, and cerebellum were all activated in both forms of reappraisal in both directions. There were also some differences related to the self- versus situation-focused instructions. For down-regulation of emotions only situation-focused strategies relating to the external situation differentially activated more lateral or outside regions of prefrontal cortex, whereas internally driven self-focused strategies activated more medial or interior regions.

The increased medial PFC involvement in self-focused reappraisal is consistent with studies showing that the mPFC is active in self-referential tasks (Gusnard, Akbudak, Shulman, & Raichle, 2001; Raichle et al., 2001). These studies have identified the mPFC as a member of the default mode network of brain activity that we discussed in chapter 8, those structures which show increases in activity when individuals are *not* engaged in an externally focused task. Gusnard and colleagues suggested that mPFC is one of the areas where neural activity is heightened during internally focused states like daydreaming and introspection. Self-focused reappraisal could have engaged this region associated with internal focus because it required monitoring the relationship to the self.

Comparing Brain Bases of Different Families of ER Strategies

The earliest studies of the brain bases of ER were mostly focused on reappraisal because it had been shown behaviorally to be the most effective strategy for altering the emotional impact of images and films. A crop of later studies compared brain activity while reappraising with the patterns found for other strategies like expressive suppression and attentional deployment.

Reappraisal/Suppression

In a 2008 neuroimaging study, Goldin and colleagues directly compared reappraisal with expressive suppression. They used 15-second film clips depicting things like surgical procedures to invoke disgust and asked the participants to simply watch (control), think objectively (reappraise), or keep their face still (suppression) while viewing them in the scanner.[7] Prefrontal areas became activated earlier in the reappraise than in the suppress condition (0 to 4.5 seconds compared to 10.5 to 15 seconds), which means that regulatory control was initiated more quickly for reappraisal, consistent with Gross's process model. Relative to the control condition, activity in regions associated with the generation of emotions, the amygdala and anterior insula, was significantly reduced in the reappraise condition but actually increased in the suppress condition, indicating a possible neural basis for the superior effectiveness of reappraisal. Surprisingly, given the increase in amygdala and insula activity, and contrary to Gross's earlier finding that expressive suppression had no effect on the experience of disgust in response to films, Goldin et al. (2008) did note a significant *decrease* in subjective ratings of the negative emotion when respondents suppressed their emotional expressions. Although it was not as large as the reduction with reappraisal, the fact that it occurred at all means that under circumstances that are less distressing (assuming that the 15-second clips evoked less disgust than Gross's earlier films that lasted approximately one minute each), suppression can regulate the experiential as well as the expressive aspects of the response. It is just not as powerful as reappraisal, in either neural or experiential terms.

Reappraisal/Attentional Deployment (Distraction)

Although we tend to think of distraction as negative when it prevents us from focusing on the task at hand, when it is deliberately used to take our attention off an upsetting or distressing problem, it is an effective regulation strategy. In order to directly compare reappraisal with the distraction form of attentional deployment, Katerina McRae and colleagues in Gross's lab asked their participants to down-regulate their responses to negative images[8] using either reappraisal or distraction at different times, and measured their brain activity (McRae et al., 2010). They were trained to reappraise by reinterpreting the situations depicted in the images in a way that made them "feel less negative" about them (p. 249). Distraction was achieved with a

---

7. The process of keeping the face still was probably aided by the bite bar and head rest used to keep the subject's head still while in the scanner.
8. Some were taken from the IAPS database and others were generated in-house.

working memory task that required the subjects to hold a six-letter string in mind while viewing the images.

Both strategies significantly decreased self-reported negative affect and supported the top-down control model: increased prefrontal and cingulate activity coupled with decreased amygdala activity. Although both strategies reduced the participants' reports of negative affect, the decreases were significantly larger with reappraisal. The patterns of brain activity also differed somewhat, giving some clues about the brain mechanisms underlying the effects of the two strategies. Brain regions associated with the processing of affective meaning were more active in reappraisal than in distraction, consistent with the notion that while meaning must be processed before it can be reappraised, it is intentionally avoided in distraction. Conversely, as you might expect, prefrontal and parietal areas previously associated with selective attention—the frontoparietal attention network discussed in the previous chapter—were more active in the distraction than in the reappraisal condition. Another notable difference between brain activations in the distraction versus reappraisal conditions was the greater *decrease* in amygdala activity for distraction. McRae et al. explained this finding in terms of amygdala activation indicating the need for further processing—the ambiguity-resolving function we discussed in chapter 4.

Reappraisal involves more elaborate, in-depth processing of the emotional stimulus, but because of this it also has more lasting effects than distraction. If a stimulus is one that will be reencountered, as when coming to terms with a personal loss or trauma, then reappraisal is more helpful, but if the distressing situation is likely to be a one-time experience, then distraction to cut short extensive processing of the stimulus can be very effective.

Another group of researchers led by Phillip Kanske in Mannheim, Germany, using addition as the distraction task and including positive as well as negative images, also found a stronger decrease in amygdala activity for distraction compared to reappraisal.[9] Although McRae et al. and Kanske, Heissler, Schönfelder, Bongers, and Wessa (2011) both found larger amygdala reductions for distraction than for reappraisal, McRae et al. found larger decreases in self-reported negative affect for reappraisal than for dis-

---

9. Other differences noted by Kanske et al. (2011) were selective OFC activation for reappraisal and dACC activation for distraction.

traction, whereas they were equally effective in reducing negative affect in the Kanske et al. study. Perhaps Kanske et al.'s addition task was more demanding than McRae et al.'s memory task, and therefore more distracting. The different strategies draw on common control mechanisms that regulate activity in emotion-generating regions, so they both have the potential to work, but their effectiveness depends upon several factors, such as the difficulty of the emotion regulation task, the time course of the emotion to be regulated (for example, whether it is chronic or more of a momentary setback), and, perhaps most important, how well individuals are able to employ the different strategies.

Individual Differences

People do differ markedly in the extent to which they use different strategies. Using a self-rating questionnaire, the Emotional Regulation Questionnaire (ERQ), Gross and John (2003) found that people's reports of the extent to which they normally employ reappraisal and expressive suppression varied markedly. Greater self-reported use of reappraisal correlated with more positive mood in general and greater overall well-being. Emily Drabant and other members of Gross's group found that self-reported reappraisal use was negatively correlated with the level of response in the amygdala in an emotional faces task (Drabant, McRae, Manuck, Hariri, & Gross, 2009). Another study from Heather Urry and her colleagues at the University of Wisconsin, Madison, connected amygdala reactivity differences with individual variation in a physiological marker of stress: the slope of salivary cortisol levels over the course of the day (Urry et al., 2006). Cortisol release exhibits a significant circadian rhythm, peaking in the early morning and falling to a low in the evening. Earlier work had demonstrated that a flattening of this rhythm, due to higher release over the day, is associated with a variety of negative factors such as higher levels of perceived stress, poorer explicit memory performance, larger waist size, and lower levels of social support (Abercrombie et al., 2004). Other studies from Gross's group linked the volume of the anterior insula with self-rated expressive suppression use (Giuliani, Drabant, Bhatnagar, & Gross, 2011) and dACC volume with self-rated reappraisal use (Giuliani, Drabant, & Gross, 2011). These correlations between differences in brain activity and structure and the favoring of particular ER strategies lead to the provocative idea that habitual use of these strategies might lead to long-term neural changes in emotional processing;

it is also possible that pre-existing differences in neural structures lead to favoring of particular ER strategies. Longitudinal studies of the changes in brain activity after extended practice of particular ER strategies, akin to the crop of recent studies demonstrating changes in neural activity and structure in long-term meditators, would illuminate this issue.

The ability to flexibly select the strategy most appropriate to the situation is a useful skill, a point that is supported by the work of George Bonanno and colleagues at Columbia University on resilience. Memory researchers were not the only group to quickly mobilize in the wake of the 9/11 attacks. Bonanno, Papa, Lalande, Westphal, and Coifman (2004) reasoned that this tense and emotionally challenging time in New York City would provide a good context for studying the emotion regulation abilities of students entering Columbia that year. Within a month of the students beginning college, they asked these students to regulate the expression of their emotions when viewing IAPS images such that another student watching from behind a one-way mirror would be either more (expression condition) or less (suppression condition) able to tell how they felt. The researchers found that the students who were able to effectively express and suppress emotions as the situation demanded were better adjusted to college two years later. Bonanno and colleagues did not specify which ER strategies their participants should use, nor did they ask for self-reports about strategies, so we are not able to relate this work directly to Gross's ER taxonomy. Rather, their study indicates that the ability to flexibly regulate the expression of emotion during emotionally trying times, however that is achieved, is correlated with better mental health.

Emotion Regulation Choice

Given the variety and potential effectiveness of the many emotion regulation strategies and the need for flexibility, how do people choose between all the possibilities? Although the majority of neuroimaging studies are silent on this matter because they specify exactly which strategy to use when, some recent work has started to address this question. Gal Sheppes, an Israeli clinical researcher, did postdoctoral work in Gross's lab, investigating emotion regulation choice. Sheppes, Schiebe, Suri, and Gross (2011) presented their participants with negative emotional images of varying intensity and allowed them to decide between reappraising the image by reinterpreting it or distracting themselves by thinking of something neutral. They found that when the images were of low negative intensity, the majority of people preferred to reappraise, but when the images were very distressing, people much more frequently opted to distract themselves. They knew that the emotion was too powerful to effectively reappraise in the moment. Different strategies are preferred at different times, and the ability to flexibly select the strategy most appropriate to the situation is a useful skill, underscoring Bonanno et al.'s findings about the importance of flexibility in emotional resilience. As we noted earlier, Gross's initial behavioral studies demonstrated that reappraisal is a highly effective strategy, but in collaboration with Sheppes, he has now shown experimentally that it can be considered too taxing or unrealizable in intensely emotional situations. Conversely, although distraction has been considered a less meaning-oriented and therefore less effective long-term strategy than reappraisal, in high-intensity situations it may be more adaptive to disengage earlier in the emotion generation process than to try to reinterpret on the spot. This new work is breaking down the idea of identifying specific strategies as either routinely adaptive or maladaptive and replacing it with a more contextually sensitive viewpoint that takes into account the situation and the individual's personal goals and preferences.

Sensitivity to the situation and flexible responsiveness to varying circumstances can break down in psychological disorders. Depression can be characterized as "getting stuck" in repetitive patterns of thought, or rumination on negative experiences (Holtzheimer & Mayberg, 2011; Nolen-Hoeksema, Wisco, & Lyubomirsky, 2008). Anxiety disorders also involve an inflexibility of response that entails repeated avoidance of anxiety-provoking stimuli, such as social settings in social anxiety disorder (Kashdan, 2010). In psychopathology, these inflexible patterns of response have become habitual and can be quite resistant to change with explicit emotion regulation strategies. As the work of Sheppes and colleagues makes clear, it is particularly difficult to engage explicit reappraisal when emotions are intense, as they often are in conditions like panic disorder or mania. Although the bulk of the research to date has focused on explicit ER strategies, especially reappraisal, in the last few years more papers have started to appear on implicit forms of emotion regulation that address the habitual and automatic regulatory processes that develop automatically over time in most people, but may become skewed in clinical conditions (Bargh & Williams, 2007; Gyurak, Gross, & Etkin, 2011; Koole & Rothermund, 2011; Mauss, Bunge, & Gross, 2007).

Implicit Emotion Regulation

Strategies like reappraisal require people to consciously and effortfully change how they are thinking about the situation that is evoking an emotional response and therefore require the use of cognitive resources like attention and working memory. Because these resources are limited, explicit ER can be cognitively costly. Implicit emotion regulation refers to ways of altering emotional experience that do not depend on conscious intentions or awareness and are therefore less resource intensive. Precisely because they are unconscious, implicit ER processes are more difficult to study experimentally than the easily instructed explicit ones. To address this issue, emotion researchers have adapted the experimental tools devised for investigating implicit memory and attitudes that show the effects of "priming" on subsequent judgments. A good example is provided by the task used by Tran, Siemer, and Joorman (2011), who biased the valence of participants' emotions by having them complete word fragments that were either all positive or all negative. In the second part of the experiment, participants were asked to identify expressions on subliminally presented faces, and were all told that they had achieved a subpar score on this test and that this was an indication of their poor emotional intelligence. Those primed by working with the negative words showed a drop in self-esteem after the fake test of social perception, but the people whose emotions were implicitly regulated with the positive words seemed to be inoculated against the self-esteem assault. The participants were not aware of the positive or negative skewing of their emotions by the word completion task, and in fact did not explicitly rate their emotions differently in the two conditions. Tran et al. interpret their study as demonstrating the malleability of implicit emotion and the ease of training implicit regulation processes to impact important mental health factors like self-esteem. The fact that biases in automatic appraisals can be altered so simply in this experimental manipulation holds promise for the incorporation of more implicit ER techniques into therapy.

The Brain's Braking System

Another body of work that converges on the importance of considering implicit as well as explicit regulation processes grew out of the self-control literature. Matthew Lieberman, codirector of the Social Cognitive Neuroscience Lab at the University of California, Los Angeles, with his wife Naomi

Eisenberger, whose work on social pain we discussed earlier in chapter 7,[10] also wondered about the applicability of experimental studies on instructed ER to everyday life (Berkman & Lieberman, 2009). In more natural circumstances, it is not just possessing the ability to regulate emotions that matters; the tendency to engage those skills is also important. The task of therapy for conditions like depression and anxiety disorders is not just to teach ER skills but to get people suffering from these conditions into the habit of applying them appropriately. The ER skills have to be practiced to become automatic. Lieberman and colleagues made two interrelated and intriguing suggestions for broadening the study of emotion regulation in light of the need to apply neuroscientific findings to everyday life and in therapeutic settings. First, they cast emotion regulation as part of a larger group of self-control processes that all depend on what they call the brain's "braking system." Next, they discovered incidental means of emotion regulation that invoke the brain's braking system that help with making ER skills more automatic.

Lieberman (2009) reviewed the literature on a wide range of self-control studies and argued that all of these seemingly disparate forms of self-discipline rely on the same neural mechanism. For example, how children perform at age five on Mischel's marshmallow study described above correlates with their later success on SATs: Those able to wait the full time (15 minutes) scored an average of 200 points higher than those who couldn't resist eating the marshmallow. Better SAT scores and marshmallow patience may not initially seem related, but they may share a common requirement to defer gratification. Many other forms of self-control have been studied that rely on a means of inhibiting impulses: motor, cognitive, financial, and perspective-taking. Motor self-control can be measured with a "go–no go" task: The "go" part of the task is to press a button whenever you see any letter on the screen except for one identified by the experimenters, and the "no go" part is to refrain from pressing only when that one particular letter appears. It is challenging to inhibit the impulse to press the button, because after several presses in a row it has become a prepotent response. Cognitive self-control can be assessed by your ability to follow explicit instructions not to think of something, such as Daniel Wegner's example of a "white bear," an attentional feat which turns out to be surprisingly difficult once the

---

10. According to Lieberman, their favorite collaboration is their son Ian James, named in part after William James (APA Early Career Award, 2007).

suggestion has been made (Wegner & Schneider, 2003). A form of financial self-control is measured by a temporal discounting task that is the adult equivalent of Mischel's marshmallows: You can choose to receive $10 immediately or wait one month for $15. The majority of people choose the immediate reward even though the $5 increase is a much better return than can be expected from other investments. Perspective-taking self-control has also been studied; this can be measured by the ability to perceive someone else's perspective when it conflicts with your own. Lieberman points out that all of these tasks, plus the more familiar emotion regulation strategies discussed above, activate one brain area in common: the right ventrolateral prefrontal cortex (rvlPFC).[11] The rvlPFC is a "hub" for self-control, or the brain's braking system.

The brain's braking system can be turned on in many diverse ways. The real surprise in Lieberman's account is that initiating the braking system in order to control any particular impulse has broader self-control effects that go beyond those intended. This is surprising, because introspectively we do not always feel as if the different forms of self-control are related. In a 2009 study conducted with two of his graduate students, Elliot Berkman and Lisa Burklund, Lieberman demonstrated that motor self-control can influence brain activity in the amygdala in a way that is reminiscent of emotion regulation even when participants are not consciously attempting to regulate their emotional response. In a clever variant of the go–no go task, they substituted emotionally expressive faces for the letters, and the participants had to press the button for one gender and resist pressing for the other. Although they were not instructed to attend to the emotional expressions of the faces, the amygdala was significantly less active in the no go condition in which they had to inhibit their tendency to push the button than in the go condition, and relative to the baseline condition of simply viewing a fixation cross. Berkman et al. interpret this finding as evidence that exerting control over motor expression has a spillover effect that looks like the model of emotion regulation we have been discussing throughout this chapter: Prefrontal control systems inhibit activity in areas related to emotional responding. Turning on the brain's braking system via motor inhibition in a situation where emotional stimuli were present had a side effect in a brain area that is

---

11. Lieberman (2009) does point out that many other brain regions are involved in the variety of self-control tasks he covers, so structures such as the dlPFC and ACC that we have discussed in association with ER are also activated in studies of other forms of control.

well known to be involved in emotional processing. However, another way of thinking about this result is that the gender identification task serves as a distraction from the emotional response, and, as we discussed earlier, distraction is correlated with reduced amygdala activity (McRae et al., 2010; Kanske et al., 2011).

Berkman et al.'s results suggest that emotion regulation can be turned on by control processes not explicitly aimed at emotional responses. This idea does not immediately gel with our subjective sense of self-control. When we try to inhibit a particular response, we feel as if we target only that particular response. The implications for kick-starting emotional regulation through other means are far-reaching. Lieberman and colleagues applied them to one ER case that has puzzled researchers: Parents and teachers frequently ask young children to "use their words" when they are upset and over-aroused. Why does simply verbally labeling feelings regulate them? To turn this into an experimental procedure, Lieberman and his coworkers devised an affect-labeling task (Lieberman et al., 2007). Adult participants were asked to view faces with negative expressions and choose an emotion word that described them. In comparison to a task where participants labeled gender rather than emotion, the rvlPFC was more active and the amygdala and other limbic structures[12] were less active. The simple act of putting feelings into words activates the brain's braking system and consequently diminishes activity in areas associated with generating emotional responses. Practice in behaviors that activate the brain's braking system, even simple actions like brushing your teeth with the nondominant hand, increases emotional self-control. This work provides a novel argument for the importance of music and physical education in schools.

The connection to mindfulness practices such as yoga and meditation is easy to make. Engaging in the precisely controlled movements of yoga poses not only activates motor self-control; if Lieberman and colleagues are right in claiming that repeatedly and voluntarily activating the brain's braking system has a spillover effect of boosting emotion regulation systems, then better control over emotional responses is likely to be induced as a side effect of the intentional and attentive positioning of the body in the practice of yoga. Similarly, with meditation, the repeated, habitual exercise of control of attention has self-control effects beyond the specific tasks engaged in

---

12. The limbic structures other than the amygdala that they listed were the vmPFC, subgenual cingulate, insula, posterior cingulate, dACC, and ventral striatum.

during the practice. Lieberman, Eisenberger, and other members of their research group have recently been studying the effects of mindfulness and its intentional cultivation on the brain's braking system (Creswell, Way, Eisenberger, & Lieberman, 2007; Dickinson, Berkman, Arch, & Lieberman, 2012). Lieberman and colleagues are recent contributors to the intensive study of mindfulness and the brain that has developed in the last decade (Fletcher, Schoendorff, & Hayes, 2010; Lazar et al., 2005; D. J. Siegel, 2007; Hölzel et al., 2011).

Mindfulness Meditation and Emotion Regulation

The heart of mindfulness practices is to repeatedly return the wandering mind to the present moment through gently exercising voluntary attentional control. Bodhipaksa, a leading meditation teacher, describes it this way:

> In this particular breath-based form of insight meditation we note the sensations of the breath arising, existing, and passing away. When distracting sensations, thoughts, and emotions arise, we bring a kindly awareness to them, similarly observing their arising, their existing, and their disappearance. (2010, p. 52)

The practice of repeatedly disengaging the attention from narrative chains of thoughts, or what Bodhipaksa calls "hypnotic bubbles," cultivates *attentional flexibility*. Heleen Slagter, Richard Davidson, and their colleagues used the attentional blink task described in chapter 8 to empirically demonstrate that meditation improves attentional flexibility. Recall that attentional blink is the inability to detect a second target if it follows the first too closely (within about a half-second window). Participants in a three-month intensive retreat at the Insight Meditation Society in Barre, Massachusetts, were significantly more likely to detect the second stimulus, thus showing a reduced attentional blink after the retreat in comparison to before, demonstrating that they were more effectively able to disengage their attention from the first stimulus in order to notice the second (Slagter et al., 2007). The attentional flexibility cultivated in mindfulness meditation practices could potentially aid in emotional regulation; the idea is that people are less likely to get caught in repetitive ruminative traps if they are more flexibly able to disengage and reengage their attention at will. We can think about the effects of meditation on emotional experience outside the actual sitting practice as a form of implicit emotion regulation. Emotional stability, or *equanimity* in Buddhist terminology, is a by-product of the practice rather than a result of consciously engaging in ER strategies like reappraisal or attentional deployment.

Studies of the neural changes that result from the practice of mindfulness meditation find that the same brain areas we have been discussing throughout this chapter are involved: bolstering of prefrontal control activity accompanied by modulation in regions associated with emotion generation. Britta Hölzel and her colleagues in Germany demonstrated that during meditation, experienced practitioners had elevated activity relative to novice controls in prefrontal areas—the dmPFC and the rostral ACC (Hölzel et al., 2007). In 2009, Hölzel, at this point working in collaboration with Lazar's group at Harvard Medical School, reported that MBSR[13] participants who reported significantly reduced stress showed decreases in basolateral amygdala gray matter density, suggesting that they are less likely to have an overactive amygdala that contributes to their emotional reactivity. In a study of nonmeditators, Gemma Modinas and her colleagues in the Netherlands found that people who scored higher on a standardized mindfulness scale[14] also had greater activity in the dmPFC during reappraisal of negative IAPS images (Modinas, Ormel, & Aleman, 2010). Further, the increased dmPFC activity was inversely correlated with amygdala activation, consistent with the broad-strokes neural ER model. Meditation practices or dispositional mindfulness acquired in some other way have the potential to shift the balance in neural networks in ways that could aid in the ongoing process of regulating emotions.

When Emotion Regulation Goes Awry: Anxiety and Depression

So far our focus has been mainly on the adaptive functioning of ER, and the majority of studies have been conducted with healthy individuals. Now we turn our attention to the nascent literature on the neural correlates of ER in psychopathology, work that returns us to our key theme of cognition–emotion interactions. As Taylor and Liberzon say in a review article, "There

---

13. MBSR—mindfulness-based stress reduction—is an eight-week intensive introductory course in mindfulness meditation practices that was devised by Jon Kabat-Zinn in 1979 at the University of Massachusetts Medical Center in Worcester for patients suffering from chronic health conditions, such as chronic pain (Kabat-Zinn, 1990, has a full description of the program).

14. The Kentucky Inventory of Mindfulness Skills (KIMS) (Baer, Smith, & Allen, 2004).

is probably no better demonstration of how thoughts and feelings bind together than psychiatric disorders" (2007, p. 413).

Implicit Emotion Regulation and Anxiety

Lieberman and colleagues' investigations of the brain's braking system indicate that implicit forms of emotion regulation can be powerful. Amit Etkin and his colleagues at Stanford and Columbia University devised a means of measuring a form of implicit ER that addresses emotional conflicts, and is specifically impaired in anxiety disorders (Egner, Etkin, Gale, & Hirsch, 2008; Etkin, Egner, Peraza, Kandel, & Hirsch, 2006; Etkin, Prater, Hoeft, Menon, & Schatzberg, 2010). Their Stroop-like emotional conflict task, known as the "facial affect identification emotional conflict task," uses happy and fearful faces overwritten with the words *fear* or *happy*. In congruent trials, the expression and word match. In incongruent trials where, for example, a happy face is overlaid with the word *fear*, subjects have to override their automatic reading of the incongruent word and identify only the facial expression. This conflict slows down subjects' responses in the incongruent trials. By analyzing the trial-to-trial patterns, Etkin et al. (2006) discovered that the incongruent responses were faster when they were preceded by an incongruent rather than a congruent trial. The exciting aspect of this result is that Etkin et al. found a way to measure *uninstructed* emotional conflict regulation; their reasoning is that the previous incongruent trial had prepared their participants to exert the control needed to override the conflicting verbal information. Importantly, their participants were completely unaware of this "emotional conflict adaptation" effect; it is an implicit and uninstructed form of regulation.

Neuroimaging of the emotional conflict task showed that the adaptation effect was correlated with negative coupling of activity in the pregenual portion of the ACC (the area of the ACC adjacent to the "genu," or knee, of the corpus callosum).[15] Increased pregenual ACC activity corresponded with decreased amygdala activity when the adaptation effect occurred, suggesting that the pregenual ACC activity could be down-regulating amygdala activity in this implicit form of emotion regulation. Importantly, the pregenual ACC–amygdala coupling was not observed in a nonemotional analog of the conflict task that required subjects to judge the gender of emotional

---

15. Brodmann's area 33.

faces while ignoring incongruent gender labels. Although the stimuli in this version of the task were still emotional faces, Etkin et al. described it as nonemotional because the conflict created in the task was not related to emotional processing. The emotional and nonemotional forms of the conflict task differed neurally in terms of the relationship between activity in the amygdala and the pregenual ACC.

When Etkin et al. (2010) ran the facial affect identification emotional conflict task with generalized anxiety disorder (GAD) patients, they found that these patients did not show the emotional conflict adaptation effect: Their responses to stimuli with incongruent facial and verbal cues did not speed up if the previous trial had also been incongruent; in other words, they were not adapting to the conflict. The imaging results showed a failure of the GAD patients to activate the pregenual ACC and a lack of pregenual ACC–amygdala connectivity. The lack of implicit and automatic regulatory processes in the anxious patients is one factor that contributes to the increased effort that they have to exert in order to regulate their emotions.

Studies like Etkin et al.'s that document a lack of implicit emotional regulation in anxiety and the corresponding specific neural patterns are important for devising targeted treatments. Despite the differences in the setup of their neural networks that result in lower pregenual ACC activation and a lack of pregenual ACC–amygdala connectivity, the adult brains of anxious people can still be altered by training. Neurofeedback involving real-time monitoring of brain activity using fMRI is a neurally based approach that has great potential for treatment of anxiety (Etkin, 2012). Several studies have demonstrated that real-time feedback about activity in the amygdala, insula, and ACC enables subjects to voluntarily modulate these usually automatic responses in order to either boost or dampen them (for a review, see deCharms, 2007). Another new approach to treatment that Etkin (2012) discussed is deep brain stimulation: physical stimulation of under- or over-active areas, something that requires specific knowledge of the brain areas involved. Helen Mayberg and her colleagues at Emory University have successfully applied this approach in cases of major depressive disorder (MDD) (Mayberg et al., 2005, Ressler & Mayberg, 2007).

Regulation of Rumination in Depression

Deep brain stimulation for treatment-resistant depression targets the subgenual ACC (sgACC), an area of the ACC that lies below the genu of the corpus callosum[16] that is thought to be excessively active in MDD. Given the importance of the sgACC in neural models of depression, University of Michigan researcher Ethan Kross was puzzled that alterations in its activation have rarely been reported in ER studies. This prompted him and his colleagues, including Ochsner, to create an experimental paradigm for generating emotions to be regulated that focused on the emotional autobiographical memories that can be so troublesome in MDD and the process of ruminating on them. Rumination, a major symptom of depression and anxiety, consists of repetitive thinking about past experiences in a negative light. Kross, Davidson, Weber, and Ochsner (2009) had healthy subjects recall highly arousing negative memories in the scanner and then do one of three things: (a) *ruminate* on them by focusing on their negative feelings, (b) *reappraise* them by actively analyzing their causes, or (c) *accept* the feelings by regarding them as "passing mental events that were psychologically distant from the self and did not control them" (p. 361). The accept strategy, which is reminiscent of mindfulness training, resulted in both the lowest reports of subjective distress and the least activity in the sgACC and mPFC. Kross et al. were able to demonstrate a connection between ER and sgACC activity using a memory-based experimental paradigm. When dealing with negative autobiographical memories, the accept strategy was better than the reappraisal strategy at freeing the subjects from excessive rumination. Kross and his collaborators, including prominently Özlem Ayduk, a professor of psychology at the University of California, Berkeley, have furthered the idea that the form of self-distancing used in the accept strategy is crucial to the benefits of mindfulness (Ayduk & Kross, 2010; Kross & Ayduk, 2011). In studies of people diagnosed with MDD, they found that the more severe the depressive symptoms, the greater the ability of participants to reduce negative affect with an instructed self-distancing strategy (Kross, Gard, Deldin, Clifton, & Ayduk, 2012). While Kross and colleagues have not yet published a neuroimaging study with MDD patients engaged in self-distancing from negative memories, this area is ripe for further clinically applicable basic research.

Concluding Comments

Substantial progress has been made in understanding the brain mechanisms of the complex, vital, and multifaceted process of emotion regula-

---

16. Brodmann's areas 24 and 25.

tion. A large number of behavioral and neuroimaging studies converge on the big-picture view of prefrontal control mechanisms modulating activity in a number of emotion-generating areas lower down the neural hierarchy. Within that big-picture view, there is variation in exactly which structures are activated or deactivated and the strength of the connections between them at different points in time with different strategies for ER. There is also substantial individual variation in the use and effectiveness of strategies. Reappraisal, a complex explicit strategy that is aimed at altering affective meaning, draws on a range of lateral and medial prefrontal areas and alters the level of activity in a number of emotion-generating regions, including the amygdala, insula, ventral striatum, and mOFC. Other explicit strategies draw on some of the same regulatory networks but also recruit and affect different brain regions. For example, the technique of self-distraction draws on many of the same cognitive control processes involved in reappraisal but in addition recruits the frontoparietal attention network, and the mindfulness strategy of acceptance has more effect on the subgenual region of the ACC than reappraisal. A smaller subset of the network of regions involved in emotion generation and regulation has been identified as important in more implicit ER adaptation effects, specifically, the connection between the pregenual subsection of the ACC and the amygdala in one set of studies.

A point that emerges clearly from contemporary studies of emotion regulation and its neural underpinnings is that people have many means of changing emotions that recruit the regulatory networks with varying degrees of effectiveness and automaticity, and in somewhat different patterns for different strategies. This multiplicity means that treatment of dysfunction in emotion regulation has many targets and avenues of approach. In their review of the neural correlates of ER in psychopathology, Taylor and Liberzon (2007) made the point that the various types of psychotherapy, such as behavioral, cognitive, and mindfulness-based interventions, act preferentially on different aspects of the total emotional response. Behavioral therapy targets the action programs producing motor behavior, cognitive therapy focuses on emotional schemas, and mindfulness more directly targets neuroendocrine and autonomic responses involved in drive and homeostasis (see their Figure 2). In other words, different therapeutic approaches address different aspects of the physiological, experiential, and behavioral components of the emotional response outlined in Gross and colleagues' model. Of course, these systems are not independent; rather, they interact with each other, and modern therapies often combine aspects of behavioral, cognitive, and mindfulness approaches to give people access to more ER tools and possibilities.

A variety of neural processes involved in control, attention, memory, and awareness are recruited and interact with each other over time in ways that we are only beginning to understand. The neuroimaging studies show both common core control mechanisms and some diversity in how different strategies are put into effect in different contexts. After an early phase of demonstrating the use of basic brain control mechanisms in explicit emotion regulation, research studies are now illuminating more about how contextually sensitive choices are made and how implicit processes also contribute to successful emotion regulation. As the field advances, we can expect to learn more about how these implicit and explicit processes interact with each other and more specifics about how dysfunctions of inflexible or ineffective emotion regulation can be treated.

What Is an Emotion—Now?

The study of emotions no longer takes place at the margins of neuroscience and psychology. As can be seen by the work presented in this book, emotion research has not only moved into the spotlight, it has spawned the development of whole new disciplines within the study of the brain; affective neuroscience, neuroeconomics, social neuroscience, and hedonics are some of the new subdisciplines we have attempted to summarize in this book. This work not only has radically revised our understanding of the importance of emotion as a brain function and in behavior, but it has also reshaped our basic conception of how the brain processes information and makes decisions. The so-called "cognitive" brain functions, such as attention, perception, learning and memory, and decision-making can no longer be seen as separate and distinct from emotions; instead, they are inextricably infused with emotional assessments and the feelings that accompany them.

We've learned that emotional reactions provide a critical summary of our past experience with a situation or event, and this summary is experienced as a "gut" feeling that provides important time and effort-saving analyses of situations that are often too complex for rational dissection. This is particularly true for the complex and inherently uncertain decisions in the social or personal realm, as demonstrated by the tragic inability of Antonio Damasio's patient Elliot to lead a productive life, despite his intact and even superior cognitive functions. Intellectual functions without accompanying emotions and feelings lack direction and purpose, clearly in contrast to the wisdom of the ages that has too often cast emotions and feelings as "animalistic" holdovers that can only disrupt "good" thinking. Nonetheless, it remains true that relying on emotions/feelings without the guidance of rational thinking can be equally disruptive; indeed, as we've learned from the study of emotion regulation, large swaths of the prefrontal cortex are devoted to making sure that our emotional responses do not run amok when a "clearer" head is needed. Again, this is especially the case in the social realm, where we are often torn between acting according to our own needs and respecting the needs and conventions of the larger social world. Understanding the intricacies and interdependence of social, cognitive, and affective aspects of brain function is a dominant theme within contemporary work. Truly, the brain is at its core an emotional and feeling brain. This means that the study of emotions is inherently integrative, so the field of affective neuroscience brings together the study of emotion, social interaction and communication, the physical body, and traditional cognitive functions to yield new insight into fundamental questions about human experience.

Looking back over the diverse topics pursued by the affective neuroscience researchers we have explored in this book gives us perspective on issues that stem from James's simple but confounding question and how to respond to it 130 years later: What is an emotion? As we discussed in the introduction, James's big question generated many other questions that have motivated the development of the field: What is the role of the body in emotion? How can we best describe the relationship between emotion and cognition? What are the brain systems involved in emotional processing? In addition, recent work has posed new and equally vital questions: What do we mean by "feelings," and how do they relate to emotions? When can we trust our emotional responses, and when might they lead us astray? How can the study of the neural processes involved in balancing emotional and cognitive functions inform our understanding of psychiatric disorders?

What Is an Emotion?

In spite of the various ways different research groups define and measure emotion, a striking common thread unites these seemingly diverse approaches and provides a solid foundation for the field as a whole: All of the researchers we have studied share a conception of emotion/feeling as fundamentally assigning value to stimuli and events. Organisms are continually bombarded by a wealth of information—from outside and inside the body and brain—and emotions provide a way of evaluating and prioritizing what to respond to. Some emotional responses may be innate; for example, rats seem to have an innate fear of the smell of cat urine. But many emotional responses, especially those of humans, have been shown to be acquired by experience, as so compellingly demonstrated by Joseph LeDoux in his exploration of fear conditioning in the amygdala. Whether innate or learned, emotional reactions coordinate rapid and often complex behavioral and bodily responses that ensure an optimal interaction with the stimulating events, thus enhancing survival.

Stimuli that have significance for the organism have valence; they are either good or bad, rewarding or punishing, and thus shape and prioritize our most basic interactions with the environment, confirming Darwin's early insight that, fundamentally, emotional responses initiate approach or avoidance behavior. Indeed, researchers such as Edmund Rolls define emotions as responses to rewards and punishments. Recent explorations into the brain systems mediating reward and punishment have led to exciting advances in the study of hedonics, the affective experiences or feelings produced by rewards and punishments, providing new insights into what happens when hedonic systems become disrupted, as in addictions. Finally, the understanding that most emotional responses are learned, and that emotional learning leads to especially powerful and enduring memories has provided critical insight into why emotional memories, as seen in post-traumatic stress disorder (PTSD), can be so disruptive and hard to overcome.

Debates over how to define the terms "emotions" or "feelings" have continued since the time James first posed his seminal question. Recently, Joseph LeDoux proposed that for scientific purposes, we should avoid the use of these difficult-to-define and imprecise common language terms (2012, 2013). He suggests instead that emotion research use the less human-laden term *survival circuits*, circuits that are shared with other animals. The function of survival circuits, which is to detect and respond to salient stimuli, seems to adequately encompass some fundamental ideas that have emerged from the study of affective neuroscience. Indeed, the modern researchers who were instrumental in the affective neuroscience paradigm shift, such as Jaak Panksepp, Joseph LeDoux, and Antonio Damasio, first made study of the feeling brain tractable through investigation of survival-related mechanisms concerned with defense, reproduction, and maintaining life.

What Is the Role of the Body in Emotion?

The characterization of emotions as survival circuits that motivate actions makes it clear that James's insistence on the role of the body in emotions was well-founded. As Öhman states, "In a very real sense, emotions reside in the body, since they mobilize the body's metabolic resources for potentially vigorous action" (2006, p. 35).

Antonio Damasio is the modern researcher who has most notably carried James's banner into current research by emphasizing the foundational role of emotions and feelings in basic biological regulation. Damasio characterizes emotions as "barometers of life management" (2010, p. 56) with the essential function of monitoring and maintaining bodily integrity. In simple organisms, homeostatic functions can be mediated reflexively by simple brain stem circuits, but as the complexity of organisms increased, the need to juggle many different homeostatic requirements, as well as to predict the consequences of potential choices, necessitated the development of more sophisticated brain mechanisms. These complex brain mechanisms, which both increase the flexibility of responses and, by storing the consequences of biological regulation of past experience, can anticipate optimal responses to new stimuli, nonetheless required that the homeostatic systems which sense and regulate the body remain intimately linked to decision-making circuits. Damasio further argues that the reenactment of the bodily responses to past experience provides subtle and nuanced feelings experienced as "gut" feelings that provide information that may be indispensable to optimal decision-making. Thus, for Damasio, the body remains the central theater of the emotions.

Another modern researcher who has refined and expanded James's ideas about the tight linkage between emotions and the body is the neuroanatomist A. D. (Bud) Craig, whose discovery and characterization of a new pathway for interoceptive processing that he suggests culminates in a representation of the sentient self in the anterior insula has also breathed new life into the notion of embodied emotions. Craig's anatomical work demonstrating a new interoceptive pathway for presumed sympathetic sensory information, and the evidence he presents for the idea that each interoceptive modality forms a discrete topographical map in the primate insula, has prompted a reconceptualization of the precision of interoceptive representations in the brain. As this information becomes integrated with other high-level information from the body, as well as information about the motivational and reward values of stimuli, Craig argues that the insula may contain the most complex representation of the body as the "sentient self" at each moment in time.

Emotional expressions have also been called the "language of the emotions" (Darwin, 1872, p. 367), and as such are at the core of social interactions in animals, including in human communication, in spite of humans' ability to make use of verbalizing emotions. Body postures and facial expressions carry important information about the intentions of the organism. Because in many cases these expressions became stylized and exaggerated as they became ritualized to serve a primarily communicative function, many emotional expressions are highly conserved across species and are readily recognized both within and between species. Darwin undertook some of the first studies to explore the idea that some human emotional expressions are universal, ideas pursued in the 20th century by Paul Ekman and his colleagues. Ekman's widely cited work on universal facial expressions of basic emotions scientifically established the power and specificity of bodily communication of emotion.

What Are the Brain Structures/Systems Involved in Emotional Processing?

Is there an emotional brain? James argued that no special brain mechanisms for emotion were required beyond the sensory and motor systems already known, a position that was challenged by his most effective early detractor, Walter Cannon. Cannon and his collaborator Bard instead emphasized specific subcortical structures, especially the thalamus and hypothalamus, as the crucial brain substrates of emotions. Building on Cannon and Bard's early work, together with Papez's important identification of a circuit of interconnected medial brain areas as the emotional brain, Paul MacLean promoted the idea of the limbic system that became widely accepted as *the* emotional system in the brain. The anatomical position of limbic structures between the more recently evolved neocortical structures and the more ancient subcortical and brain stem structures that mediated the automatic homeostatic reactions necessary for survival in MacLean's now discredited triune brain model had wide appeal. In MacLean's model, the limbic system was especially important in early social interactions that over time came to be modulated by learning and subject to deliberative processes, such as the need to conform to social standards. The localization of emotion in primarily subcortical structures beneath the neocortex also provided anatomical confirmation that emotion and reason were distinct evolutionary developments.

The emotional functions of many of these limbic structures have been amply verified by research in affective neuroscience over the last few decades: The cingulate gyrus featured in Papez's original circuit has proven to be important in many studies of emotion and its regulation; the amygdala, included in MacLean's expanded limbic system, is vital for fear learning, as explored in depth by LeDoux and colleagues, and for emotional salience in general; the body-minded insula that Craig put firmly on the map was also part of MacLean's extended limbic system; in addition, the reward systems of the nucleus accumbens, ventral pallidum, and orbitofrontal cortex, also identified as "limbic" by MacLean, have been intimately connected with the emotional valuing of stimuli. Contemporary critiques of the limbic system concept do not challenge the important emotional roles of these limbic structures; rather, they question the notion of the brain as composed of modular structures, some of which are exclusively devoted to emotion and are distinct from brain systems involved in other functions.

The groundbreaking work of Damasio profoundly challenged the designation of a circumscribed limbic system by arguing that emotional processes permeate so-called cognitive functions. His work has shown that both cognitive and emotional functions require the coordinated activity of neocortical, limbic, and brain stem structures. Rather than conceiving of emotions as carried out by an isolated, encapsulated brain process, as suggested by MacLean's triune brain, Damasio argues that emotions provide the basic set of preferences by which all decisions must be evaluated, and, as such, prioritize and guide all decisions. Even scientific discoveries that are seemingly based on the highest forms of reason are biased and guided by intuitions and hunches about promising directions to search for solutions, and those intuitions grow out of the emotional systems that represent the full sum of past experience. Thus, Damasio would extend emotion functions throughout many levels of the brain, even into the prototypical cognitive regions of the dorsolateral prefrontal cortex.

Extensions of the emotional system in the other direction—further down into the brain stem—have long been championed by Jaak Panksepp, who emphasizes the role of brain stem structures in what he defines as his seven core emotional systems. More recently, Damasio, particularly in his latest book *Self Comes to Mind*, has also emphasized the role of life regulation mechanisms based in the brain stem in establishing affective responses.

Expansions of the emotional brain upward and downward are consistent with the wealth of contemporary evidence about the brain bases of emotion, which has stressed the pervasive interconnectedness of brain systems involved in emotional processing. Indeed, a characteristic feature that unites the emotion-related brain structures that we have reviewed is their role as massive integrators of information. They function as "hubs" or "convergence zones" that bring together information from multiple sensory systems with information about their biological value. To mediate basic bioregulatory functions, emotions must integrate an assessment of the needs of the body with an evaluation of what is available in the external environment. And that is a job for the whole brain, not just an isolated emotional subsection.

A final argument against the limbic system concept comes from Joseph LeDoux, who points out that there are no agreed-upon criteria that can be used to determine limbic system membership. Without such criteria, the concept remains so vague as to be meaningless. In addition, he forcefully argues against the concept of a single "emotional brain" that mediates all emotional responses. Instead, he argues that each emotional system has evolved in response to specific survival pressures. Rather than continuing to debate the vaguely defined emotional brain, LeDoux instead urges researchers to focus on identifying the brain substrates for each of the many defined emotional responses, or what he has most recently defined as "survival circuits."

Note that LeDoux is not arguing for the idea that each of the basic emotions has its own brain region devoted to it; rather, he is encouraging investigation of the particulars of possibly distinct neural circuits that support different types of survival-related behaviors. Recent meta-analytic studies of human brain responses to emotional stimuli, albeit couched in the human-laden terms that LeDoux is encouraging us to move away from, provide support for his focus on working at the network level. Early neuroimaging work had linked fear with the amygdala, disgust with the insula, anger with the orbitofrontal cortex, and sadness with the subgenual ACC. Current work, however, suggests that the story is more complicated; the amygdala, for example, is activated by many salient stimuli, including rewarding stimuli, not just fear-invoking ones. Every emotional response may require the participation of many brain regions—a brain network. Different emotion networks may share some brain structures, and specific brain regions may participate in multiple emotions, making it difficult to find a unique brain signature for each basic emotion. More work on the connectivity between different brain regions during tasks evoking different types of emotional responses is needed before the hypothesis of discriminable neural signatures for basic emotions can be assessed more definitively.

In spite of many cogent arguments against it, the concept of the limbic system remains a convenient shorthand when referring to those brain structures that seem most intimately tied to the assessment of biological relevance and value and the prioritization of behavioral responses, and it remains a functional concept within the research field as well as continuing to have resonance in the popular culture. As research continues to refine our understanding of the emotional functions of the brain and more firmly establishes how fully integrated they are with other brain functions, however, this terminology may eventually disappear from scientific and popular discourse.

What Is the Relationship between Emotion and Cognition?

Plato's image of passion and intellect as battling horses pulling in different directions continues to be a powerful descriptor of how we persist in dichotomizing emotion and reason in everyday life. Descriptions of the "hot" emotions overwhelming our "cooler" reasoning powers, and the metaphors used to describe our struggles to contain our emotions as battling storms, tempests, and hurricanes, seem to confirm the conflict between emotion and reason. Although the scientific study of emotion has begun to undermine this entrenched viewpoint, and research in affective neuroscience has provided evidence for the alternative view that emotion and cognition often support and amplify rather than oppose each other, we continue to adhere to emotion/cognition opposition in our scientific as well as our everyday lives.

The development of cognitive psychology in the middle of the last century was crucial in making the needed break with the radical behaviorism that dominated the early part of the century. However, the adoption of the computer as a metaphor for the mind by cognitive psychology effectively marginalized the study of emotions, and led to the assignment of mental functions such as attention, perception, and memory as fundamentally "cognitive" brain functions. The insight that perception is influenced by personal and social values, emotions, and motivations that was central to the midcentury "New Look" work in perception spearheaded by an important player in the cognitive revolution, Jerome Bruner, seemed to be forgotten once the cognitive approach became well established. Recent work in affective neuroscience addresses this omission by showing that our emotional state and the context in which a stimulus is perceived fundamentally shape cognitive functions from the earliest stages of perceptual processing. As we saw in chapters 9 and 10, positive and negative emotional states can physically increase or decrease the field of visual perception and attention, altering what is seen and even influencing whether it is "seen" at all, as dramatically illustrated in the gorilla suit experiment discussed in chapter 8. Our expectations and emotions profoundly shape the processing of stimuli, and ultimately, our view of the world.

Antonio Damasio's research with neurological patients such as Elliot directly confronted the separation of emotions and reason. Far from regarding emotions as disruptive and antagonistic to sound reasoning, his research has shown that damage to brain structures that disrupt the ability to make use of emotional processes also disrupt the ability to make effective personal and social decisions. Emotional summaries stored in the vmPFC represent our accumulated "wisdom" about a situation, which pares down decision options to the few choices which can be most efficiently analyzed using reason. Without them, our reasoning systems become overwhelmed.

What Is the Relationship between Emotions and Feelings?

James conflated these two terms in his oft-quoted definition: "*Our feeling of the same [bodily] changes as they occur IS the emotion*" (1884, p. 190, capitalization and italics in original). We seldom take time to reflect on the differences between these words in our everyday language. As we have seen, however, the importance of differentiating between emotions and feelings is now widely accepted in the field of emotion research. Emotion researchers reserve the term *feelings* for the experience or the awareness of an emotional response, especially as it is "felt" in the body, which is what James called an emotion, while the term *emotion* refers to the suite of responses precipitated by an encounter with a salient stimulus. Most researchers also agree that emotional responses may take place entirely outside the realm of conscious awareness, even in humans. In contrast, feelings require some element of awareness. Although many researchers see an important role for the awareness of the emotional response, there is much less agreement on where and how such feelings occur.

Damasio was one of the first researchers to insist that the terms *feelings* and *emotions* should refer to distinct processes that are each associated with an important brain function. For Damasio, feelings are a bodily experience, a position which helped usher in the neo-Jamesian movement in emotion research. Like James, Damasio realized that these bodily feelings provoked by an emotional response would be recorded in the somatosensory cortices, a designation which for him includes the insula as well as primary and secondary somatosensory cortices. Together, the somatosensory cortices record both external (exteroceptive) and internal (interoceptive) aspects of bodily sensation and bring them together in a complete representation of the physiological state of the entire body. Craig's elegant and detailed anatomical work has extended Damasio's ideas about how the body is represented in the brain and the role of the body maps in feelings and a sense of self. For Damasio, the bringing together of internal and external somatic events, which is lateralized to the right somatosensory cortices, also provides a continuous barometer of the state of the body, which he refers to as background feelings. Although these feelings are often unattended, they can be consciously sensed, and provide a key component of our sense of self. The more intense feelings that occur in response to an emotional event also provide information about the detailed and nuanced consequences of an emotional stimulus and are used to help direct further behavior needed to maintain or restore homeostatic balance. Thus, for Damasio, feelings play a critical role in biological regulation and evolved hand in hand with emotions. In complex organisms, both background feelings and feelings of emotions continue to play a critical role in decision-making as well as contribute to the full conscious awareness of self. For Damasio, feelings emerge as a way to monitor the state of the body as needed to maintain homeostatic balance, and thus can be found as part of most nervous systems.

LeDoux, on the other hand, sees feelings as something that emerged only with the evolution of consciousness, and thus may be restricted to humans. He is critical of human emotion research that overly relies on conscious feelings and reports, which in his mind misses what is core in emotions. The reliance on reportable feelings excludes much of the biology that is shared between humans and other animals and seriously constrains the scientific study of emotions as an evolutionary function that is widely conserved in the animal world. As mentioned above, he now argues (LeDoux, 2013) that common language terms like *fear, anger,* and *love* are legitimate only in reference to humans. Such human feeling–laden terms should be replaced with the more specific and precise language of the survival circuits that are widely shared among animals; the term *fear* should be replaced with "threat-induced defensive reactions," for example, which are found across the animal kingdom, while the word *fear* should be reserved for the feelings aspect of emotions, which may be present only in humans.

LeDoux's position on where feelings occur clearly puts him at odds with many of the other major theorists we have covered, who, like Damasio, argue that feelings play a significant and distinct role in the behavior of many animals, and are part and parcel of the evolution of emotions. Jaak Panksepp, for example, argues that the conserved core brain stem and sub-cortical circuits that he has studied experimentally in a variety of mammals represent the "ancestral tools for living" (Panksepp & Biven, 2012, p. 63) and generate "affective" or "primary" feelings. For Panksepp, as for Dama-sio, these core feelings guide behavior toward rewards and away from threats to survival. Thus, Panksepp and Damasio agree that affective feel-ings emerged early in animal evolution as a way to assess the goodness or badness of stimuli and thus critically assist survival. They would argue that feelings are a crucial component of LeDoux's survival circuits.

The role of feelings as a way to monitor basic homeostatic function is also key in the work of Craig, but in his view, awareness of feelings only emerged with the development of detailed interoceptive maps that have been exten-sively integrated with a full analysis of external events, which first emerges in the primate anterior insula and related frontal cortex. For Craig, the insula is where external and internal information meet to provide the most complete representation of the body, and thus the insula is crucial for sen-tience and basic self-awareness. As discussed in chapter 7, although Dama-sio and Craig see a similar function for feelings, they differ in where they are located. Damasio, like Panksepp, stresses the brain stem origins of pri-mordial feelings, noting that the first place where interoceptive information forms topographic maps is in the upper brain stem. In Damasio's view, the upper brain stem regions are the first level of an extended network of struc-tures that are important for complex feelings and self-awareness. Damasio acknowledges the importance of Craig's work in identifying the interocep-tive pathways that illuminate the vital role of the human insula in feelings of all kinds and agrees that "at the level of the cerebral cortex, the main region involved in feelings is the insular cortex" (Damasio, 2010, p. 117). However, he disagrees with Craig's designation of the insula as *the* single structure necessary for feelings. He points to his Patient B., who lacked any insular cortex yet still experienced feelings. Instead, Damasio proposes that feelings require a distributed network that contains many structures, a model consistent with other neurobiological theories of awareness.

The use of feelings to guide behavior is also an important part of the "feelings-as-information" approach of Norbert Schwarz, Gerald Clore, and their colleagues, whose argument that feelings provide us with an integrative evaluation of our ongoing experience is strikingly similar to that of Damasio. This role for feelings is also the focus of researchers working in the field of neuroeconomics, who use feelings like aversion to loss to explain otherwise irrational economic decisions.

When Can We Trust Our Emotions, and When Do They Lead Us Astray?

We have learned that emotions are vital in many basic mental functions, suggesting that there are many reasons to trust our emotional intuitions. Our gut reactions may be especially important when there are many possibilities to consider and much uncertainty about potential consequences. Coming to decisions always seems to involve following our emotional intuitions at some level. A lack of trust in our emotions, or a lack of awareness of them, can lead to indecisiveness and apathy. Work in the feelings-as-information field has even shown that lack of trust in feelings decreases people's accuracy in predicting future outcomes in politics, sports events, and financial decisions. There is also often good reason to trust the impact of emotions on our memories, because they aid us in selecting what really matters to us. Recall of emotional material has repeatedly been shown to be better than recall of less emotionally stimulating or neutral material, and we now understand some of the brain processes involved in this emotional enhancement of memory. In planning for the future, we often draw upon our remembered past experiences and their emotional impact to guide our imaginations about what will come. Amnesia for the emotionally significant personal past impairs the ability to anticipate and plan for the future. Emotions crucially guide our attention to important aspects of our external environments, setting off alarm bells about important survival-related needs or signaling the presence of rewards. Signals associated with bodily needs, such as hunger, thirst, extremes of temperature, pain, and fatigue, motivate us to find ways to meet those needs.

So there are many reasons to trust emotions to guide our decision-making, memory, future planning, and attention, but there are also ways in which they can lead us astray. Overreliance on emotional signals can lead to impulsiveness in decision-making; going with your gut instinct despite complicating factors that you are explicitly aware of, or failing to seek out other explicit sources of information because you are content to follow your instinctual feelings, can lead to choices that are just as poor as those made without the benefit of emotional intuitions. As discussed in chapter 9, feelings are most useful as information when they are based on extensive experience and are subjected to the same kinds of cognitive analyses used to arrive at good logical inferences. Good decisions require a balance of feelings and cognitive analysis.

In many psychiatric disorders, emotional systems may no longer be trustworthy. In PTSD and other anxiety disorders, the alarm system function of emotions has shifted from being adaptive to being too readily triggered. In addictive behaviors, the craving for substances of abuse far outstrips the actual pleasure derived from them, and will be pursued to the exclusion of other basic needs. The "sticky" emotions of panic in anxiety disorders, despair in depressive disorders, and out-of-control wanting or seeking in addictive disorders reveal the dangers of intense emotions unanchored by appropriate cognitive assessments.

How Can We Better Balance Emotional and Cognitive Functions?

The dichotomous view of the unruly hot passions acting in opposition to levelheaded cool reason can at times overemphasize the conception of psychopathology as an overwhelming of cognition by emotion. Although there is some merit to this way of thinking, as suggested in the section above, it places the focuses on the control processes needed to effectively suppress strong emotional responses rather than emphasizing the understanding being developed in contemporary affective neuroscience that emotions are adaptive and often vital for decision-making. Viewing emotions as adaptive and informative prompts a different view of how best to balance and use them effectively. The emotional reactions that we have to distressing situations are not in themselves inappropriate or irrational; they only become so when they escalate and cannot run their natural course. Emotions are intensely energy-consuming reactions that are meant to be brief responses to salient stimuli. They are not meant to persist once the direct threat or need has been met. Ironically, it is often the case that intense emotions are maintained by thought processes. The ruminative cycles of depression and anxiety, where sadness and fear are fueled by repetitive negative thoughts, are a disturbing example of a maladaptive interaction of emotions and cognition. The interactive view of emotion and cognition that has emerged from the work reviewed here suggests ways of thinking about how to best balance them.

Research in emotion regulation has shown that because emotions are such an essential part of many brain functions, there are a variety of ways that inappropriate or unnecessary emotional reactions and experiences can be regulated. Maladaptive emotion–cognition cycles of interaction can be disrupted by making use of our human ability to articulate to ourselves and others; the simple use of words to label emotions activates brain regions such as the ventrolateral prefrontal cortex, which directly or indirectly reduces activity in subcortical systems involved in more automatic emotional responses. We can make use of our ability to mentally time travel, and train ourselves to imagine a desirable or productive future; this "imagining" can establish or strengthen brain patterns that again act to reduce more habitual and often unproductive emotional reactions. Meditation training as well as cognitive behavioral therapy teaches people how to redirect cognitive processes such as attention that may be acting to ignite unwanted or disruptive emotional responses, as seen in PTSD and anxiety disorders. These techniques also act over time to strengthen pathways needed to modulate unwanted or excessive emotional responses. These multiple means of achieving emotion/cognitive balance reinforce each other and act to balance the integrative patterns of brain activity needed both to strengthen our emotional life, allowing us to reap its many benefits, and to ensure the most optimal use of emotional and cognitive interactions. Recognizing the essentially emotional nature of the brain does not mean that we are ruled by passion; on the contrary, it encourages us to understand the usefulness and flexibility of emotion–cognition interactions.

References

Abercrombie, H. C., Giese-Davis, J., Sephton, S., Epel, E. S., Turner-Cobb, J. M., & Spiegel, D. (2004). Flattened cortisol rhythms in metastatic breast cancer patients. *Psychoneuroendocrinology, 29,* 1082–1092.

Adolphs, R. (2008). Fear, faces and the human amygdala. *Current Opinion in Neurobiology, 18,* 166–172.

Adolphs , R. (2010) What does the amygdala contribute to social cognition? *Annals of the New York Academy of Sciences: The Year in Cognitive Neuroscience, 1191,* 42–61.

Adolphs, R., Baron-Cohen, S., & Tranel, D. (2002). Impaired recognition of social emotions following amygdala damage. *Journal of Cognitive Neuroscience, 14,* 1264–1274.

Adolphs, R., Gosselin, F., Buchanan, T. W., Tranel, D., Schyns, P., & Damasio, A. R. (2005). A mechanism for impaired fear recognition after amygdala damage. *Nature, 433,* 68–72.

Adolphs, R., Tranel, D., & Buchanan, T. W. (2005). Amygdala damage impairs emotional memory for gist but not details of complex stimuli. *Nature Neuroscience, 8,* 512–518.

Adolphs, R., Tranel, D., Damasio, H., & Damasio, A. (1994). Impaired recognition of emotion in facial expressions following bilateral damage to the human amygdala. *Nature, 372,* 669–672.

Aldridge, J. W., & Berridge, K. C. (2010). Neural coding of pleasure: "Rose-tinted glasses" of the ventral pallidum. In M. L. Kringelbach & K. C. Berridge (Eds.), *Pleasures of the brain* (pp. 62–73). New York, NY: Oxford University Press.

Allman, J. M., Tetreault, N. A., Hakeem, A. Y., Manye, K. F., Semendeferi, K., Erwin, J. M., . . . Hof, P. R. (2010). The von Economo neurons in frontoinsular and anterior cingulate cortex in great apes and humans. *Brain Structure and Function, 214,* 495–517.

Allman, J. M., Watson, K. K., Tetrault, N. A., & Hakeem, A. Y. (2005). Intuition and autism: A possible role for von Economo neurons. *Trends in Cognitive Science, 9,* 367–373.

Andero, R., & Ressler, K. J. (2012). Fear extinction and BDNF: Translating animal models of PTSD to the clinic. *Genes, Brain and Behavior, 11,* 503–512.

Anders, S., Eippert, F., Weiskopf, N., & Veit, R. (2008). The human amygdala is sensitive to the valence of pictures and sounds irrespective of arousal: An fMRI study. *SCAN, 2,* 233–243.

Anderson, A. K. (2005). Affective influences on the attentional dynamics supporting awareness. *Journal of Experimental Psychology: General, 134,* 258–281.

Anderson, A. K., & Phelps, E. A. (2001). Lesions of the human amygdala impair enhanced perception of emotionally salient events. *Nature, 411,* 305–309.

Anderson, E., Siegel, E. H., & Barrett, L. F. (2011). What you feel influences what you see: The role of affective feelings in resolving binocular rivalry. *Journal of Experimental Social Psychology, 47,* 856–860.

Apkarian, A. V., Sosa, Y., Krauss, B. R., Thomas, P. S., Fredrickson, B. E., Levy, R. E., . . . Chialvo, D. R. (2004). Chronic pain patients are impaired on emotional decision-making task. *Pain, 108,* 129–136.

Arias, A. J., Steinberg, K., Banga, A., & Trestman, R. L. (2006). Systematic review of the efficacy of meditation techniques as treatments for medical illness. *Journal of Alternative and Complementary Medicine, 12,* 817–832.

Arnold, M. B. (1960). *Emotion and personality: Vol. I. Psychological aspects; Vol. 2. Neurological and physiological aspects.* New York, NY: Columbia University Press.

Attar, C. H., & Muller, M. M. (2012). Selective attention to task-irrelevant emotional distracters is unaffected by the perceptual load associated with a foreground task. *PLoS ONE, 7,* e37186. doi: 10.1371/journal.pone.0037186

Ayduk, O., & Kross, E. (2010). Asking why without ruminating: The role of self-distancing in enabling adaptive self-reflection. *Social and Personality Psychology Compass, 4,* 841–854.

Azar, B. (2011). Oxytocin's other side. *APA Monitor on Psychology, 42,* 40.

Baddeley, A. D. (2007). *Working memory, thought and action.* New York, NY: Oxford University Press.

Badre, D., & Wagner, A. D. (2007). Left ventrolateral prefrontal cortex and the cognitive control of memory. *Neuropsychologia, 45,* 2883–2901.

Baer, R. A. (2003). Mindfulness training as a clinical intervention: A conceptual and empirical review. *Clinical Psychology: Science and Practice, 10,* 125–143.

Baer, R. A., Smith, G. T., & Allen, K. B. (2004). Assessment of mindfulness by self-report: The Kentucky inventory of mindfulness skills. *Assessment, 11,* 191–206.

Bahrick, H. P. (1984). Semantic memory content in permastore: Fifty years of memory for Spanish learned in school. *Journal of Experimental Psychology: General, 113,* 1–29.

References

Bard, P. (1928). A diencephalic mechanism for the expression of rage with special reference to the sympathetic nervous system. *American Journal of Physiology, 84,* 490–516.

Bargh, J. A., & Williams, L. E. (2007). The nonconscious regulation of emotion. In J. J. Gross (Ed.), *Handbook of emotion regulation* (pp. 429–445). New York, NY: Guilford Press.

Bartels, A., & Zeki, S. (2004). The neural correlates of maternal and romantic love. *Neuroimage, 21,* 1155–1166.

Bartlett, F. C. (1995). *Remembering: A study in experimental and social psychology.* New York, NY: Cambridge University Press. (Original work published 1932)

Barrett, L. F. (2006). Valence as a basic building block of emotional life. *Journal of Research in Personality, 40,* 35–55.

Barrett, L. F. (2007). The science of emotion. White paper commissioned for the National Research Council Committee on Opportunities in Basic Research in the Behavioral and Social Sciences for the U.S. Military, pp. 189–217.

Barrett, L. F., Lindquist, K., Bliss-Moreau, E., Duncan, S., Gendron, M., Mize, J., & Brennan, L. (2007). Of mice and men: Natural kinds of emotion in the mammalian brain? *Perspectives on Psychological Science, 2,* 297–312.

Barrett, L. F., & Russell, J. A. (1999). The structure of current affect: Controversies and emerging consensus. *Current Directions in Psychological Science, 8,* 10–14.

Baumann, N., & Kuhl, J. (2005). Positive affect and flexibility: Overcoming the precedence of global over local processing of visual information. *Motivation and Emotion, 29,* 123–134.

Baumeister, A. A. (2000). The Tulane electrical brain stimulation program: A historical case study in medical ethics. *Journal of the History of Neuroscience, 9,* 262–278.

Baylis, L. L., Rolls, E. T., & Baylis, G. C. (1995). Afferent connections of the caudolateral orbitofrontal cortex taste area of the primate. *Neuroscience, 64,* 801–812.

Becker, M. W. (2009). Panic search: Fear produces efficient visual search for nonthreatening objects. *Psychological Science, 20,* 435–437.

Bechara, A. (2005). Decision making, impulse control and loss of willpower to resist drugs: A neurocognitive perspective. *Nature Reviews Neuroscience, 3,* 563–573.

Bechara, A., & Damasio, A. R (2005). The somatic marker hypothesis: A neural theory of economic decision. *Games and Economic Behavior, 52,* 336–372.

Bechara, A., & Damasio, H. (2002). Decision-making and addiction: Part I. Impaired activation of somatic states in substance dependent individuals when pondering decisions with negative future consequences. *Neuropsychologia, 40,* 1675–1689.

Bechara, A., Damasio, H., & Damasio, A. R. (2000). Emotion, decision making and the orbitofrontal cortex. *Cerebral Cortex, 10,* 295–307.

Bechara, A., Damasio, H., & Damasio, A. R. (2003). Role of the amygdala in decision-making. *Annals of the New York Academy of Science, 985,* 356–369.

Bechara, A., Damasio, A. R., Damasio, H., & Anderson, S. (1994). Insensitivity to future consequences following damage to human prefrontal cortex. *Cognition, 50,* 7–12.

Bechara, A., Damasio, H., Tranel, D., & Damasio, A. R. (1997). Deciding advantageously before knowing the advantageous strategy. *Science, 275,* 1293–1295.

Bechara, A., Damasio, H., Tranel, D., & Damasio, A. R. (2005). The Iowa gambling task and the somatic marker hypothesis: Some questions and answers. *Trends in Cognitive Science, 9,* 159–162.

Bechara, A., Dolan, S., & Hindes, A. (2002). Decision-making and addiction: Part II. Myopia for the future or hypersensitivity to reward? *Neuropsychologia, 40,* 1690–1705.

Bejani, B. P., Damier, P., Arnulf, I., Thivard, L., Bonnet, A.-M., Dormont, D., . . . Agid, Y. (1999). Transient acute depression induced by high-frequency deep-brain stimulation. *New England Journal of Medicine, 340,* 1476–1480.

Berkman, E. T., Burklund, L., & Lieberman, M. D. (2009). Inhibitory spillover: Intentional motor inhibition produces incidental limbic inhibition via right inferior frontal cortex. *Neuroimage, 47,* 705–712.

Berkman, E. T., & Lieberman, M. D. (2009). Using neuroscience to broaden emotion regulation: Theoretical and methodological considerations. *Social and Personality Psychology Compass, 3,* 475–493.

Berman, M., Nee, D., Peltier, S., Kross, E., Deldin, P., & Jonides, J. (2010). Depression, rumination, and the default network. *Social Cognitive Affective Neuroscience, 6,* 548–555.

Berns, G. S., Chappelow, J., Cekic, M., Zink, C. F., Pagnoni, G., & Martin-Kruski, M. E. (2006). Neurobiological substrates of dread. *Science, 312,* 754–758.

Berridge, K. C. (2003). Pleasures of the brain. *Brain and Cognition, 52,* 106–128.

Berridge, K. C. (2004). Simple pleasures. *Psychological Science Agenda.* Retrieved from http://www.apa.org/science/psa/sb-berridgeprt.html

Berridge, K. C. (2007). The debate over dopamine's role in reward: The case for incentive salience. *Psychopharmacology, 191,* 391–431.

Berridge, K. C. (2009). Wanting and liking: Observations from the neuroscience and psychology laboratory. *Inquiry, 52,* 378–398.

Berridge, K.C. (2012). From prediction error to incentive salience: mesolimbic computation of reward motivation. *European Journal of Neuroscience, 35,* 1124–1143.

Berridge, K. C., Ho, C.-Y., Ricard, J. M., & DiFeliceantonio, A. G. (2010). The tempted brain eats: Pleasure and desire circuits in obesity and eating disorders. *Brain Research, 1350,* 43–64.

Berridge, K. C., & Kringelbach, M. L. (2013). Neuroscience of affect: brain mechanisms of pleasure and displeasure. *Current Opinion in Neurobiology, 23,* 294–303.

Berridge, K. C., & Robinson, T. E. (1995). The mind of an addicted brain: Neural sensitization of "wanting" versus "liking." *Current Directions in Psychological Science, 4,* 71–76.

Berridge, K. C., & Robinson, T. E. (2003). Parsing reward. *Trends in neurosciences, 26,* 507–513.

Berridge, K. C., Robinson, T. E., & Aldridge, J. W. (2009). Dissecting components of reward: 'Liking', 'wanting', and learning. *Current Opinion in Pharmacology, 9,* 65–73.

Berridge, K. C., & Winkielman, P. (2003). What is an unconscious emotion: The case for unconscious 'liking.' *Cognition and Emotion, 17,* 181–211.

Bijleveld, E., Custers, R., & Aarts, H. (2012). Human reward pursuit: From rudimentary to higher-level function. *Psychological Science, 21,* 194–199.

Bishop, S. J. (2007). Neurocognitive mechanisms of anxiety: an integrative account. *Trends in Cognitive Sciences, 11,* 307–316.

Bishop, S. J. (2009). Trait anxiety and impoverished prefrontal control of attention. *Nature Neuroscience, 12,* 92–98.

Bless, H., Bohner, G., Schwarz, N., & Strack, F. (1990). Mood and persuasion: A cognitive response analysis. *Personality and Social Psychology Bulletin, 16,* 331–345.

Bless, H., Clore, G. L., Schwartz, N., Golisano, V., Rabe, C., & Wölk, M. (1996). Mood and the use of scripts: Does a happy mood really lead to mindlessness? *Journal of Personality and Social Psychology, 71,* 665–679.

Blood, A. J., & Zatorre, R. J. (2001). Intensely pleasurable responses to music correlate with activity in brain regions implicated in reward and emotion. *Proceedings of the National Academy of Sciences, 98,* 11818–11823.

Bocanegra, B. R., Huijding, J., & Zeelenberg, R. (2012). Beyond attentional bias: A perceptual bias in a dot-probe task. *Emotion, 12,* 1362–1366.

Bocanegra, B., & Zeelenberg, R. (2009). Emotion improves and impairs early vision. *Psychological Science, 20,* 707–713.

Bodhipaksa. (2010). *Living as a river.* Boulder, CO: Sounds True.

Bonanno, G. A., Papa, A., Lalande, K., Westphal, M., & Coifman, K. (2004). The importance of being flexible: The ability to both enhance and suppress emotional expression predicts long-term adjustment. *Psychological Science, 15,* 482–487.

Botvinick, M. M., Cohen, J. D., & Carter, C. S. (2004). Conflict monitoring and anterior cingulate cortex: An update. *Trends in Cognitive Science, 8,* 539–546.

Brefzynski, J. A., & DeYoe, E. (1999). A physiological correlate of the "spotlight" of visual attention. *Nature Neuroscience, 2,* 370–374.

Bremner, J. D., Randall, P., Scott, T. M., Bronen, R. A., Seibyl, J. P., Southwick, S. M., . . . Innis, R. B. (1995). MRI-based measurement of hippocampal volume in patients with combat-related posttraumatic stress disorder. *American Journal of Psychiatry, 152,* 973–981.

Bremner, J. D., Randall, P., Vermetten, E., Staib, L., Bronen, R. A., Capelli, S., . . . Charney, D. S. (1997). MRI-based measurement of hippocampal volume in posttraumatic stress disorder related to childhood physical and sexual abuse: A preliminary report. *Biological Psychiatry, 4,* 23–32.

Bremner, J. D., Vythilingam, M., Vermetten, E., Southwick, S. M., McGlashan, T., Nazeer, A., . . . Charney, D. S. (2003a). MRI and PET study of deficits in hippocampal structure and function in women with childhood sexual abuse and posttraumatic stress disorder (PTSD). *American Journal of Psychiatry, 160,* 924–932.

Bremner, J. D., Vythilingam, M., Vermetten, E., Southwick, S. M., McGlashan, T., Staib, L., . . . Charney, D. S. (2003b). Neural correlates of declarative memory for emotionally valenced words in women with posttraumatic stress disorder (PTSD) related to early childhood sexual abuse. *Biological Psychiatry, 53,* 289–299.

Brooks, J. C., Zambreanu, L., Godinez, A., Craig, A. D., & Tracey, I.(2005). Somatotopic organization of the human insula to painful heat studied with high resolution functional imaging. *Neuroimage, 27,* 201–209.

Brosch, T., Pourtois, G., Sander, D., & Vuilleumier, P. (2011). Additive effects of emotional, endogenous, and exogenous attention: Behavioral and electrophysiological evidence. *Neuropsychologia, 49,* 1779–1787.

Brown, R., & Kulik, J. (1977). Flashbulb memories. *Cognition, 5,* 73–99.

Brunet, A., Orr, S. P., Tremblay, J., Robertson, K., Nader, K., & Pitman, R. K. (2008). Effect of post-retrieval propranolol on psychophysiological responding during subsequent script-driven traumatic imagery in post-traumatic stress disorder. *Journal of Psychiatric Research, 42,* 503–506.

Brunet, A., Poundja, J., Tremblay, J., Bui, E., Thomas, E., Orr, S. P., . . . Pitman R. K. (2011). Trauma reactivation under the influence of propranolol decreases posttraumatic stress symptoms and disorder: 3 open-label trials. *Journal of Clinical Pharmacology, 31,* 547–550.

Buckner, R. L., Andrews-Hanna, J. R., & Schacter, D. L. (2008). The brain's default network: Anatomy, function, and relevance to disease. *Annals of the New York Academy of Sciences, 1124,* 1–38.

Buckner, R. L., & Carroll, D. C. (2008). Self-projection and the brain. *Trends in Cognitive Science, 11,* 49–57.

Buhle, J. T. , Kober, H., Ochsner, K. N., Mende-Siedlecki, P., Weber, J., Hughes, B. L., . . . Wager, T. D. (2012). Common representations of pain and negative emotion in the midbrain periaqueductal gray. *Social, Cognitive and Affective Neuroscience, 7,* 609–616. doi: 10.1093/scan/nss038

Burgdorf, J., Panksepp, J., & Moskal, J. R. (2011). Frequency-modulated 50kHz ultrasonic vocalizations: A tool for uncovering the molecular substrates of positive affect. *Neuroscience and Biobehavioral Reviews, 35,* 1831–1836.

Burgdorf, J., Wood, P. L., Kroes, R. A., Moskal, J. R., & Panksepp, J. (2007). Neurobiology of 50-kHz vocalizations in rats: Electrode mapping, lesion, and pharmacology studies. *Behavioural Brain Research, 182,* 274–283.

References

Burghardt, N. S., Sigurdsson, T., Gorman, J. M., McEwen, B. S., & LeDoux, J. E. (2013). Chronic antidepressant treatment impairs the acquisition of fear extinction. *Biological Psychiatry, 73,* 1078–1086.

Bush, G., Luu, P., & Posner, M. I. (2000). Cognitive and emotional influences in anterior cingulate cortex. *Trends in Cognitive Science, 4,* 215–222.

Cabanac, M. (1971). Physiological role of pleasure. *Science, 173,* 1103–1107.

Cabanac, M. (2010). The dialectics of pleasure. In M. L. Kringelbach & K. C. Berridge (Eds.), *Pleasures of the brain* (pp. 113–124). New York, NY: Oxford University Press.

Cahill, L., Babinsky, R., Markowitsch, H. J., & McGaugh, J. L. (1995). The amygdala and emotional memory. *Nature, 377,* 295–296.

Cahill, L., & McGaugh, J. L. (1995). A novel demonstration of enhanced memory associated with emotional arousal. *Consciousness and Cognition, 4,* 410–421.

Calder, A. J., Beaver, J. D., Davis, M. H., van Ditzhuijzen, J., Keane, J., & Lawrence, A. D. (2007). Disgust sensitivity predicts the insula and pallidal response to pictures of disgusting foods. *European Journal of Neuroscience, 25,* 3422–3428.

Cameron, O. G. (2001). Interoception: The inside story—a model for psychosomatic processes. *Psychosomatic Medicine, 63,* 697–710.

Campos, J. J., Campos, R. G., & Barrett, K. C. (1989). Emergent themes in the study of emotional development and emotion regulation. *Developmental Psychology, 25,* 394.

Canli, T., Zhao, Z., Brewer, J., Gabrieli, J. D. E., & Cahill, L. (2000). Event-related activation in the human amygdala associates with later memory for individual emotional response. *Journal of Neuroscience, 20,* 1–5.

Cannon, W. B. (1915). Bodily changes in pain, hunger, fear and rage. New York, NY: Appleton.

Cannon, W. B. (1927). The James-Lange theory of emotions: A critical examination and an alternative theory. *American Journal of Psychology, 39,* 106–124.

Cannon, W. B. (1929). Organization for physiological homeostasis. *Physiological Review, 9,* 399–431.

Cereda, C., Ghika, J., Maeder, P., & Bougousslavsky, J. (2002). Strokes restricted to the insular cortex. *Neurology, 59,* 1950–1955.

Chan, W. Y. M, Leung, H. T., Westbrook, F., & McNally, G. P. (2010). Effects of recent exposure on extinction of Pavlovian fear conditioning. *Learning and Memory, 17,* 512–521.

Chartrand, T. L., & Bargh, J. A. (1999). The chameleon effect: The perception–behavior link and social interaction. *Journal of Personality and Social Psychology, 76,* 893–910.

Chermahini, S. A., & Hommel, B. (2012). More creative through positive mood? Not everyone! *Frontiers in Human Neuroscience, 6,* doi: 10.3389/fnhum.oo319

Ciesielski, B. G., Armstrong, T., Zald, D. H., & Olatunji, B. O. (2010). Emotion modulation of visual attention: Categorical and temporal characteristics. *PLoS ONE, 5,* e13860. doi: 10.1371/journal.pone.0013860

Clore, G. L., & Colcombe, S. (2003). The parallel worlds of affective concepts and feelings. In J. Musch & K. C. Klauer (Eds.), *The Psychology of Evaluation: Affective Processes in Cognition and Emotion* (pp. 335–370). Mahwah, NJ: Erlbaum.

Clore, G. L., & Huntsinger, J. R. (2007). How emotions inform judgment and regulate thought. *Trends in Cognitive Science, 11,* 395–399.

Clore, G. L., & Huntsinger, J. R. (2009). How the object of affect guides its impact. *Emotion Review, 1,* 39–54.

Clore, G. L., & Storbeck, J. (2006). Affect as information about liking efficacy and importance. In Joseph Forgas (Ed.), *Hearts and Minds: Affective influences on social cognition and behavior* (pp. 123–144). New York, NY: Psychology Press.

Cochrane, C. E., Brewerton, T. D., Wilson, D. B., & Hodges, E. L. (1993). Alexithymia in eating disorders. *International Journal of Eating Disorders, 14,* 219–222.

Coenen, W., Panksepp, J., Hurwitz, T. A., Urbach, H., & Madler, B. (2012). Human medial forebrain bundle (MFB) and anterior thalamic radiation (ATR): Imaging of two major subcortical pathways and the dynamic balance of opposite affects in understanding depression. *Journal of Neuropsychiatry and Clinical Neuroscience, 24,* 223–236.

Cohen, J. D. (2005). The vulcanization of the human brain: A neural perspective on interactions between cognition and emotion. *Journal of Economic Perspectives, 19,* 3–24.

Corkin, S. (2002). What's new with the amnesic patient H. M.? *Nature Reviews Neuroscience, 3,* 153–160.

Corkin, S. (2013). *Permanent present tense: The unforgettable life of the amnesic patient, H. M.* New York, NY: Basic Books.

Craig, A. D. (2002). How do you feel? Interoception: The sense of the physiological condition of the body. *Nature Reviews Neuroscience, 3,* 655–666.

Craig, A. D. (2003). Interoception: The sense of the physiological condition of the body. *Current Opinion in Neurobiology, 13,* 500–505.

Craig, A. D. (2004a). A new view of pain as a homeostatic emotion. *Trends in Neuroscience, 26,* 303–307.

Craig, A. D. (2004b). Human feelings: Why are some more aware than others? *Trends in Cognitive Science, 8,* 239–241.

Craig, A. D. (2005). Forebrain emotional asymmetry: A neuroanatomical basis? *Trends in Cognitive Sciences, 9,* 566–571.

Craig, A. D. (2008). Interoception and emotion: A neuroanatomical perspective. In M. Lewis, J. M. Haviland-Jones, & L. F. Barrett (Eds.), *Handbook of emotions* (3rd ed., pp. 272–288). New York, NY: Guilford.

Craig, A. D. (2009a). How do you feel—now? The anterior insula and human awareness. *Nature Reviews Neuroscience, 10,* 59–70.

References

Craig, A. D. (2009b). Emotional moments across time: A possible neural basis for time perception in the anterior insula. *Philosophical Transactions of the Royal Society, 364*, 1933–1942.

Craig, A. D. (2010). The sentient self. *Brain Structure and Function, 214*, 563–577.

Craig, A. D. (2011). Significance of the insula for the evolution of human awareness of feelings from the body. *New York Academy of Sciences, 1225*, 72–82.

Craig, A. D., Chen, K., Bandy, D., & Reiman, E. M. (2000). Thermosensory activation of insular cortex. *Nature Neuroscience, 3*, 184–190.

Creswell, D., Way, B., Eisenberger, N. I., & Lieberman, M. D. (2007). Neural correlates of dispositional mindfulness during affect labeling. *Psychosomatic Medicine, 69*, 560–565.

Critchley, H. (2005). Neural mechanisms of autonomic, affective, and cognitive integration. *Journal of Comparative Neurology, 493*, 154–166.

Critchley, H. D., Wiens, S., Rothstein, P., Öhman, A., & Dolan, R. J. (2004). Neural systems supporting interoceptive awareness. *Nature Neuroscience, 7*, 189–195.

Cromie, W. (2006, July 24). How Darwin's finches got their beaks. *Harvard Gazette.* Retrieved from http://www.news.harvard.edu/gazette/2006/08.24/31-finches.html

Cukor, J., Spitalnick, J., Difede, J., Rizzo, A., & Rothbaum, B. O. (2009). Emerging treatments for PTSD. *Clinical Psychology Review: Special Issue: PTSD, Iraq, and Afghanistan, 29*, 715–726.

Dalgleish, T. (2004). The emotional brain. *Nature Reviews Neuroscience, 5*, 582–589.

Dalgleish, T., Hauer, B., & Kuyken, W. (2008). The mental regulation of autobiographical recollection in the aftermath of trauma. *Current Directions in Psychological Science, 17*, 259–263.

Damasio, A. (1994). *Descartes' error: Emotion, reason, and the human brain.* New York, NY: Grosset/Putnam.

Damasio, A. (1996). The somatic marker hypothesis and the possible functions of the prefrontal cortex. *Philosophical Transactions of the Royal Society, 351*, 1413–1420.

Damasio, A. (2003). Feelings of emotion and the self. *Annals of the New York Academy of Science, 1001*, 253–261.

Damasio, A. (2010). *Self comes to mind: Constructing the conscious brain.* New York, NY: Pantheon Books.

Damasio, A., & Carvalho, G. B. (2013). The nature of feelings: Evolutionary and neurobiological origins. *Nature Reviews Neuroscience, 14*, 143–152.

Damasio, A., Damasio, H., & Tranel, D. (2013). Persistence of feelings and sentience after bilateral damage of the insula. *Cerebral Cortex, 23*, 833–846.

Damasio, A., Grabowski, T. J., Bechara, A., Damasio, H., Ponto, L. L. B., Parvizi, J., & Hitchwa, R. D. (2000). Subcortical and cortical brain activity during the feeling of self-generated emotions. *Nature Neuroscience, 3*, 1049–1056.

Damasio, H., Grabowski, T., Frank, R., Galaburda, A. M., & Damasio A. R. (1994b).

The return of Phineas Gage: Clues about the brain from the skull of a famous patient. *Science, 264,* 1102–1105.

Darwin, C. (1872). *The expression of the emotions in man and animals.* London, UK: John Murray.

Davidson, R. J., Ekman, P., Saron, C. D., Senulis, J. A., & Friesen, W. V. (1990). Approach-withdrawal and cerebral asymmetry: Emotion expression and brain physiology I. *Journal of Personality and Social Psychology, 58,* 330–341.

Davis, H. P. & Squire, L. R. (1984). Protein synthesis and memory: a review. *Psychological Bulletin, 96,* 518–559.

Deacon, T. (2006). The aesthetic faculty. In Mark Turner (Ed.), *The artful mind: Cognitive science and the riddle of human creativity* (pp. 21–53). New York, NY: Oxford University Press.

Decety, J., & Jackson, P. L. (2006). A social neuroscience perspective on empathy. *Current Directions in Psychological Science, 15,* 54–58.

deCharms, R. C. (2007). Reading and controlling human brain activation using real-time functional magnetic resonance imaging. *Trends in Cognitive Science, 11,* 473–481.

De Martino, B., Camerer, C. F., & Adolphs, R. (2010). Amygdala damage eliminates monetary loss aversion. *Proceedings of the National Academy of Sciences, 107,* 3788–3792.

De Martino, B., Kumaran, D., Seymour, B., & Dolan, R. J. (2006). Frames, biases and rational decision-making in the human brain. *Science, 313,* 684–687.

Diamond, A., & Amso, D. (2008). Contributions of neuroscience to our understanding of cognitive development. *Current Directions in Psychological Science, 17,* 136–141.

Diamond, D. M., Campbell, A. M., Park, C. R., Halonen, J., & Zoladz, P. R. (2007). The temporal dynamics model of emotional memory processing: A synthesis on the neurobiological basis of stress-induced amnesia, flashbulb and traumatic memories, and the Yerkes-Dodson law. *Neural Plasticity.* Vol. 2007, Article ID 60803, doi: 10.1155/2007/60803

Dickinson, A., & Balleine, B. (2010). Hedonics: The cognitive-motivational interface. In M. L. Kringelbach & K. C. Berridge (Eds.), *Pleasures of the brain* (pp. 74–84). New York, NY: Oxford University Press.

Dickinson, J., Berkman, E. T., Arch, J., & Lieberman, M. D. (2012). Neural correlates of focused attention during a brief mindfulness induction. SCAN. doi: 10.1093/scan/nss030

Dijksterhuis, A., & Aarts, H. (2010). Goals, attention and (un)consciousness. *Annual Review of Psychology, 61,* 1467–1490.

Dolcos, F., Iordan, A. D., & Dolcos, S. (2011). Neural correlates of emotion–cognition interactions: A review of evidence from brain imaging investigations. *Journal of Cognitive Psychology, 23,* 669–694.

References

Dolcos, F., LaBar, K. S., & Cabeza, R. (2004). Interaction between the amygdala and the medial temporal lobe memory system predicts better memory for emotional events. *Neuron, 42,* 855–863.

Dolcos, F., LaBar, K. S., & Cabeza, R. (2005). Remembering one year later: Role of the amygdala and the medial temporal lobe memory system in retrieving emotional memories. *Proceedings of the National Academy of Sciences, 102,* 2626–2631.

Drabant, E. M., McRae, K., Manuck, S. B., Hariri, A. R., & Gross, J. J. (2009). Individual differences in typical reappraisal use predict amygdala and prefrontal responses. *Biological Psychiatry, 65,* 367–373.

Duerden, E. G., Arsalidou, M., Lee, M., & Taylor, M. J. (2013). Lateralization of affective processing in the insula. *Neuroimage, 78,* 159–175.

Duman, R. S., Nakagawa, S., & Malberg, J. (2001). Regulation of adult neurogenesis by anti-depressant treatment. *Neuropsychopharmacology, 25,* 836–44.

Dunn, B. D., Dalgleish, T., & Lawrence, A. D. (2006). The somatic marker hypothesis: A critical evaluation. *Neuroscience Biobehavioral Review, 30,* 239–271.

Dutton, D. G., & Aron, A. P. (1974). Some evidence for heightened sexual attraction under conditions of high anxiety. *Journal of Personality and Social Psychology, 30,* 510–517.

Easterbrook, J. A. (1959). The effect of emotion on cue utilization and the organization of behavior. *Psychological Review, 66,* 183–201.

Egner, T. (2011). Surprise! A unifying model of dorsal anterior cingulate function? *Nature Neuroscience, 14,* 1219–1220.

Egner, T., Etkin, A., Gale, S., & Hirsch, J. (2008). Dissociable neural systems resolve conflict from emotional versus nonemotional distracters. *Cerebral Cortex, 18,* 1475–1484.

Egner, T., & Hirsch, J. (2005). Cognitive control mechanisms resolve conflict through cortical amplification of task-relevant information. *Nature Neuroscience, 8,* 1784–1790.

Ekman, P. (1992). Are there basic emotions?. *Psychological Review, 99,* 550–553.

Ekman, P. (1994). All emotions are basic. In P. Ekman & R. J. Davidson (Eds.), *The Nature of Emotion* (pp. 15–19). New York, NY: Oxford University Press.

Ekman, P. (1999). Basic emotions. In T. Dalgleish & M. Power (Eds.), *Handbook of cognition and emotion* (pp. 45–60). New York, NY: Wiley.

Ekman, P., & Friesen, W. (1976). Measuring facial movement. *Environmental Psychology and Nonverbal Behavior, 1,* 56–75. doi: 10.1007/BFo115465

Ekman, P., Levenson, R., & Friesen, W. V. (1983). Autonomic nervous system activity distinguishes among emotions. *Science, 221,* 1208–1210.

Ekman, P., Sorenson, E. R., & Friesen, W. V. (1969). Pan-cultural elements in facial displays of emotion. *Science, 164,* 86–88.

Eisenberger, N. I., & Lieberman, M. D. (2004). Why rejection hurts: A common neural alarm system for physical and social pain. *Trends in Cognitive Science, 8,* 294–300.

Eisenberger, N. I., Lieberman, M., & Williams, K. (2003). Does rejection hurt: An fMRI study of social exclusion. *Science, 302,* 290–292.

Enoch, M. (2013). The first steps on the path toward genomic predictors of behavioral therapy for posttraumatic stress disorder. *Biological Psychiatry, 73,* 1039–1040.

Etkin, A. (2012). Neurobiology of anxiety: From neural circuits to novel solutions? *Depression and Anxiety, 29,* 355–358.

Etkin, A., Egner, T., & Kalisch, R. (2011). Emotional processing in anterior cingulate and medial prefrontal cortex. *Trends in Cognitive Sciences, 15,* 85–93.

Etkin, A., Egner, T., Peraza, D., Kandel, E., & Hirsch, J. (2006). Resolving emotional conflict: A role for the rostral anterior cingulate cortex in modulating activity in the amygdala. *Neuron, 51,* 871–882.

Etkin, A., Prater, K. E., Hoeft, F., Menon, V., & Schatzberg, A. F. (2010). Failure of anterior cingulate activation and connectivity with the amygdala during implicit regulation of emotional processing in generalized anxiety disorder. *American Journal of Psychiatry, 167,* 545–554.

Fancher, R. E. (1996). *Pioneers of psychology.* New York, NY: Norton.

Fancher, R. E. & Rutherford, A. (2011). *Pioneers of psychology: A history.* New York, NY: Norton.

Fanselow, M. S. (2013). Fear takes a double hit from vagal nerve stimulation. *Biological Psychiatry 73,* 1043–1044.

Faure, A. Reynolds, S.M., Richard, J.M. & Berridge, K.C. (2008). Mesolimbic dopamine in desire and dread: Enabling motivation to be generated by localized glutamate disruptions in nucleus accumbens. *Journal of Neuroscience, 28,* 7184–7192.

Faure, A., Richard, J.M. & Berridge, K.C. (2010). Desire and dread from the nucleus accumbens: Cortical glutamate and subcortical GABA differentially generate motivation and hedonic impact in the rat. *PLoS ONE. 5*(6): e11223.

Fanselow, M. S. (2013). Fear and anxiety take a double hit from vagal nerve stimulation. *Biological Psychiatry, 73,* 1043–1044.

Feinstein, J., Adolphs, R., Damasio, A., & Tranel, D. (2011). The human amygdala and the induction and experience of fear. *Current Biology, 21,* 34–38.

Felmingham, K. L., Dobson-Stone, C., Schofield, P. R., Quirk, G. J., & Bryant, R. A. (2013). The brain-derived neurotrophic factor Val66Met polymorphism predicts response to exposure therapy in posttraumatic stress disorder. *Biological Psychiatry, 73,* 1059–1063.

Finger, S. (1994). *Origins of neuroscience: A history of explorations into brain function.* New York, NY: Oxford University Press.

Fletcher, L. B., Schoendorff, B., & Hayes, S. C. (2010). Searching for mindfulness in the brain: A process-oriented approach to examining the neural correlates of mindfulness. *Mindfulness, 1,* 41–63.

Forgas, J. P. (2008). Affect and cognition. *Perspectives on Psychological Science, 3,* 94–101.

References

Forgas, J. P. (2013). Don't worry, be sad! On the cognitive, motivational, and interpersonal benefits of negative mood. *Current Directions in Psychological Science, 22,* 225–232.

Franklin, T. R., Acton, P. D., Maldjian, J. A., Gray, J. D., Croft, J. R., Dackis, C. A., . . . Childress, A. R. (2002). Decreased gray matter concentration in the insular, orbitofrontal, cingulate, and temporal cortices of cocaine patients. *Biological Psychiatry, 51,* 134–142.

Fredrickson, B. L. (2001). The role of positive emotions in positive psychology: The broaden-and-build theory of positive emotions. *American Psychologist, 56,* 218–226.

Fredrickson, B. L., & Branigan, C. (2005). Positive emotions broaden the scope of attention and thought-action repertoires. *Cognition and Emotion, 19,* 315–322.

Fredrickson, B. L., & Losada, M. F. (2005). Positive affect and the complex dynamics of human flourishing. *American Psychologist, 60,* 678–686.

Fresco, D. M., Mennin, D. S., Heimberg, R. G., & Ritter, M. (2013). Emotion regulation therapy for generalized anxiety disorder. *Cognitive and Behavioral Practice, 20,* 282–300. doi: 10.1016/j.cbpra.2013.02.00

Friedman, B. H. (2010). Feelings and the body: The Jamesian perspective on autonomic specificity of emotion. *Biological Psychology, 84,* 383–393.

Friedman, R. S., & Förster, J. (2010). Implicit affective cues and attentional tuning: An integrative review. *Psychological Bulletin, 136,* 875–893.

Frijda, N. H. (2010). On the nature and function of pleasure. In Morten L. Kringelbach & Kent C. Berridge (Eds.), *Pleasures of the brain* (pp. 99–112). New York, NY: Oxford University Press.

Frith, U. (2003). *Autism: Explaining the enigma.* Cambridge, MA: Blackwell.

Gable, P., & Harmon-Jones, E. (2009). Neural activity underlying the effect of approach-motivated positive affect on narrowed attention. *Psychological Science, 20,* 406–409.

Gable, P., & Harmon-Jones, E. (2010a). The motivational dimensional model of affect: Implications for breadth of attention, memory and cognitive categorization. *Cognition and Emotion, 24,* 322–337.

Gable, P., & Harmon-Jones, E. (2010b). The blues broaden but the nasty narrows: Attentional consequences of negative affects low and high in motivational intensity. *Psychological Science, 21,* 211–215.

Gallese, V. (2003). The roots of empathy: The shared manifold hypothesis and the neural basis of intersubjectivity. *Psychopathology, 36,* 171–180.

Gallese, V., & Goldman, A. (1998). Mirror neurons and the simulation theory of mind-reading. *Trends in Cognitive Science, 2,* 493–501.

Gasper, K., & Clore, G. L. (2002). Attending to the big picture: Mood and global versus local processing of visual information. *Psychological Science, 13,* 33–39.

Gendron, M., & Barrett, L. F. (2009). Reconstructing the past: A century of ideas about emotion in psychology. *Emotion Review, 1,* 316–339.

Gigerenzer, G., & Gaissmaier, W. (2011). Heuristic decision making. *Annual Review of Psychology, 62,* 451–482.

Gilbertson, M. W., Shenton, M. E., Ciszewski, A., Kasai, K., Lasko, N. B., Orr, S. P., & Pitman, R. K. (2002). Smaller hippocampal volume predicts pathologic vulnerability to psychological trauma. *Nature Neuroscience, 5,* 1242–1247.

Giuliani, N., Drabant, E. M., Bhatnagar, R., & Gross, J. J. (2011). Emotion regulation and brain plasticity: Expressive suppression use predicts anterior insula volume. *Neuroimage, 58,* 10–15.

Giuliani, N. R., Drabant, E. M., & Gross, J. J. (2011). Anterior cingulate cortex volume and emotion regulation: Is bigger better? *Biological Psychology, 86,* 379–382.

Giuliani, N., & Gross, J. J. (2009). Reappraisal. In D. Sander & K. Scherer (Eds.), *Oxford companion to the affective sciences.* New York, NY: Oxford University Press.

Glimcher, P.W. (2011). Understanding dopamine and reinforcement learning: The dopamine reward prediction error hypothesis. *Proceedings of the National Academy of Sciences, 108,* Suppl 3: 15647–15654.

Gohm, C. L., & Clore, G. L. (2002). Affect as information: An individual-difference approach. In L. Barrett & P. Salovey (Eds.), *The wisdom of feeling: Psychological processes in emotional intelligence* (pp. 89–113). New York, NY: Guilford Press.

Gold, P. E. (2008). Protein synthesis inhibition and memory: formation vs. amnesia. *Neurobiology of Learning and Memory, 89,* 201–211.

Goldin, P. R., McRae, K., Ramel, W., & Gross, J. J. (2008). The neural bases of emotion regulation: Reappraisal and suppression of negative emotion. *Biological Psychiatry, 63,* 577–586.

Goldstein, R. Z., Craig, A. D., Bechara, A., Garavan, H., Childress, A. R., Paulus, M. P., & Volkow, N. D. (2009). The neurocircuitry of impaired insight in drug addiction. *Trends in Cognitive Sciences, 13,* 372–380.

Golkar, A., Bellander, M., Olsson, A., & Öhman, A. (2012). Are fear memories erasable? Reconsolidation of learned fear with fear-relevant and fear-irrelevant stimuli. *Frontiers in Behavioral Neuroscience, 6,* 80.

Goode, E. (2002, November 5). A conversation with Daniel Kahneman: On profit, loss and the mysteries of the mind. *New York Times.*

Gould, E., Beylin, A., Tanapat, P., Reeves, A., & Shors, T. J. (1999). Learning enhances adult neurogenesis in the hippocampal formation. *Nature Neuroscience, 2,* 260–265.

Gray, M. A., Harrison, N. A., Weins, S., & Critchley, H. D. (2007). Modulation of emotional appraisal by false physiological feedback during fMRI. *PLoS ONE, 6,* e546. doi: 10.1371/journal.pone.0000456.

Grecucci, A., Giorgetta, C., van't Wout, M., Bonini, N., & Sanfey, A. G. (2013). Reappraising the ultimatum: An fMRI study of emotion regulation and decision making. *Cerebral Cortex, 23,* 399–410.

Greene, J. D., Somerville, R. B., Nystrom, L. E., Darley, J. M., & Cohen, J. D. (2001). An fMRI investigation of emotional engagement in moral judgment. *Science, 293,* 2015–2108.

Greenfield, S. (2008). *ID: The quest for meaning in the 21st century.* New York, NY: Hodder & Staughton.

Greeson, J., & Brantley, J. (2009). Mindfulness and anxiety disorders: Developing a wise relationship with the inner experience of fear. In F. Didonna (Ed.), *Clinical handbook of mindfulness* (pp. 171–188). New York, NY: Springer.

Griefeneder, R., Bless, H., & Pham, M. T. (2011). When do people rely on affective and cognitive feelings in judgments? A review. *Personality and Social Psychology Review, 15,* 107–141.

Griffiths, T. D., Warren, J. D., Dean, J. L., & Howard, D. (2007). "When the feeling's gone": A selective loss of musical emotion. *Journal of Neurology, Neurosurgery, and Psychiatry, 75,* 341–345.

Gross, J. J. (1998a). The emerging field of emotion regulation: An integrative review. *Review of General Psychology, 2,* 271–299.

Gross, J. J. (1998b). Antecedent- and response- focused emotion regulation: Divergent consequences for experience, expression, and physiology. *Journal of Personality and Social Psychology, 74,* 224–237.

Gross, J. J. (Ed.). (2007). *Handbook of emotion regulation.* New York, NY: Guilford Press.

Gross, J. J., & Barrett, L. F. (2011). Emotion generation and emotion regulation: One or two depends on your point of view. *Emotion Review, 3,* 8–16.

Gross, J. J., & John, O. (2003). Individual differences in two emotion regulation processes: Implications for affect, relationships, and well-being. *Journal of Personality and Social Psychology, 85,* 348–362.

Gurvits, T. V., Shenton, M. E., Hokama, H., Ohta, H., Lasko, N. B., Gilbertson, M. W., . . . Pitman, R. K. (1996). Magnetic resonance imaging study of hippocampal volume in chronic, combat-related posttraumatic stress disorder. *Biological Psychiatry, 40,* 1091–1099.

Gusnard, D. A., Akbudak, E., Shulman, G. L., & Raichle, M. E. (2001). Medial prefrontal cortex and self-referential mental activity: Relation to a default mode of brain function. *Proceedings of the National Academy of Sciences, USA, 98,* 4259–4264.

Gyurak, Gross, J. J., & Etkin, A. (2011). Explicit and implicit emotion regulation: A dual process framework. *Cognition and Emotion, 25,* 400–412.

Haberman, J., & Whitney, D. (2009). Seeing the mean: Ensemble coding for sets of faces. *Journal of Experimental Psychology: Human Perception and Performance, 35,* 718–717.

Hajek, T., Kopecek, M., & Hoschl, C. (2012). Reduced hippocampal volumes in healthy carriers of brain-derived neurotrophic factor Val66Met polymorphism: Meta-analysis. *The World Journal of Biological Psychiatry, 13,* 178–187.

Hamann, S. (2012). Mapping discrete and dimensional emotions onto the brain: Controversies and consensus. *Trends in Cognitive Sciences, 16*, 458–466.

Harber, K. (2005). Self-esteem and affect-as-information. *Personality and Social Psychology Bulletin, 31*, 276–288.

Hare, T. A., Camerer, C. F., & Rangel, A. (2009). Self-control in decision-making involves modulation of the vmPFC valuation system. *Science, 324*, 646–648.

Harlow, H. (1958). The nature of love. *American Psychologist, 13*, 673–685.

Harlow, J. M. (1868). Recovery from the passage of an iron bar through the head. *Publications of the Massachusetts Medical Society, 2*, 327–347.

Harmon-Jones, E., Gable, P. A., & Price, T. F. (2013). Does negative affect always narrow and positive affect always broaden the mind? Influence of motivational intensity on cognitive scope. *Current Directions in Psychological Science, 22*, 301–307.

Hart, A. S., Rutledge, R. B., Glimcher, P. W. and Phillips, P. E.M. (2014). Phasic dopamine release in rat nucleus accumbens symmetrically encodes a reward prediction error term. *Journal of Neuroscience, 34*, 689–704

Hartley, C. A., Fischl, B., & Phelps, E. A. (2011). Brain structure correlates of individual differences in the acquisition and inhibition of conditioned fear. *Cerebral Cortex, 21*(9), 1954–1962.

Hartley, C. A., & Phelps, E. A. (2010). Changing fear: The neurocircuitry of emotion regulation. *Neuropsychopharmacology, 35*, 136–146.

Hartley, C. A., & Phelps, E. A. (2012). Anxiety and decision-making. *Biological Psychiatry, 72*, 113–118.

Hayes, S. C., Follette, V. M., & Linehan, M. M. (Eds.). (2004). *Mindfulness and acceptance: Expanding the cognitive-behavioral tradition.* New York, NY: Guilford Press.

Heath, R. (1972). Pleasure and brain activity in man: Deep and surface electroencephalograms during orgasm. *Journal of Nervous and Mental Disease, 154*, 3–18.

Hennenlotter, A., Schroeder, U., Erhard, P.. Haslinger, B., Stahl, R., Weindl, A., . . . Ceballos-Bauman, A. O. (2004). Neural correlates associated with impaired disgust processing in pre-symptomatic Huntington's disease. *Brain, 127*, 1446–1453.

Henrich, J., Heine, S. J., & Norenzayan, A. (2010). The weirdest people in the world? *Behavioral and Brain Sciences, 33*, 61–83.

Het, S., Ramlow, G., & Wolf, O. T. (2005). A meta-analytic review of the effects of acute cortisol administration on human memory. *Psychoneuroendrocrinology, 30*, 771–784.

Heuer, F., & Reisberg, D. (1990). Vivid memories of emotional events: The accuracy of remembered minutiae. *Memory and Cognition, 18*, 496–506.

Hickok, G. (2014). *The Myth of Mirror Neurons: The Real Neuroscience of Communication and Cognition.* New York: Norton.

Hirst, W., Phelps, E. A., Buckner, R. L., Budson, A. E., Cuc, A., Gabrieli, J. D. E., . . . Vaidya, C.J. (2009). Long-term memory for the terrorist attack of September 11:

References

Flashbulb memories, event memories, and the factors that influence their retention. *Journal of Experimental Psychology: General, 138,* 161–176.

Hirst, W., Phelps, E. A., Meskin, R., Vaidya, C. J., Johnson, M. K., Mitchell, K. J. . . . (2014). A ten-year follow-up of a study of memory for the attack of September 11, 2001: Flashbulb memories and memories for flashbulb events. In press.

Holden, C. (1979). Paul MacLean and the triune brain. *Science, 204,* 1066–1068.

Holtzheimer, P. E., & Mayberg, H. S. (2011). Stuck in a rut: Rethinking depression and its treatment. *Trends in Neurosciences, 34*(1), 1–9.

Hölzel, B. K, Carmody, J., Evans, K. C., Hoge, E. A., Dusek, J. A., Morgan, L., . . . Lazar, S. W. (2009). Stress reduction correlates with structural changes in the amygdala. *Social Cognitive and Affective Neuroscience, 5,* 11–17.

Hölzel, B. K., Lazar, S. W., Gard, T., Schuman-Olivier, Z., Vago, D. R., & Ott, U. (2011). How does mindfulness meditation work? Proposing mechanisms of action from a conceptual and neural perspective. *Perspectives on Psychological Science, 6,* 537–559.

Hölzel, B. K., Ott, U., Hempel, H., Hackl, A., Wolf, K., Stark, R., & Vaitl, D. (2007). Differential engagement of anterior cingulate and adjacent medial frontal cortex in adept meditators and non-meditators. *Neuroscience Letters, 421,* 16–21.

Hua, L. H., Strigo, I. A., Baxter, L. C., Johnson, S. C., & Craig, A. D. (2005). Anteroposterior somatotopy of innocuous cooling activation focus in human dorsal posterior insular cortex. *American Journal of Physiology: Regulatory, Integrative and Comparative Physiology, 289,* R319–R325.

Human Connectome Project. (2013). Retrieved from http://www.humanconnectomeproject.org/

Huntsinger, M., Isbell, L. M., & Clore, G. (2012). Sometimes happy people focus on the trees and sad people focus on the forest: Context-dependent effects of mood in impression formation. *Personality and Social Psychology Bulletin, 38,* 220–232.

Hupbach, A., & Fieman, R. (2012). Moderate stress enhances immediate and delayed retrieval of educationally relevant material in healthy young men. *Behavioral Neuroscience, 126,* 819–825.

Isen, A. M. (2008). Some ways in which positive affect influences decision making and problem solving. In M. Lewis, J., Haviland-Jones, & L. F. Barrett (Eds.), *Handbook of emotions* (3rd ed., p. 548–573). New York, NY: Guilford Press.

Izard, C. E. (2007). Basic emotions, natural kinds, emotion schemas, and a new paradigm. *Perspectives on Psychological Science, 2,* 260–280.

Izard, C. E. (2009). Emotion theory and research: Highlights, unanswered questions, and emerging issues. *Annual Review of Psychology, 60,* 1–25.

Jabbi, M., Swart, M., & Keysers, C. (2007). Empathy for positive and negative emotions in the gustatory cortex. *Neuroimage, 34,* 1744–1781.

Jackson, P. I., Brunet, E., Meltzoff, A. N., & Decety, J. (2006). Empathy examined through the neural mechanisms involved in imagining how I feel versus how you feel pain: An event-related fMRI study. *Neuropsychologia, 44,* 752–761.

James, W. (1884). What is an emotion? *Mind, 9,* 188–205.

James, W. (1890). *The principles of psychology.* New York, NY: Dover.

Johnson, K. J, Waugh, C. E., & Fredrickson, B. L. (2010). Smile to see the forest: Facially expressed positive emotions broaden cognition. *Cognition and Emotion, 24,* 299–321.

Jones, C. L., Ward, J., & Critchley, H. D. (2010). The neuropsychological impact of insular cortex lesions. *Journal of Neurology, Neurosurgery and Psychiatry, 81,* 611–618.

Kabat-Zinn, J. (1990). *Full catastrophe living.* New York, NY: Delacorte Press.

Kabat-Zinn, J. (2003). Mindfulness-based interventions in context: Past, present, and future. *Clinical Psychology: Science and Practice, 10,* 144–156.

Kahneman, D. (2003). A perspective on judgment and choice: Mapping the bounded rationality. *American Psychologist, 58,* 697–720.

Kahneman, D. (2011). *Thinking, fast and slow.* New York, NY: Farrar, Strauss, Giroux.

Kahneman, D., & Tversky, A. (1984). Choices, values and frames. *American Psychologist, 39,* 341–350.

Kahneman, D., & Tversky, A. (1996). On the reality of cognitive illusions. *Psychological Review, 103,* 582–591.

Kalin, N. H., Shelton, S. E., Fox, A. S., Rogers, J., Oakes, T. R., & Davidson, R. J. (2008). The serotonin transporter genotype is associated with intermediate brain phenotypes that depend on the context of eliciting stressor. *Molecular psychiatry, 13,* 1021–1027.

Kanske, P., Heissler, J., Schönfelder, S., Bongers, A., & Wessa, M. (2011). How to regulate emotion? Neural networks for reappraisal and distraction. *Cerebral Cortex, 21,* 1379–1388.

Kashdan, T. B. (2010). Psychological flexibility as a fundamental aspect of health. *Clinical Psychology Review, 30,* 865–878.

Kaspar, K., & Konig, P. (2012). Emotions and personality traits as high-level factors in visual attention: A review. *Frontiers in Human Neuroscience, 6,* Article 321, 1–14.

Kaye, W. H., Wierenga, C. E., Bailer, U. F., Simmons, A. N., & Bischoff-Grethe, A. (2013). Nothing tastes as good as skinny feels: The neurobiology of anorexia nervosa. *Trends in Neurosciences, 36,* 110–120.

Kelly, V. C. (2009). *A primer of affect psychology.* Retrieved from http://tomkins.org/uploads/Primer_of_Affect_Psychology.pdf

Kennedy, D. P., Gläscher, J., Tyszka, J. M., & Adolphs, R. (2009). Personal space regulation by the human amygdala. *Nature Neuroscience, 10,* 1226–1227.

Kensinger, E. A., & Schacter, D. L. (2008). Memory and emotion. In M. Lewis, J. M. Haviland-Jones, & L. F. Barrett (Eds.), *Handbook of emotions* (3rd ed., pp. 601–617). New York, NY: Guilford Press.

References

Kim, S. H., & Hamann, S. (2007). Neural correlates of positive and negative emotion regulation. *Journal of Cognitive Neuroscience, 19,* 776–798.

Kim, M., Justin, G., Sylan, G., Loucks, R. A., Davis, F.C. & Whalen, P. J. (2011). Anxiety dissociates dorsal and ventral medial prefrontal cortex functional connectivity. *Cerebral Cortex, 21,* 1667–1673.

Kindt, M., & Soeter, M. (2013). Reconsolidation in a human fear conditioning study: A test of extinction as an updating mechanism. *Biological Psychology, 92,* 43–50.

Kitayama, N., Vaccarino, V., Kutner, M., Weiss, P., & Bremner, J. D. (2005). Magnetic resonance imaging (MRI) measurement of hippocampal volume in posttraumatic stress disorder: A meta-analysis. *Journal of Affective Disorders, 88,* 79–86.

Knapska, E., Macias, M., Mikosza, M., Nowaka, A., Owczarekb, D., Wawrzyniakb, M., ... & Kaczmarek, L. (2012). Functional anatomy of neural circuits regulating fear and extinction. *Proceedings of the National Acadxemy of Sciences, 109,* 17093–17098.

Knudsen, E. I. (2007). Fundamental components of attention. *Annual Review of Neuroscience, 30,* 57–78.

Knutson, B., & Greer, S.M. (2008). Anticipatory affect: Neural correlates and consequences for choice. *Philosophical Transactions of the Royal Society B, 363,* 3771–3786.

Koenigs, M., Huey, E. D., Raymont, V., Cheon, B., Solomon, J., Wassermann, E. M., & Grafman, J. (2008). Focal brain damage protects against post-traumatic stress disorder in combat veterans. *Nature Neuroscience, 11,* 232–237.

Kok, B. E., Coffey, K. A., Cohn, M. A., Catalino, L. I., Vacharkulksemsek, T., Algoe, S. B., ... Fredrickson, B. L. (2013). How positive emotions build physical health: Perceived positive social connections account for the upward spiral between positive emotions and vagal tone. *Psychological Science, 24,* 1123–1132.

Koole, S. (2009). The psychology of emotion regulation: An integrative review. *Cognition and Emotion, 23,* 4–41.

Koole, S. L., & Rothermund, K. (2011). "I feel better but I don't know why": The psychology of implicit emotion regulation. *Cognition and Emotion, 25,* 389–399.

Kosfeld, M., Heinrichs, M., Zak, P. J., Fischbacher, U., & Fehr, E. (2005). Oxytocin increases trust in humans. *Nature, 435,* 673–676.

Kuhnen, C., & Knutson, B. (2005). The neural basis of financial risk taking. *Neuron, 47,* 763–770.

Kringelbach, M. (2005). The human orbitofrontal cortex: Linking reward to hedonic experience. *Nature Reviews Neuroscience, 6,* 691–702.

Kringelbach, M., O'Doherty, J., Rolls, E. T., & Andrews, C. (2003). Activation of the human orbitofrontal cortex to a liquid food stimulus is correlated with its subjective pleasantness. *Cerebral Cortex, 13,* 1064–1071.

Kringelbach, M. L., & Rolls, E. T. (2004). The functional neuroanatomy of the human orbitofrontal cortex: Evidence from neuroimaging and neuropsychology. *Progress in Neurobiology, 72,* 341–372.

Kross, E., & Ayduk, O. (2011). Making meaning out of negative experiences by self-distancing. *Current Directions in Psychological Science, 20,* 187–191.

Kross, E., Davidson, M., Weber, J., & Ochsner, K. (2009). Coping with emotions past: The neural bases of regulating affect associated with negative autobiographical memories. *Biological Psychiatry, 65,* 361–366.

Kross, E., Gard, D., Deldin, P., Clifton, J., & Ayduk, O. (2012). Asking why from a distance: Its cognitive and emotional consequences for people with major depressive disorder. *Journal of Abnormal Psychology, 121,* 559–569.

Kumsta, R., & Heinrichs, M. (2013). Oxytocin, stress, and social behavior: neurogenetics of the human oxytocin system. *Current Opinion in Neurobiology, 2,* 11–16.

Kuyken, W., & Brewin, C. R. (1995). Autobiographical memory functioning in depression and reports of early abuse. *Journal of Abnormal Psychology, 104,* 585–591.

Lambert, K. G. (2003). The life and career of Paul MacLean: A journey toward neurobiological and social harmony. *Physiology and Behavior, 79,* 343–349.

Lane, R. D., Fink, G. R., Chau, P. M., & Dolan, R. J. (1997). Neural activation during selective attention to subjective emotional states. *NeuroReport, 8,* 3969–3972.

Lang, P. J., & Bradley, M. M. (2010). Emotion and the motivational brain. *Biological Psychology, 84,* 437–450.

Lang, P. J., Bradley, M. M., & Cuthbert, B. N. (2008). *International affective picture system (IAPS): Affective ratings of pictures and instruction manual* (Technical Report A-8). University of Florida, Gainesville, FL.

Lange, C. G. (1912). The mechanisms of emotion. In B. Rand (Trans.), *The classical psychologists* (pp. 672–684). Boston, MA: Houghton Mifflin. Retrieved from http://psychclassics.yorku.ca/Lange/ (Original work published 1884)

Lautin, A. (2001). *The limbic brain.* New York, NY: Springer.

Lazar, S. W., Kerr, C., Wasserman, R. H., Gray, J. R., Greve, D., Treadway, M. T., . . . Fischl, B. (2005). Meditation experience is associated with increased cortical thickness. *NeuroReport, 16,* 1893–1897.

Lazarus, R. S., & Alfert, E. (1964). Short-circuiting of threat by experimentally altering cognitive appraisal. *Journal of Abnormal and Social Psychology, 69,* 195–205.

LeDoux, J. E. (1996). *The emotional brain: The mysterious underpinnings of emotional life.* New York, NY: Simon & Schuster.

LeDoux, J. E. (2000). Emotion circuits in the brain. *Annual Review of Neuroscience, 23,* 155–184.

LeDoux, J. L. (2002). *Synaptic self.* New York, NY: Penguin.

LeDoux, J. E. (2003). The emotional brain, fear and the amygdala. *Cellular and Molecular Neurobiology, 23,* 727–734.

LeDoux, J. E. (2007). The amygdala. *Current Biology, 17,* R8868–R8874.

LeDoux, J. E. (2012). Rethinking the emotional brain. *Neuron, 73,* 653–676.

LeDoux, J. E. (2013). The slippery slope of fear. *Trends in Cognitive Science, 17,* 155–156.

References

LeDoux, J. E., & Phelps, E. A. (2008). Emotional networks in the brain. In M. Lewis, J. M. Haviland-Jones, & L. F. Barett (Eds.), *Handbook of emotions* (3rd ed., pp. 159–179). New York, NY: Guilford Press.

Leibenluft, E., Gobbini, M. I., Harrison, T., & Haxby, J. V. (2004). Mothers' neural activation in response to pictures of their own children and other children. *Biological Psychiatry, 56,* 225–232.

Lerner, J. S., & Tiedens, L.Z. (2006). Portrait of the angry decision maker: How appraisal tendencies shape anger's influence on cognition. *Journal of Behavioral Decision Making, 19,* 115–137.

Levine, L. J., & Pizarro, D. A. (2004). Emotion and memory research: A grumpy overview. *Social Cognition, 22,* 530–554.

Levy, D. J., & Glimcher, P. W. (2012). The root of all value: a neural common currency for choice. *Current Opinion in Neurobiology, 22,* 1027–1038.

Leyton, M. (2010). The neurobiology of desire: Dopamine and the regulation of mood and motivational states in humans. In M. L. Kringelbach K. C. Berridge (Eds.), *Pleasures of the brain* (pp. 222–243). New York, NY: Oxford University Press.

Li, W., Howard, J. D., Parrish, T. B., & Gottfried, J. A. (2008). Aversive learning enhances perceptual and cortical discrimination of indiscriminable odor cues. *Science, 319*(5871), 1842–1845.

Lieberman, M. D. (2009). The brain's braking system (and how to "use your words" to tap into it). *Neuroleadership, 2,* 9–14.

Lieberman, M. D. (2013). *Social: Why our brains are wired to connect.* New York, NY: Crown.

Lieberman, M. D., Eisenberger, N. I., Crockett, M. J., Tom, S. M., Pfeifer, J. H., & Way, B. M. (2007). Putting feelings into words: Affect labeling disrupts amygdala activity to affective stimuli. *Psychological Science, 18,* 421–428.

Lim, S.-L., Padmala, S., & Pessoa L. (2009). Segregating the significant from the mundane on a moment-to-moment basis via direct and indirect amygdala contributions. *Proceedings of the National Academy of Sciences, 106,* 16841–16846.

Lim, M. M., Wang, Z., Olazabal1, D. E., Ren, X., Terwilliger, E. F. & Young, L. J. (2004). Enhanced partner preference in a promiscuous species by manipulating the expression of a single gene. *Nature, 429,* 754–757.

Lin, C.-H., Chiu, Y.-C., Cheng, C.-M. & Hsieh, J.-C. (2008). Brain maps of Iowa gambling task. *BMC Neuroscience, 9,* 72.

Linden, D. J. (2011). *The compass of pleasure: How our brains make fatty foods, orgasm, exercise, marijuana, generosity, vodka, learning, and gambling feel so good.* New York, NY: Viking.

Lindquist, K. A., & Barrett, L. F. (2012). A functional architecture of the human brain: Emerging insights from the science of emotion. *Trends in Cognitive Sciences, 16,* 533–540.

Lindquist, K. A., Wager, T. D., Kober, H., Bliss-Moreau, E., & Barrett, L. F. (2012). The brain basis of emotion: A meta-analytic review. *Behavioral and Brain Sciences, 35,* 121–143.

Linehan, M. M. (1993). *Cognitive-behavioral treatment of borderline personality disorder.* New York, NY: Guilford Press.

Ljungberg, T., Apicella, P., & Schultz, W. (1992). Responses of monkey dopamine neurons during learning of behavioral reactions. *Journal of Neurophysiology, 67,* 145–163.

Loewenstein, G. (2006). The pleasures and pains of information. *Science, 312,* 705–707.

Londsdorf, T. B., Weike, A. I., Golkar, A., Schalling, M., Hamm, A. O., & Öhman, A. (2010). Amygdala-dependent fear conditioning in humans is modulated by BDNFval66met polymorphism. *Behavioral Neuroscience 124,* 9–15.

Luine, V., Villegas, M., Martinez, C., & McEwen, B. S. (1994). Repeated stress causes reversible impairments of spatial memory performance. *Brain Research, 639,* 167–170.

Lutz, A., Brefczynski-Lewis, J., Johnstone, T., & Davidson, R. J. (2008). Regulation of the neural circuitry of emotion by compassion meditation: Effects of meditative expertise. *PLoS ONE, 3,* e1897. doi: 10.1371/journal.pone.0001897

Lutz, A., McFarlin, D. R., Perlman, D. M., Salomons, T. V., & Davidson, R. J. (2013). Altered anterior insula activation during anticipation and experience of painful stimuli in expert meditators. *Neuroimage, 64,* 538–546.

MacLean, P. D. (1949). Psychosomatic disease and the "visceral brain": Recent developments bearing on the Papez theory of emotion. *Psychosomatic Medicine, 11,* 338–353.

MacLean, P. D. (1952). Some psychiatric implications of physiological studies on frontotemporal portion of the limbic system (visceral brain). *Electroencephalography and Clinical Neurophysiology, 4,* 407–418.

MacLean, P. D. (1964). Man and his animal brains. *Modern Medicine, 12,* 95–106.

MacLean, P. D. (1984). Brain evolution relating to family, play, and the separation call. *Archives of General Psychiatry, 42,* 405–417.

Macmillan, M. (2000). *An odd kind of fame: Stories of Phineas Gage.* Cambridge, MA: MIT Press.

Macmillan, M. (2008). Phineas Gage: Unravelling the myth. *The Psychologist (British Psychological Society), 21,* 828–831.

Mahan, A. L. & Ressler, K. J. (2012). Fear conditioning, synaptic plasticity and the amygdala: implications for posttraumatic stress disorder. *Trends in Neurosciences, 35,* 24–36.

Mahler, S. V., Smith, K. S., & Berridge, K. C. (2007). Endocannabinoid hedonic hotspot for sensory pleasure: Anandamide in nucleus accumbens shell enhances 'liking' of a sweet reward. *Neuropsychopharmacology, 32,* 2267–2278.

Mak, A. K., Hu, Z. G., Zhang, J. X., Xiao, Z. W., & Lee, T. M. (2009). Neural correlates of regulation of positive and negative emotions: An fMRI study. *Neuroscience Letters, 457,* 101–106.

Malberg, J. E., Eisch, A. J., Nestler, E. J., & Duman, R. S. (2000). Chronic antidepressant treatment increases neurogenesis in adult rat hippocampus. *Journal of Neuroscience, 20,* 9104–9110.

Maren, S. (2011). Seeking a spotless mind: Extinction, deconsolidation, and erasure of fear memory. *Neuron, 70,* 830–845.

Maren, S. (2014). Fear of the unexpected: Hippocampus mediates novelty-induced return of extinguished fear in rats. *Neurobiology of Learning and Memory, 108,* 88–95.

Mauss, I. B., Evers C., Wilhelm F. H., & Gross J. J. (2006). How to bite your tongue without blowing your top: Implicit evaluation of emotion regulation predicts affective responding to anger provocation. *Personality and Social Psychology Bulletin, 32,* 589–602.

Mauss, I. B., Bunge, S. A., & Gross, J. J. (2007). Automatic emotion regulation. *Social and Personality Psychology Compass, 1,* 146–167.

Mayberg, H. S., Lozano, A., Voon, V., Mcneely, H., Seminowicz, D., Hamani, C., . . . Kennedy, S. H. (2005). Deep brain stimulation for treatment-resistant depression. *Neuron, 45,* 651–660.

McEwen, B. S. (2000). The neurobiology of stress: From serendipity to clinical relevance. *Brain Research, 886,* 172–189.

McEwen, B. S., & Sapolsky, R. (1995). Stress and cognitive function. *Current Opinion in Neurobiology, 5,* 205–216.

McGaugh, J. L. (2000). Memory: A century of consolidation. *Science, 287,* 248–251.

McGaugh, J. (2003). *Memory and emotion: The making of lasting memories.* New York, NY: Columbia University Press.

McGaugh, J. L., & Cahill, L. (2003). Emotion and memory: Central and peripheral contributions. In R. Davidson, K. Scherer, & H. Goldsmith (Eds.), *Handbook of affective sciences* (pp. 93–116). New York, NY: Oxford University Press.

McRae, K., Hughes, B., Chopra, S., Gabrieli, J. D., Gross, J. J., & Ochsner, K. N. (2010). The neural bases of distraction and reappraisal. *Journal of Cognitive Neuroscience, 22,* 248–262.

Meyer-Lindenberg, A., Domes, G., Kirsch, P., & Heinrichs, M. (2011). Oxytocin and vasopressin in the human brain: social neuropeptides for translational medicine. *Nature Reviews Neuroscience, 12,* 524–535.

Milad, M. R., Pitman, R. K., Ellis, C. B., Gold, A. L, Shin, L. M, Lasko, N. B., . . . (2009). Neurobiological basis of failure to recall extinction memory in posttraumatic stress disorder. *Biological Psychiatry, 66,* 1075–1082.

Milad, M. R., Quinn, B. T., Pitman, R. K., Orr, S. P., Fischl, B., & Rauch, S.L. (2005). Thickness of ventromedial prefrontal cortex in humans is correlated with extinction memory. *Proceedings of the National Academy of Sciences, 102,* 10706–10711.

Milad M. R., Quirk, G. J. (2012). Fear Extinction as a Model for Translational Neuro-science: Ten Years of Progress. *Annual Review of Psychology, 63,* 129–151.

Miller, E. K., & Cohen, J. D. (2001). An integrative theory of prefrontal cortical function. *Annual Review of Neuroscience, 24,* 167–202.

Miller, G. A. (1956). The magical number seven plus or minus two: Some limits on our capacity for processing information. *Psychological Review, 63,* 81–97.

Miller, G. A. (1991). *Psychology: The science of mental life.* New York, NY: Penguin Books.

Miller, G. A., Galanter, E., & Pribram, K. (1960). *Plans and the structure of behavior.* New York, NY: Holt, Rinehart and Winston.

Milner, B., Corkin, S., & Teuber, H.-L. (1968). Further analysis of the hippocampal amnesic syndrome: 14-year follow-up study of H. M. *Neuropsychologia, 6,* 215–234.

Mischel, W., Ebbesen, E. B., & Zeiss, A. R. (1972). Cognitive and attentional mechanisms in delay of gratification. *Journal of Personality and Social Psychology, 21,* 204–218.

Miu, A., Heilman, R., & Houser, D. (2008). Anxiety impairs decision-making: Psycho-physiological evidence from an Iowa gambling task. *Biological Psychology, 77,* 353–358.

Mobbs, D., Lau, H. C., Jones, O. D., & Frith, C. D. (2007). Law, responsibility and the brain. *PLoS Biology, 5,* 693–700.

Modinas, G., Ormel, J., & Aleman, A. (2010). Individual differences in dispositional mindfulness and brain activity involved in reappraisal of emotion. *Social Cognitive and Affective Neuroscience, 5,* 369–377.

Molendijk, M. L., van Tol, M-J., Penninx, B. W. J. H., van der Wee, M. J. A., Aleman, A., Veltman, D. J., . . .& Elzinga, B. M. (2012). BDNF val66met affects hippocampal volume and emotion-related hippocampal memory activity. *Translational Psychiatry, 2,* e74.

Monfils, M. H., Cowansage, K. K., Klann, E., & LeDoux, J. E. (2009). Extinction reconsolidation boundaries: Key to persistent attenuation of fear memories. *Science, 324,* 952–955.

Morris, R. (1984). Developments of a water-maze procedure for studying spatial learning in the rat. *Journal of Neuroscience Methods, 11,* 47–60.

Muller, N. G., Bartelt, O. A., Donner, T. H., Villringer, A., & Brandt, S. A. (2003). A physiological correlate of the "zoom lens" of visual attention. *Journal of Neuroscience, 23,* 3561–3565.

Murphy, F. C., Nimmo-Smith, I., & Lawrence, A. D. (2003). Functional neuroanatomy of emotion: A meta-analysis. *Cognitive, Affective, and Behavioral Neuroscience, 3,* 207–233.

Myers, K. M., & Davis, M. (2007). Mechanisms of fear extinction. *Molecular Psychiatry, 12,* 120–150.

Nader, K. (2003). Memory traces unbound. *Trends in Neuroscience, 26,* 65–72.

References

Nader, K., & Einarsson, E. O. (2010). Memory reconsolidation: An update. *Annals of the New York Academy of Science, 1191,* 27–41.

Nader, K., Schafe, G. E., & LeDoux, J. E. (2000). Fear memories require protein synthesis in the amygdala for reconsolidation after retrieval. *Nature, 406,* 722–726.

Nahm, F. L. D., & Pribram, K. H. (1998). *Heinrich Kluver: A biographical memoir.* National Academies Press: Washington, DC.

Naqvi, N. H., & Bechara, A. (2009).The hidden island of addiction: The insula. *Trends in Neuroscience, 32,* 56–57.

Naqvi, N. H., & Bechara, A. (2010). The insula and drug addiction: An interoceptive view of pleasure, urges, and decision making. *Brain Structure and Function, 214,* 435–450.

Naqvi, N. H., Rudrauf, D., Damasio, H., & Bechara, A. (2007). Damage to the insula disrupts addiction to cigarette smoking. *Science, 315,* 531–534.

Neisser, U. (1982). Snapshots or benchmarks. In Ulric Neisser (Ed.), *Memory observed: Remembering in Natural Contexts.* New York, NY: W. H. Freeman.

Neisser, U., & Harsch, N. (1992). Phantom flashbulbs: False recollections of hearing the news about the Challenger. In E. Winograd & Ulric Neisser (Eds.), *Affect and accuracy in recall: Studies of "flashbulb" memories: Vol. 4. Emory symposia in cognition* (pp. 9–31). New York, NY: Cambridge University Press.

Neisser, U., Winograd, E., Bergman, E. T., Schreiber, C. A., Palmer, S. E., & Weldon, M. S. (1996). Remembering the earthquake: Direct experience vs. hearing the news. *Memory, 4,* 337–357.

Nettle, D., & Bateson, M. (2012). The evolutionary origins of mood and its disorders. *Current Biology, 22,* R712–R721.

Niedenthal, P. (2007). Embodying emotion. *Science, 316,* 1002–1005.

Nolen-Hoeksema, S., Wisco, B. E., & Lyubomirsky, S. (2008). Rethinking rumination. *Perspectives in Psychological Science, 3,* 400–424.

Ochsner, K. N., Bunge, S. A., Gross, J. J., & Gabrieli, J. D. E. (2002). Rethinking feelings: An fMRI study of the cognitive regulation of emotion. *Journal of Cognitive Neuroscience, 14,* 1215–1229.

Ochsner, K. N., & Gross, J. J. (2008). Cognitive emotion regulation: Insights from social cognitive and affective neuroscience. *Current Directions in Psychological Science, 17,* 153–158.

Ochsner, K. N., & Phelps, E. (2007). Emerging perspective on emotion–cognition interactions. *Trends in Cognitive Science, 11,* 317–318.

Ochsner, K. N., Ray, R. R., Cooper, J. C., Robertson, E. R., Chopra, S., Gabrieli, J. D. E., & Gross, J. J. (2004). For better or for worse: Neural systems supporting the cognitive down- and up-regulation of negative emotion. *Neuroimage, 23,* 483–499.

Ochsner, K. N., Silvers, J. A., & Buhle, J. T. (2012). Functional imaging studies of emotion regulation: A synthetic review and evolving model of the cognitive control of emotion. *Annals of the New York Academy of Sciences, 1251,* E1–E24.

Oei, N. Y., Elzinga, B. M., Wolf, O. T., de Ruiter, M. B., Damoiseaux, J. S., Kuijer, J. P., . . . Rombouts, S. A. (2007). Glucocorticoids decrease hippocampal and prefrontal activation during declarative memory retrieval in young men. *Brain Imaging and Behavior, 1,* 31–41.

Öhman, A. (2000). Fear and anxiety: Evolutionary, cognitive, and clinical perspectives. In M. Lewis & J. M. Haviland-Jones (Eds.), *Handbook of emotions* (pp. 573–593). New York, NY: Guilford Press.

Öhman, A. (2005). The role of the amygdala in human fear: Automatic detection of threat. *Psychoneurendocrinology, 30,* 952–958.

Öhman, A. (2006). Making sense of emotion: evolution, reason & the brain. *Daedalus, 135*(3), 33–45.

Öhman, A., & Mineka, S. (2001). Fears, phobias and preparedness: Toward an evolved module of fear and fear learning. *Psychological Review, 108,* 483–522.

Olausson, H., Lamarre, Y., Backlund, H., Morin, C., Wallin, B. G., Starck, G., . . . Bushnell, M. C. (2002). Unmyelinated tactile afferents signal touch and project to insular cortex. *Nature Neuroscience, 5,* 900–904.

Olds, J. (1958). Self-stimulation of the brain. *Science, 127,* 315–324.

Olsson, A., Nearing, K. I., & Phelps, E. A. (2007). Learning fears by observing others: The neural systems of social fear transmission. *Social, Cognitive and Affective Neuroscience, 2,* 3–11.

Oppenheimer, S. M., Gelb, A., Girvin, J. P., & Hachinski, V. C. (1992). Cardiovascular effects of human insular cortex stimulation. *Neurology, 42,* 1727–1732.

Ortony, A., & Turner, T. J. (1990). What's basic about basic emotions? *Psychological Review, 97*(3), 315.

Orsini, C. A., & Maren, S. (2012). Neural and cellular mechanisms of fear and extinction memory formation. *Neuroscience and Biobehavioral Reviews. 36,* 1773–1802.

Osgood, C. E. (1952). The nature and measurement of meaning. *Psychological Bulletin, 49,* 197–237.

Ousdal, O. T., Jensen, J., Server, A., Hariri, A. R., Nakstad, P. H., & Andreassen, O. A. (2008). The human amygdala is involved in general behavioral relevance detection: Evidence from an event-related functional magnetic resonance imaging go–no go task. *Neuroscience, 156,* 450–455.

Packard, M. G., Cahill, L., & McGaugh, J. L. (1994). Amygdala modulation of hippocampal-dependent and caudate nucleus-dependent memory processes. *Proceedings of the National Academy of Sciences, USA, 91,* 8477–8481.

Padmala, S., & Pessoa, L. (2008). Affective learning enhances visual detection and responses in primary visual cortex. *Journal of Neuroscience, 28,* 6202–6210.

Panksepp, J. (1998). *Affective neuroscience: The foundations of animal and human emotions.* New York, NY: Oxford University Press.

Panksepp, J. (2005). On the embodied neural nature of core emotional affects. *Journal of Consciousness Studies, 12,* 158–184.

Panksepp, J. (2007). Neurologizing the psychology of affects: How appraisal-based constructivism and basic emotion theory can coexist. *Perspectives on Psychological Science, 2,* 281–296.

Panksepp, J. (2010a). Interview with Virginia Campbell on Brain Science Podcasts. Episode 65. Originally aired on January 31, 2010. Retrieved from http://www.brain sciencepodcast.com/bsp/2010/1/13/affective-neuroscience-with-jaak-panksepp-bsp-65.html

Panksepp (2010b). Affective neuroscience of the emotional BrainMind: Evolutionary perspectives and implications for understanding depression. *Dialogues in Clinical Neuroscience, 12,* 533–545.

Panksepp, J. (2011). The basic emotional circuits of mammalian brains: Do animals have affective lives? *Neuroscience and Biobehavioral Reviews, 35,* 1791–1804.

Panksepp, J., & Biven, L. (2012). *Archaeology of mind: Neuroevolutionary origins of human emotions.* New York, NY: Norton.

Panksepp, J., Fuchs, T., & Iacobucci, P. (2011). The basic neuroscience of emotional experiences in mammals: The case of subcortical fear circuitry and implications for clinical anxiety. *Applied Animal Behaviour Science, 129,* 1–17.

Panksepp, J., & Watt, D. (2011). What is basic about basic emotions? Lasting lessons from affective neuroscience. *Emotion Review, 3,* 387–396.

Pape, H. C., & Pare, D. (2010). Plastic synaptic networks of the amygdala for the acquisition, expression, and extinction of conditioned fear. *Physiological Review, 90,* 419–463.

Papez, J. W. (1937). A proposed mechanism of emotion. *Archives of Neurology and Psychiatry, 79,* 725–743.

Patel, R., Spreng, R. N., Shin, L. M., & Girard, T. A. (2012). Neurocircuitry models of post-traumatic stress disorder and beyond: A meta-analysis of functional neuroimaging studies. *Neuroscience and Biobehavioral Reviews, 36,* 2130–2142.

Paulus, M. P., Potterat, E. G., Taylor, M. K., Van Orden, K. F., Bauman, J., Momen, N., . . . Swain, J. L. (2009). A neuroscience approach to optimizing brain resources for human performance in extreme environments. *Neuroscience and Biobehavioral Reviews, 33,* 1080–1088.

Paulus, M. P., Rogalsky, C., Simmons, A., Feinstein, J. S., & Stein, M. B. (2003). Increased activation in the right insula during risk-taking decision making is related to harm avoidance and neuroticism. *NeuroImage, 19,* 1439–1448.

Paulus, M. P., & Stein, M. B. (2006). An insular view of anxiety. *Biological Psychiatry, 60,* 383–387.

Paulus, M. P., & Stein, M. B. (2010). Interoception in anxiety and depression. *Brain Structure and Function, 214,* 451–463.

Peciña, S. & Berridge, K. C. (2000). Opioid site in nucleus accumbens shell mediates food intake and hedonic 'liking': map based on microinjection fos plumes. *Brain Research, 863,* 71–86.

Peciña, S., & Berridge, K. C. (2005). Hedonic hot spot in nucleus accumbens shell: Where do mu-opioids cause increased hedonic impact of sweetness? *Journal of Neuroscience, 25,* 11777–11786.

Peña, D. F., Engineer, N. D., & McIntyre, C. K. (2013). Rapid remission of conditioned fear expression with extinction training paired with vagus nerve stimulation. *Biological Psychiatry, 73,* 1071–1077.

Penfield, W., & Boldrey, E. (1937). Somatic motor and sensory representations in the cerebral cortex of man as studied by electrical stimulation. *Brain, 60,* 389–443.

Penfield, W., & Faulk, M. E. (1955). The insula: Further observations on its function. *Brain, 78,* 445–470.

Pereira, M. G., de Oliveira, L., Erthal, F. S., Joffily, M., Mocaiber, I. F., Volchan, E., & Pessoa L. (2010). Emotion affects action: Midcingulate cortex as a pivotal node of interaction between negative emotion and motor signals. *Cognitive, Affective and Behavioral Neuroscience, 10,* 94–106.

Pereira, M. G., Volchan, E., de Souza, G. G. L., de Oliveira, L., Campagnoli, R., Pinheiro, W. M., & Pessoa, L. (2006). Sustained and transient modulation of performance induced by emotional picture viewing. *Emotion, 6,* 622–634.

Pessoa, L. (2005). To what extent are emotional visual stimuli processed without attention and awareness? *Current Opinion In Neurobiology, 15,* 188–196.

Pessoa, L. (2008). On the relationship between emotion and cognition. *Nature Reviews Neuroscience, 9,* 148–158.

Pessoa, L. (2010). Emergent processes in cognitive-emotional interactions. *Dialogues in Clinical Neuroscience, 12,* 433–448.

Pessoa, L. (2012). Beyond brain regions: Network perspective of cognition–emotion interactions. *Behavioral and Brain Sciences, 35,* 158–159.

Pessoa, L., Kastner, S., & Ungerleider, L. G. (2002). Attentional control of the processing of neutral and emotional stimuli. *Cognitive Brain Research, 15,* 31–45.

Pessoa, L., McKenna, M., Gutierrez, E., & Ungerleider, L. G. (2002). Neural processing of emotional faces requires attention. *Proceedings of the National Academy of Sciences, 99,* 11458–11463.

Pessoa L., Oliveira L., & Pereira M. G. (2010). Attention and emotion. *Scholarpedia* J. 5, 6314.10.4249/scholarpedia.6314

Peters, J., Dieppa-Perea, L .M., Melendez, L. M., & Quirk, G. J. (2010). Induction of fear extinction with hippocampal-infralimbic BDNF. *Science, 328,* 1288– 1290

Petersen, S. E., & Posner, M. I. (2012). The attention system of the human brain: 20 years after. *Annual Review of Neuroscience, 35,* 73–89.

Pham, M. T., Lee, L., & Stephen, A. T. (2012). Feeling the future: The emotional oracle effect. *Journal of Consumer Research, 39,* 461–477.

Phan, K. L., Wager, T. D., Taylor, S. F., & Liberzon, I. (2002). Functional neuroanatomy of emotion: A meta-analysis of emotion activation studies in PET and fMRI. *Neuroimage, 16,* 331–348.

Phelps, E. A. (2006). Emotion and cognition: Insights from studies of the human amygdala. *Annual Review of Psychology, 57,* 27–53.

Phelps, E. A., Delgado, M. R., Nearing, K. I., & LeDoux, J. E. (2004). Extinction learning in humans: Role of the amygdala and vmPFC. *Neuron, 43,* 897–905.

Phelps, E. A., & LeDoux, J. E. (2005). Contributions of the amygdala to emotion processing: From animal models to human behavior. *Neuron, 48, 175–187.*

Phelps, E. A., Ling, S., & Carrasco, M. (2006). Emotion facilitates perception and potentiates the perceptual benefits of attention. *Psychological Science, 17,* 292–299.

Phelps, E. A., & Sharot, T. (2008). How (and why) emotion enhances the subjective sense of recollection. *Current Directions in Psychological Science, 17,* 147–152.

Pichon, S., de Gelder, B., & Grèzes, J. (2012). Threat prompts defensive brain responses independently of attentional control. *Cerebral Cortex, 22,* 274–285.

Pitman, R. K., Sanders, K. M., Zusman, R. M., Healy, A. R., Cheema, F., Lasko, N. B., . . . Orr, S. P. (2002). Pilot study of secondary prevention of posttraumatic stress disorder with propranolol. *Biological Psychiatry, 51,* 189–192.

Ploghaus, A., Tracey, I., Gati, J. S., Clare, S., Menon, R. S., Matthews, P. M., & Rawlins, J. N. P. (1999). Dissociating pain from its anticipation in the human brain. *Science, 284,* 1979–1981.

Pollatos, O., Kurz, A. L., Albrecht, J., Schreder, T., Kleemann, A. M., Schöpf, V., . . . Schandry, R. (2008). Reduced perception of bodily signals in anorexia nervosa. *Eating Behaviors, 9,* 381–388.

Pourtois, G., Schettino, A., & Vuilleumier, P. (2012). Brain mechanisms for emotional influences on perception and attention: What is magic and what is not. *Biological Psychology, 92,* 492–512.

Price, T. F., & Harmon-Jones, E. (2010). Approach motivational body postures lean towards left frontal brain activity. *Psychophysiology, 48,* 718–722.

Proffitt, D. R. P., Bhalla, M., Gossweiler, R., & Midgett, J. (1995). Perceiving geographical slant. *Psychonomic Bulletin and Review, 2,* 409–428.

Quirk, J. J., & Beer, J. S. (2006). Prefrontal involvement in the regulation of emotion: Convergence of rat and human studies. *Current Opinion in Neurobiology, 16,* 723–727.

Raichle, M., MacLeod, A. M., Snyder, A. Z., Powers, W. J., Gusnard, D. A., & Shulman, G. L. (2001). A default mode of brain functioning. *Proceedings of the National Academy of Sciences, 98,* 676–682.

Rainville, P., Bechara, A., Naqvi, N., & Damasio, A. R. (2006). Basic emotions are associated with distinct patterns of cardiorespiratory activity. *International Journal of Psychophysiology, 61,* 5–18.

Rauch, S. L., Savage, C. R., Alpert, N. M., Fischman, A. J., & Jenike, M. A. (1997). The functional neuroanatomy of anxiety: A study of three disorders using positron emission tomography and symptom provocation. *Biological Psychiatry, 42,* 446–452.

Rauch, S. L., Shin, L. M., & Phelps, E. A. (2006). Neurocircuitry models of posttraumatic stress disorder and extinction: Human neuroimaging research—past, present and future. *Biological Psychiatry, 60,* 376–382.

Ray, R., & Zald, D. H. (2012). Anatomical insights into the interaction of emotion and cognition in the prefrontal cortex. *Neuroscience and Biobehavioral Reviews, 36,* 479–501.

Reiner, C. R., Stefanucci, J. K., Proffitt, D. R., & Clore, G. (2011). An effect of mood on the perception of geographical slant. *Cognition and Emotion, 25,* 174–182.

Ressler, K. J., & Mayberg, H. (2007). Targeting abnormal neural circuits in mood and anxiety disorders: From the laboratory to the clinic. *Nature Neuroscience, 10,* 1116–1124.

Reynolds, S. M., & Berridge, K. C. (2008). Emotional environments retune the valence of appetitive versus fearful functions in nucleus accumbens. *Nature Neuroscience, 11,* 423–425.

Richard, J. M., Castro, D. C., DiFeliceantonio, A. G., Robinson, M. J. F., & Berridge, K. C. (2013). Mapping brain circuits of reward and motivation: In the footsteps of Ann Kelley. *Neuroscience and Biobehavioral Reviews, 37,* 1919–1931.

Richards, J. M., & Gross, J. J. (2000). Emotion regulation and memory: The cognitive costs of keeping one's cool. *Journal of Personality and Social Psychology, 79,* 410–424.

Richardson, R. (2006). *William James and the maelstrom of American modernism.* New York, NY: Houghton Mifflin.

Rilling, J. K., Gutman, D. A., Zeh, T. R., Pagnoni, G., Berns, G. S., & Kilts, C. D. (2002). A neural basis for social cooperation. *Neuron, 35,* 395–405.

Rivers, W. H. R. (1918) The repression of war experience. *Proceedings of the Royal Society of Medicine, 11,* 1–20.

Rizzolatti, G., & Craighero, L. (2004). The mirror-neuron system. *Annual Review of Neuroscience, 27,* 169–192.

Rizzolatti, G., Fadiga, L., Gallese, V., & Fogassi, L. (1996). Premotor cortex and the recognition of motor actions. *Cognitive Brain Research, 3,* 131–141.

Robinson, T. E., & Berridge, K. C. (1993). The neural basis of drug craving: An incentive sensitization theory of addiction. *Brain Research Reviews, 18,* 247–291.

Robinson, T. E., & Berridge, K. C. (2008). The incentive sensitization theory of addiction: Some current issues. *Philosophical Transactions of the Royal Society B, 363,* 3137–3146.

Roediger, H., & McDermott, K. (1995). Creating false memories: Remembering words not presented in lists. *Journal of Experimental Psychology: Learning, Memory, and Cognition, 21,* 803–814.

Roiser J. P., de Martino, B., Tan G. C., Kumaran, D., Seymour B., Wood N. W., & Dolan R. J. (2009). A genetically mediated bias in decision making driven by failure of amygdala control. *Journal of Neuroscience, 29,* 5985–5991.

References

Rolls, E. T. (1999). *The brain and emotion*. New York, NY: Oxford University Press.

Rolls, E. T. (2000). The orbitofrontal cortex and reward. *Cerebral Cortex, 10,* 284–294.

Rolls, E. T., & Grabenhorst, F. (2008). The orbitofrontal cortex and beyond: From affect to decision making. *Progress in Neurobiology, 86,* 216–244.

Roozendaal, B. (2002). Stress and memory: Opposing effects of glucocorticoids on memory consolidation and memory retrieval. *Neurobiology of Learning and Memory, 78,* 578–595.

Roozendaal, B., McEwen, B. S., & Chattarji, S. (2009). Stress, memory and the amygdala. *Nature Reviews Neuroscience, 10,* 423–433.

Rosas-Vidal, L. E., Do-Monte, F. H., Sotres-Bayon, F., & Quirk, G. J. (2014). Hippocampal-prefrontal BDNF and memory for fear extinction. *Neuropsychopharmacology, 39,* 2161–2169.

Rosen, J. B. (2004). The neurobiology of conditioned and unconditioned fear: A neurobehavioral system analysis of the amygdala. *Behavioral and Cognitive Neuroscience Reviews, 3,* 23–41.

Rosenbaum, R. S., Köhler, S., Schacter, D. L., Moscovitch, M., Westmacott, R., Black, S. E., . . . Tulving, E. (2005). The case of K. C.: Contributions of a memory-impaired person to memory theory. *Neuropsychologia, 43*(7), 989–1021.

Rowe, G., Hirsch, J. B., & Anderson, A. K. (2006). Positive affect increases the breadth of attentional selection. *Proceedings of the National Academy of Sciences, 104,* 383–388.

Russell, J. A. (1994). Is there universal recognition of emotion from facial expression? A review of the cross-cultural studies. *Psychological Bulletin, 115,* 102–141.

Russell, J. (2012). Curriculum vitae. Retrieved October 2, 2013, from http://www.bc.edu/content/dam/files/schools/cas_sites/psych/pdf/cv_russell_2012_dec.pdf

Salmon, P., Sephton, S., Weissbecker, I., Hoover, K., Ulmer, C., & Studts, J. L. (2004). Mindfulness meditation in clinical practice. *Cognitive and Behavioral Practice, 11,* 434–446.

Samanez-Larkin, G. R., Hollon, N. G., Carstensen, L. L., & Knutson, B. (2008). Individual differences in insular sensitivity during loss anticipation predict avoidance learning. *Psychological Science, 19,* 320–323.

Sander, D., Grafman, J., & Zalla, T. (2003). The human amygdala: An evolved system for relevance detection. *Reviews in the Neurosciences, 14,* 303–316.

Sanfey, A. G., & Chang, L. J. (2008). Multiple systems in decision making. *Annals of the New York Academy of Sciences, 1128,* 53–62.

Sanfey, A. G., Rilling, J. K., Aronson, J. A., Nystrom, L. E., & Cohen, J. D. (2003). The neural basis of economic decision-making in the Ultimatum Game. *Science, 200,* 1755–1758.

Saplosky, R. (2004). *Why zebras don't get ulcers.* New York, NY: Henry Holt & Company. Third Edition.

Schacter, D.L. (1996). *Searching for memory: The brain, the mind, and the past.* New York, NY: BasicBooks.

Schacter, D. L., & Addis, D. R. (2007). Constructive memory: The ghosts of past and future. *Nature, 445,* 27.

Schachter, S., & Singer, J. E. (1962). Cognitive, social, and physiological determinants of emotional state. *Psychological Review, 69,* 379–399.

Schafe, G. E., & LeDoux, J. E. (2000). Memory consolidation of auditory Pavlovian fear conditioning requires protein synthesis and protein kinase A in the amygdala. *Journal of Neuroscience, 20,* RC96.

Scherer, K. R. (2012). Neuroscience findings are consistent with appraisal theories of emotion; but does the brain "respect" constructionism? *Behavioral and Brain Sciences, 35,* 163–164.

Schiller, D., Kanen, J. W., LeDoux, J. E., Monfils, M.-H., & Phelps, E. A. (2013). Extinction during reconsolidation of threat memory diminishes prefrontal cortex involvement. *Proceedings of the National Academy of Sciences, 110,* 20040–20045.

Schiller, D., Monfils, M.-H., Raio, C. M., Johnson, D. C., LeDoux, J. E., & Phelps, E. A. (2010). Preventing the return of fear in humans using reconsolidation update mechanisms. *Nature, 463,* 49–53.

Schultz, W. (2007). Behavioral dopamine signals. *Trends in Neurosciences, 30,* 203–210.

Schultz, W., Dayan, P., & Montague, P. R. (1997). A neural substrate of prediction and reward. *Science, 275,* 1593–1599.

Schwabe, L., Nader, K., & Pruessner, J. C. (2014). Reconsolidation of human memory: Brain mechanisms and clinical relevance. *Biological Psychiatry,* in press.

Schwarz, N. (2012). Feelings-as-information theory. In P. Van Lange, A. Kruglanski, & E. T. Higgins (Eds.), *Handbook of theories of social psychology* (pp. 289–308). Thousand Oaks, CA: Sage.

Schwarz, N., & Clore, G. (1983). Mood, misattribution, and judgments of well-being: Informative and directive functions of affective states. *Journal of Personality and Social Psychology, 45,* 513–523.

Schwarz, N., Strack, F., Kommer, D., & Wagner, D. (1987). Soccer, rooms, and the quality of your life: Mood effects on judgments of satisfaction with life in general and with specific life-domains. *European Journal of Social Psychology, 17,* 69–79.

Seeley, W. W. (2010). Anterior insula degeneration in frontotemporal dementia. *Brain Structure and Function, 214,* 465–475.

Seeley, W. W., Carlin, D. A., Allman, J. M., Macedo, M. N., Bush, C., Miller, B. L., & Dearmond, S. J. (2006). Early frontotemporal dementia targets neurons unique to apes and humans. *Annals of Neurology, 60,* 660–667.

Seeley, W. W., Menon, V., Schatzberg, A. F., Keller, J., Glover, G. H., Kenna, H., . . . Greicius, M. D. (2007). Dissociable intrinsic connectivity networks for salience processing and executive control. *Journal of Neuroscience, 27,* 2349–2356.

References

Seligman, M. E. P. (1971). Phobias and preparedness. *Behavior Therapy, 2,* 307–320.

Sevy, S., Burdick, K. E., Viswewaraiah, H., Abdelmessih, S., Lukin, M., Yechiam, E., & Bechara, A. (2007). Iowa gambling task in schizophrenia: A review and new data in patients with schizophrenia and co-occurring cannabis use disorders. *Schizophrenia Research, 92,* 74–84.

Sexton, M. C., Sunday, S. R., Hurt, S., & Halmi, K. A. (1998). The relationship between alexithymia, depression, and Axis II psychopathology in eating disorder inpatients. *International Journal of Eating Disorders, 23,* 277–286.

Shackman, A. J., Salomons, T. S., Slagter, H. A., Fox, A. S., Winter, J. J., & Davidson, R. J. (2011). The integration of negative affect, pain and cognitive control in the cingulate cortex. *Nature Reviews Neuroscience, 12,* 154–167.

Sharot, T., Delgado, M. R., & Phelps, E. A. (2004). How emotion enhances the feeling of remembering. *Nature Neuroscience, 12,* 1376–1380.

Sharot, T., Martorella, E. A., Delgado, M. R., & Phelps, E. A. (2007). How personal experience modulates the neural circuitry of memories of September 11. *Proceedings of the National Academy of Sciences, 104,* 389–394.

Shephard, G.M. (2004). The human sense of smell: Are we better than we think? *PLOS Biology,* 2: e146. doi:10.1371/journal.pbio.0020146.

Sheppes, G., Schiebe, S., Suri, G., & Gross, J. J. (2011). Emotion-regulation choice. *Psychological Science, 22,* 1391–1396.

Shin, L. M., & Liberzon, I. (2010). The neurocircuitry of fear, stress, and anxiety disorders. *Neuropsychopharmacology, 35,* 169–191.

Shulman, G. L., Fiez, J. A., Corbetta, M., Buckner, R. L., Miezen, F. M., Raichle, M. E., & Petersen, S. E. (1997). Common blood flow changes across visual tasks: II. Decreases in cerebral cortex. *Journal of Cognitive Neuroscience, 9,* 648–666.

Siegel, D. J. (2007). *The mindful brain.* New York, NY: Norton.

Siegel, E. H., & Stefanucci, J. K. (2011). A little bit louder now: Negative affect increases perceived loudness. *Emotion, 11,* 1006–1011.

Sienkiewicz-Jarosz, H., Scinska, A., Kuran, W., Ryglewicz, D., Rogowski, A., Wrobel, E., . . . Bienkowski, P. (2005). Taste responses in patients with Parkinson's disease. *Journal of Neurology, Neurosurgery and Psychiatry, 76,* 40–46.

Simons, D. J., & Chabris, C. F. (1999). Gorillas in our midst: Sustained inattentional blindness for dynamic events. *Perception, 28,* 1059–1074.

Singer, T., Critchley, H. D., & Preuschoff, K. (2009). A common role of insula in feelings, empathy and uncertainty. *TICS, 13,* 334–340.

Singer, T., Seymour, B., O'Doherty, J., Kaube, H., Dolan, R. J., & Frith, C. D. (2004). Empathy for pain involves the affective but not sensory components of pain. *Science, 303,* 1157–1161.

Slagter, H. A., Lutz, A., Greischar, L. L., Francis, A. D., Nieuwenhuis, S., Davis, J. M., & Davidson, R. J. (2007). Mental training affects use of limited brain resources. *PLoS Biology, 5,* e138.

Slovic, P., Finucane, M., Peters, E., & MacGregor, D. G. (2002). The affect heuristic. In T. Gilovich, D. Griffin, & D. Kahneman (Eds.), *Heuristics and biases: The psychology of intuitive judgment* (pp. 397–420). Cambridge, UK: Cambridge University Press.

Small, D. M., Zatorre, R. J., Dagher, A., Evans, A. C., & Jones-Gotman, M. (2001). Changes in brain activity related to eating chocolate: From pleasure to aversion. *Brain, 124,* 1720–1733.

Smith, K. S., Berridge, K. C., & Aldridge, J. W. (2011). Disentangling pleasure from incentive salience and learning signals in brain reward circuitry. *PNAS Plus, Proceedings of the National Academy of Sciences, 108,* e255–264.

Smith, K. S., Mahler, S. V., Pecina, S., & Berridge, K. C. (2010). Hedonic hotspots: Generating sensory pleasure in the brain. In M. L. Kringelbach & K. C. Berridge (Eds.), *Pleasures of the brain* (pp. 27–49). New York, NY: Oxford University Press.

Smith, K. S., Tindell, A. J., Aldridge, J. W., & Berridge, K. C. (2009). Ventral pallidum roles in reward and motivation. *Behavioural Brain Research, 196,* 155–167.

Smits, J. A. J., Rosenfield, D., Otto, M. W., Powers, M. B., Hofmann, S. G., Telch, M. J., . . . Tart, C. D. (2013). D-cycloserine enhancement of fear extinction is specific to successful exposure sessions: Evidence from the treatment of height phobia. *Biological Psychiatry, 73,* 1054–1058.

Snyder, P. J., Kaufman, R., Harrison, J. J., & Maruff, P. (2010). Charles Darwin's emotional expression "experiment" and his contribution to modern neuropharmacology. *Journal of the History of the Neurosciences, 19,* 158–170.

Sokol-Hessner, P., Hsu, M., Curley, N. G., Delgado, M., Camerer, C. F., & Phelps, E. A. (2009). Thinking like a trader selectively reduces individuals' loss aversion. *Proceedings of the National Academy of Sciences, 106,* 5035–5040.

Soliman, F., Glatt, C. E., Bath, K. G., Levita, L., Jones, R. M., Pattwell, S. S., . . . Casey, B. J. (2010). A genetic variant BDNF polymorphism alters extinction learning in both mouse and human. *Science, 327,* 863–865.

Sotres-Bayon, F., Cain, C. K., & Ledoux, J. E. (2006). Brain mechanisms of fear extinction: Historical perspectives on the contribution of prefrontal cortex. *Biological Psychiatry, 60,* 329–336.

Specter, M. (2014, May 19). Parial recall: Can neuroscience help us rewrite our most traumatic memories? *The New Yorker,* 38–48.

Speranza, M., Corcos, M., Loas, G., Stéphan, P., Guilbaud, O., Perez-Diaz, F., . . . Jeammet, P. (2005). Depressive personality dimensions and alexithymia in eating disorders. *Psychiatry Research, 135,* 153–163.

Spreng, R. N., Mar, R. A., & Kim, A. S. N. (2009). The common neural basis of autobiographical memory, prospection, navigation, theory of mind and the default mode: A quantitative meta-analysis. *Journal of Cognitive Neuroscience, 21,* 489–510.

Squire, L. R. (2004). Memory systems of the brain: A brief history and current perspective. *Neurobiology of Learning and Memory, 82,* 171–177.

References

Standing, L. (1973). Learning 10000 pictures. *Quarterly Journal of Experimental Psychology, 25,* 207–222.

Steinberg, E. E., Keiflin, R., Boivin, J., Witten, I. B., Deisseroth, K., & Janak, P. H. (2013). A causal link between prediction errors, dopamine and learning. *Nature Neuroscience. 16,* 966–972.

Stevens, F. L., Hurley, R. A., & Taber, K. H. (2011). Anterior cingulate cortex: Unique role in cognition and emotion. *Journal of Neuropsychiatry and Clinical Neuroscience, 23,* 121–125.

Storbeck, J., & Clore, G. L. (2005). With sadness comes accuracy; With happiness, false memory mood and the false memory effect. *Psychological Science, 16*(10), 785–791.

Storbeck, J., & Clore, G. L. (2011). Affect influences false memories at encoding: Evidence from recognition data. *Emotion, 14,* 981–989.

Stout. J., Rodawalt, W. C., & Siemers, E. R. (2001). Risky decision making in Huntington's disease. *Journal of the International Neuropsychological Society, 7,* 92–101.

Strigo, I., Matthews, S. C., Simmons, A. N., Oberndorfer, T., Klabunde, M., Reinhardt, L. E., & Kaye, W. H. (2013). Altered insula activation during pain anticipation in individuals recovered from anorexia nervosa: Evidence of interoceptive dysregulation. *International Journal of Eating Disorders, 46,* 23–33.

Stroop, J. R. (1935). Studies of interference in serial verbal reactions. *Journal of Experimental Psychology, 18,* 643–662.

Suri, G., Sheppes, G., & Gross, J. J. (2012). Predicting affective choice. *Journal of Experimental Psychology: General, 142,* 627–633.

Susskind, J. M, Lee, D. H., Cusi, A., Feiman, R., Grabski, W., & Anderson, A. K. (2008). Expressing fear enhances sensory acquisition. *Nature Neuroscience, 11,* 843–850.

Tabibnia, G., Satpute, A. B., & Lieberman, M. D. (2008). The sunny side of fairness: Preference for fairness activates reward circuitry (and disregarding unfairness activates self-control circuitry). *Psychological Science, 19,* 339–347.

Talarico, J. M., & Rubin, D. C. (2003). Confidence, not consistency, characterizes flashbulb memories. *Psychological Science, 14,* 455–461.

Taylor, S. F., & Liberzon, I. (2007). Neural correlates of emotion regulation in psychopathology. *Trends in Cognitive Science, 11,* 413–418.

Thompson, C. P., & Cowan, T. (1986). Flashbulb memories: A nicer interpretation of a Neisser recollection. *Cognition, 22,* 199–200.

Tindell, A. J., Berridge, K. C., & Aldridge, J. W. (2004). Ventral pallidal representation of Pavlovian cues and reward: Population and rate codes. *Journal of Neuroscience, 24,* 1058–1069.

Tindell, A. J., Berridge, K. C., Zhang, J., Pecina, S., & Aldridge, W. (2005) Ventral pallidal neurons code incentive motivation: amplification by mesolimbic sensitization and amphetamine. *European Journal of Neuroscience. 22,* 2617–2634.

Tindell, A. J., Smith, K. S., Peciña, S., Berridge, K. C., & Aldridge, J. W. (2006). Ventral pallidum firing codes hedonic reward: When a bad taste turns good. *Journal of Neurophysiology. 96,* 2399–2409.

Todd, R. M., Talmi, D., Schmitz, T. W., Susskind, J., & Anderson, A. K. (2012). Psychophysical and neural evidence for emotion-enhanced perceptual vividness. *Journal of Neuroscience, 32,* 11201–11212.

Tom, S., Fox, C. R., Poldrak, R. A., & Trepel, C. (2007). The neural basis of loss aversion in decision-making under risk. *Science, 315,* 515–518.

Torta, D. M., & Cauda, F. (2011). Different functions in the cingulate cortex: A meta-analytical connectivity modeling study. *Neuroimage, 56,* 2157–2172.

Tracy, J., & Randles, D. (2011). Four models of basic emotions: A review of Ekman and Cordaro, Izard, Levenson, and Panksepp and Watt. *Emotion Review, 3,* 397–405.

Tran, T. B., Siemer, M., & Joorman, J. (2011). Implicit interpretation biases affect emotional vulnerability: A training study. *Cognition and Emotion, 25,* 546–558.

Tranel, D., Gullickson, G., Koch, M., & Adolphs, R. (2006). Altered experience of emotion following bilateral amygdala damage. *Cognitive Neuropsychiatry, 11,* 219–232.

Treisman, A. (1986). Features and objects in visual processing. *Scientific American, 254,* 114–125.

Tsakiris, M., Hesse, M. D., Boy, C., Haggard, P., & Fink, G. R. (2007). Neural signatures of body ownership: A sensory network for bodily self-consciousness. *Cerebral Cortex, 17,* 2235–2244.

Tsakiris, M., Tajadura-Jimenez, A., & Costantini, M. (2011). Just a heartbeat away from one's body: Interoceptive sensitivity predicts malleability of body-representations. *Proceedings of the Royal Society B, 278,* 2470–2476.

Tulving, E. (1972). Episodic and semantic memory. In E. Tulving & W. Donaldson (Eds.), *Organization of memory* (pp. 382–402). New York, NY: Academic Press.

Tulving, E. (1985). Memory and consciousness. *Canadian Psychology, 26,* 1–12.

Unkelbach, C., Forgas, J. P., & Denson, T. F. (2008). The turban effect: The influence of Muslim headgear and induced affect on aggressive responses in the shooter bias paradigm. *Journal of Experimental Social Psychology, 44,* 1409–1413.

Urry, H. L., van Reekum, C. M., Johnstone, T., Kalin, N. H., Thurow, M. E., Schaefer, H. S., . . . Davidson, R. J. (2006). Amygdala and ventromedial prefrontal cortex are inversely coupled during regulation of negative affect and predict the diurnal pattern of cortisol secretion among older adults. *Journal of Neuroscience, 26,* 4415–4425.

Valenstein, E. (1973). *Brain control: Critical examination of brain stimulation and psychosurgery.* New York, NY: Wiley.

Verdejo-García, A., & Bechara, A. (2009). A somatic marker theory of addiction. *Neuropharmacology, 56,* 48–62.

Verdejo-García, A., Clark, L., & Dunn, B. D. (2012). The role of interoception in addiction: A critical review. *Neuroscience and Biobehavioral Reviews, 36,* 1857–1869.

References

Vermetten, E., Vythilingam, M., Southwick, S. M., Charney, D. S., & Bremner, J. D. (2003). Long-term treatment with paroxetine increases verbal declarative memory and hippocampal volume in posttraumatic stress disorder. *Biological Psychiatry, 54,* 693–702.

Vrtička, P., Sander, D., & Vuilleumier, P. (2011). Effects of emotion regulation strategy on brain responses to the valence and social content of visual scenes. *Neuropsychologia, 49,* 1067–1082.

Vuilleumier, P. (2005). How brains beware: Neural mechanisms of emotional attention. *Trends in Cognitive Science, 9,* 585–594.

Vuilleumier, P., Armony J. L., Driver, J., & Dolan R. J. (2001). Effects of attention and emotion on face processing in the human brain: An event-related fMRI study. *Neuron, 30,* 829–841.

Vuilleumier, P., & Driver, J., (2007). Modulation of visual processing by attention and emotion: Windows on causal interactions between human brain regions. *Philosophical Transactions of the Royal Society London B: Biological Sciences, 362,* 837–855.

Vuilleumier, P., & Huang, Y. M. (2009). Emotional attention: Uncovering the mechanisms of affective biases in perception. *Current Directions in Psychological Science, 18,* 148–152.

Vytal, K., & Hamann, S. (2010). Neuroimaging support for discrete neural correlates of basic emotions: A voxel-based meta-analysis. *Journal of Cognitive Neuroscience, 22,* 2864–2885.

Wagner, A., Aizenstein, H., Mazurkewicz, L., Fudge, J., Frank, G. K., Putnam, K., . . . Kaye, W. H. (2008). Altered insula response to a taste stimulus in individuals recovered from restricted-type anorexia nervosa. *Neuropsychopharmacology, 33,* 513–523.

Wegner, D. M., & Schneider, D. J. (2003). The white bear story. *Psychological Inquiry, 14,* 326–329.

Weinberger, N. M. (2004). Specific long-term memory traces in primary auditory cortex. *Nature Neuroscience, 5,* 279–290.

Werner, N. S., Duschek, S., & Schandry, R. (2009). Relationships between affective states and decision-making. *International Journal of Psychophysiology, 74,* 259–265.

Whalen, P. J., Rauch, S. L., Etcoff, N. L., McInerney, S. C., Lee, M. B., & Jenike, M. A. (1998). Masked presentations of emotional facial expressions modulate amygdala activity without explicit knowledge. *Journal of Neuroscience, 18,* 411–418.

Wheeler, M. A., Stuss, D. T., & Tulving, E. (1997). Toward a theory of episodic memory: The frontal lobes and autonoetic consciousness. *Psychological Bulletin, 121,* 331–354.

Wicker, B., Keysers, C., Plailly, J., Royet, J. P., Gallese, V., & Rizzolatti, G. (2003). Both of us disgusted in my insula: The common neural basis of seeing and feeling disgust. *Neuron, 40,* 655–664.

Wiens, S. (2005). Interoception in emotional experience. *Current Opinion in Neurology, 18*, 442–447.

Wiens, S., Mezzacappa, E. S., & Katkin, E. S. (2000). Heartbeat detection and the experience of emotions. *Cognition and Emotion, 14*, 417–427.

Williams, J. M. G., Barnhofer, T., Crane, C., Hemans, D., Raes, F., Watkins, E., & Dalgleish, T. (2007). Autobiographical memory specificity and emotional disorder. *Psychological Bulletin, 133*, 122–148.

Williams, J. M. G., & Kabat-Zinn, J. (2011). Mindfulness: Diverse perspectives on its meaning, origins, and multiple applications at the intersection of science and dharma. *Contemporary Buddhism, 12*, 1–18.

Williams, J. M. G., & Kuyken, W. (2012). Mindfulness-based cognitive therapy: A promising new approach to preventing depressive relapse. *British Journal of Psychiatry, 200*, 359–360. doi: 10.1192/bjp.bp.111.104745

Winkielman, P., & Berridge, K. (2004). Unconscious emotion. *Current Directions in Psychological Science, 13*, 120–123.

Winkielman, P., Knutson, B., Paulus, M., & Trujillo, J. L. (2007). Affective influence on judgments and decisions: Moving toward core mechanisms. *Review of General Psychology, 11*, 170–192.

Wolf, O. T. (2009). Stress and memory in humans: Twelve years of progress? *Brain Research, 1293*, 142–154.

Wolfe, J. M. (2010). Visual search. *Current Biology, 20*, R346–R349.

Wu, C. C., Sacchet, M. D., & Knutson, B. (2012). Toward an affective neuroscience of financial risk taking. *Frontiers in Neuroscience, 6*, 1–10.

Xu, P., Gu, R., Broster, L. S., Wu, R., Van Dam, N. T., Jiang, Y., . . .(2013). Neural Basis of Emotional Decision Making in Trait Anxiety. *Journal of Neuroscience 33*, 18641–18653.

Xue, Y.-X., Luo, Y.-X., Wu, P., Shi, H.-S., Xue, L.-F., Chen, C., . . . Lu, L. (2012). A memory retrieval-extinction procedure to prevent drug craving and relapse. *Science, 336*, 241–245.

Yerkes, R. M., & Dodson, J. D. (1908). The relation of strength of stimulus to rapidity of habit-information. *Journal of Comparative Neurology of Psychology, 18*, 459–482.

Young, L. J., Lim, M. M., Gingrich, B., & Insel, T. R. (2001). Cellular mechanisms of social attachment. *Hormones and Behavior, 40*, 133–138.

Zajonc, R. B. (1980). Feeling and thinking: Preferences need no inferences. *American psychologist, 35*, 151–175.

Zak, P. J., Stanton, A. A., & Ahmadi, S. (2007). Oxytocin increases generosity in humans. *PLoS ONE, 2*, e1128.

Zaki, J., Davis, J. I., & Ochsner, K. N. (2012). Overlapping activity in anterior insula during interoception and emotional experience. *Neuroimage, 62*, 493–499.

References

Zhao, X., Wang, P., Li, C., Hu, Z., Xi, Q., Wu, W., & Tang, X. (2007). Altered default mode network activity in patient with anxiety disorders: An fMRI study. *European Journal of Radiology, 63,* 373–378.

Zonnevylle-Bender, M. J. S., van Goozen, S. H. M., Cohen-Kettenis, P. T., van Elburg, T. A., & van Engeland, H. (2004). Emotional functioning in adolescent anorexia nervosa patients. *European Child and Adolescent Psychiatry, 13,* 28–34.

Index

In this index, the following designations are used:
b for box, *f* for figure, *n* for note, and *t* for table.